NOTABLE
AFRICAN AMERICAN
WRITERS

MAGILL'S CHOICE

NOTABLE
AFRICAN AMERICAN
WRITERS

Volume 2

Nikki Giovanni — Ishmael Reed

443 – 900

from

THE EDITORS OF SALEM PRESS

SALEM PRESS, INC.

Pasadena, California   Hackensack, New Jersey

Essays originally appeared, in whole or in part, in *Critical Survey of Drama* (2003), *Critical Survey of Poetry* (2003), *Critical Survey of Short Fiction* (2001), and *Critical Survey of Long Fiction* (2000), and *Magill's Choice: 100 Masters of Mystery and Detective Fiction* (2001). New material has been added.

Library of Congress Cataloging-in-Publication Data
Notable African American writers.
    p. cm. — (Magill's choice)
Includes bibliographical references and indexes.
ISBN-13: 978-1-58765-272-1 (set : alk. paper)
ISBN-10: 1-58765-272-2 (set : alk. paper)
ISBN-13: 978-1-58765-274-5 (v. 2 : alk. paper)
ISBN-10: 1-58765-274-9 (v. 2 : alk. paper)
[etc.]
    1. American literature—African American authors—Dictionaries.
2. African American authors—Biography—Dictionaries.   3. African Americans in literature—Dictionaries.   4. African Americans—Intellectual life—Dictionaries.   I. Title.   II. Series.
    PS153.N5N68 2006
    810.9'89607303—dc22

                                                                2006002916

First Printing

PRINTED IN CANADA

Contents

Complete List of Contents

Volume 1

Volume 2

Volume 3

NOTABLE
AFRICAN AMERICAN
WRITERS

Nikki Giovanni

Poet

Born: Knoxville, Tennessee; June 7, 1943

POETRY: *Black Feeling, Black Talk*, 1968; *Black Judgement*, 1968; *Black Feeling, Black Talk, Black Judgement*, 1970; *Re: Creation*, 1970; *Poem of Angela Yvonne Davis*, 1970; *Spin a Soft Black Song: Poems for Children*, 1971, revised 1987 (juvenile); *My House*, 1972; *Ego-Tripping, and Other Poems for Young Readers*, 1973 (juvenile); *The Women and the Men*, 1975; *Cotton Candy on a Rainy Day*, 1978; *Vacation Time*, 1980 (juvenile); *Those Who Ride the Night Winds*, 1983 (juvenile); *Knoxville, Tennessee*, 1994 (juvenile); *Life: Through Black Eyes*, 1995; *The Genie in the Jar*, 1996 (juvenile); *The Selected Poems of Nikki Giovanni*, 1996; *The Sun Is So Quiet*, 1996 (juvenile); *Love Poems*, 1997; *Blues: For All the Changes*, 1999; *Quilting the Black-Eyed Pea: Poems and Not Quite Poems*, 2002; *The Collected Poetry of Nikki Giovanni, 1968-1998*, 2003; *Just for You! The Girls in the Circle*, 2004 (juvenile).

NONFICTION: *Gemini: An Extended Autobiographical Statement on My First Twenty-five Years of Being a Black Poet*, 1971; *A Dialogue: James Baldwin and Nikki Giovanni*, 1973; *A Poetic Equation: Conversations Between Nikki Giovanni and Margaret Walker*, 1974; *Sacred Cows . . . and Other Edibles*, 1988; *Conversations with Nikki Giovanni*, 1992 (Virginia C. Fowler, editor); *Racism 101*, 1994; *The Prosaic Soul of Nikki Giovanni*, 2003 (includes *Gemini*, *Sacred Cows*, and *Racism 101*).

EDITED TEXTS: *Night Comes Softly: Anthology of Black Female Voices*, 1970; *Appalachian Elders: A Warm Hearth Sampler*, 1991 (with Cathee Dennison); *Grand Mothers: Poems, Reminiscences, and Short Stories About the Keepers of Our Traditions*, 1994; *Shimmy Shimmy Shimmy Like My Sister Kate: Looking at the Harlem Renaissance Through Poems*, 1996; *Grand Fathers: Reminiscences, Poems, Recipes, and Photos of the Keepers of Our Traditions*, 1999.

Achievements

Nikki Giovanni has earned an impressive array of honors throughout her literary career. In the late 1960's she won grants from the Ford Foundation, National Endowment for the Arts, and the Harlem Cultural Council. She was named one of ten "Most Admired Black Women" by the *The New York Amsterdam News* in 1969. In 1971 she won an outstanding achievement award from *Mademoiselle,* an Omega Psi Phi Fraternity Award for outstanding contribution to arts and letters, and a Prince Matchabelli Sun Shower Award; in 1972, a life membership and scroll from the National Council of Negro Women and a National Association of Radio and Television Announcers Award for her recording of *Truth Is on Its Way,* and Woman of the Year Youth Leadership Award from *Ladies' Home Journal;* in 1973, a National Book Award nomination for *Gemini* and a Best Books for Young Adults citation from the American Library Association for *My House.* In the 1980's, she won a Woman of the Year citation from the Cincinnati Chapter of the Young Women's Christian Association, was elected to the Ohio Women's Hall of Fame, received an Outstanding Woman of Tennessee citation, won the Post-Corbett Award, and was named Woman of the Year from the National Association for the Advancement of Colored People (Lynchburg chapter). In the 1990's, she won the Jeanine Rae Award for the Advancement of Women's Culture and a Langston Hughes Award.

She has received numerous honorary degrees from academic institutions, including Wilberforce University, Fisk University, the University of Maryland (Princess Anne Campus), Ripon University, Smith College, Indiana University, Albright College, Cabrini College, and Allegheny College. Several cities have honored her with keys to the city, including Dallas, New York City, Cincinnati, Miami, New Orleans, and Los Angeles.

Biography

Yolande Cornelia Giovanni was born on June 7, 1943, in Knoxville, Tennessee, but grew up in Wyoming and Lincoln Heights, Ohio, suburbs of Cincinnati, where she currently resides. She described her childhood as "quite happy" in the poem "Nikki-Rosa," and her reminiscences in *Gemini* testify to her devotion to relatives, especially her sister Gary (who nicknamed her "Nikki") and her grandparents, John Brown Watson, one of the first graduates of Fisk University, and his wife Louvenia, whose strength of character she admired and emulated. Giovanni herself entered Fisk at sixteen and was graduated magna cum laude in 1967 with a bachelor of arts degree in history. At Fisk, her independent spirit led to her being expelled after one semester; but when she reentered in 1964, she immediately became involved in politics, reestablishing the university's chapter of the Student Nonviolent Coordinating Committee (SNCC). She also became greatly interested in literature and participated in John Oliver Killens's writers' workshop. She also briefly attended the School of Social Work at the University of Pennsylvania. It was black politics and black art, however, that held her interest. In 1967, a Ford Foundation grant enabled her to complete and publish her first book of poetry, *Black Feeling, Black Talk,* and its success led to a National Foundation of the Arts grant on which

(© by Jill Krementz)

she attended Columbia University's School of Fine Arts in 1968. Instead of completing her proposed novel or work toward a graduate degree, she continued to work on a volume of poetry, *Black Judgement*, published through a grant by the Harlem Cultural Council on the Arts.

Her impact on black American literature was immediate and electric. Her celebration of blackness and her militancy placed her in the avant-garde of black letters. Hailed as the "Princess of Black Poetry," she began touring the United States, lecturing to college audiences, spreading her message of black cultural nationalism, "ego-tripping," and love. To raise black cultural awareness and to foster black art, she became an assistant professor of black studies at Queens College, Flushing, New York in 1968 and taught creative writing at Livingston College, Rutgers University, from 1968 to 1970. She organized the Black Arts Festival in Cincinnati in 1967, editing *Love Black*, a magazine of the people—"what the brother thought and felt"; participated in the 1970 National Educational Television program "Soul!"; and took part in the two-week black festival "Soul at the Center" at Lincoln Center in New York in 1972.

The core of Giovanni's life and work is love and service; the focus is the family: her own, the black community, humanity. In 1969, her son Thomas Watson Giovanni was born: Her concern for him—indeed, for all children—was the springboard for her volumes of children's poetry, which include *Spin a Soft Black Song, Ego-Tripping, and Other Poems for Young Readers, Vacation Time*, and *The Genie in the Jar.* She also worked with the Reading Is Fundamental (RIF) Program in Harlem, the Jackie Robinson Foundation, and the President's Committee on the International Year of the Child (1979). Her poetry reflects a life of meditation and domesticity. She is also an active member of black service organizations and an editorial consultant and columnist for *Encore American and Worldwide News Magazine*, a black news monthly with a Third World focus.

In the 1980's and 1990's she taught at a number of colleges and universities throughout the country, as both a faculty member and a visiting professor, including College of Mount St. Joseph on the Ohio, Mount St. Joseph, Ohio, as professor of creative writing; Ohio State University, Columbus, as visiting professor of English; and Texas Christian University, as visiting professor in humanities. She started her long tenure as professor at Virginia Tech, Blacksburg, Virginia in 1987. She also contributes a great deal of her time to public service and directing a variety of art festivals and writing workshops. She directs the Warm Hearth Writer's Workshop, was appointed to the Ohio Humanities Council in 1987, served from 1990 to 1993 as a member of the board of directors for Virginia Foundation for Humanities and Public Policy, and participated in the Appalachian Community Fund from 1991 to 1993 and the Volunteer Action Center from 1991 to 1994. She was a featured poet at the International Poetry Festival in Utrecht, Holland, in 1991. She gives numerous poetry readings and lectures worldwide and appears on numerous television talk shows.

Analysis: Poetry

From the beginning of her career, Nikki Giovanni has combined private with public concerns, and her development has been toward the exploration of the inner life of one black female—herself—as a paradigm for black women's aspirations in contemporary America. An individualist who early admired Ayn Rand's concept of rational self-interest, Giovanni has a unique black identity. Her example of self-actualization embodied in her poetry has been not only influential but also inspirational, especially to black youth.

In *The Souls of Black Folk* (1903), W. E. B. Du Bois expressed the dilemma of the black American writer—a double consciousness of being both an American and a black. Nikki Giovanni, however, has never felt this division. In *Gemini* she asserts, "I've always known I was colored. When I was Negro I knew I was colored; now that I'm Black I know which color it is. Any identity crisis I may have had never centered on race." The transition from Negro to black represents for her, as for Amiri Baraka and other adherents of the Black Consciousness movement, a transvaluation: black becomes a "sacrament." It is an outward and visible sign of an inward and spiritual grace, making a po-

447

etry reading a "service" and a play a "ritual." Rather than a mask that prevents the inner man from being seen, as in Ralph Ellison's *Invisible Man* (1952), color becomes a sign of worth itself. In her early poems and pronouncements, she proves herself a true Gemini, dividing the world into either/or, into mutually exclusive categories. Everything is literally black or white: "Perhaps the biggest question in the modern world is the definition of a genus—huemanity. And the white man is no hueman." Her concerns, in her first two books of poems, like the audience she both addresses and represents, are exclusively black. Her early ideas about poetry are closely connected with her ideas about race. In her essay "The Weather as a Cultural Determiner" she elaborates on the thesis that black people are naturally poets: Indeed "we are our own poems": "Poetry is the culture of a people. We are poets even when we don't write poems; just look at our life, our rhythms, our tenderness, our signifying, our sermons and our songs." Her poems were originally composed for polemical, not lyrical, ends—for the black community: Poetry is "just a manifestation of our collective historical needs. And we strike a responsive chord because the people will always respond to the natural things."

Political Poems
Throughout her poetry run two main themes, revolution and love—one destructive, the other creative. Even in her earliest verse both strands are evident; only the emphasis shifts from the former to the latter. For example, in an early poem, "Detroit Conference of Unity and Art (For HRB)," the "most valid" of the resolutions passed "as we climbed Malcolm's ladder" was "Rap chose me." The revolution that she calls for in *Black Judgement* is, on one level, literal: In "Reflections on April 4, 1968," the date of the assassination of Martin Luther King, Jr., even her poetic structure collapses in the face of the need for violence:

> What can I, a poor Black woman, do to destroy America?
> This is a question, with appropriate variations, being
> asked in every Black heart. There is one answer—I can kill.
> There is one compromise—I can protect those who kill.

448

> There is one cop-out—I can encourage others to kill. There
> are no other ways.

The revolution is also symbolic, striking out at the poisonous racial myths that have devalued blacks in America. In "Word Poem
(Perhaps Worth Considering)" she writes: "as things be/come/
let's destroy/ then we can destroy/ what we be/come/ let's
build/ what we become/ when we dream." The destruction
here is of values and attitudes, seemingly in accord with the
statement in *Gemini:* "Nobody's trying to make the system Black;
we're trying to make a system that's human so that Black folks
can live in it. This means we're trying to destroy the existing
system." Giovanni's poems attack the American political establishment in a sweeping, generalized way; her analysis is simple—
exterminate the white beast. Her real contempt is directed toward "Negroes" still in the service of white America: "The True
Import of Present Dialogue, Black vs. Negro" is "Can you kill/
Can you kill a white man/ Can you kill the nigger/ in you." Her
"Black Judgement" is upon " . . . niggerish ways." Aware that with
children lies the future, she urges in "Poem for Black Boys" new
revolutionary games:

> Ask your mother for a Rap Brown gun
> Santa just may comply if you wish hard enough
> Ask for CULLURD instead of Monopoly
> DO NOT SIT IN DO NOT FOLLOW KING
> GO DIRECTLY TO STREETS
> This is a game you can win.

Poetry of denial, vilification, and decreation (what she calls
her "nigger-nigger" phrase) is essentially dead-ended; the main
rhetorical problem of the new black poets was how to restore
value to the black experience. Giovanni has accomplished such
a restoration through the affirmation of her own life and the
transforming power of poetry. In her volume *Cotton Candy on a
Rainy Day,* "The Beep Beep Poem" has a "song of herself" almost
like Walt Whitman's:

> i love the aloneness of the road
> when I ascend descending curves

> the power within my toes delights me
> and i fling my spirit down the highway
> i love the way i feel
> when i pass the moon and i holler to the stars
> i'm coming through

Such elation, however, is unusual. The tone of "Nikki-Rosa," "Mothers," and "Legacies" is more bittersweet. Giovanni gradually realized that writing itself is creative of value: She says in "Boxes," "i write/ because/ i have to." In the 1960's, writing appeared to be a luxury: In "For Saundra," she notes:

> maybe i shouldn't write
> at all
> but clean my gun
> and check my kerosene supply
> perhaps these are not poetic
> times
> at all.

My House

In the 1960's, poetry was to be a witness of the times—"it's so important to record" ("Records"), but her poetry proved to be her house: *My House* shows her assimilation and transformation of the world into her castle. In "Poem (For Nina)" from that volume, she begins by asserting that "We are all imprisoned *in the castle of our skins*"; though her imagination will color her world "Black Gold": "my castle shall become/ my rendezvous/ my courtyard will bloom with hyacinths and jack-in-the-pulpits/ my moat will not restrict me but will be filled/ with dolphins . . . ." In "A Very Simple Wish" she wants through her poetry to make a patchwork quilt of the world, including all that seems to be left behind by world history: "i've a mind to build/ a new world/ want to play."

In *My House* Giovanni began to exhibit increased sophistication and maturity. Her viewpoint had broadened beyond a rigid black revolutionary consciousness to balance a wide range of social concerns. Her rhymes had also become more pronounced, more lyrical, more gentle. The themes of family love, loneliness, and frustration, which Giovanni had defiantly explored in her earlier works, find much deeper expression in *My House*. Her change from an incendiary radical to a nurturing poet is traced in the poem "Revolutionary Dreams": from dreaming "militant dreams/ of taking over america," she

> . . . awoke and dug
> that if i dreamed natural
> dreams of being a natural
> woman doing what a woman
> does when she's natural
> i would have a revolution

This changed perspective accords with the conclusion of "When I Die": "And if ever i touched a life i hope that life knows/ that i know that touching was and still is and will/ always be the true/ revolution." Love and sex form the subject matter of many of her poems. She will "scream and stamp and shout/ for more beautiful beautiful beautiful/ black men with outasight afros" in "Beautiful Black Men" and propose "counterrevolutionary" sex in "Seduction" and "That Day": "if you've got the dough/ then i've got the heat/ we can use my oven/ til it's warm and sweet."

This bold and playful manner, however, is usually modulated by the complications of any long-term relationship between men and women. While she explains in *Gemini*: "to me sex is an essence . . . . It's a basic of human relationships. And sex is conflict; it could be considered a miniwar between two people," marriage is "'give and take—you give and he takes.'" In "Woman" her acknowledgment of the difficulty of a black man maintaining his self-respect in America has led to her acceptance of his failings: "she decided to become/ a woman/ and though he still refused/ to be a man/ she decided it was all/ right."

Cotton Candy on a Rainy Day

This poem, like many others in *Cotton Candy on a Rainy Day*, bespeaks the tempering of her vision. When Giovanni published *Cotton Candy on a Rainy Day*, critics viewed it as one of her most somber works. They noted the focus on emotional ups and downs, fear and insecurity, and the weight of everyday responsibilities. The title poem tells of "the gray of my mornings/ Or the blues of every night" in a decade known for "loneliness." Life is likened to nebulous cotton candy: "The sweet soft essence/ of possibility/ Never quite maturing." Her attitude tired, her potential stillborn, she is unable to categorize life as easily as before, "To put a three-dimensional picture/ On a one-dimensional surface."

One reason for her growth in vision seems to be her realization of the complexity of a woman's life. The black woman's negative self-image depicted in "Adulthood" was not solved by adopting the role of Revolutionary Black Poet. In "Woman Poem," "Untitled," "Once a Lady Told Me," "Each Sunday," and "The Winter Storm," the women with compromised lives are other women. In "A Poem Off Center," however, she includes herself in this condition: "maybe i shouldn't feel sorry/ for myself/ but the more i understand women/ the more i do." A comparison of "All I Gotta Do" ("is sit and wait") to "Choice," two poems alike in their subject matter and their syncopated beat, shows that a woman's only choice is to cry.

Africa and Black Music

Two other themes in her poetry also ally Giovanni with the new black poets—Africa and black music. The romantic and exotic Africa of the Harlem Renaissance writers appears only in "Ego-Tripping," where Africa is personified as a beautiful woman. Her own African experience has produced poems that give a balanced recognition of the African's separate identity. In "They Clapped," African Americans are treated like any other tourists and African life is seen realistically.

> they stopped running when they learned the packages
> on the women's heads were heavy and that babies didn't
> cry and disease is uncomfortable and that villages are fun
> only because you knew the feel of good leather on good pavement.

Her conclusion—"despite the dead/ dream they saw a free future"—opens the way for a new hope in "Africa": "i dream of black men and women walking/ together side by side into a new world/ described by love and bounded by difference."

Black music forms the basis of many of her poems: Aretha Franklin emerges as her personal idol, lines from popular songs are woven into "Revolutionary Music" and "Dreams," and several of her poems are based on traditional black American music. She has written a blues tune, "Master Charge Blues," in which a modern woman lets her credit card cure her troubles, and a song which could be set to music, "The Only Song I'm Singing."

The use of the ballad stanza in "On Hearing 'The Girl with the Flaxen Hair'" is effective in building a narrative about white and black art: The girl with flaxen hair gets a song; the black woman does not because her man is tired after working. Her most successful adaptation of musical form comes in "The Great Pax White" which recalls gospel music (indeed, on her recording she read this poem to the tune of "Peace be still," which is also a refrain in the poem). Here Pax Whitie (a bitter parody of the Pax Romana) is described first in an inversion of the words beginning St. John's gospel: The word "was death to all life." Western history, its wars and brutality, is recounted with two alternating calls and responses: "ain't they got no shame?" and "ain't we got no pride?" Her historical account is heavily ironic:

> So the great white prince
> Was shot like a nigger in texas
> And our Black shining prince was murdered
> like that thug in his cathedral
> While our nigger in memphis
> was shot like their prince in dallas.

The irony here and in other political poems, such as "Oppression," will be directed in *Cotton Candy on a Rainy Day* toward herself in "Being and Nothingness" and "The New Yorkers."

Human Relationships

As Giovanni's poems turned toward human relationships, there was a marked increase in her lyricism and especially in her use of imagery, both decorative and structural. Her lover's hands are compared to butterflies in "The Butterfly"; she feels like a falling leaf after a night of passion in "Autumn Poems"; getting rid of a lover is just so much "Housecleaning." "Make Up" sustains the image of cosmetics to talk about the life of pretense that a woman must live. On the whole, her verse descends from William Carlos Williams and Langston Hughes, but her voice is her own. While she is not a stylistic innovator, nor a stunning image-maker, she has an ingratiating style, one that proceeds from the energy of her personality, and an increasingly sure command of phrasing.

In "The Wonder Woman (A New Dream—for Stevie Wonder)," Giovanni reviewed her life up to 1971: "i wanted to be/ a sweet inspiration in my dreams/ of my people but the times/ require that i give/ myself willingly and become/ a wonder woman." If her subsequent history has fallen short of this ideal, it is still her strong clear voice that one remembers after reading her poetry; her poems are ultimately the self-expression of a black woman who has discovered that "Black love is Black wealth" and who has brought many people, both black and white, to poetry.

Children's Poetry
Giovanni devoted much of her writing to children's poetry in the 1980's and early 1990's. She describes her writing for children as an opportunity to "share a bit of the past with children. Black kids deserve to hear their history. My kids books are serious but not dour." Her movement toward this type of poetry reflected her time spent as a mother and time spent enjoying her extended family. More than anything, the poems in her children's collection *Vacation Time* showcased her growing lightness of spirit and inner stability. Similarly, *Those Who Ride the Night Winds* revealed a new and innovative form and brought forth Giovanni's heightened self-knowledge and imagination. In *Those Who Ride the Night Winds*, she echoed the political activism of her early verse as she dedicated various pieces to Phillis Wheatley, Martin Luther King, Jr., and Rosa Parks. A decade passed between the publication of *Those Who Ride the Night Winds* and her 1994 title *Knoxville, Tennessee*, a time during which she devoted energy to public causes and arts development, wrote essays, and contributed to edited texts.

The Middle Years

During the 1980's and the 1990's—Giovanni's "middle years"—her work continued to reflect her changing concerns and perspectives. *The Selected Poems of Nikki Giovanni,* which spans the first three decades of her career, was lauded by critics as a "rich synthesis [that] reveals the evolution of Giovanni's voice and charts the course of the social issues that are her muses, issues of gender and race."

Her collection titled *Love Poems* has an interesting pop-culture twist to it. Ever an unwavering supporter of black youth, Giovanni was devastated by the murder of rap singer Tupac Shakur in 1997 and had the words "Thug Life" tattooed on her left forearm in his honor. She then dedicated *Love Poems* to Shakur. "A lover whose love was often misunderstood," begins the dedication. Giovanni noted in an interview that she was frustrated with those who would confuse the message and the messenger:

> Rap is expressing the violence that's there, and we weren't even looking at that until rap came up and talked about it. It gave voice to the conditions that people are living under.

While there are somber, sociopolitical pieces here—the burning of black churches and the aforementioned role of "gansta rap"—most of the poems find Giovanni upbeat and domestic. Most of the poems are about friendship and sexuality, children and motherhood, loneliness and sharing, "beautiful black men" and "our faith and our energy and loving our mamas and ourselves and the world and all the chances we took in trying to make everything better." Her celebration of creative energy and the family spirit of African American communities dominates this collection.

Blues: For All the Changes

As the twentieth century came to a close, readers found a bit of the younger, more political Giovanni in several of the poems of her collection *Blues: For All the Changes.* While sociopolitical commentary in poetry often fails because it loses touch with humanity, Giovanni continues to keep focus on people: Here she spars with ills that confront Americans, but every struggle has a human face. There is a real estate developer who is destroying the woodland adjacent to Giovanni's home in preparation for a new housing development ("Road Rage"). There is a young basketball star ("Iverson"), who, when harassed for his youth and style, finds a compassionate but stern sister in Giovanni. And there is President Bill Clinton, who is subject to Giovanni's opinions ("The President's Penis"). Giovanni writes in this collection with an authority informed by experience and shared with heart-stealing candor.

Pop culture and pleasure find a place in the collection as well. She writes about tennis player Pete Sampras and her own tennis playing; pays tribute to Jackie Robinson, soul singer Regina Belle, the late blues singer Alberta Hunter, and Betty Shabazz, the late widow of Malcolm X. She also writes fondly of her memories of going to the ballpark with her father to see the Cincinnati Reds.

Her battle with illness is captured in "Me and Mrs. Robin," which deals with Giovanni's convalescence from cancer surgery and the family of robins she observed with delight and sympathy from her window. Yet this gentle poem also revisits the real estate developer, who, the poem notes, has destroyed trees and "confused the birds and murdered the possum and groundhog." As she identifies with an injured robin, Giovanni's language invokes a gnostic cosmogony: God takes care of individuals; Mother Nature wreaks havoc left and right. "No one ever says 'Mother Nature have mercy.' Mother nature don't give a damn," Giovanni says; "that's why God is so important."

Other Literary Forms

Besides her volumes of verse, Nikki Giovanni has made several poetry recordings. Some, such as *Truth Is on Its Way* (Right On Records, 1971), have gospel music accompaniment. Her recordings, as well as her many public performances, have helped to popularize the black oral poetry movement. Her two books of conversations with older, established black writers, *A Dialogue:*

James Baldwin and Nikki Giovanni and *A Poetic Equation: Conversations Between Nikki Giovanni and Margaret Walker,* offer the contrasting attitudes of two generations of black American writers on the aims of black literature in white America. The first book is especially interesting for its spirited discussion about the changing relationships between black men and black women, a topic of many of Giovanni's poems. The second clarifies her literary development and contains an impassioned plea for blacks to seize control of their destinies.

Gemini: An Extended Autobiographical Statement on My First Twenty-five Years of Being a Black Poet, which was nominated for a National Book Award in 1973, offers scenes from her life as a child and mother. While little is seen of the experiences and influences that shaped her art and thought, the book does contain essays about the black cultural revolution of the 1960's that serve as companion pieces to her poems. She has edited several texts, written syndicated columns—"One Woman's Voice" (*The New York Times*) and "The Root of the Matter" (*Encore American and Worldwide News Magazine*); and contributed essays to many black magazines and journals. *Sacred Cows . . . and Other Edibles* collects a number of her essays. A collection of her work has been established at the Muger Memorial Library at Boston University.

Bibliography

Baldwin, James, and Nikki Giovanni. *A Dialogue: James Baldwin and Nikki Giovanni.* Philadelphia: Lippincott, 1973. Based on a conversation aired by the Public Broadcasting Service as *Soul!* in 1971, this friendly, informal conversation sheds light on Giovanni's opinions regarding race and gender identity in America—foundational themes in much of her poetry. Includes a foreword by Ida Lewis and an afterword by Orde Coombs.

Bigsby, C. W. E. *The Second Black Renaissance: Essays in Black Literature.* Westport, Conn.: Greenwood Press, 1980. Bigsby analyzes many recent contributions to African American literature, including the work of Giovanni. Useful to any student of contemporary African American literature. Contains bibliographical references and an index.

Fowler, Virginia C. *Nikki Giovanni.* New York: Twayne, 1992. An introductory biography and critical study of selected works by Giovanni. Includes bibliographical references and index.

Giovanni, Nikki. "Author Spotlight: Nikki Giovanni." *Ebony* 59, no. 2 (December, 2003): 30-32. An interview with the author that centers on her recent work, particularly her work about her experience with cancer, as well as her views on creative writing and its relationship to hip-hop.

_____. *Conversations with Nikki Giovanni.* Interviews by Virginia C. Fowler. Jackson: University Press of Mississippi, 1992. A collection of interviews with Giovanni containing invaluable biographical information and insights into her writing.

_____. "Nikki Giovanni." http://nikki-giovanni.com/. Accessed September 1, 2005. In addition to a very complete summary of her works, this Web site contains a biography, video clips, photographs, and Giovanni's vitae.

_____. "Nikki Giovanni Gets Real." *Essence* 33, no. 7 (November, 2002): 130-131. Giovanni talks about the late rap artist Tupac Shakur, basketball player Allen Iverson, and how both have been misrepresented in the media. She also gives advice to women on raising boys and young men.

Giovanni, Nikki, and Gloria Naylor. "Conversation: Gloria Naylor and Nikki Giovanni." *Callaloo* 23, no. 4 (Fall, 2000): 1395-1409. Naylor and Giovanni discuss the importance of black people raising their tolerance of one another and resisting the stereotypes that suggest black men cannot be close to one another.

Gould, Jean. "Nikki Giovanni." In *Modern American Women Poets.* New York: Dodd, Mead, 1984. As treatments of this affable, self-confident poet are wont to be, Gould's discussion of Giovanni is warm and personal. Stresses her biography and particularly her precocious personal achievements; provides little direct examination of the poetry.

Madhubuti, Haki R. *Dynamite Voices.* Detroit: Broadside Press, 1971. Radical African American poet Madhubuti offers a history and criticism of some poets of the 1960's, of which Giovanni was one. Valuable, because he offers a contemporary look at the African American poetry scene. Contains a bibliography.

Walters, Jennifer. "Nikki Giovanni and Rita Dove: Poets Redefining." *The Journal of Negro History* 85, no. 3 (Summer, 2000): 210-217. The poetry of Nikki Giovanni and Rita Dove is discussed. Both women are examples of self-defined African American women who found a voice through writing.

White, Evelyn C. "The Poet and the Rapper." *Essence* 30, no. 1 (May, 1999): 122-124. Discusses Nikki Giovanni and cultural rapper and actor Queen Latifah, racism, rap music, and politics, topics which have abundantly influenced Giovanni's poetry.

— Sarah Hilbert; Honora Rankine-Galloway

Alex Haley

Biographer and novelist

Born: Ithaca, New York; August 11, 1921
Died: Seattle, Washington; February 10, 1992

LONG FICTION: *Roots: The Saga of an American Family*, 1976; *A Different Kind of Christmas*, 1988; *Alex Haley's Queen: The Story of an American Family*, 1993 (with David Stevens); *Mama Flora's Family*, 1998 (with Stevens).
TELEPLAY: *Palmerstown, U.S.A.*, 1980.
NONFICTION: *The Playboy Interviews*, 1993 (Murray Fisher, editor).
EDITED TEXT: *The Autobiography of Malcolm X*, 1965.

Achievements

Alex Haley received widespread recognition in 1964 for the publication of *The Autobiography of Malcolm X* "as told to Alex Haley." This work presents the life of the militant and controversial Nation of Islam leader Malcolm X in his own words, and its vast success undoubtedly was driven in part by Malcolm X's assassination in February, 1965. *The Autobiography of Malcolm X* earned its place in literary history for providing a glimpse into the mind of the self-proclaimed "angriest black man in America."

After publishing *The Autobiography of Malcolm X*, Haley worked for the next ten years on the project that became the best-selling novel *Roots*. A fictionalized account of the lives of Haley's African American ancestors over the course of seven generations, *Roots* gained immediate popularity and launched a genealogy craze among Americans of all ethnicities, not just African Americans. *Roots* also was turned into a miniseries that was viewed in 1977 by 130 million people, making it one of the biggest television events of all time.

Both works, although different in form, breached the racial divide in popular culture and brought important American racial issues to the attention of a mass audience that included people of all colors. This achievement is reflected in the honors that Haley received for these two works. *The Autobiography of Malcolm X* was named by *Time* magazine as one of the ten most important nonfiction books of the twentieth century. Following the publication of *Roots,* which received a 1977 National Book Award, Haley was awarded a Pulitzer Prize and the the Spingarn Medal of the National Association for the Advancement of Colored People (NAACP) for outstanding achievement by a black American.

Biography

Alex Haley was born in Ithaca, New York, in 1921 to Bertha George Palmer and Simon Alexander Haley, graduate students at Cornell University. As a young boy, Haley moved with his family back to his parents' hometown of Henning, Tennessee. Growing up in Henning surrounded by a large extended family, Haley and his younger brothers enjoyed listening to their grandmother and aunts tell stories about their family's history. One story that particularly fascinated Haley was the tale of a slave ancestor named Kunta Kinte, also referred to as "the African," who had arrived on a ship that landed in a place called "Naplis"—which Haley much later learned was Annapolis, Maryland—and worked on a plantation in Spotsylvania County, Virginia.

After attending teacher's college in North Carolina for two years, Haley joined the U.S. Coast Guard in 1939. In 1941, he married Nannie Branch, with whom he had two children, Lydia and William. Haley served as a mess boy and later as a cook at the beginning of his Coast Guard career, but he took up writing as a hobby when he found that his writing skills were in demand among coworkers who needed help composing love letters. This experience led Haley to try his hand as a romance writer, and he submitted numerous romance stories to popular magazines, but without success. Undaunted, Haley next tried his hand at history, writing mainly about the history of the Coast Guard, and he published several of these articles in magazines. In 1949, Haley was promoted to the position of Coast Guard

(AP/Wide World Photos)

journalist, a position that he held until his retirement from service in 1958.

After retiring from the Coast Guard, Haley authored a successful series of articles in *Playboy* magazine about prominent African Americans, including jazz musician Miles Davis, boxer Cassius Clay (later known as Muhammad Ali), and Nation of Islam leader Malcolm X, among others. His *Playboy* interview with Malcolm X led Haley to take on a larger project, which became his first book, *The Autobiography of Malcolm X*, published in 1965. Haley met with Malcolm X frequently over a two-year period to conduct the interviews for the book, which sold six million copies and was translated into eight languages. Its critical and popular acclaim helped Haley obtain a contract with the publisher Doubleday to write his next book, *Roots*.

Haley's first marriage ended in 1964, and he married Juliette Collins, with whom he had one child, Cynthia, before their divorce in 1972. Between the publication of *The Autobiography of*

Malcolm X in 1965 and *Roots* in 1976, Haley spent most of his time conducting the painstaking historical and genealogical research for *Roots*. His research ultimately led him to Gambia, West Africa, where he met a *griot*, or ancestral storyteller, who told Haley the African side of his family's stories about Kunta Kinte. Haley describes this encounter as the "peak experience" of his life.

In 1976, *Roots* was published and immediately became a bestseller. Almost overnight, the book sparked a genealogy fad among Americans of all ethnicities but particularly among African Americans. Read by millions, the story of *Roots* became even more well known in 1977 when it was adapted for television as a miniseries that was viewed by 130 million people.

Not long after the publication of *Roots* and the airing of the miniseries, several writers brought plagiarism lawsuits against Haley. Although judges dismissed two of the suits, Haley paid $650,000 in an out-of-court settlement to Harold Courlander, author of a 1967 novel called *The African*. Some people believe that Haley's settlement payment was an admission of guilt; others believe that Haley agreed to the payment simply to avoid a lengthy trial. A few years later, several historians questioned whether *Roots* was historically accurate and whether Haley's genealogical research was reliable. However, despite questions about its authenticity, *Roots* continues to be important for its influence on popular culture and for its realistic portrayal of slavery and the lives of African Americans.

Alex Haley died of cardiac arrest in 1992 in Seattle, Washington. He was seventy years old.

Analysis: Nonfiction

To conduct the interviews that would become *The Autobiography of Malcolm X*, Alex Haley met with Malcolm X almost daily throughout 1963 and 1964. According to Haley, Malcolm insisted that the story be told in his own words, with no "biographical interpretation" on Haley's part. This limited Haley's role as a biographer: Because he followed Malcolm's ban on interpretation, the reader learns only what Malcolm chooses to reveal.

However, despite this rather significant limitation, Haley's work is a success. He managed to take the raw data of hundreds of hours of interviews and weave together a life story that is not only coherent but powerfully lucid, revealing to a great extent the logical development of Malcolm X's theories about race and religion. However misguided some of Malcolm X's racial beliefs seem, Haley's articulate writing serves to create understanding—understanding of how these beliefs make a great deal of sense in the world inhabited by Malcolm X and millions of other young men like him.

The Autobiography of Malcolm X

Malcolm X was born Malcolm Little in 1925. His father was involved in the black separatist movement, and the family was forced to move several times when Malcolm was young in order to escape racially motivated violence. In 1929, the growing family settled in East Lansing, Michigan. Malcolm's childhood changed dramatically when his father died in 1931, attacked by white men who despised and feared his political beliefs. Plunged into grinding poverty, the family of eight struggled to stay together, but within a few years, Malcolm's mother suffered a nervous breakdown and was institutionalized. After a stint in a juvenile detention home, Malcolm was sent to live with an older half-sister in Boston.

In Boston, and later in Harlem, New York, Malcolm learned how to live "on the street," surviving by selling drugs, "running numbers" (working for an illegal lottery), pimping, and stealing. Finally caught and sent to jail in 1946, Malcolm underwent a prison conversion to Islam and began corresponding regularly with Elijah Muhammad, the leader of the Nation of Islam. Before long, Malcolm was a devout believer in Elijah Muhammad's teachings, including the controversial ideas that black people are a superior race and white people are "devils."

With access to the prison library, and time on his hands, Malcolm began to study history and literature, and his reading convinced him that white people had mistreated people of color throughout history and had often used Christianity as a tool to oppress people of color. This self-education reinforced

Malcolm's commitment to Nation of Islam teachings, and when he was released from prison in 1952, he began working for Elijah Muhammad, recruiting followers and starting new temples in cities all across the country, eventually becoming the head minister of the New York City Temple.

Working for the Nation of Islam, Malcolm discovered his gift for public speaking, and during the twelve years that he served as a highly visible spokesman for the Nation of Islam, its membership and its profile increased immensely. During this time, Malcolm also became a highly divisive figure. His passionate speeches about black pride, black superiority, and white "devils" typically had one of two effects on his audiences. Many black people felt empowered by Malcolm's black pride message and angered by his revelations about the system of oppression that served to keep black people "in their place." However, many people of all skin colors felt that Malcolm's teachings were just as racist as the system of oppression that he was fighting, and that encouraging separatism was taking a step backward in race relations.

In late 1963, Malcolm and Elijah Muhammad had a disagreement, leading Malcolm X to leave the Nation of Islam and found a new group, the Muslim Mosque. In 1964, Malcolm made two extensive trips to Africa and the Middle East, including a pilgrimage to the Islamic holy city of Mecca in Saudi Arabia and a speaking tour of many African capitals. During the pilgrimage, when he witnessed Muslims of all skin colors worshipping together, Malcolm underwent a "second conversion"—a fundamental change in his beliefs about race. When he returned to the United States, Malcolm began teaching that a "brotherhood of all races" just might be possible after all.

However, Malcolm did not live long enough to spread this new teaching very far. He was assassinated in 1965 at the age of 39.

Robert Penn Warren, discussing *The Autobiography of Malcolm X* in an essay from the *Yale Review* in 1966, writes

> He was the black man who looked the white man in the eye and
> forgave nothing. . . . [He] let the white man see what, from a cer-

tain perspective, he, his history, and his culture looked like. It was possible to say that this perspective was not the only one, that it did not give the whole truth about the white man . . . but it was not possible to say that the perspective did not carry *a* truth. . . . As one reads the *Autobiography*, one feels that, whatever the historical importance of Malcolm Little, his story has permanence.

This is perhaps the most significant contribution of *The Autobiography of Malcolm X*: Haley's masterful transcription of Malcolm X's words articulates the mission and meaning of the life of a controversial and often misunderstood activist.

Analysis: Long Fiction

Some critics have found it difficult to evaluate *Roots* because it is unclear whether the book is essentially fact or essentially fiction. Although based on genealogical and historical research, it is not a book of history, because most of its details and dialogue are (by necessity) invented. However, unlike most historical fiction, *Roots* is much more than a fictional story placed against a real historical background, with a few famous historical figures making cameo appearances. Haley himself called the book "faction," a mix of fact and fiction.

Roots

Roots opens with the birth of Kunta Kinte in 1750 and tells the story of his childhood in a Muslim family, part of a Mandinka tribe in the small Gambian village of Juffure in West Africa. One day when Kunta is about seventeen, he is captured and endures the horrors of the Middle Passage—the voyage across the Atlantic Ocean on a crowded, stinking, disease-ridden slave ship, an experience shared by perhaps 20 million Africans over the four hundred years of the slave trade.

Landing at Annapolis and arriving at a plantation in Virginia, Kunta is shocked to find that the other black people there are not Africans—they speak English, practice Christianity, and, worst of all, seem to accept the fact that they are slaves. Kunta vows never to assimilate, and for this, he endures unspeakably brutal treatment. His African ways and stubborn individuality become the tales and legends of his descendants: his daughter Kizzy, who is sold away from her parents as a teenager; Kizzy's son, the colorful character Chicken George, born of rape by Kizzy's plantation owner; and all the generations down to Alex Haley's own grandparents, aunts, and parents, who share stories about Kunta, "the African," with Haley and his brothers.

Critics who consider *Roots* to be a work of history have sometimes faulted it for containing historical inaccuracies. For instance, it is unlikely that Kunta's village, Juffure, was as peaceful and democratic in the eighteenth century as Haley portrays it, and it is also doubtful whether Kunta's northern Virginia plantation would have produced cotton in the late 1700's. These kinds of factual errors bother some critics, but others overlook them and judge the book on its literary merits rather than its historical correctness.

The literary merits of *Roots* are many. Most important is the skill with which Haley portrays the reality of slavery and the slave trade. Haley's writing shatters the myth of the happy-go-lucky slave who loves his master and has no desire to be freed. Haley was not the first writer to portray slavery realistically, but he was the first to reach a mass audience of Americans of all colors and ethnicities. This feat was partly the result of perfect timing. The Civil Rights movement of the 1960's had made some progress in changing mainstream attitudes toward African Americans, so *Roots* was able to find a wide audience that might not have been ready to hear the book's message twenty years earlier. However, the book's success also is a result of its compelling story line and characters. Haley's skillful writing easily draws readers in, helping them identify with and care about the characters' triumphs and sorrows.

Roots also succeeds in its resonance with African Americans whose family histories were lost or obscured by the institution of slavery. The book elicited a very personal response among many African Americans, who felt that *Roots* had returned their identity to them. Beyond the personal scale, however, the novel changed American culture by demonstrating that it was possible to do serious historical research into African American history and genealogy. Indeed, the study of African American history in schools and colleges became commonplace only after the publication of *Roots*.

Roots has a universal appeal that accounts for its commercial success. Although it tells the unique story of African Americans, it also tells a story with which all Americans can identify. Most Americans' ancestors originally were settlers from other continents. Just like Haley's family, many American families tell stories about their forebears and raise their children to know their roots. Finally, all Americans can sympathize with what many believe to be the worst horror of slavery—not the beatings or the lack of freedom, but the forced separation of families. For these reasons, *Roots* found a receptive audience not only among African Americans but also among Americans of all ethnicities and backgrounds.

Bibliography

Garraty, John A., and Mark C. Carnes, eds. *American National Biography.* Vol. 9. New York: Oxford University Press, 1999. Contains a thorough discussion of Haley's life and works.

Kern-Foxworth, Marilyn. "Alex Haley." In *Dictionary of Literary Biography,* edited by Thadious M. Davis and Trudier Harris. Vol. 38 in *Afro-American Writers After 1955: Dramatists and Prose Writers.* Detroit: Gale Research, 1985. Relates Haley's life to his writings. Includes a bibliography.

Massaquoi, Hans J. "Alex Haley: The Man Behind *Roots.*" *Ebony* 32, no. 6 (April, 1977): 33-39. Discusses the writing of *Roots* and the making of the television miniseries. Includes black-and-white and color photographs.

Shirley, David. *Alex Haley.* New York: Chelsea House, 1994. This biography includes black-and-white photographs and an introduction by Coretta Scott King.

Warren, Robert Penn. "Malcolm X: Mission and Meaning." *Yale Review* 56, no. 2 (Winter, 1966): 161-171. A review of *The Autobiography of Malcolm X* that discusses its political and ideological ramifications.

— Karen Antell

Virginia Hamilton

Novelist and biographer

Born: Yellow Springs, Ohio; March 12, 1936
Died: Dayton, Ohio; February 19, 2002

NONFICTION: *W. E. B. Du Bois: A Biography*, 1972; *Paul Robeson: The Life and Times of a Free Black Man*, 1974.

CHILDREN'S/YOUNG ADULT LITERATURE: *Zeely*, 1967; *The House of Dies Drear*, 1968; *The Planet of Junior Brown*, 1971; *M. C. Higgins the Great*, 1974; *Justice and Her Brothers*, 1978; *Dustland*, 1980; *Jahdu*, 1980; *The Gathering*, 1981; *Sweet Whispers, Brother Rush*, 1982; *Willie Bea and the Time the Martians Landed*, 1983; *The People Could Fly: American Black Folktales*, 1985; *The Mystery of Drear House*, 1987; *A White Romance*, 1987; *Anthony Burns: The Defeat and Triumph of a Fugitive Slave*, 1988; *In the Beginning: Creation Stories from Around the World*, 1988; *Bells of Christmas*, 1989; *The Dark Way: Stories from the Spirit World*, 1990; *Cousins*, 1990; *Many Thousand Gone: African Americans from Slavery to Freedom*, 1992; *Plain City*, 1993; *Her Stories: African American Folktales, Fairy Tales, and True Tales*, 1995; *When Birds Could Talk and Bats Could Sing*, 1996; *A Ring of Tricksters: Animal Tales from America, the West Indies, and Africa*, 1997; *The Magical Adventures of Pretty Pearl*, 1998; *Second Cousins*, 1998; *Bluish*, 1999; *The Girl Who Spun Gold*, 2000; *Wee Winnie Witch's Skinny: An Original Scare Tale for Halloween*, 2001; *Time Pieces: The Book of Times*, 2002.

Achievements

Virginia Hamilton has been called one of the best writers of children's fiction in the twentieth century. Her output has been prodigious, and the number of awards and honors she received attests not only to her popularity and commercial success but also to her artistry and skill. She has been given over forty honors, and in many instances she has received the same award for more than one book. For instance, she has the American Library Association Notable Book award for fifteen different books. The American Library Association Best Book for Young Adults award went to six of her books. Among the many other awards her books have received are the American Library Association's Coretta Scott King Award, The Horn Book Fanfare Honor Book Award, the Hans Christian Anderson Award (an international award), the National Book Award, the Newbery Medal and Honor Book Awards, the 1996 Honor Titles Storytelling World Award, and many others. Her body of work was honored with such awards as the Ohio Governor's Award of 2000, the Ohioana Award in 1984 and its Career Medal in 1991. Other honors include Distinguished Visiting Professorships at Queens College, New York (1986-1987 and 1987-1988) and at Ohio State University (1988-1989), and honorary degrees from Bank Street College of Education in New York, Ohio State University, Wright State University (Ohio), and Kent State University (Ohio). One of the most prestigious awards she has been given is the John D. and Catherine C. MacArthur Fellowship, which she received in 1995. She was the first children's author recipient of this so-called genius award.

Biography

Virginia Esther Hamilton, the youngest of five children, was born and raised in Yellow Springs, Ohio, a descendent of an African American man who escaped to Ohio from slavery. Her parents were Kenneth James Hamilton, a musician, and Etta Belle Perry Hamilton. She attended school in Yellow Springs, graduating with honors, and went on to Yellow Springs's Antioch College on a full scholarship. Her writing courses there reinforced her longstanding conviction that becoming an author was her destiny. She completed further study at Ohio State University and The New School for Social Research in New York.

In New York, she supported herself through various activities, including work as a singer in obscure nightclubs. She mingled with other writers, musicians, and artists and ultimately met her future husband, poet Arnold Adoff, whom she married in March 1960. The two traveled to Spain and North Africa, destinations she had long wanted to visit. It was after this lengthy trip (lasting several months) that she wrote her first book, *Zeely*. She had tried to write, even at a very early age, and had concentrated her efforts on short stories. But an editor at Macmillan Publishing Company (with whom she had attended Antioch College) suggested that she try book-length fiction for young adults. *Zeely* was the result of Hamilton's efforts to transform a short story she had written in college into a short novel.

The success of her award-winning first book was balanced with a few critics' comments on flaws in the novel's character development. Still, she was encouraged to continue, knowing that she had begun to establish a reputation for an impressive style and imaginative narratives. Her second book came out in 1968, and she had produced seven more by 1974, interspersing her fiction with biographies of the notable African Americans W. E. B. Du Bois and Paul Robeson. She chose these biographical subjects because they fit in with her strong belief in the ability of African Americans to survive against unfair odds and in the importance of nurturing African American racial pride. These concepts are prominent themes in many of her fictional works.

Though her husband had been a teacher in New York and she had lived there while attending school and working in different capacities (one of her jobs was as a cost accountant for an engineering firm), after fifteen years of off-and-on residence, Hamilton felt the city was so mentally stimulating that it was difficult for her to find the meditative quiet she needed as a writer. Consequently, she moved with her husband and their two children back to Ohio and settled on land that had been owned by her family since the late nineteenth century. Hamilton and Adoff built a large redwood and glass home, where they both worked at their craft. She produced more than thirty books, most of them award winners, before dying of breast cancer in 2002. She was sixty-five years old.

Analysis: Children's Literature

Virginia Hamilton is known internationally for the major contributions her young adult fiction makes to the fields of children's literature and African American literature. Her dozens of fiction and nonfiction works portray the African American experience in a unique and honest way that had rarely been attempted by another American writer. Her main characters are solemn children who are faced with situations or conditions that are at least peculiar, and often bizarre or even perilous. These children face their circumstances with purpose and dignity, and eventually come to understand what it means to be African American in America and to be worthy human beings.

Zeely

Zeely Tayber is an older girl who lives on a farm and raises hogs. Over six feet tall, she is regal and mysterious, and to the young girl, Geeder, visiting a neighboring farm with her brother, she seems as marvelous as a Watutsi queen, like one pictured in a magazine Geeder reads in her uncle's house. Geeder sees Zeely as a proud and dignified role model and wants to be like her and to become her friend. When the two finally meet, first at a disastrous hog market and later when Zeely summons her to a catalpa forest, Geeder at last learns about Zeely's mysterious background.

Zeely was Hamilton's first book. It was named one of the American Library Association's Notable Books and also received a Nancy Block Award. Some critics, however, took exception with her character development and to certain episodes that they felt were anticlimactic. For example, in one scene the hogs are brought to market and Geeder is slightly injured; this scene was critiqued as insufficiently realized. The author was praised, however, for her use of language and her ability to create a story and style that appeals to young female readers.

The House of Dies Drear

Written in 1968, *The House of Dies Drear* tells the story of a family that relocates from North Carolina to a house in an Ohio town that was an Underground Railroad station. The father, a history professor, is fascinated by the house and the legends surrounding it. But his thirteen-year-old son Thomas and the rest of the family are uneasy living in a house where, as legend has it, the former owner, a Dutch immigrant abolitionist named Drear, and two runaway slaves were murdered. The ghosts of the slaves and Drear are supposed to be haunting the house. Thomas explores the tunnels and secret passageways in and around the house and encounters the old caretaker, Mr. Pluto, who seems evil to Thomas. The youth is convinced the house is dangerous, and the family is warned that they must leave before disaster strikes. But Thomas and his father join forces, and together they try to unlock the mystery of the house.

This book received the Ohioana Book Award and the Edgar Allan Poe Award for best juvenile mystery. A sequel, *The Mystery of Drear House: The Conclusion of the Dies Drear Chronicles*, was written eighteen years later and revealed the house's mysteries. A movie based on the book was made in 1984; Hamilton wrote the screenplay.

The Planet of Junior Brown

Junior Brown is a neurotic, three-hundred-pound eighth grader with musical talent. His family circumstances are miserable: a sickly, overprotective mother and an often-absent father. Music is the one bright spot in his life, but, despite his talent, his music teacher won't allow him to practice his lessons on the grand piano in her apartment. The excuses she offers only increase the fantasies that gradually consume the boy. His friends are few: There is only Mr. Pool, the school janitor, and Buddy Clark. Buddy is an orphan who has lived most of his young life on the streets. He and Junior so rarely go to school that on the infrequent occasions when they do show up, some teachers don't recognize them. Life becomes so complicated for them that Junior begins to lose his grip on reality, and Buddy and Mr. Pool are the only people with the loyalty and affection to support him in his decision to run away from home and in his encounter with his piano teacher's mysterious "relative."

Some critics consider the characters Junior and Buddy to be as memorable and original as any in modern fiction written for young readers. The story is one of courage in the face of despair and of heroism and survival, and it promotes the notion that human beings must be interdependent. *The Planet of Junior Brown*, with its themes of the brotherhood of man and the indomitability of the human spirit, won Hamilton's first Newbery Honor Book award.

M. C. Higgins the Great

Mayo Cornelius Higgins, nicknamed M. C., is a youngster living with his family on land that has been in the family since his great-grandmother came there as a runaway slave. When stripmining on the nearby mountain threatens to ruin their land, M. C. envisions escaping with his family to a better place. However, strangers come to the area, bringing with them the possibility that M. C. can do something to try to save the mountain that is part of their home instead of merely trying to escape the impending ugliness.

Called by some reviewers a brilliantly conceived novel, *M. C. Higgins the Great* has the elements of a rite-of-passage story, showing a youngster coping with conflicts with a difficult father and dealing with the need to grow up and show more maturity and responsibility. Though it won a Newbery Medal, a National Book Award, and the Boston Globe Award, it also received some criticism. Its opening passages were said to be "almost impenetrable" because of the "heavy prose." Still, others commend it as a fine piece of writing, "moving, poetic, and unsentimental," "warm, humane, and hopeful."

Cousins and Second Cousins

Two books follow the story of cousins Cammy, Patty Ann, and Elodie, whose relationship is marred by the perception that Patty Ann is not only smart and beautiful but spoiled, selfish, and rude. In *Cousins*, Cammy has to deal with guilt when Patty Ann drowns soon after Cammy wishes she were dead. Some of her despair comes from the circumstances surrounding the drowning: Patty Ann dies rescuing Elodie. Family, especially Cammy's grandmother, help her deal with her remorse. *Second Cousins* picks up the story a year later, with Cammy and Elodie still recovering from their feelings about Patty Ann's untimely death. A family reunion introduces them to yet another cousin, through whom a long-hidden family secret is disclosed.

These two books were written eight years apart; the first in 1990, the second in 1998. *Cousins* received five awards, among them the American Library Association's Notable Book and the Notable Children's Trade Book in the Field of Social Studies.

Other Literary Forms

Though fiction for children and young adults is her strong suit, Virginia Hamilton has also produced works of nonfiction, picture books, articles, essays, and edited anthologies. Her nonfiction work includes biographies of W. E. B. Du Bois and Paul Robeson. *Many Thousand Gone: African Americans from Slavery to Freedom* and *Anthony Burns: The Defeat and Triumph of a Fugitive Slave* are books about somewhat-obscure African Americans. The former contains vignettes and short narratives about black people whose lives reveal the realities of slavery, the fugitive experience, and the hard-won freedom during and after the Civil War. *Anthony Burns* recounts the Boston trial of one black man under the Fugitive Slave Law and reveals the appalling conditions faced by slaves in antebellum America. Hamilton collected many folktales about Africans and African Americans, as well as other ethnic groups, in such works as *Her Stories: African American Folktales, Fairy Tales, and True Tales*; *In the Beginning: Creation Stories from Around the World*; *The People Could Fly: American Black Folktales*; and *A Ring of Tricksters: Animal Tales from America, the West Indies, and Africa*. Her articles have appeared in the journals *Elementary English* and *Horn Book*.

Bibliography

Hamilton, Virginia. "A Conversation with Virginia Hamilton." Interview by Marilyn Apseloff. *Children's Literature in Education*, n.s. 14, no. 4 (Winter, 1983): 204-213. An interview with author Virginia Hamilton, who discusses her life and her work.

_____. "Creative Geography in the Ohio Novels of Virginia Hamilton." *Children's Literature Association Quarterly* 8, no. 1 (Spring, 1983): 17-20. Discusses Virginia Hamilton's use of actual locations and landscapes of her Yellow Springs, Ohio, hometown to create the details of mood in her novels set in Ohio.

_____. "Virginia Hamilton: Welcome to My World!" http://www.virginiahamilton.com/. Accessed September 1, 2005. Maintained by Hamilton's husband, this site details Hamilton's life and work, and also contains photos, video clips, information on the conferences named in her honor, and jokes and activities for children.

Langton, Jane. "Virginia Hamilton the Great." *Horn Book* 50 (December, 1974): 671-673. A commendatory appraisal of Hamilton's Newbery Award-winning *M. C. Higgins the Great.* Also analyzes the book's style.

Mikkelsen, Nina. *Virginia Hamilton.* New York: Twayne, 1994. Discusses Hamilton's writing life and habits, her early life as she prepared to become a writer, and her life after the peak of her writing career.

Review of *The People Could Fly,* by Virginia Hamilton. *Kirkus Reviews* 51, no. 21 (November, 2004): 1044. A very positive review of Hamilton's book; makes special note of its power and dreamlike qualities.

Spears-Bunton, Linda. "Welcome to My House: Student Responses to Virginia Hamilton's *House of Dies Drear." Journal of Negro Education* 59, no. 4 (1990): 566-576. The article discusses how the cultural backgrounds of students from varying ethnic and socioeconomic groups influence their comprehension in reading Hamilton's book, which is used in a study in conjunction with Nathaniel Hawthorne's *Scarlet Letter.*

Trites, Robert. "'I Double Never Ever Never Lie to My Chil'ren': Inside People in Virginia Hamilton's Narratives." *African American Review* 32, no. 1 (1998): 147-156. Author discusses the characters in Hamilton's novels and how they relate to each other within the narrative structure of the stories.

Ward, Doug. "The Aboveground Railroad." Review of *The People Could Fly,* by Virginia Hamilton. *The New York Times,* November 14, 2004, p. 45. A review of one of Hamilton's most well-known contributions to the field of children's literature.

—*Jane L. Ball*

Lorraine Hansberry

Playwright

Born: Chicago, Illinois; May 19, 1930
Died: New York, New York; January 12, 1965

DRAMA: *A Raisin in the Sun*, pr., pb. 1959; *The Sign in Sidney Brustein's Window*, pr. 1964, pb. 1965; *To Be Young, Gifted, and Black*, pr. 1969, pb. 1971; *Les Blancs*, pr. 1970, pb. 1972; *The Drinking Gourd*, pb. 1972; *What Use Are Flowers?*, pb. 1972; *Les Blancs: The Collected Last Plays of Lorraine Hansberry*, pb. 1972 (includes *Les Blancs*, *The Drinking Gourd*, and *What Use Are Flowers?*; Robert Nemiroff, editor).

NONFICTION: *The Movement: Documentary of a Struggle for Equality*, 1964 (includes photographs); *To Be Young, Gifted, and Black: Lorraine Hansberry in Her Own Words*, 1969 (Robert Nemiroff, editor).

Achievements

Lorraine Hansberry's career was very brief: Only two of her plays were produced in her lifetime, yet she recorded some very impressive theatrical achievements. She was only twenty-nine when *A Raisin in the Sun* appeared on Broadway, and its great success earned for her recognition that continues to this day. When *A Raisin in the Sun* was voted best play of the year by the New York Drama Critics Circle, she became the first black person as well as the youngest person to win the award. In 1973, a musical was adapted from *A Raisin in the Sun*, entitled *Raisin* (with libretto by Robert Nemiroff); it won a Tony Award as best musical of the year. She was respected and befriended by such figures as Paul Robeson and James Baldwin, and she helped in an active way to further the work of the Civil Rights movement. Though her later work has received far less recognition than her first play, *A Raisin in the Sun* continues to enjoy broad popularity.

Biography

Lorraine Vivian Hansberry was born on May 19, 1930, in the South Side of Chicago, the black section of the city. Her parents, Carl and Mamie Hansberry, were well-off. Her father was a United States deputy marshal for a time and then opened a successful real estate business in Chicago. Despite her family's affluence, they were forced by local covenants to live in the poor South Side. When Hansberry was eight years old, her father decided to test the legality of those covenants by buying a home in a white section of the city. Hansberry later recalled one incident that occurred shortly after the family's move to a white neighborhood: A mob gathered outside their home, and a brick, thrown through a window, barely missed her before embedding itself in a wall.

In order to stay in the house, to which he was not given clear title, Carl Hansberry instituted a civil rights suit against such restrictive covenants. When he lost in Illinois courts, he and the National Association for the Advancement of Colored People (NAACP) carried an appeal to the United States Supreme Court, which, on November 12, 1940, reversed the ruling of the Illinois supreme court and declared the local covenants illegal. Thus, Lorraine had a consciousness of the need to struggle for civil rights from a very young age. Her father, despite his legal victory, grew increasingly pessimistic about the prospects for change in the racial situation, and he finally decided to leave the country and retire in Mexico City. He had a stroke during a visit to Mexico, however, and died in 1945.

Hansberry's uncle, William Leo Hansberry, was also an important influence on her. A scholar of African history who taught at Howard University, his pupils included Nnamdi Azikewe, the first president of Nigeria, and Kwame Nkrumah of Ghana. Indeed, William Leo Hansberry was such a significant figure in African studies that in 1963, the University of Nigeria named its College of African Studies at Nsakka after him. While Lorraine was growing up, she was frequently exposed to the perspectives of young African students who were invited to family dinners, and this exposure helped to shape many of the attitudes later found in her plays.

Lorraine, the youngest of four children, was encouraged to excel and was expected to succeed. After attending Englewood High School, she enrolled in the University of Wisconsin as a journalism student. She did not fare very well at the university, however, and felt restricted by the many requirements of the school. After two years, she left Wisconsin and enrolled in the New School for Social Research in New York, where she was permitted greater leeway in choosing courses.

Once in New York, Hansberry began writing for several periodicals, including *Freedom*, Paul Robeson's monthly magazine. She quickly became a reporter and then an associate editor of the magazine. In New York, she met Robert Nemiroff, then a student at New York University, and they were married in June of 1953. By this time, Hansberry had decided to be a writer, and

(Library of Congress)

although the bulk of her energies went into writing, she did hold a variety of jobs during the next few years. When Nemiroff acquired a good position with music publisher Phil Rose, she quit working and began writing full-time.

Hansberry's first completed work was *A Raisin in the Sun*, which, after an initial struggle for financial backing, opened on Broadway at the Ethel Barrymore Theatre on March 11, 1959. The play, starring Sidney Poitier, Ruby Dee, Louis Gossett, Jr., and Claudia McNeil, was an enormous success, running for 530 performances, and in May, it won for Hansberry the New York Drama Critics Circle Award.

Soon thereafter, Hansberry and Nemiroff moved from their apartment in Greenwich Village to a home in Croton, New York, in order for Hansberry to have more privacy for her work. At the same time, her success made her a public figure, and she used her newfound fame to champion the causes of civil rights and African independence. She made important speeches in a variety of places and once confronted then Attorney General Robert Kennedy on the issue of civil rights.

It was not until 1964 that Hansberry produced another play, *The Sign in Sidney Brustein's Window*, and by that time she was seriously ill. The play opened at the Longacre Theatre on October 15, 1964, to generally good but unenthusiastic reviews, and Nemiroff had to struggle to keep it open, a number of times placing advertisements in newspapers asking for support, accepting financial support from friends and associates, and once accepting the proceeds from a spontaneous collection taken up by the audience when it was announced that without additional funds, the play would have to close. On this uncertain financial basis, production of the play continued from week to week.

Hansberry's life continued in much the same way. While the play struggled, she was in a hospital bed dying of cancer. She once lapsed into a coma and was not expected to recover, but for a brief time she did rally, recovering all of her faculties. Her strength gave out, however, and on January 12, 1965, she died. That night, the Longacre Theatre closed its doors in mourning, and *The Sign in Sidney Brustein's Window* closed after 101 performances.

Analysis: Drama

Lorraine Hansberry claimed Sean O'Casey as one of the earliest and strongest influences on her work and cited his realistic portrayal of character as the source of strength in his plays. In *To Be Young, Gifted, and Black*, she praised O'Casey for describing

> the human personality in its totality. O'Casey never fools you about the Irish . . . the Irish drunkard, the Irish braggart, the Irish liar . . . and the genuine heroism which must naturally emerge when you tell the truth about people. This . . . is the height of artistic perception . . . because when you believe people so completely . . . then you also believe them in their moments of heroic assertion: you don't doubt them.

In her three most significant plays, *A Raisin in the Sun*, *The Sign in Sidney Brustein's Window*, and *Les Blancs*, one can see Hansberry's devotion to the principles that she valued in O'Casey. First, she espoused realistic drama; second, she believed that the ordinary individual has a capacity for heroism; and finally, she believed that drama should reveal to the audience its own humanity and its own capacity for heroism.

Hansberry claimed that her work was realistic rather than naturalistic, explaining that

> naturalism tends to take the world as it is and say: this is what it is . . . it is "true" because we see it every day in life . . . you simply photograph the garbage can. But in realism . . . the artist . . . imposes . . . not only what *is* but what is *possible* . . . because that is part of reality too.

For Hansberry, then, realism involved more than a photographic faithfulness to the real world. She sought to deliver a universal message but realized that "in order to create the universal you must pay very great attention to the specific. Universality . . . emerges from truthful identity of what is." This concern for realism was present from the very beginning of Hansberry's career and persists in her work, though she did occasionally depart from it in small ways, such as in the symbolic rather than literal presence of "The Woman" in *Les Blancs*, that character symbolizing the spirit of liberty and freedom that lives inside humanity.

Essential to Hansberry's vision of reality was the belief that the average person has within him or her the capacity for heroism. Hansberry believed that each human being is not only "dramatically interesting" but also a "creature of stature," and this is one of the most compelling features of her drama. Like O'Casey, Hansberry paints a full picture of each character, complete with flaws and weaknesses, yet she does not permit these flaws to hide the characters' "stature." Perhaps she expressed this idea best in *A Raisin in the Sun*, when Lena Younger berates her daughter Beneatha for condemning her brother, Walter Lee. Lena says, "When you start measuring somebody, measure him right, child, measure him right. Make sure you done taken into account what hills and valleys he come through before he got to wherever he is." For Hansberry, each character's life is marked by suffering, struggle, and weakness, yet in each case, the final word has not been written. Just as Beneatha's brother can rise from his degradation, just as Sidney (in *The Sign in Sidney Brustein's Window*) can overcome his ennui, so each of her characters possesses not only a story already written but also possibilities for growth, accomplishment, and heroism. Hansberry permits no stereotypes in her drama, opting instead for characters that present a mixture of positive and negative forces.

Hansberry's realistic style and her stress on the possibilities for heroism within each of her characters have everything to do with the purpose that she saw in drama. As James Baldwin observed, Hansberry made no bones about asserting that art has a purpose, that it contains "the energy that could change things." In *A Raisin in the Sun*, Hansberry describes a poor black family living in Chicago's South Side, her own childhood home, and through her realistic portrayal of their financial, emotional, and racial struggles, as well as in her depiction of their ability to prevail, she offers her audience a model of hope and perseverance and shows the commonality of human aspirations, regardless of color. In *The Sign in Sidney Brustein's Window*, she takes as her subject the disillusioned liberal Sidney Brustein, who has lost faith in the possibility of creating a better world. After all of his disillusionment, he realizes that despair is not an answer, that the only answer is hope despite all odds and logic, that change depends on his commitment to it. So too, in *Les Blancs*, Hansberry gives her audience a character, Tshembe Matoseh, who has a comfortable, pleasant, secure life and who seeks to avoid commitment to the cause of African independence, though he believes in the justness of that cause. He learns that change comes about only through commitment, and that such commitment often means the abandonment of personal comfort on behalf of something larger.

A Raisin in the Sun

Hansberry's earliest play, *A Raisin in the Sun*, is also her finest and most successful work. The play is set in the South Side of Chicago, Hansberry's childhood home, and focuses on the events that transpire during a few days in the life of the Younger family, a family headed by Lena Younger, the mother; the other family members are her daughter, Beneatha, her son, Walter Lee, and his wife, Ruth, and son, Travis. The play focuses on the problem of what the family should do with ten thousand dollars that Lena receives as an insurance payment after the death of her husband, Walter Lee, Sr. The money seems a blessing at first, but the family is torn, disagreeing on how the money should be spent.

The play's title is taken from Langston Hughes's poem "Harlem" and calls attention to the dreams of the various characters, and the effects of having those dreams deferred. The set itself, fully realistic, emphasizes this theme from the first moment of the play. The furniture, once chosen with care, has been well cared for, yet it is drab, undistinguished, worn out from long years of service. The late Walter Lee, Sr., was a man of dreams, but he could never catch up with them, and he died, exhausted and wasted, worn out like the furniture, at an early age. His family is threatened with the same fate, but his insurance money holds out hope for the fulfillment of dreams. Lena and Walter Lee, however, disagree about what to do with the money. Walter Lee hates his job as a chauffeur and plans to become his own man by opening a liquor store with some friends, but Lena instead makes a down payment on a house with one-third of the money, and plans to use another third to finance Beneatha's medical studies. After the two argue, Lena realizes that she has not permitted her son to be a man and has stifled him, just as the rest of the world has. In order to make up for the past, she entrusts him with the remaining two-thirds of the money, directing him to take Beneatha's portion and put it into a savings account for her, using the final third as he sees fit. Walter Lee, however, invests all the money in a foolhardy scheme and discovers shortly thereafter that one of his partners has bilked him of the money.

The house that Lena has purchased is in a white neighborhood, and a Mr. Lindner has approached the Youngers, offering to buy back the house—at a profit to the Youngers—because the members of the community do not want blacks living there. Walter Lee at first scornfully refuses Lindner's offer, but once he has lost all the money he is desperate to recoup his losses and calls Lindner, willing to sell the house. The family is horrified at how low Walter has sunk, but when Beneatha rejects him, claiming there is "nothing left to love" in him, Lena reminds her that "There is always something to love. And if you ain't learned that, you ain't learned nothing." Lena asks Beneatha, "You give him up for me? You wrote his epitaph too—like the rest of the world? Well, who give you the privilege?" The epitaph is indeed premature, for when Lindner arrives and Walter is forced to speak in his son's presence, Walter gains heroic stature by rejecting the offer, telling Lindner in simple, direct terms that they will move into their house because his father "earned it." It is a moment during which Walter comes into manhood, and if it has taken him a long while to do so, the moment is all the richer in heroism.

The theme of heroism found in an unlikely place is perhaps best conveyed through the symbol of Lena's plant. Throughout the play, Lena has tended a small, sickly plant that clings tenaciously to life despite the lack of sunlight in the apartment. Its environment is harsh, unfavorable, yet it clings to life anyway— somewhat like Walter, whose life should long ago have extinguished any trace of heroism in him. Hansberry gives her audience a message of hope.

Hansberry also reminds her audience of the common needs and aspirations of all humanity, and she does so without oversimplification. None of the characters in the play is a simple type, not even Lindner, who might easily have been presented as an incarnation of evil. Instead, Lindner is conveyed as a human being. When asked why she portrayed Lindner in this manner, Hansberry replied "I have treated Mr. Lindner as a human being merely because he is one; that does not make the meaning of his call less malignant, less sick." Here is where Hansberry calls her audience to action. She reminds the audience of what it is to be human and enjoins them to respect the dignity of all their fellows.

An interesting subtheme in the play, one that would be developed far more fully later in *Les Blancs,* is introduced by Joseph Asagai, an African student with a romantic interest in Beneatha. Some of the most moving speeches in the play belong to Asagai, and when Beneatha temporarily loses hope after Walter has lost all the money, Asagai reminds her of her ideals and the need to keep working toward improvement in the future. When Beneatha asks where it will all end, Asagai rejects the question, asking, "End? Who even spoke of an end? To life? To living?" Beneatha does not fully understand Asagai's argument at the time, but its meaning must be clear enough to the audience, who will see at the end of the play that Walter's victory is not an end, but rather one small, glorious advance. There will be other trials, other problems to overcome, but, as Asagai says, any other problem "will be the problem of another time."

The Sign in Sidney Brustein's Window

Hansberry's second play, *The Sign in Sidney Brustein's Window,* never matched the success of her first, but it, too, uses a realistic format and was drawn from her own life. Instead of South Side Chicago, it is set in Greenwich Village, Hansberry's home during the early years of her marriage with Robert Nemiroff, and the central character is one who must have resembled many of Hansberry's friends. He is Sidney Brustein, a lapsed liberal, an intellectual, a former insurgent who has lost faith in his ability to bring about constructive change. As the play opens, Sidney moves from one project, a nightclub that failed, to another, the publication of a local newspaper, which Sidney insists will be apolitical. His motto at the opening of the play is "Presume no commitment, disavow all engagement, mock all great expectations. And above all else, avoid the impulse to correct." Sidney's past efforts have failed, and his lost faith is much the same as Beneatha's in *A Raisin in the Sun*.

The surrounding environment goes a long way toward explaining Sidney's cynicism. His wife, Iris, has been in psychoanalysis for two years, and her troubled soul threatens their marriage. Iris's older sister, Mavis, is anti-Semitic, and her other sister, Gloria, is a high-class call girl who masquerades as a model. Sidney's upstairs neighbor, David Ragin, is a homosexual playwright whose plays invariably assert "the isolation of the soul of man, the alienation of the human spirit, the desolation of all love, all possible communication." Organized crime controls politics in the neighborhood, and drug addiction is rampant; one of Sidney's employees at the defunct nightclub, Sal Peretti, died of addiction at the age of seventeen, despite Sidney's efforts to help him. Faced with these grim realities, Sidney longs to live in a high, wooded land, far from civilization, in a simpler, easier world.

The resultant atmosphere is one of disillusionment as characters lash out in anger while trying to protect themselves from pain. One of the targets of the intellectual barbs of the group is Mavis, an average, settled housewife who fusses over Iris and pretends to no intellectual stature. When the wit gets too pointed, though, Mavis cuts through the verbiage with a telling remark: "I was taught to believe that creativity and great intelligence ought to make one expansive and understanding. That if ordinary people . . . could not expect understanding from artists . . . then where indeed might we look for it at all." Only Sidney is moved by this remark; he is unable to maintain the pretense of cynicism, admitting, "I *care*. I care about it all. It takes too much energy *not* to care." Thus, Sidney lets himself be drawn into another cause, the election of Wally O'Hara to public office as an independent, someone who will oppose the drug culture and gangster rule of the neighborhood.

As Sidney throws himself into this new cause, he uses his newspaper to further the campaign, and even puts a sign, "Vote for Wally O'Hara," in his window. Idealism seems to have won out, and indeed Wally wins the election, but Sidney is put to a severe test as Iris seems about to leave him, and it is discovered that Wally is on the payroll of the gangsters. Added to all this is Gloria's suicide in Sidney's bathroom. Her death brings Sidney to a moment of crisis, and when Wally O'Hara comes into the room to offer condolences and to warn against any hasty actions, Sidney achieves a clarity of vision that reveals his heroism. Sidney says,

> *This world*—this swirling, seething madness—which you ask us to accept, to maintain—has done this . . . maimed my friends . . . emptied these rooms and my very bed. And now it has taken my sister. *This* world. Therefore, to live, to breathe—I shall *have* to fight it.

When Wally accuses Sidney of being a fool, he agrees:

> A fool who believes that death is waste and love is sweet and that the earth turns and that men change every day . . . and that people wanna be better than they are . . . and that I hurt terribly today, and that hurt is desperation and desperation is energy and energy can *move* things.

In this moment, Sidney learns true commitment and his responsibility to make the world what it ought to be. The play closes with Iris and Sidney holding each other on the couch, Iris crying in pain, with Sidney enjoining her: "Yes . . . weep now, darling, weep. Let us both weep. That is the first thing: to let ourselves feel again . . . then, tomorrow, we shall make something strong of this sorrow."

As the curtain closes, the audience can scarcely fail to apply these closing words to themselves. Only if they permit themselves to feel the pain, Hansberry claims, will it be possible to do anything to ease that pain in the future. James Baldwin, referring to the play, said, "it is about nothing less than our responsibility to ourselves and to others," a consistent theme in Hansberry's drama. Again and again, she reminds the audience of their responsibility to act in behalf of a better future, and the basis for this message is her affirmative vision. Robert Nemiroff says that she found reason to hope "in the most unlikely place of all: the lives most of us lead today. Precisely, in short, where *we* cannot find it. It was the mark of her respect for us all."

Les Blancs

Hansberry's last play of significance, *Les Blancs*, was not in finished form when she died and did not open onstage until November 15, 1970, at the Longacre Theatre, years after her death. Nemiroff completed and edited the text, though it is to a very large degree Hansberry's play. It was her least-successful play, running for only forty-seven performances, but it did spark considerable controversy, garnering both extravagant praise and passionate denunciation. Some attacked the play as advocating racial warfare, while others claimed it was the best play of the year, incisive and compassionate. The play is set not in a locale drawn from Hansberry's own experience but in a place that long held her interest: Africa.

Les Blancs is Hansberry's most complex and difficult play. It takes as its subject white colonialism and various possible responses to it. At the center of the play are the members of the Matoseh family: Abioseh Senior, the father, who is not actually part of the play, having died before it opens, but who is important in that his whole life defined the various responses possible (acceptance, attempts at lawful change, rebellion); in addition, there are his sons, Abioseh, Eric, and, most important, Tshembe. Hansberry attempts to shed some light on the movement for African independence by showing the relationships of the Matosehs to the whites living in Africa. The whites of importance are Major Rice, the military commander of the colony; Charlie Morris, a reporter; Madame Neilsen, and her husband, Dr. Neilsen, a character never appearing onstage but one responsible for the presence of all the others.

Dr. Neilsen has for many years run a makeshift hospital in the jungle; he is cut in the mold of Albert Schweitzer, for he has dedicated his life to tending the medical ills of the natives. It is because of him that all the other doctors are there and because of him, too, that Charlie Morris is in Africa, for Charlie has come to write a story about the famous doctor.

Whereas Charlie comes to Africa for the first time, Tshembe and Abioseh are called back to Africa by the death of their father. Abioseh comes back a Catholic priest, having renounced his African heritage and embraced the culture and beliefs of the colonialists. Tshembe, too, has taken much from the colonial culture, including his education and a European bride. He has not, however, rejected his heritage, and he is sensitive to the injustice of the colonial system. Though he sees colonialism as evil, he does not want to commit himself to opposing it. He wants to return to his wife and child and lead a comfortable, secure life.

For both Charlie and Tshembe, the visit to Africa brings the unexpected, for they return in the midst of an uprising, called "terror" by the whites and "resistance" by the blacks. Charlie gradually learns the true nature of colonialism, and Tshembe, after great struggle, learns that he cannot avoid his obligation to oppose colonialism actively.

While Charlie waits for Dr. Neilsen to return from another village, he learns from Madame Neilsen that the doctor's efforts seem to be less and less appreciated. When Tshembe comes on the scene, Charlie is immediately interested in him and repeatedly tries to engage the former student of Madame Neilsen and the doctor in conversation, but they fail to understand each other. Tshembe will accept none of the assumptions that Charlie has brought with him to Africa: He rejects the efforts of Dr. Neilsen, however well-intentioned, as representing the guilty conscience of colonialism while perpetrating the system. He also rejects Charlie's confident assumption that the facilities are so backward because of the superstitions of the natives. Charlie, on the other hand, cannot understand how Tshembe can speak so bitterly against colonialism yet not do anything to oppose it. Tshembe explains that he is one of those "who see too much to take sides," but his position becomes increasingly untenable. He is approached by members of the resistance and is asked to lead them, at which point he learns that it was his father who conceived the movement when it became clear that the colonialists, including Dr. Neilsen, saw themselves in the position of father rather than brother to the natives and would never give them freedom.

Still, Tshembe resists the commitment, but Charlie, as he leaves the scene, convinced now that the resistance is necessary, asks Tshembe, "Where are you running, man? Back to Europe? To watch the action on your telly?" Charlie reminds Tshembe that "we do what we can." Madame Neilsen herself makes Tshembe face the needs of his people. Tshembe by this time knows what his choice must be, but he is unable to make it. In his despair, he turns to Madame Neilsen, imploring her help. She tells him, "You have forgotten your geometry if you are despairing, Tshembe. I once taught you that a line goes into infinity unless it is bisected. Our country needs *warriors*, Tshembe Matoseh."

In the final scene of the play, Tshembe takes up arms against the colonialists, and Hansberry makes his decision all the more dramatic by having him kill his brother Abioseh, who has taken the colonial side. Yet, lest anyone misunderstand the agony of his choice, Hansberry ends the play with Tshembe on his knees before the bodies of those he has loved, committed but in agony, deeply engulfed by grief that such commitment is necessary.

Les Blancs is less an answer to the problem of colonialism than it is another expression of Hansberry's deep and abiding belief in the need for individual commitment, and in the ability of the individual, once committed, to bring about positive change for the future, even if that requires suffering in the present. Surely her commitment to her writing will guarantee her work an audience far into the future.

Other Literary Forms

As a result of her involvement in the Civil Rights movement, Lorraine Hansberry wrote the narrative for *The Movement: Documentary of a Struggle for Equality*, a book of photographs, for the

Student Nonviolent Coordinating Committee (SNCC). Because she died at such a young age, Hansberry left much of her work unpublished, but her husband, Robert Nemiroff, the literary executor of her estate, edited and submitted some of it for publication and, in the case of *Les Blancs*, production. In addition, he arranged excerpts from Hansberry's various writings into a seven-and-a-half-hour radio program entitled *To Be Young, Gifted, and Black*, which was broadcast on radio station WBAI in 1967. This program was later adapted for the stage, opening at the Cherry Lane Theatre in New York on January 2, 1969, and becoming the longest running production of the 1968-1969 season. Many readers know Hansberry through the anthology of her writings edited by Nemiroff, *To Be Young, Gifted, and Black: Lorraine Hansberry in Her Own Words*, a book that has enjoyed very wide circulation.

Bibliography

Austin, Gayle. "Black Women Playwrights Exorcizing Myths." *Phylon* 48 (Fall, 1997): 229-239. Examines the work of Alice Childress, Hansberry, and Ntozake Shange in dispelling stereotypical myths of African American characters, such as the tragic mulatto and the comic Negro, and in presenting new constructions, such as the black militant and the evolving black woman.

Brown-Guillory, Elizabeth. *Their Place on the Stage: Black Women Playwrights in America*. Westport, Conn.: Greenwood Press, 1988. Contains summaries and comparisons of the work of Alice Childress, Hansberry, and Ntozake Shange.

Carter, Steven R. *Hansberry's Drama: Commitment amid Complexity*. Urbana: University of Illinois Press, 1991. An examination of Hansberry's plays from the political standpoint. Bibliography and index.

Cheney, Anne. *Lorraine Hansberry*. New York: Twayne, 1994. A basic biography of Hansberry that examines her life and works. Bibliography and index.

Domina, Lynn. *Understanding "A Raisin in the Sun": A Student Casebook to Issues, Sources, and Historical Documents*. Westport, Conn.: Greenwood Press, 1998. A study that places Hansberry's works and life in context and examines her portrayal of African Americans in literature. Bibliography and index.

Effiong, Philip U. *In Search of a Model for African American Drama: A Study of Selected Plays by Lorraine Hansberry, Amiri Baraka, and Ntozake Shange.* Lanham, Md.: University Press of America, 2000. A study of the plays of three prominent African Americans, including Hansberry. Bibliography and index.

Hansberry, Lorraine, and Langston Hughes. "A Raisin in the Sun." *Literary Cavalcade* 56, no. 8 (May, 2004): 8-14. Provides a summary of the play, biographical information about the playwright, and a discussion of the work's transition from poem to play.

Kappel, Lawrence, ed. *Readings on "A Raisin in the Sun."* San Diego, Calif.: Greenhaven Press, 2001. A collection of essays that deal with aspects of Hansberry's most famous work. Bibliography and index.

Keppel, Ben. *The Work of Democracy: Ralph Bunche, Kenneth B. Clark, Lorraine Hansberry, and the Cultural Politics of Race.* Cambridge, Mass.: Harvard University Press, 1995. Keppel examines race relations and the Civil Rights movement, including a discussion of Hansberry's role in the movement. Bibliography and index.

Leeson, Richard M. *Lorraine Hansberry: A Research and Production Sourcebook.* Westport, Conn.: Greenwood Press, 1997. This sourcebook focuses on Hansberry as a dramatist, examining her portrayal of African Americans in literature. Bibliography and index.

Literary Cavalcade. "Lorraine Hansberry: Personal Struggles." 57, no. 8 (May, 2005): 22-24. A short biography and summary of *A Raisin in the Sun.*

Scheader, Catherine. *Lorraine Hansberry: A Playwright and Voice of Justice.* Springfield, N.J.: Enslow, 1998. A biography that examines Hansberry's dual roles as civil rights advocate and dramatist. Bibliography and index.

Steyn, Mark. "Raisin' Cain." *New Criterion* 22, no. 10 (June, 2004): 32-37. Analysis of *A Raisin in the Sun*'s themes, characters, and basic plot structure.

— *Katherine Lederer; Hugh Short*

Michael S. Harper

Poet

Born: Brooklyn, New York; March 18, 1938

POETRY: *Dear John, Dear Coltrane*, 1970; *History Is Your Own Heartbeat*, 1971; *Photographs, Negatives: History as Apple Tree*, 1972; *Song: I Want a Witness*, 1972; *Debridement*, 1973; *Nightmare Begins Responsibility*, 1974; *Images of Kin: New and Selected Poems*, 1977; *Rhode Island: Eight Poems*, 1981; *Healing Song for the Inner Ear*, 1985; *Honorable Amendments*, 1995; *Songlines in Michaeltree: New and Collected Poems*, 2000.

EDITED TEXTS: *Chant of Saints: A Gathering of Afro-American Literature, Art, and Scholarship*, 1979 (with Robert B. Stepto); *The Carleton Miscellany: A Ralph Ellison Festival*, 1980 (with John Wright); *The Collected Poems of Sterling A. Brown*, 1980; *Every Shut Eye Ain't Asleep: An Anthology of Poetry by African Americans Since 1945*, 1994 (with Anthony Walton); *The Vintage Book of African American Poetry*, 2000 (with Walton); *Selected Poems*, 2002 (edited and introduced by Ronald A. Sharp).

Achievements

Formal recognition of Michael S. Harper's poetry has been consistent from the publication of his first collection of poems, *Dear John, Dear Coltrane*, which was nominated for the National Book Award in 1971. After *History Is Your Own Heartbeat*, his second collection, received the Poetry Award of the Black Academy of Arts and Letters in 1972, other grants and awards followed: a National Institute of Arts and Letters Creative Writing Award (1972), a Guggenheim Fellowship (1976), a National Endowment for the Arts grant (1977), and the Massachusetts Council of Creative Writing Award (1977). In 1977, Harper's seventh book, *Images of Kin*, received the Melville Cane Award and was nominated in 1978 for the National Book Award. Harper was appointed the poet laureate of Rhode Island in 1988 and was named a Phi Beta Kappa scholar in 1990.

In accordance with his literary and cultural stature, Harper was invited to read in the bicentenary exchange with England in 1976, at the Library of Congress in 1975 and 1976, and in several African countries—Senegal, Ghana, Gambia, Zaire, Zambia, Tanzania, Botswana, and South Africa—in 1977.

Harper has been honored with visiting professorships at Harvard and Yale Universities and distinguished professorships at Carleton College and the University of Cincinnati. In 1970 he began his employment at Brown University. Promoted to full professor at the age of thirty-six in 1974, Harper received the endowed chair of the Israel J. Kapstein Professorship in 1983.

Biography

Michael Steven Harper was born on March 18, 1938, in Brooklyn, New York, and his birth brought with it particular pressures to succeed: He was the first male born on either side of the family, and he was delivered at his parent's home by his grandfather, Roland R. Johnson. His father, Walter Harper, was a postal worker and supervisor; his mother, Katherine Johnson, worked as a medical stenographer. While not wealthy, the Harper family did enjoy a middle-class income that permitted the acquisition of a good record collection, interesting the young Harper in music and serving as a source for his later development as a poet.

At thirteen, Harper and his family, including his younger brother Jonathan and his sister Katherine, moved to a predominantly white neighborhood in West Los Angeles, an area in which several black families were to have their houses bombed in the early 1950's. Enrolling shortly thereafter in Susan Miller Dorsey High School, Harper was assigned to an industrial arts course of study rather than to an academic one, presumably because he was black, and only his father's intervention with a counselor reversed the institutional assumptions about his abilities. Suffering from extreme asthma in 1951, Harper spent the summer confined to the house and, also because of his asthma, later refused to undress for gym class, for which he failed the class and was kept off the honor roll. Always having been encouraged to study medicine in the tradition of his grandfather and his great-grandfather Dr. John Albert Johnson, an African Methodist Episcopal Church bishop and missionary in South Africa from 1907 to 1916, Harper used the incident to escape the family's pressures and to turn his attention from the classroom and his interests in medicine, literature, and history to the ordinary life in the streets and neighborhoods around him. While not a disciplined student, he was a good test-taker, and he was graduated from high school in 1955.

From 1956 to 1961, Harper pursued a premedical course at Los Angeles State College (now California State University at Los Angeles) while at the same time working full-time as a postal worker. In college, a zoology professor discouraged his study of medicine, assuming that blacks were incapable of sustaining the rigors of medical school. On the job, Harper encountered well-educated blacks who were unable to advance—not because they lacked merit, but because they were black. Together, these two experiences of racism, experienced at first hand, helped shape his sense that American society was essentially schizophrenic: It celebrated free competition based on merit, but it barred blacks from an equal chance to participate in the culture—color was too often more consequential than character.

While Harper was in college, two books in particular, *The Letters of John Keats* (1958) and Ralph Ellison's *Invisible Man* (1952), and a course, "The Epic of Search," which offered a historical view of the human quest for self-assertion from *The Odyssey* (c. ninth century B.C.E.) to *Invisible Man*, rekindled his desire to write. In high school, he had experimented with poetry, short fiction, and drama, but he had abandoned those early attempts. Deprived of encouragement to study medicine, Harper enrolled in the Iowa Writers' Workshop in 1961. Restricted to segregated housing, he became increasingly aware of the fragmentation in American cultural life. As the only black enrolled in both poetry and fiction classes, Harper began to write poetry seriously, receiving encouragement from the writer Ralph Dickey and the painter Oliver Lee Jackson. In 1962, turning his attention to teaching, Harper left Iowa to teach at Pasadena City College, armed at twenty-four with a long-standing knowledge of black music and a newly developing expertise in black history, writing, and painting—all of which would come to inform his new commitment to his principal mode of expression: poetry.

The following year, 1963, Harper returned to Iowa and, although he had been in the Creative Writers' Program, he passed the comprehensive examinations in English, receiving his master's degree. He taught then at Contra Costa College, San Pablo, California, from 1964 to 1968. After teaching the following year at Reed College and Lewis and Clark College in Oregon, he taught as associate professor of English at California State College at Hayward in 1969-1970. Although receiving a tenured appointment as an associate professor at Brown University in 1970, Harper spent 1970-1971 at the University of Illinois, pursuing a postdoctoral fellowship at the Center for Advanced Studies. In 1971, Harper began teaching at several universities as a visiting professor while being employed at Brown University, where he served as director of the Graduate Creative Writing Program from 1974 to 1983. He was appointed to an endowed chair at Brown in 1983, and he served as Rhode Island's poet laureate from 1988-1993.

Analysis: Poetry

Michael S. Harper's oeuvre has established his stature as a significant voice in contemporary poetry. As an African American poet, Harper explores the historical and contemporary duality of consciousness that was first expressed by Frederick Douglass in the nineteenth century and W. E. B. Du Bois in the early twentieth century: What it means to be both black and American, and how one survives as both. While using to a limited extent a narrative frame, Harper's lyricism pays homage to the heroic endurance of family members, unsung musicians, and historical activists through a consciously developed technique that affirms the African American literary tradition, grounded in the oral tradition of storytelling and the musical heritage of spirituals, blues, and jazz. Avoiding the sometimes strident, polemical tones of black poetry in the 1960's and 1970's, Harper nevertheless fashions an ethically powerful voice, marked not only by a passion in exposing the tragedy of black history in America but also by a compassion for the individuals who have sought to endure and to create out of the cauldron of racism. His distinctive voice and all-embracing vision have evoked praise from both black and white reviewers and critics.

In an interview with Abraham Chapman, Michael Harper identifies the poetic technique of much of his work as "modality," an abstract musical concept that he uses as a metaphor for his ethical vision as well as for his subjective principle of composition. Many of Harper's poems lend themselves to performance; they are meant to be read aloud. In hearing them, one hears, through a range of idiom, dialect, and individual voices, the past fused with the contemporary, the individual speaking forth from communal experience and the black American's kinship, simultaneously tragic and heroic, to the whole of American cultural values. Rooted in classic jazz patterns from such musicians as Duke Ellington, Charlie Parker, and John Coltrane, modality is "about relationships" and "about energy, energy irreducible and true only unto itself." As a philosophical, ethical perspective, modality is a "particular frequency" for expressing and articulating "the special nature of the Black man and his condition and his contributions" to the American synthesis of cultural values. As such, modality refutes "the Western orientation of division between denotative/connotative, body/mind, life/spirit, soul/body, mind/heart" and affirms a unity of being and experience: "*modality is always about unity.*" Consequently, Harper's poetry gathers fragments from private and public experience, past and present, and seeks to rejuvenate spiritual forces historically suppressed by bringing them to the surface in a poetry of "tensions resolved through a morality worked out between people."

Dear John, Dear Coltrane

In the early poems of *Dear John, Dear Coltrane,* Harper's modal experiments succeed in a variety of forms that nevertheless remain unified in the power of his particular voice. In "Brother

John," Harper eulogizes Charlie Parker, the "Bird/ baddest nightdreamer/ on sax in the ornithology-world," Miles Davis, "bug-eyed, unspeakable,/ Miles, sweet Mute,/ sweat Miles, black Miles," and John Coltrane, who serves as a mythic center for the poem and the volume as well as several later poems. Typical of Harper's multiple allusions in naming, however, both the poem and the volume also eulogize John O. Stewart, a friend and fiction writer; nor is Coltrane merely a mythic figure, for Harper maintained a personal friendship with him until his death in 1967; in addition, the name "John" also conjures echoes from Harper's great-grandfather, who spent several years in South Africa, and, further, evokes John Brown, who figures prominently in later poems by Harper. Thus, from early in his work, Harper uses modality to reconcile past and present, myth and history, and private and public; personal mourning becomes part of a universal experience and a communal celebration. Drawing inspiration from both the suffering and the achievement of jazz artists in this poem and in subsequent poems in his career, Harper establishes the modal wordplay that affirms his philosophical stance as an activist of the conscience, "I'm a black man; I am;/ black; I am; I'm a black/ man; I am; I am," and his own cry of being, refusing any limiting universality of humanness that is blind to ethnic heritage and experience: "I am; I'm a black man;/ I am."

In other poems from that first volume, Harper links past and present as well as private and public by exploring larger patterns of history. In "American History," Harper asserts the invisibility of black suffering to mainstream America by juxtaposing "Those four black girls blown up/ in that Alabama church" with "five hundred/ middle passage blacks,/ in a net, under water . . . so *redcoats* wouldn't find them." Concluding in an ironic but colloquial idiom, he asks: "Can't find what you can't see/ can you?" In "Reuben, Reuben," Harper uses the death of his own son to overcome his pain in the transcendence of creative energy, just as blues singers have always done when faced with the horror of loss: "I reach from pain/ to music great enough/ to bring me back . . . we've lost a son/ the music, *jazz*, comes in."

History Is Your Own Heartbeat

Harper's early poems test the possibilities of modality, and, in such techniques as concrete imaging, literary allusions, sprung syntax, enjambment, blues refrains, idioms, variable line lengths, and innovative cadences, he discovers in modality a formalism strong enough to bear diverse experiments in free-verse forms and yet a visionary field large enough to draw from virtually any relationship, however intimate or distant, however painful or joyful, for individual affirmation. In his second collection, *History Is Your Own Heartbeat*, Harper uses modality to reconstruct personal history, integrating it with a mythic sense of spiritual unity. Divided into three sections, the book begins with a twenty-poem sequence, "Ruth's Blues," which employs his white mother-in-law's physical deterioration as an extended metaphor for the denial of black and white kinship. In tribute to Ruth's endurance in her quest for physical and psychological health, Harper shows the potential for a unified American sensibility, one which respects cultural differences yet realizes from the pain of division that American experience "is all a well-knit family;/ *a love supreme*," if one chooses to affirm multiple origins. The following two sections, "History as Personality" and "High Modes," pay homage, respectively, to influential personalities such as Martin Luther King, Jr., and Gwendolyn Brooks and, in the latter, to the painter Oliver Lee Jackson. Throughout these sections, Harper emphasizes the unity of a historical and cultural continuum that reaches back to Africa and comes forward to his own family, claiming his own past and an American history that is freed of its delusions, confronting its origins in the slavery of Africans and the genocide of Native Americans, to whom Harper also unearths literal kinship. In several ways, then, this volume, as the title suggests, builds from literal links of kinship with a diversity of races and cultures to a holistic view of American values, in contrast to the exclusive emphasis on European origins characteristic of traditional American history. By healing himself of narrow stereotypes, Harper offers "a love supreme" to his fellow citizens, asserting kinship even where citizenship has been denied and is diminished by racism.

Song: I Want a Witness
Subsequent books extend Harper's sense of kinship and develop the aesthetic of modality. In *Song: I Want a Witness*, he explores the black American religious heritage, using the metaphor of testifying, and conceptualizes the literary process as
essentially one of an ethical affirmation of heroic character.
Tracing American culture back both to Native America, by a link
with a great-great-grandmother who was Chippewa, and to the
Puritan legacies of Roger Williams and John Winthrop, by a link
to the spirit of place where he lives, Harper, in "History as
Appletree," develops an organic metaphor that embodies history and family while also bringing the negative, through an extended photographic metaphor of those ignored by history, to
present light and image. In this vision, the fruit of the tree,
American culture itself, blossoms with the fertility of long-
forgotten bones whose dust nurtures the root system.

Debridement
The collection *Debridement*, a medical term for cutting away
the dead flesh of a wound so that it will not infect the healthy
body and a metaphor for revising stereotyped versions of American history, honors the heroic actions of John Brown, Richard
Wright, and the fictional John Henry Louis. Together, the three
sections, each revolving around its respective persona, correct
the myth that Americans who have fought against racism were
insane, zealous, hysterical. Instead, Harper argues through the
modality of these poems, they were—and are—themselves the
victims of racism, surviving because they have pursued a truth
that has for the most part been hidden from them.

Nightmare Begins Responsibility
In *Nightmare Begins Responsibility*, the poet extends a logic that
runs through the previous two books. Once one realizes that the
pejorative American myth is false, then one must act to overcome the cultural insensitivity of racism and the apathy toward
the land, both as physical and cultural environment. Alienation
and isolation yield only to courageous, often unpopular action,
and the American Dream and manifest destiny are concepts of

death riddled with literal exploitation and genocide unless one replaces them with the values of kinship and acts to establish historical knowledge and contemporary intimacy as the basis for defining oneself as an American.

Images of Kin and Healing Song for the Inner Ear
Harper's insistence that one accept both unity and diversity, both pain and love, continues in *Images of Kin*, which reverses the chronological order of the selections which represent an anthology of his earlier poetry. By beginning with new poems and working back to the earlier ones, Harper testifies to the imperative for reconstructing American myth and history. *Healing Song for the Inner Ear* expands the modality of celebrating friends, family, musicians, and poets by bringing them into Harper's constantly expanding vision of history. Functioning much like his first book, this collection moves both backward and forward, but it also moves toward a more international perspective than that found in any of his earlier collections. From the American perspective of "Goin' to the Territory," which salutes the influence of Ralph Ellison and witnesses his aesthetic endurance, and "The Pen," which gives voice to an oral tradition become literary artifact, embodying values inherent in both black American and Native American lives, a modality in which "patterns of the word fling out into destiny/ as a prairie used to when the Indians/ were called Kiowa, Crow, Dakota, Cheyenne," to a series of poems set in South Africa, Harper explores the complexity of image and story embedded in history and the enduring truth of experience excavated in modal expression.

"The Militance of a Photograph . . . "
In the poem "The Militance of a Photograph in the Passbook of a Bantu Under Detention," Harper meditates on the history behind the photograph that identifies a black South African from Soweto, and he asserts "This is no simple mug shot/ of a runaway boy in a training/ film. . . . " Harper senses his own history here; the runaway might have been a nineteenth century slave, the training film could well serve as a powerful tool for the suppression of historical facts, and the mug shot suggests that color

itself (since only blacks must carry passbooks) is the crime. Personally, Harper must also unite his great-grandfather's experience in South Africa with the strategies of apartheid, and, in uniting the past personal association with the contemporary public policies of racism, Harper affirms the courage of the oppressed: "The Zulu lullaby/ I cannot sing in Bantu/ is this song in the body/ of a passbook/ and the book passes/ into a shirt/ and the back that wears it." Perhaps the modality of such a link between Americans and South Africans, between forgotten language and forgotten people, serves as the celebration of Harper's enduring theme, as in the epigraph to the poem: "Peace is the active presence of Justice."

Songlines in Michaeltree

In Harper's retrospective collection, which culls poetry from eight previous volumes, he returns to his characteristic progressive, improvisatory power that respects a variety of traditions in the arts. He celebrates the accomplishments of outstanding figures of the African American community while also tenderly exploring the "Michaeltree," an emblem of his own life, with deeply felt poems about members of his family. Serving as figurative bookends to the volume is a poem of six stanzas, each line repeated three times, beginning with the triad, "when there is no history," followed by an image of "a blind nation in a storm," that is "belted in these ruins." Here Harper asserts a reclamation from silent and suppression of the many-centuried struggle of African Americans in the United States, and sets the tone for the collection.

Poems from past collections are balanced by Harper with additional material to assist the reader in understanding his life of teaching and writing. "Notes to the Poem" functions as a teaching text and provides background to Harper's familiar themes, elucidating his use of historical data that might be obscure to those who don't share his expertise. "To the Reader" invites the reader on a journey that explores the evolution of his creative consciousness. Here he acknowledges his debt to the "pioneering writers: Robert Hayden, Sterling A. Brown, and Ralph Ellison." He also notes the influences of family members and, through anecdotal notes, that of his experiences with publicly reading his poetry. Finally, "Notes on Form and Fictions" examines his poetic technique and the derivations of his innovations. He notes, "I began to write poems because I could not see those elements of my life that I considered sacred reflected in my courses of study: scientific, literary, and linguistic." The reader thus better understands his overriding attraction to African American music as a source for shape, language, rhythms, and the near-mythic hero-figures of his poetry.

Other Literary Forms

Michael Harper works almost exclusively as a poet, but, in collaboration with Robert B. Stepto, he has edited one of the most influential anthologies of African American letters since Alain Locke's anthology from the Harlem Renaissance, *The New Negro: An Interpretation* (1925). Like Locke's anthology, *Chant of Saints: A Gathering of Afro-American Literature, Art, and Scholarship* represents a substantial accomplishment in defining the importance of African American artists and writers to American culture. This was followed by *Every Shut Eye Ain't Asleep: An Anthology of Poetry by African Americans Since 1945* and *The Vintage Book of African American Poetry*. In addition to his poetry and these anthologies, Harper has published several essays, including "My Poetic Technique and the Humanization of the American Audience," in *Black American Literature and Humanism.* Harper also edited *The Collected Poems of Sterling A. Brown.*

Bibliography

Antonucci, Michael. "The Map and the Territory: An Interview with Michael S. Harper." *African American Review* 34, no. 3 (Fall, 2000): 501-508. This interview refers back to Harper's statements in earlier interviews and allows for clarifications of his position on poets as historians and other matters. Comments on Robert Hayden, the legacy of John Brown, Ralph Ellison, African American cultural heroes, and several of Harper's own poems.
Breslin, Paul. "Some Early Returns." *Poetry* 134 (May, 1979): 107-

114. In this review of *Images of Kin: New and Selected Poems*, Breslin admits to liking Harper's work—noting that his style is distinctive—but has reservations about his ability to realize each poem fully. Nevertheless, he appreciates Harper for the range of his voice and his desire for completeness.

Brown, Joseph A. "Their Long Scars Touch Ours: A Reflection on the Poetry of Michael Harper." *Callaloo* 9, no. 1 (1986): 209-220. One of the several pieces on Harper to be found in this particular journal, this one provides a succinct, useful overview of Harper's themes and sense of history.

Forbes, Calvin. Review of *Honorable Amendments*, by Michael S. Harper. *African American Review* 32, no. 3 (Fall, 1998): 508-510. Forbes questions the reasons for Harper's retreat to secondary status, feeling he is no longer numbered among the indispensable African American literary artists. He takes Harper's lack of literary awards as one kind of evidence. Forbes examines Harper's fondness for the iambic measure and wonders if this dimension of his work, along with Harper's admiration for general humanistic values like hard work, has somehow alienated him politically. Forbes concludes, "Harper at his best is the personification of the black literary mainstream poet doing his thing."

Jackson, Richard. *Acts of Mind: Conversations with Contemporary Poets*. University: University of Alabama Press, 1983. The interview with Harper, recorded here and titled "Magic: Power: Activation: Transformation," discusses, among other things, the lyricism in his poetry and his kinship with people. In this conversation, Harper explains how he constructs his poems and how magic and power shape the world. Useful in providing insight into Harper's motivations.

Lerner, Ben. *To Cut Is to Heal: A Critical Companion to Michael S. Harper's "Debridement."* Providence, R.I.: Paradigm Press, 2000. Includes an interview with Harper, an essay by Scott Saul, and bibliographical references.

Lieberman, Laurence. *Unassigned Frequencies: American Poetry in Review, 1964-77*. Chicago: University of Illinois Press, 1977. In his commendable essay "The Muse of History," Lieberman reviews Harper's *Debridement* and considers it one of Harper's best works to date, calling him a poet of "musical richness and density of style in the short, compact lyric." Commends Harper for his restraint and freedom from emoting in contrast with the intensity of his subjects. The essay also critiques Derek Walcott's *Another Life* (1973), drawing parallels between the works of these two poets.

Turner, Alberta T., ed. *Fifty Contemporary Poets: The Creative Process.* New York: David McKay, 1977. Harper discusses how he wrote "Grandfather." He says: "I have always been a poet who had a pattern for a poem at conception. . . . " This volume contains some relevant background information about this poem, as well as some insights into Harper's approach to his art.

— *Michael Loudon; Philip K. Jason; Sarah Hilbert*

Robert Hayden

Poet

Born: Detroit, Michigan; August 4, 1913
Died: Ann Arbor, Michigan; February 25, 1980

POETRY: *Heart-Shape in the Dust*, 1940; *The Lion and the Archer*, 1948 (with Myron O'Higgins); *Figure of Time: Poems*, 1955; *A Ballad of Remembrance*, 1962; *Selected Poems*, 1966; *Words in the Mourning Time*, 1970; *The Night-Blooming Cereus*, 1972; *Angle of Ascent: New and Selected Poems*, 1975; *American Journal*, 1978; *The Legend of John Brown*, 1978; *Collected Poems*, 1985, revised 1996.

NONFICTION: *Collected Prose*, 1984.

EDITED TEXTS: *Kaleidoscope: Poems by American Negro Poets*, 1967; *Afro-American Literature: An Introduction*, 1971 (with David J. Burrows and Frederick R. Lapides).

Achievements

In 1976, Robert Hayden became the first African American to be appointed as poetry consultant to the Library of Congress. He twice won the Hopwood Award for Poetry at the University of Michigan and has been awarded the Academy of American Poets Fellowship, the Lenore Marshall Poetry Prize, the National Book Award for Poetry, and the Shelley Memorial Award. His strength as a poet lay in his convincingly ambivalent vision of the world, the consistent philosophical basis of that outlook, and the quietly effective language with which he renders it.

Biography

Robert Earl Hayden was born in Detroit, Michigan, on August 4, 1913, as Asa Bundy Sheffey. His natural parents divorced while he was young, and he was reared by William and Sue Ellen Hayden, taking their name and thinking that he had been legally adopted. His natural mother sometimes lived next door to the Haydens, and he has described his childhood environment as angry and disrupted. Hayden suffered from extremely poor eyesight, and even as a child, he spent more time in reading poetry—and later in writing it—than in more physical activities.

From 1932 to 1936, Hayden attended Detroit City College (now Wayne State University). There he had the first of three important meetings with famous poets: Langston Hughes came for a reading, and Hayden was able to have the more established poet read and evaluate some of his work. After graduation, and while he was briefly married, Hayden met Countée Cullen; later, working on a master's degree at the University of Michigan, Hayden was able to study poetry under W. H. Auden.

During this period he married again, to Erma Morris, and in 1946, he and his family moved to Nashville, where Hayden began a twenty-two year teaching career at Fisk University. By this

(Library of Congress)

point in his life, he had published some of his most famous poems ("Middle Passage," for example) and had twice won the Hopwood Award for Poetry at the University of Michigan. He and his wife had also converted to the Baha'i faith, a worldview which underlies much of Hayden's poetry, especially in its reconciliation of the oneness of God with the multiplicity of his historical manifestations and in the sustaining faith that the dark side of humankind's existence, evidenced by such events as the assassinations of which Hayden writes in "Words in the Mourning Time," "are process, major means whereby/ oh dreadfully, our humanness must be achieved."

From the time he left Fisk in 1968 until his death in 1980, Hayden was a professor of English at the University of Michigan. In 1976, he became the first African American to be appointed as poetry consultant to the Library of Congress.

Analysis: Poetry

Suggesting a Neoplatonic world of faultless knowledge and harmony that human beings once possessed, and often casting a wistful backward glance toward that lost perfection, while at the same time dreaming of an equally perfect future harmony where the difficulties of this world can be transcended, Robert Hayden nevertheless focused his poetic attention on this world, on the shifting and equivocal present. Calling himself a "realist who distrusts so-called reality," Hayden wrote with a clear realistic bent: His work centers on the natural and human of this place and time. These he lovingly describes, yet he also distrusts them; for the present reality is, both factually and poetically, one that betrays the hopes and dreams of human beings.

Because of this ambivalence, Hayden's poetry has always a slightly distant, reserved quality, and although the tone gives way sometimes to simple weariness, other times to wistfulness, the dominant tone is ironic acceptance. Even though many of Hayden's poems are on specifically black themes, using such archetypal images of black literature as flight, and although many celebrate the historical heroes of black American life, Hayden's detachment was often at odds, particularly during the 1970's, with the dominant mood of black culture. Hayden's poetry may occasionally have a political subject, and it is always critical of the cruelties and hypocrisies of America's past, but it is not polemical or didactic, and Hayden's appeal resides perhaps more among other artists and academicians than among a large popular audience. Indeed, despite the consistency of Hayden's output, he was not published by a major press in America until Liveright published *Angle of Ascent* in 1975.

Daedalus Poems

In his early "O Daedalus, Fly Away Home" and the other later poem about Daedalus, "For a Young Artist," Robert Hayden describes his view of the task of poetry, its relationship to the reader, and the stance of the poet. "For a Young Artist," based on a story by Gabriel García Márquez, begins with a protagonist, the artist, trapped in a pigsty. His condition is a tragic one, but he subsists on the meager fare that he scavenges from nature, rejecting the charity of society. Much of the focus of the poem is on that society: It finds the fallen artist at once baffling and prophetic. The people curse him but ask for his blessing, unable to decide whether he is "actual angel? carny freak?"

The uncertainty of their vision is characteristic in Hayden's world, where one struggles to make sense of his drastically reduced and often deceitful surroundings. The artist himself, however, is proud, refusing charity, refusing to hide his nakedness. His struggle—and this is the distinctive motif in Hayden's poetry—is for ascent. His transformation from ugliness to beauty, his attempt at flight is a difficult one, but after many failures, he finally achieves the "angle of ascent" in a "silken rustling" of air. In "O Daedalus, Fly Away Home," a more impressionistic poem, the main character also makes for himself a set of wings; struggling there against the powers of night, he weaves together "a wish and a weariness" in order to rise above the evil spell and fly home.

Transformations of Reality

Hayden's poetry is always about such transformations of reality. For him the world is confusing and contradictory. All that human beings can know is the darkness of this world: Their former and their future knowledge remain merely clouds. One knows only shadows, as in Plato's cave. The human attitude is thus a wish for the light that lies beyond, a weariness for the light that humankind has lost. The human need is a search to reconcile the two, to balance the two shadowy worlds or to transform this world.

In either case, Hayden's poetry is always dialectic: Each poem arises out of such conflicts as time and timelessness, art and history, dream and memory, past and present, flight and descent. What the artist must do is weave together those opposites into a set of poetic wings, synthesize the two into a oneness, itself a vision of the ultimate oneness, so that the reader understands better the necessary but frightening, terrible but beautiful position that human beings occupy in the world.

Poetry of Balance

Hayden's poetry, with its careful balance between a world he loves and lives in and must describe and his dissatisfaction with its failures and limitations and with his vision of what life was and must be again, teases the reader with its doubled perspective and its delicate and supple language. The poems themselves are often traditional in their narrative structure and regular rhythm. Paradox and pun, both suggesting tension, are frequent devices, and irony, an attitude of approving distance, is the most common tone. Hayden's poetry is a world observed with wit and disappointment, with love and sorrow. His strongest work makes the reader reobserve the world, set in the context of history and art, of philosophy and poetics. Hayden is a black poet in his specific attention to black myths and heroes, if not in an attempt to capture the distinctive voices of black culture. He is also, however, simply a poet, for the themes he works through and the voices with which he speaks make real a universally human perception of this world.

A characteristic posture for Hayden's poetic figures is, then, one of balance. Hayden gives this theme witty representation in the poem "The Performers," where the persona watches literal balancers, "two minor Wallendas," who are washing windows seven stories up in space. The persona identifies with them and their dangerous situation until he sees himself falling. The window washers enter his office, thanking him for his understanding of their position, as he thanks them for making him see once more his own precarious yet protected location. They are like the poet-juggler in Richard Wilbur's poem "Juggler," and their job too, like that of Wilbur's poet-persona, is to make others see the world again in both its freshness and its gravity.

Although the balance may be between the two attractive opposites of past and future perfection, since they are but shadows, it is more frequently between present, human realities. In "Moose Wallow," for example, the protagonist feels the shadowy presence of moose watching him from either side, while he experiences both hope and fear. In "The Broken Dark," a rabbi describes "Demons on the left. Death on either side,/ . . . the way of life between." Within this world, the poet finds himself both alien and at home, both struggling to accept the world and attempting to flee it. The need for acceptance leads to the strong realistic feeling of Hayden's work: the attention to detail, the careful visual imagery, and the strong characterization and narration. Indeed, some of Hayden's most vivid poetry depends on the brilliant creation of character and on his storytelling ability.

Romanticism vs. Realism
The struggle to flee the world, however, leads to an equally pervasive attraction to myth, history, and art—alternatives to the time-drenched present—and to philosophical abstraction, as in the emphasis on Platonic reflections, that gives the poetry an equally consistent romantic quality. If in his realism Hayden resembles a poet like Wilbur, in his Romanticism he most resembles William Butler Yeats. There are specific similarities: The twelve-year-old girl of "The Peacock Room," who becomes a cadaver caught up in the folds of a fluttering peacock, recalls several of the poems about Maud Gonne. "Dance the Orange" concludes with a Yeatsian merging of the dancer and the dance. "Lear Is Gay" uses the metaphor of time as a scarecrow. The similarity is more than incidental, however: It is essential to Hayden's vision, and one of the powers of Hayden's poetry arises

from this tension between his Romantic underpinnings and his realistic surface.

This tension is evident in "Monet's 'Waterlilies,'" the first section of which is a meditation on the "poisonous news" from Selma and Saigon. From this reality, the poet retreats to art, to the painting that he loves, where space and time are reconciled; then "The seen, the known/ dissolve in iridescence." Looking at the painting, the poet discovers the "aura of that world/ each of us has lost." Then reality gives way, and the painting becomes the "shadow" of the joy of that lost world. Indeed, several of Hayden's poems suggest his attraction to the static visual arts and his conviction that poetry is like painting: "Richard Hunt's 'Arachne,'" "Kodachromes of the Island," "Butterfly Piece," "The Peacock Room"—these and several others have as their subject humankind's attempt to transform reality into something more nearly resembling the ultimate presence than its human and temporal manifestation.

In "Butterfly Piece," the poet examines Brazilian butterflies that have been preserved and encased as works of art, and it seems he can find no higher praise than to compare them with Fabergé enamel work: Nature may mirror art, but the movement of the poem is away from this assurance. In the second stanza, Hayden focuses on how their bright colors resemble those of the human world, colors so bright that they burden, that they break. Finally then, he comments that this wild beauty has been killed and sold "to prettify," a distinct diminishment of the original implication. Thus art provides for Hayden one alternative to the human world, where lives are too often burdened, too often break. Yet if perfect art can in its serene reconciliation of time and space rekindle memories of a more perfect vision, it can also be a diminution of reality; even here, then, Hayden maintains the ambivalence of his vision.

Historical Urge
Like art, history provides an alternative to present patterns. Sometimes the history is personal, as in "Beginnings," the poem that opens *Angle of Ascent* and that itself opens simply with the names of Hayden's ancestors; this calling the roll suggests the

search for identity that is another theme in Hayden's work, one obviously related to his own confused childhood identity. More often the history is public, as in the events of the American past, and particularly those of black American history, representing a time outside the uneasy present.

The historical urge is most clearly seen in Hayden's narrative poetry, such as in "Middle Passage," a long poem in which the coming of slaves to America is told by a series of different voices. That poem, too—and it is among Hayden's finest—begins with a list of names: the hopeful and religious names of the slave ships, Hayden writes, bright and ironical compared with the grim cargo of human beings they are delivering. The voices include those of the ship's log and of a deponent at a trial. Ariel's song from *The Tempest* (1611), a song used by T. S. Eliot for different purposes in *The Waste Land* (1922), suggests that those who have been drowned have been transformed, not into pearl or coral as in William Shakespeare's vision, but into New England pews and altar lights.

Hymns enter, as well as the voice of the slave trader himself. In the climactic third section, the poet himself speaks, first describing the horrible historic voyage "through death" and contrasting with the voice of a white slave trader who has survived the *Amistad* mutiny, when blacks did in fact mutiny and take over a ship. The self-justifying voice of that narrator counterpoints the bravery of Cinquez, the prince who led the mutiny and transformed the horror of confinement by using the terrible liberating force of rebellion. This is, the poet says at last, the "deep immortal human wish/ the timeless will"; it is that of transfiguration, of life out of death, a living death redeemed into new life. In this historical vision, Hayden creates his most powerful narrative image of humankind's potential transformation—for Hayden, all life is a voyage, all human beings are confined, all worthwhile acts are attempts to be free.

Dream and Memory

As well as the balance between the present reality and such timeless entities as myth, history, and art, Hayden presents the balance between dream, the longing for a perfect future, and memory, the dimly recalled past, as alternatives to the present. "The Dream (1863)," contrasts the dreams of liberation of a Southern slave who envisions her liberators as heroic and mythic figures with excerpts from letters of a Union soldier who is among her real liberators. Although the letters are often hackneyed and sentimental, their humor stale, they have a human bravery and modesty that is attractive. As always, Hayden's vision of them is ambivalent, but it is finally affirmative. The dreams, however beautiful in their abstract imaginings, are inappropriate to the reality, and the dreamer sinks to the ground at the end, attempting to rise, but failing.

Distrusting the present, Hayden creates in his poetry a tension between it and timeless worlds—art, history, myth, memory, and desire. Out of those tensions, he finds the movement of his poetry. Thus there is in his work, as in the human lives he describes, a constant choice, an alternation of poetic attention and human needs, so that his characters, like the poet, are always at once alien to and at home in this world, making an uneasy peace, living in delicate balance.

Motifs of Transformation
There is in Hayden another way of dealing with dialectical opposition: not the balancing of the two, but the movement from one to another. As often as his poems depict stasis and balance, so also do they suggest synthesis through process, an equal possibility for working through humans' ambiguous place in the world. Thus transformation and metamorphosis become major motifs in his work. In "Theme and Variation," which—as the title suggests—indicates the large direction of Hayden's work, he writes that "all things alter . . . become a something more,/ a something less." In "Richard Hunt's 'Arachne,'" for example, he captures the movement downward. Here Arachne is caught in the moment of her transformation from human to arachnid—not yet changed to unthinking animal, no longer fully woman. Horrible as the surface is, however, Hayden's attitude remains detached: If she is on one hand "dying," she is on the other "becoming."

The theme of transformation informs and unifies Hayden's

long poem "An Inference of Mexico." Like many of his works, this poem involves travel. Hayden writes about "the migratory habits of the soul," but it is clear that the body migrates through the world as well. (The contrast with the settledness of Hayden's own adult life is interesting.) In this poem the light of Mexico, strange and savage, causes the persona to reexamine his world. The first section involves a burial, the putting away of the old life; as he watches a funeral, he looks upward to see "graveblack vultures," which are "transformed by steeps of flight." An anonymous voice urges him to flee, but when, in the second section, he looks at the mountains, they are equally dark and seem themselves to be "imploring a god." In the third section, "Veracruz," he looks at the ocean where tourists ignore "the bickering spray." Then at the center of this section, the poet indicates humankind's choices: flight and escape—"Leap now/ and cease from error"—or acceptance, a turning shoreward, "accepting all—/ the losses and farewells,/ the long warfare with self,/ with God." For the persona, reality itself becomes a dream, and he chooses to escape; he turns to leap, to cease from error, and in the next section his heart turns heavenward in praise of pagan gods, followed by a section contrasting the Christian and pagan deities that coexist in the Mexican culture. The escape cannot last, however; the poet is inextricably tied to things of this world, and so in the sixth section he finds himself back in the market, where he is surrounded by tourists and beggars, asking for charity while the fire-king god looks blankly on. The last section, "La Corrida," contrasting bull and matador, sun and shadow, again suggests humanity's awful power and dilemma; it is the poet's own voice that now begs for charity, that all human beings be redeemed and delivered from what they are "yet cannot be" and from their past, all they know "and do not wish/ to know."

"An Inference of Mexico" also employs Hayden's two favorite images for the human predicament. The first is war. Superficially, "Locus," too, describes a landscape, and, like "An Inference of Mexico," it is rich in descriptive detail of flora and fauna, of people and events. The trees are those of "an illusionist," however, and the human position in this world is one of antagonism: spies watch Hernando de Soto's troops, runagates hide from Southern masters. Here nature thrives, but it thrives on spareness, nature itself doing what Hayden asks of humanity: accepting a world that gives one less than one needs and more than one can often bear. The flowers "twist into grace"; the houses are symbols of dreams dying prolonged and painful deaths. The past remains, then, "adored and/ unforgiven." It is not merely landscape, but "soulscape," and this soulscape is a "battleground/ of warring shades whose weapons kill."

Even in "On Lookout Mountain," where the Civil War battleground has been converted into an unimportant tourist spot, where choices once daring and dangerous have become selections of souvenirs and trivia, the cries of Kilroy, like those of Civil War soldiers and even those of the present, are concentric. Although on one level the present insignificance contrasts with the momentous past, on another they are only versions of the same story; the cries of past generations remain audible in "the warfare of our peace."

Flight and Descent

The image which recurs most frequently throughout Hayden's poetry, however, is flight, in tension with its opposite, descent, but also used as a pun for a further tension, the noun formed from both "to flee" and "to fly." Descent, that transformation to something less, is a dangerous alternative to flight. In "The Dream," Sinda, the dreamer, sinks to the ground at the end; in "The Performers," the observer of the window washers stays with them in his imagination until he sees himself falling with no safety strap to hold him up. In "The Ballad of Nat Turner" it is the dream of falling angels that confirms Turner's destructive but liberating vision. The poem which best exemplifies descent is "The Diver." It opens with the diver sinking through the sea's "easeful/ azure." That descent is an escape from the present, with its warring shadows, its balances and choices. The creatures that the diver sees remind him of "lost images," but he sinks beyond them. It is as "dreams of/ wingless flight." The goal of this descent is a ship, but the treasures that the diver finds there are "voracious life." His flashlight probing "fogs of water," everything seems eerie, a game of hide and seek. The diver's longing is to throw off everything, to yield to the rapturous deep, "have/ done with self and/ every dinning/ vain complexity." This deep, which once seemed so easeful, now becomes frenzied, canceling, numbing. Whether by reflex or by will, the persona begins to struggle. He escapes somehow, manages the "measured rise" to the surface. Like Robert Frost's "Stopping by Woods on a Snowy Evening," "The Diver" shows how restful the dark can seem, how the strange beauty of this deep and dark alternative can entice one to leave behind the promises and battles of his own disappointing world. Here, too, as in Frost's poem, although with considerably more effort, the poet-persona rejects escape; ascent for the diver is only a return to the surface of life, but it is as difficult as the ascent in any of Hayden's poems.

Another kind of escape may be fleeing—the flight, say, of an escaping slave, of another who flees a reality that certainly burdens and threatens to break him. This is the kind of escape that Hayden describes in "The Ballad of Sue Ellen Westerfield" or "Runagate Runagate," an escape which is not the treacherous evasion of "The Diver" but the attempt to be free. The flight is thus a punning ascent, as in "Runagate Runagate," where slaves rise "from their anguish and their power," willing to be free. Sue Ellen Westerfield escapes slavery, a burning ship, and a white lover—all escapes that are necessary in her difficult attempt at freedom.

The final transformation, that which the soul aspires to and which the poet ultimately embraces, is what Hayden, in the title of his collected poems, calls "the angle of ascent." Flight is, of course, a prominent motif in black literature. For Hayden it is the most important of all images, for it suggests not merely escape, but meaningful escape, not merely transformation, but transfiguration, so that present reality becomes an image of the perfect reality for which human beings long. In both poems about Daedalus, Hayden aptly uses this metaphor, and what the poet-personae do is rise. After their struggle they achieve that angle of ascent in order to find a resting place where they are not at all alien. The treatment of the metaphor is sometimes less serious. In "Unidentified Flying Object," the main character seems to have climbed aboard a UFO, leaving her life in total disorder, her face "transformed" into something that the man who observes her has never seen before. Although the poem ends with a hint that Mattie Lee may have suffered a darker fate, the ambiguous ending can only slightly modify the witty assertion of the earlier movement of the poem—an ascent that leaves behind radios and roasts, churches and suitors, gossips and sheriffs. In "'Summertime and the Living. . . .'" the living is not easy, and the characters' dreams and hopes contrast with the vividly depicted reality of their lives. The city dwellers find the summer a time for poor folks, when they can sit on stoops and talk, when they share their common dream, here a fantasy of Ethiopia, the Africa of remembered past and longed-for future, which spreads across them "her gorgeous wings." Their lives, too, are for a moment "transformed by steeps of flight."

Other Literary Forms

Robert Hayden also edited two volumes of black literature: *Kaleidoscope: Poems by American Negro Poets* and *Afro-American Literature: An Introduction*, the latter with David J. Burrows and Frederick R. Lapides.

Bibliography

Bloom, Harold, ed. *Robert Hayden*. Philadelphia: Chelsea House, 2005. A volume in the Bloom's Modern Critical Views series. Includes an introduction by Bloom; essays by such scholars as Lewis Turco, Fred M. Fetrow, Vera M. Kutzinski, Brian Conniff, and Pontheolla T. Williams; and a chronology.

Conniff, Brian. "Robert Hayden and the Rise of the African American Poetic Sequence." *African American Review* 33, no. 3 (Fall, 1999): 487-506. A discussion of Hayden's development in the poem "Middle Passage" of an experimental poetics that could examine racism by telling an episode of its history in a number of contending voices.

Davis, Arthur P. "Robert Hayden." In *From the Dark Tower: Afro-American Writers, 1900 to 1960*. Washington, D.C.: Howard University Press, 1982. This study emphasizes the craftsmanship of Hayden. Davis illustrates the variety of verse forms and techniques used in the later poems and discusses in detail a few poems. Although some of Hayden's best poems deal with racial subject matter, his technical mastery raises them above the level of protest.

Davis, Charles T. "Robert Hayden's Use of History." In *Modern Black Poets: A Collection of Critical Essays,* edited by Donald B. Gibson. Englewood Cliffs, N.J.: Prentice-Hall, 1973. This clear, well-illustrated study examines Hayden's lifelong preoccupation with African American history. Davis traces in individual poems the changing emphasis from physical to spiritual liberation, in subjects ranging from Nat Turner to Malcolm X.

Fetrow, Fred M. "Portraits and Personae: Characterization in the Poetry of Robert Hayden." In *Black American Poets Between Worlds, 1940-1960,* edited by R. Baxter Miller. Knoxville: University of Tennessee Press, 1986. This illuminating study approaches Hayden's poetry through his portraits of real and imagined persons. Two groups of African American historical figures are fighters for freedom and artists and entertainers. Fictional characters are also studied for insights into Hayden's personality.

_____. *Robert Hayden.* Boston: Twayne, 1984. The first book-length study of Hayden, this volume is a good introduction to his work. After tracing his life, Fetrow studies the poems chronologically according to subject matter: confession, description of people and places, black heritage, and spiritual transcendence. Supplemented by a chronology, notes, a select bibliography (including a list of secondary sources with brief annotations), and an index.

Gikandi, Simon. "Race and the Idea of the Aesthetic." *Michigan Quarterly Review* 40, no. 2 (Spring, 2001): 318-350. Gikandi discusses Hayden's lifelong struggle with the relationship between the question of race and the idea of the aesthetic, and with questions concerning how the moral lines and social boundaries of modernity are drawn.

Glaysher, Frederick, ed. *Collected Prose: Robert Hayden.* Foreword by William Meredith. Ann Arbor: University of Michigan Press, 1984. This excellent one-volume collection of Hayden's prose includes previously unpublished or inaccessible pieces. Four interviews are especially helpful in clarifying Hayden's intentions in specific poems.

Su, Adrienne. "The Poetry of Robert Hayden." *Library Cavalcade* 52, no. 2 (October, 1999): 8-11. A brief profile of Hayden and a critique of "Those Winter Sundays," "The Prisoners," and "Monet's 'Waterlilies.'"

Williams, Pontheolla T. *Robert Hayden: A Critical Analysis of His Poetry.* Foreword by Blyden Jackson. Urbana: University of Illinois Press, 1987. In one of the most thorough studies to date, Williams examines all aspects of Hayden's poetry. An opening biographical summary clarifies poetic influences and remaining chapters chronologically treat all published works. Supplemented by a comprehensive bibliography (including an unannotated list of secondary sources), copies of key poems discussed in the text, a chronology, notes, and an index.

— Howard Faulkner

Chester Himes

Novelist and short-story writer

Born: Jefferson City, Missouri; July 29, 1909
Died: Moraira, Spain; November 12, 1984

LONG FICTION: *If He Hollers Let Him Go*, 1945; *Lonely Crusade*, 1947; *Cast the First Stone*, 1952 (unexpurgated edition pb. as *Yesterday Will Make You Cry*, 1998); *The Third Generation*, 1954; *The Primitive*, 1955 (unexpurgated edition pb. as *The End of a Primitive*, 1997); *For Love of Imabelle*, 1957 (revised as *A Rage in Harlem*, 1965); *Il pluet des coups durs*, 1958 (*The Real Cool Killers*, 1959); *Couché dans le pain*, 1959 (*The Crazy Kill*, 1959); *Dare-dare*, 1959 (*Run Man Run*, 1966); *Tout pour plaire*, 1959 (*The Big Gold Dream*, 1960); *Imbroglio negro*, 1960 (*All Shot Up*, 1960); *Ne nous énervons pas!*, 1961 (*The Heat's On*, 1966; also pb. as *Come Back Charleston Blue*, 1974); *Pinktoes*, 1961; *Une affaire de viol*, 1963 (*A Case of Rape*, 1980); *Retour en Afrique*, 1964 (*Cotton Comes to Harlem*, 1965); *Blind Man with a Pistol*, 1969 (also pb. as *Hot Day, Hot Night*, 1970); *Plan B*, 1983.
SHORT FICTION: *The Collected Stories of Chester Himes*, 1990.
NONFICTION: *The Quality of Hurt: The Autobiography of Chester Himes, Volume I*, 1972; *My Life of Absurdity: The Autobiography of Chester Himes, Volume II*, 1976.
MISCELLANEOUS: *Black on Black: "Baby Sister" and Selected Writings*, 1973.

Achievements

Best known for the series of detective stories called the Harlem Domestic, Chester Himes wrote in many genres and with an impressive variety of techniques and themes. Because throughout his career, even after he had emigrated abroad, he confronted without flinching the wrenching effects of racism in the United

States, he is sometimes categorized into the group of protest writers. What distinguishes him is his humor, often necessarily grotesque in the grimmest of circumstances.

Upon the publication of *The Collected Stories of Chester Himes*, a brief review in the magazine *Essence* recommended his stories, written over a forty-year span, because he showed African Americans to themselves as they really are, in all facets of their lives. Such relevance suggests that he captured an essence of African American life, one that is often tragic and violent, and also passionate, tender, sensual. He was awarded the Rosenwald Fellowship in 1944 and the Grand Prix de Littérature Policière in 1958.

Biography

Chester Bomar Himes was born on July 29, 1909, in Jefferson City, Missouri, the youngest of three sons born to Estelle Charlotte Bomar and Joseph Sandy Himes, a professor of blacksmithing and wheelwrighting and head of the Mechanical Arts Department at Lincoln University. In 1921 Himes's father obtained a position at Normal College in Pine Bluff, Arkansas, and Chester and his brother Joe were enrolled in first-year studies there (with classmates ten years their senior). In the same year Joe was permanently blinded while conducting a chemistry demonstration he and Chester had prepared. The local hospital's refusal to admit and treat his brother's injury (presumably because of racial prejudice)—one of several such incidents experienced in his youth—made a lasting impression upon Chester and contributed to his often-cited "quality of hurt" (the title of the first volume of his autobiography). In the next two years Himes attended high schools in St. Louis, Missouri, and Cleveland, Ohio, experiencing the loneliness, isolation, and violence frequently accorded the outsider in adolescence (in schoolyard battles he received chipped teeth, lacerations to the head, and a broken shoulder which never healed properly). Himes was graduated, nevertheless, from Cleveland's Glenville High School in January, 1926. Preparing to attend Ohio State University in the fall, he took a job as a busboy in a local hotel. Injured

(Library of Congress)

by a fall down an elevator shaft, Himes was awarded a monthly disability pension which allowed him to enter the university directly.

Early enthusiasm for collegiate life turned quickly to personal depression and alienation, undermining Himes's academic fervor and success. This discontent led to his flirtation with illicit lifestyles and his subsequent expulsion from the university. Returning to Cleveland, Himes was swept into the dangers and excitement of underworld activities which, as he noted in his autobiography, exposed him to many of the strange characters who populate his detective series.

After two suspended sentences for burglary and fraud (because of the personal appeals of his parents for leniency), Himes was arrested in September, 1928, charged with armed robbery, and sentenced to twenty to twenty-five years of hard labor at Ohio State Penitentiary. His serious writing began in prison. By the time he was paroled to his mother in 1936, Himes's stories about the frustrations and contradictions of prison life had appeared in *Esquire* and numerous African American newspapers and magazines. In 1937, Himes married Jean Johnson, his sweetheart before imprisonment. Finding employment first as a laborer, then as a research assistant in the Cleveland Public Library, Himes was finally employed by the Ohio State Writers' Project to work on a history of Cleveland. With the start of World War II, Himes moved to Los Angeles, California. His first two novels, *If He Hollers Let Him Go* and *Lonely Crusade*, were based on these experiences. Following trips to New York, back to Los Angeles, and then to New York, where his third novel, *Cast the First Stone*, was published, Himes divorced Jean and left for Europe in 1953, sensing the possibility of a new beginning.

The French admired his life, particularly appreciating the satire of *Pinktoes*, a ribald novel proposing the solution to racial tensions through indiscriminate sexual relationships. It was his French editor who encouraged Himes to write the detective novels set in Harlem, featuring Grave Digger Jones and Coffin Ed Johnson. Himes wrote these in a hurry, desperate for the money, but they turned out to be the perfect match of form and content. Increasingly pessimistic about the violence of his native country, Himes wrote more and more about the radical solution to the racial problem—violence. The Harlem of his detectives, the detectives themselves, the people among whom they move are all caught up, trapped in a cycle of violent behavior from which they cannot escape.

With so much pain, personal and cultural, experienced from the beginning of his life, Himes did what talented artists do: He confronted it, fashioned it into a personal vision, and, living fully, even found the love and humor in it. Between 1953 and 1957, Himes lived in Paris, London, and Majorca while finishing work on *The Third Generation* and *The Primitive*. Following the international success of his Harlem Domestic series, Himes moved permanently to Spain in 1969 and, with the exception of brief trips to the United States and other parts of Europe, lived there with his second wife, Lesley Packard, until his death on November 12, 1984.

Analysis: Long Fiction

Chester Himes began his Harlem Domestic series with the publication of *For Love of Imabelle,* following a suggestion by his French publisher, Marcel Duhamel, to contribute to the popular *Série noire.* Written in less than two weeks, while he was "living in a little crummy hotel in Paris" under very strained emotional and economic circumstances, the novel, when translated and published in Paris in 1958, was awarded a French literary prize, the Grand Prix de Littérature Policière. Rescued from economic dependency and the obscurity of exile, Himes wrote the next four volumes in the series—*The Crazy Kill, The Real Cool Killers, All Shot Up,* and *The Big Gold Dream*—all within the next two years. Each successive volume represents a significant expansion and development of essential aspects of Himes's evolving artistic and ideological vision.

Inspired by two detectives Himes met in Los Angeles in the 1940's, Grave Digger Jones and Coffin Ed Johnson are serious and, as their nicknames imply, deadly enforcers of social order and justice. Maintaining balance through a carefully organized network of spies disguised as junkies, drunks, and even nuns soliciting alms for the poor at the most unusual times and places, Grave Digger and Coffin Ed are aggressive, fearless, and genuinely concerned with the community's welfare and improvement. They wage a relentless, unorthodox, and often-personal battle against Harlem's criminal elements. Fiercely loyal to each other, they are forced to be "tough" and mutually protective: They operate in an arena where most people consider policemen public enemies. Honest, dedicated to their profession, and motivated largely by a moral conscience—tinged with a certain amount of cynicism—they possess a code of ethics comparable (although not identical) to those of the Hammett/Chandler heroes.

Only in the first book of the series is there any implication of venality or dishonesty:

> They took their tribute, like all real cops, from the established
> underworld catering to the essential needs of the people—
> gamekeepers, madams, streetwalkers, numbers writers, num-
> bers bankers. But they were rough on purse snatchers, muggers,
> burglars, con men, and all strangers working any racket.

Except for this brief reference—explained perhaps by the fact
that Himes had not fully developed their characters, a possibility suggested by their absence in almost the first half of the
novel—all the subsequent narratives are explicit in emphasizing
their honesty and integrity as detectives.

Grave Digger and Coffin Ed are often brutal in their search
for the guilty; this aspect of their characters, however, is directly
related to the principal issues of the series and to Himes's vision
of the essence of American life: violence. In a discussion of his
perception of the detective genre with the novelist John A. Williams, Himes shed some light on the reasons for the pervasive
presence of often-hideous forms of physical violence in his
works:

> It's just plain and simple violence in narrative form, you know.
> 'Cause no one, *no one*, writes about violence the way that Ameri-
> cans do. As a matter of fact, for the simple reason that no one
> understands violence or experiences violence like the Ameri-
> can civilians do. . . . American violence is public life, it's a public
> way of life, it became a form, a detective story form.

Indeed, more than one critic has attacked Himes's novels on
the basis of gratuitous physical violence. When practiced by
Grave Digger and Coffin Ed, however, brutal outbursts are,
more often than not, justifiable: Caught between the dangers inherent in their quest for a better community and the long arm
of the white institution which supposedly protects them, Grave
Digger Jones and Coffin Ed Johnson are forced to be coldly effective through the only means at their disposal. Certainly their
role as black representatives of the white power structure defines the very tenuous nature of their relationship to the Harlem community and accounts for most of the novels' uncertainties and much of their suspense.

526

On another level, however, the excessive physical violence in Himes's novels is related to another aspect of the author's artistic and ideological perspectives—namely, the concern for place, real and imaginary. Harlem represents the center and circumference of the African American experience: It is the symbolic microcosm and the historical matrix of Himes's America. Isolated, besieged by the outside world, and turning inward upon itself, Harlem is, on one hand, a symbol of disorder, chaos, confusion, and self-perpetuating pain and, on the other, an emblem of cultural and historical achievement. The duality and contradiction of its identity is the source of the tension which animates Himes's plots and propels them toward their often-incredible resolutions. At the core of Harlem's reality, moreover, is violence—physical and psychological.

In a speech delivered in 1948 and subsequently published as "The Dilemma of the Negro Novelist in the U.S." in *Beyond the Angry Black* (1966), a compilation edited by John A. Williams, Himes noted: "The question the Negro writer must answer is: How does the fear he feels as a Negro in white American society affect his, the Negro personality?" Not until this question is addressed by the writer, Himes went on to say, can there be the slightest understanding of any aspect of black life in the United States: crime, marital relations, spiritual or economic aspirations—all will be beyond understanding until the dynamics of this fear have been exposed behind the walls of the ghetto, "until others have experienced with us to the same extent the impact of fear upon our personalities." It is this conception of fear and its psychological corollary, rage, that sustains Himes's detective stories and links them ideologically to his earlier, non-mystery fiction. (It is significant that the first novel in the series, *For Love of Imabelle*, was published in the United States as *A Rage in Harlem*.)

The Crazy Kill
The connection between the image of Harlem and the violence which derives from fear is particularly apparent in *The Crazy Kill*. The Harlem of this novel is a place, in the words of Coffin Ed, "where anything can happen," and from the narrative's bizarre

opening incident to the very last, that sense of the incredibly plausible pervades. When the theft of a bag of money from a grocery store attracts the attention of the Reverend Short, Mamie Pullen's minister and a participant at the wake held across the street for Mamie's husband, the notorious gambler Big Joe Pullen, the storefront preacher leans too far out of a bedroom window under the influence of his favorite concoction, opium and brandy, and falls out. He lands, miraculously, in a basket of bread outside the bakery beneath. He picks himself up and returns to the wake, where he experiences one of his habitual "visions." When Mamie later accompanies the Reverend Short to the window as he explains the circumstances of his fall, she looks down and sees the body of Valentine "Val" Haines, a young hood who has been living with Sister Dulcy and her husband Johnny "Fishtail" Perry, Big Joe's godson. The earlier vision has become reality: a dead man with a hunting knife in his heart.

Grave Digger and Coffin Ed are summoned to discover who murdered Val and, with Detective Sergeant Brody, an Irishman, begin questioning all possible suspects. Perhaps it was Johnny, whose temper is as infamous as his gambling prowess. Perhaps it was Charlie Chink, whose girlfriend, Doll Baby, appeared to be the recent target of Val's affections. Still, why the exotic hunting knife? Why the basket of bread? What conspiracy of silence connects the Reverend Short, Johnny's girl Sister Dulcy, and Mamie Pullen, forcing Johnny to travel to Chicago before returning to Harlem and murdering Charlie Chink?

After the initial several hours of questioning, Sergeant Brody, despite his years of experience, is too dumbfounded to explain the web of illogical complications in this case. Grave Digger tells him, in a statement that recurs throughout the novel and the entire series, epitomizing Himes's vision of the city: "This is Harlem. . . . ain't no other place like it in the world. You've got to start from scratch here, because these folks in Harlem do things for reasons nobody else in the world would think of."

The plot unravels through a series of mysterious events, including scenes of rage and violence that are the physical consequences of emotional brutalization. Johnny wakes up to find

Charlie Chink wandering around nude in his apartment and shoots him six times, stomps his bloody body until Chink's teeth are "stuck in his calloused heel," and then leans over and clubs Chink's head "into a bloody pulp with his pistol butt." These explosions, Himes's work suggests, derive from the most sublimated forms of frustration and hatred; the same forces can be seen in the degree of murderous intent which accompanies Coffin Ed's frequent loss of equilibrium. The repeated examples of "murderous rage" and the number of characters in the series whose faces are cut or whose bodies are maimed are related to this vision of Harlem as a dehumanizing prisonlike world. Even the apparently comic purposes of character description tend to underscore this perspective (the Reverend Short, for example, is introduced as having a "mouth shaped like that of a catfish" and eyes that "protrude behind his gold-rimmed spectacles like a bug's under a microscope").

Himes's evocation of a sense of place, however, is not limited to bizarre scenes of physical violence and rage. Beyond the scores of defiant men who are reminders of the repressed nature of manhood in the inner cities, the author gives abundant images of Harlem's social life (rent parties, fish fries, and wakes), its cultural past (Duke Ellington, Billy Eckstein, the Apollo Theatre), its economic and political hierarchies (civil servants, politicians, underworld celebrities), and its peculiar lifestyles and institutions (street gangs, professional gamblers, numbers runners, the homosexual subculture, the heroin trade, evangelists' churches, and soapbox orators). All of this is done with the aplomb of a tour guide whose knowledge of the terrain is complete and whose understanding of the cultural codes of behavior permits explanation to the uninitiated.

A bittersweet, tragicomic tone alternating with an almost Rabelaisian exuberance characterizes Himes's descriptions of the sights, rhythms, and sounds of life in Harlem. Even the diverse enticements and rich peculiarities of African American cooking are a part of Harlem's atmosphere, and the smells and tastes are frequently explored as Himes moves his two detectives through the many greasy spoons that line their beat (at one point in *Crazy Kill* the author duplicates an entire restaurant menu, from entrees to beverages, from "alligator tail and rice" to "sassafras-root tea").

Humor (if not parody) is reflected in the many unusual names of Himes's characters: Sassafras, Susie Q., Charlie Chink Dawson, H. Exodus Clay, Pigmeat, and Fishtail Perry; it is also reflected in the many instances of gullibility motivated by greed which account for the numerous scams, stings, and swindles that occur.

Himes accomplishes all of this with a remarkable economy of dialogue and language, an astute manipulation of temporal sequence, and a pattern of plots distinguished by a marvelous blend of fantasy and realism: a sense of the magically real which lurks beneath the surface of the commonplace. "Is he crazy or just acting?" asks Sergeant Brody about the Reverend Short's vision. "Maybe both," Grave Digger answers.

The last three novels in the series—*Cotton Comes to Harlem*, *The Heat's On*, and *Blind Man with a Pistol*—continue the character types, stylistic devices, and thematic concerns of the earlier novels. Each one represents a deepening of Himes's artistic control over his material; each one further enhanced his reputation in the genre and increased his notoriety and popularity among the American public. The first two of these were adapted for the screen—*Cotton Comes to Harlem* and *Come Back Charleston Blue*—and the third, reissued in the United States as *Hot Day, Hot Night*, was received as the "apotheosis" of Himes's detective novels. Its author was described (on the jacket cover) as "the best black American novelist writing today."

Analysis: Short Fiction

Chester Himes's short stories, he believed, served as his apprenticeship as a writer. They were the first of his writings to be published, and he continued in the genre intermittently for more than forty years. When an anthology of his short fiction was proposed in 1954, he revealed in his autobiography that he could not feel proud of it. The anthology finally published in 1973, *Black on Black: Baby Sister and Selected Writings*, was highly selective, concentrating on the stories of the first two decades of his career. A 1990 edition, *The Collected Stories of Chester Himes,* contains sixty-one pieces, ranging from 1933 to 1978, with nine updated. Many are prison stories, and not all are of even quality, but as a whole, they demonstrate Himes's remarkably versatile range of techniques and the ongoing themes and preoccupations of his longer pieces.

"His Last Day"

Prison life, horrible as it was, gave Himes the subject of several short stories. "His Last Day," about a condemned man's last few hours before the electric chair, already shows some of Himes's trademarks. Spats, a hardened, ruthless criminal who is condemned to death for killing a police officer, reflects wryly that he would not have been identified if the one person left alive during his robbery of a club had not recognized his fawn-colored spats. Even when he manages to hide out for a few days, he is finally trapped—by his past and by a woman. An old sweetheart whom he had abandoned in her pregnancy shoots the man who had provided Spats with refuge, thus attracting the police. Rivetingly grim, this early effort is marred by the dated slang, but even so, Himes's characteristic grisly humor comes through.

"Her Whole Existence"

James Baldwin wrote of Himes that he was the only black writer to describe male-female relationships in terms other than violence. One of Himes's earliest love stories, "Her Whole Existence: A Story of True Love," verges on parody in its clichéd language but also shows Himes's imaginative skill. Written from the point of view of Mabel Miles, the beautiful daughter of a successful African American politician, the story leaps suddenly from the romanticism of Mabel's attraction for Richard Riley, an ambitious, successful, and handsome criminal, to an analysis of class conflict. Trapped between the respect for law instilled by her family and her own passion, Mabel first betrays Richard and then helps him to escape. It is the first of Himes's portrayals of unpredictable but strong women.

"A Nigger"

"A Nigger" suggests, with its shockingly simple denouement, Himes's bitter observations about the sexual relationship between blacks and whites. Mr. Shelton, a rich old white man, drops in unexpectedly on Fay, a black prostitute who lives with a light-skinned common-law husband and who is currently involved with another black man, Joe Wolf. Taken by surprise, Fay shoves Joe into the closet to receive her white lover. Joe hears her cajole and flatter Mr. Shelton out of two hundred dollars and, crouched in the dark, recalls other tired, unattractive white men he has known who have turned to black women not in appreciation but in exhaustion. Such men have convinced themselves, he thinks, that it is only black flesh they touch, animal flesh that has no mind or power to judge. When he is ready to leave, Mr. Shelton opens the door of the closet by mistake, looks in, turns away, and leaves. While Fay is jubilant that Joe was not detected, Joe is so furious that he tries to strangle her. He knows that the white man saw him and simply refused to recognize his existence. Back in his own tiny room, he reflects bitterly that he must count himself a "nigger" for allowing his poverty and dependence on a prostitute to rob him of his manhood.

"Headwaiter"

Though many of Himes's stories—and novels—ram home the pain of being black in the United States, there are other works that portray individuals who can carve a dignified niche in the limited ways available to them. "Headwaiter" presents Dick Small, an African American man in charge of an old-fashioned dining room patronized by a regular white clientele. Imperturbable in this familiar atmosphere, Dick watches over everyone in his care, remembering the personal details of individual customers, waiters, and busboys. In his small way, he does what he can for the less fortunate. When the diners are horrified to learn that one of the best waiters is a former convict, Dick stands firmly by his decision to give the man a second chance, and his polite firmness quells the furor. He is unable, however, to save another waiter who acts drunk; when he has to dismiss him, he does so with sympathy and compassion.

"Lunching at the Ritzmore"

The complementary story "Lunching at the Ritzmore" differs in tone. A satiric view of the laws that required separate public establishments for blacks and whites, this story suggests, lightheartedly, what Himes was seriously to advocate later: the power that lies in a large crowd to hurl down racist barriers. In "the mecca of the motley" in Pershing Square, Los Angeles, a young college student from Vermont argues that there is no discrimination against Negroes. A drifter in the crowd bets him the price of dinner that a young brown-skinned Negro, an unemployed mechanic, will be refused service if the three eat at a restaurant. As the three set off in search of a suitably challenging place to eat, the crowd around them grows and grows because people think that a free giveaway must be the goal of such a gathering. A policeman follows them, wanting to arrest them but not being able to think of a good reason to do so. Finally, an enormous crowd halts outside the very fancy Ritzmore Hotel; there, the debate shifts slightly from race to class, as none of the three is dressed well enough. The diners, the waiters, and the cooks, however, are so stunned by the crowd that the three men are immediately served the only item that they can read on the French menu—ironically enough, it is apple pie. The student wins his bet but has to pay because the drifter is broke.

"All He Needs Is Feet"

Few other stories exhibit such lighthearted irony in the face of racial discrimination. "All He Needs Is Feet" is ironic, in the horrifying, brutal way that shocks the reader into realizing why Himes later saw violence as the only solution for African Americans, because they are mistreated so violently by a violent society. Ward, a black man, walking down the sidewalk in Rome, Georgia, steps off to let a white woman and two white men pass. One white man bumps into Ward anyway and provokes him to fight. A crowd that gathers, thinking a lynching is too severe, pours gasoline on Ward's feet and sets him on fire. In jail for assault with a deadly weapon, Ward has his feet amputated. He goes to Chicago with money sent by his family and learns to use crutches and knee pads to work at shining shoes, saving enough money to buy war bonds. In a theater, his crutches tucked out of everyone's way under the seats, Ward cannot stand up for the national anthem at the end of the film. A big, burly man from Arkansas hits him for disrespect to the flag. The ultimate cruelty of the story comes as a punch line, when a policeman arrests the white man: The man from Arkansas blubbers that he could not stand a "nigger" sitting through the national anthem, even if he did not have feet.

The issue of patriotism became very complex for African Americans during World War II, especially for those who fought for democracy against Adolf Hitler and his blatantly racist and fascist goals of a super race and then had to reflect on the racism in their own democracy. Several of Himes's war stories, such as "Two Soldiers," reveal a man struggling to remain patriotic and optimistic. The most effective of these, "So Softly Smiling," springs from the war atmosphere but is really a beautiful love story. Roy Jonny Squires, a lieutenant in the U.S. Army, returns to Harlem for thirty days. Exhausted by the warfare in North Africa, he heads for a bar late at night and meets Mona Morrison, a successful poet. Her "tawny skin like an African veld at sunset" exactly fulfills the ache for love that fiery raids at dawn have brought upon him. This delicate love story is punctuated throughout with dramatic reminders that the lovers' time together is very short, and their courtship and married life proceed at breakneck speed. It is in this story that Himes touches on the race issue during war, lightly, positively; Roy says that he finally enlisted because he heard someone say that the United States belonged to the Negro as much as it did to anyone.

"Tang"

More than two decades later, Himes seemed to have lost such patriotic optimism. In "Tang," a tired, hungry couple sit watching television in their cold-water slum flat in Harlem, when a long cardboard box with a florist's label is delivered to them. They discover inside it an M-14 army gun and a typewritten sheet warning them to learn how to use their weapon and wait for instructions, for freedom is near. The man, T-bone Smith, who had used such a weapon in the Korean War, is absolutely terrified and wants to report the gun to the police. The woman, Tang, once a beautiful, softly rounded woman who has become hard and angular from her life as a poor prostitute, is ecstatic. She hugs the gun as if it were a lover and cherishes the thought that the gun could chop up a white policeman. She is ready to fight for freedom, even pointing the gun at T-bone to stop him from calling the police. Her defiance enrages him; he whips out a spring-blade knife and slashes her to death, crying that he might not be free of whitey, but he is now free of her.

Writing twenty years before Himes's death, the critic Edward Margolies noted that Himes's characters tend to be reflective, interested in ideas and in intellectualizing the predicaments in which they find themselves. As such, they are quite different from such characters as Bigger Thomas, with whom Richard Wright shocked the United States in his *Native Son* (1940). Wright's success trapped other African American writers whom the literary establishment then automatically described as, or expected to be, "protest" writers. Certainly, the range of Himes's short fiction is so vast that it includes stories of strong protest. He wrote, however, stories of individuals caught up in a web of many circumstances. Race is clearly an issue in his fiction, but so are love, sex, poverty, class, war, prison, violence, success, failure, and humor. His short fiction is not only a prelude to his better known novels but also a rewarding world in itself.

Bibliography

Benson, Christopher. "What's Behind the Boon in Black Mystery Writers?" *Ebony* 58, no. 11 (September, 2003): 110-113. An informative discussion of the increasingly popular African American mystery novel, written to coincide with the eighth annual Chester Himes Black Mystery Writers Conference and Awards Program.

Breu, Christopher. "Freudian Knot or Gordian Knot? The Contradictions of Racialized Masculinity in Chester Himes's *If He Hollers Let Him Go.*" *Callaloo* 26, no. 3 (Summer, 2003): 766-796. A valuable discussion of the novel and its interpretation of racism, masculinity, sexuality, and violence in postwar America.

Bunyan, Scott. "No Order from Chaos: The Absence of Chandler's Extra-Legal in the Detective Fiction of Chester Himes and Walter Mosley." *Studies in the Novel* 35, no. 3 (Fall, 2003): 339-366. Studies Himes's *Blind Man with a Pistol* and *Plan B* and discusses the importance of extralegal space in the novels.

Calloway, Catherine. "Fiction: The 1930s to the 1960s." *American Literature* 77, no. 2 (June, 2005): 349-368. This chapter examines Himes's work and compares it to that of four other major American authors: James Baldwin, Ralph Ellison, John Steinbeck, and Richard Wright.

Cochran, David. "So Much Nonsense Must Make Sense: The Black Vision of Chester Himes." *The Midwest Quarterly* 38 (Autumn, 1996): 1-30. Examines Himes's creation of the hard-boiled cop figure as a reflection of his own experience in Harlem. Argues that he presents Harlem as the underside of American capitalism.

Crooks, Robert. "From the Far Side of the Urban Frontier: The Detective Fiction of Chester Himes and Walter Mosley." *College Literature* 22 (October, 1995): 68-90. Analyzes the emergence of African American detective fiction in the works of Walter Mosley and Chester Himes. Shows how Himes develops a strategy for disrupting the frontier narrative in a way that lays it bare.

Fabré, Michel, Robert E. Skinner, and Lester Sullivan, comps. *Chester Himes: An Annotated Primary and Secondary Bibliography.* Westport, Conn.: Greenwood Press, 1992. This is a comprehensive annotated bibliography of writings by and about Himes.

Himes, Chester. *Conversations with Chester Himes.* Edited by Michel Fabré and Robert Skinner. Jackson: University Press of Mississippi, 1995. This collection of interviews with Himes provides information about his life and work.

Itagaki, Lynn M. "Transgressing Race and Community in Chester Himes's *If He Hollers Let Him Go.*" *African American Review* 37, no. 1 (Spring, 2003): 65-81. An insightful article that places Himes's novel in an autobiographical context, placing particular focus on dealing with racism and other painful experiences.

Lundquist, James. *Chester Himes.* New York: Frederick Ungar, 1976. An introductory volume to Himes's life and works, with chapters on the war novels, confessional novels, and detective novels. The first chapter, "November, 1928," describes the armed robbery for which Himes was arrested and his subsequent arrest and trial, in detail. Chronology, notes, bibliography of primary and secondary sources, index.

Margolies, Edward. "Race and Sex: The Novels of Chester Himes." In *Native Sons: A Critical Study of Twentieth-Century Negro American Authors.* Philadelphia: J. B. Lippincott, 1968. A discussion of the major novels. The author sees Himes as considerably different from the group of protest writers following Richard Wright and believes that his European sojourn weakened his writings about the United States. Bibliography and index.

Margolies, Edward, and Michel Fabré. *The Several Lives of Chester Himes.* Jackson: University Press of Mississippi, 1997. This full-length biography of Himes is indispensable for information about his life.

Milliken, Stephen F. *Chester Himes: A Critical Appraisal.* Columbia: University of Missouri Press, 1976. Contains an excellent chapter, "Take a Giant Step," on Himes's short stories. This study includes sections on the protest, autobiographical, and detective novels. Chronology, bibliography of primary sources, and annotated bibliography of secondary sources.

Muller, Gilbert. *Chester Himes.* Boston: Twayne, 1989. An excellent introduction to Himes's life and works. Traces the evolution of Himes's grotesque, revolutionary view of life in the United States for African Americans, in several literary modes, culminating in his detective fiction. Chronology, appendix, index, and annotated bibliographies of primary and secondary works.

Rosen, Steven J. "African American Anti-Semitism and Himes's *Lonely Crusade.*" *MELUS* 20 (Summer, 1995): 47-68. Discusses an anti-Semitic streak that runs through Himes's work alongside an anxiety to assert masculinity. Shows how Himes used Jewish characters or formulated Jewish traits as a foil to black American masculinity.

Rosenblatt, Roger. "The Hero Vanishes." In *Black Fiction.* Cambridge, Mass.: Harvard University Press, 1974. Briefly compares Himes's hero to Richard Wright's *Native Son* (1940). Particularly interesting is the introduction, which provides a broad-ranging discussion of the relationship of black literature to American literature as a whole. Index, bibliography.
— *Roland E. Bush; Shakuntala Jayaswal*

Langston Hughes
Poet, critic, and playwright

Born: Joplin, Missouri; February 1, 1902
Died: New York, New York; May 22, 1967

LONG FICTION: *Not Without Laughter,* 1930; *Tambourines to Glory,* 1958.

SHORT FICTION: *The Ways of White Folks,* 1934; *Simple Speaks His Mind,* 1950; *Laughing to Keep from Crying,* 1952; *Simple Takes a Wife,* 1953; *Simple Stakes a Claim,* 1957; *The Best of Simple,* 1961; *Something in Common, and Other Stories,* 1963; *Simple's Uncle Sam,* 1965.

DRAMA: *Troubled Island,* pr. 1935 (opera libretto); *Mulatto,* pb. 1935; *Little Ham,* pr. 1935; *Don't You Want to Be Free?,* pb. 1938; *Freedom's Plow,* pb. 1943; *Street Scene,* pr., pb. 1947 (lyrics; music by Kurt Weill and Elmer Rice); *Simply Heavenly,* pr. 1957 (opera libretto); *Black Nativity,* pr. 1961; *Tambourines to Glory,* pr., pb. 1963; *Five Plays,* pb. 1963 (Walter Smalley, editor); *Jerico-Jim Crow,* pr. 1964; *The Prodigal Son,* pr. 1965.

SCREENPLAYS: *Way Down South,* 1939 (with Clarence Muse).

POETRY: *The Weary Blues,* 1926; *Fine Clothes to the Jew,* 1927; *Dear Lovely Death,* 1931; *The Negro Mother,* 1931; *The Dream Keeper, and Other Poems,* 1932; *Scottsboro Limited: Four Poems and a Play in Verse,* 1932; *A New Song,* 1938; *Shakespeare in Harlem,* 1942; *Jim Crow's Last Stand,* 1943; *Lament for Dark Peoples,* 1944; *Fields of Wonder,* 1947; *One Way Ticket,* 1949; *Montage of a Dream Deferred,* 1951; *Selected Poems of Langston Hughes,* 1959; *Ask Your Mama: Or, Twelve Moods for Jazz,* 1961; *The Panther and the Lash: Or, Poems of Our Times,* 1967; *The Poems, 1921-1940,* 2001 (volume 1 of *The Collected Works of Langston Hughes;* Dolan Hubbard, editor); *The Poems, 1941-1950,* 2001 (volume 2 of *The Collected Works of Langston Hughes;* Hubbard, editor); *The Poems, 1951-1967,* 2001 (volume 3 of *The Collected Works of Langston Hughes;* Hubbard, editor).

NONFICTION: *The Big Sea: An Autobiography*, 1940; *Famous American Negroes*, 1954; *Famous Negro Music Makers*, 1955; *The Sweet Flypaper of Life*, 1955 (photographs by Roy De Carava); *A Pictorial History of the Negro in America*, 1956 (with Milton Meltzer); *I Wonder as I Wander: An Autobiographical Journey*, 1956; *Famous Negro Heroes of America*, 1958; *Fight for Freedom: The Story of the NAACP*, 1962; *Black Magic: A Pictorial History of the Negro in American Entertainment*, 1967 (with Meltzer); *Black Misery*, 1969 (illustrations by Arouni); *Arna Bontemps—Langston Hughes Letters*, 1980; *Remember Me to Harlem: The Letters of Langston Hughes and Carl Van Vechten, 1925-1964*, 2001 (Emily Bernard, editor).

CHILDREN'S/YOUNG ADULT LITERATURE: *Popo and Fijina: Children of Haiti*, 1932 (story; with Arna Bontemps); *The First Book of Negroes*, 1952; *The First Book of Rhythms*, 1954; *The First Book of Jazz*, 1955; *The First Book of the West Indies*, 1955; *The First Book of Africa*, 1960.

EDITED TEXTS: *The Poetry of the Negro, 1746-1949*, 1949 (with Arna Bontemps); *The Book of Negro Folklore*, 1959 (with Bontemps); *New Negro Poets: U.S.A.*, 1964; *The Book of Negro Humor*, 1966; *The Best Short Stories by Negro Writers: An Anthology from 1899 to the Present*, 1967.

TRANSLATIONS: *Masters of the Dew*, 1947 (of Jacques Roumain; with Mercer Cook); *Cuba Libre*, 1948 (of Nicolás Guillén; with Ben Carruthers); *Gypsy Ballads*, 1951 (of Federico García Lorca); *Selected Poems of Gabriela Mistral*, 1957.

MISCELLANEOUS: *The Langston Hughes Reader*, 1958; *The Collected Works of Langston Hughes*, 2001 (12 volumes).

Achievements

Langston Hughes has been acknowledged—both before and after his death—as the most influential African American writer in the English-speaking world. As a leader of the Harlem Renaissance, he not only wrote in a variety of genres but also edited and encouraged the literary, dramatic, and musical productions of other people of color. Recognition came during his lifetime as early as 1925, when he won the Poetry Prize given by *Opportu-*

nity magazine and the Spingarn prizes of *Crisis* magazine for both poetry and essay writing. His novel *Not Without Laughter* won the Harmon Gold Medal in 1931. That year he received his first Rosenwald Fellowship, an award repeated in 1941. The John Simon Guggenheim Memorial Foundation Fellowship in 1935, the National Academy of Arts and Letters Award for Literature in 1946, and the Ainsfield-Wolf Award in 1953 continued to keep him in the forefront of the literary community, particularly in New York, throughout his life. His alma mater, Lincoln University, awarded him an honorary doctorate in 1943, and he received others from Howard University and Case Western Reserve University in 1963 and 1964, respectively.

All of his works illustrate the depth of Langston Hughes's commitment to a celebration of black American life in all its forms and make immediately evident the reason why he has been proclaimed "The Poet Laureate of Black America." His stature as a humorist grew from his creation of Jesse B. Semple, also known as Simple, a Harlem barstool philosopher in the tradition of American folk humor ranging from Davy Crockett to Mr. Dooley. Hughes wrote about Simple in columns published in the *Chicago Defender,* begun in the 1940's and continuing into the 1960's. His Simple columns also appeared in the *New York Post* between 1962 and 1965. Publication of his five books of Simple sketches increased the readership of that sage of Harlem with his views on life in white America.

Although Hughes never had any one big seller, his efforts in so many fields of literary endeavor earned for him the admiration and respect of readers in all walks of life. Certainly, too, Hughes is a major poetic figure of his time and perhaps the best black American poet.

Biography

James Mercer Langston Hughes (the first two names were soon dropped) was born in Joplin, Missouri, on February 1, 1902. His parents, James Nathaniel and Carrie Mercer Langston Hughes, separated when Hughes was young; by the time he was twelve, he had lived in several cities: Buffalo, Cleveland, Lawrence and

(Library of Congress)

Topeka, Kansas, Colorado Springs, and Mexico City (where his father lived). Until 1914, however, Hughes lived mainly with his maternal grandmother in Lawrence.

Hughes began writing poetry during his grammar school days in Lincoln, Illinois. While attending Cleveland's Central High School (1916-1920), Hughes wrote his first short story, "Mary Winosky," and published poems in the school's literary publications. The first national publication of his work came in 1921, when *The Crisis* published "The Negro Speaks of Rivers." The poem had been written while Hughes was taking a train on his way to see his father in Mexico City, a visit that the young man dreaded making. His hatred for his father, fueled by his father's contempt for poor people who could not make anything of themselves, actually led to Hughes's being hospitalized briefly in 1919.

Hughes's father did, however, send his son to Columbia University in 1921. Although Hughes did not stay at Columbia, his experiences in Harlem laid the groundwork for his later love affair with the city within a city. Equally important to Hughes's later work was the time he spent at sea and abroad during this period of his life. His exposure to American blues and jazz players in Paris nightclubs and his experiences in Europe, and especially in Africa, although brief, provided a rich source of material that he used over the next decades in his writing.

The years between 1919 and 1929 have been variously referred to as the Harlem Renaissance, the New Negro Renaissance, and the Harlem Awakening. Whatever they are called, they were years of rich productivity within the black artistic community, and Hughes was an important element in that Renaissance. While working as a busboy in the Wardman Park Hotel in Washington, D.C., in 1925, Hughes showed some of his poems—"Jazzonia," "Negro Dancers," and "The Weary Blues"—to Vachel Lindsay, who read them during one of his performances that same evening. The next day, Hughes was presented to the local press as "the busboy poet." With that introduction, and with the aid of people such as writer Carl Van Vechten and Walter White (of the NAACP), Hughes's popularity began to grow. He published *The Weary Blues* in 1926 and entered Lincoln University in Pennsylvania, where he completed his college education. The 1920's also saw the publication of his second volume of poems, *Fine Clothes to the Jew*, and the completion of his first novel, *Not Without Laughter*.

During much of the early 1930's, Hughes traveled abroad. He went to Cuba and Haiti during 1931-1932 and joined a group of young writers and students from Harlem on a film-making trip to Russia in 1932-1933. Publishing articles in Russian journals enabled him to extend his own travels in the Far East; he also began to write short stories during that time. By 1934, he had written the fourteen stories that he included in *The Ways of White Folks*.

During the mid-1930's, several of Hughes's plays were produced, *Mulatto* and *Little Ham* among them. In the course of having these plays performed, Hughes started the Harlem Suitcase Theatre in 1938, the New Negro Theatre in Los Angeles (1939), and the Skyloft Players of Chicago (1941).

After the publication of his first autobiographical volume, *The Big Sea*, Hughes spent time in Chicago with the group he had founded there. When America entered World War II, Hughes produced material for the war effort, ranging from "Defense Bond Blues" to articles on black American participation in the war. In addition, during the 1940's, he began work on his translations of the poetry of Cuban poet Nicolás Guillén, wrote essays for such diverse magazines as the *Saturday Review of Literature* and *Negro Digest*, wrote the lyrics for *Street Scene*, and published the volumes of poetry *Shakespeare in Harlem, Fields of Wonder*, and *One Way Ticket*.

Also in the 1940's, Hughes "discovered" Jesse B. Semple. Drawing inspiration from a conversation he had in a bar with a worker from a New Jersey war plant—during which the man complained to his nagging girlfriend, "You know white folks don't tell colored folks what cranks crank"—Hughes developed the framework for his Simple stories. He combined his own authorial voice, the voice of Simple's learned interrogator (eventually named Boyd), and the voice of Simple himself to weave a mixture of folk humor that has direct ties back to the "old southwest" humor of Mark Twain and his contemporaries.

The next decades saw continued production of poetry and other writing by Hughes. He wrote his pictorial histories and his "first books" for children. He continued his public readings, often accompanied by piano and/or jazz orchestra—a prototype of the Beat poets. His second volume of autobiography, *I Wonder as I Wander*, was published in 1956, and *The Langston Hughes Reader*, an extensive collection of his work in several genres, appeared two years later. The last two volumes of his new poetry, *Ask Your Mama* and *The Panther and the Lash*, continued his experimentation with incorporating jazz and folk elements into his poetry.

Hughes spent the last years of his life living and working in Harlem. He encouraged younger black writers, publishing several stories by newcomers in his *The Best Short Stories by Negro Writers*, as well as including works by established older writers such as Ralph Ellison and Richard Wright. Hughes died on May 22, 1967, in Harlem, the city that so inspired and informed his best work. No one caught the magic that Harlem represented during his lifetime in quite the way that Hughes did.

Analysis: Short Fiction

Langston Hughes records in *The Big Sea: An Autobiography* his feelings upon first seeing Africa: " . . . when I saw the dust-green hills in the sunlight, something took hold of me inside. My Africa, Motherland of the Negro peoples! And me a Negro! The real thing!" The trip to Africa confirmed what he already knew—that the subject matter of his writings would reflect his desire "to write seriously and as well as I knew how about the Negro people." Most of Hughes's short stories concern themselves with black people presented from many different perspectives and in both tragic and comic dimensions. Even when the protagonist of a story is white, as in "Little Dog," the gentle black man to whom Miss Briggs is attracted is given special focus. Hughes, however, is not racist in his presentation. People, regardless of their racial background, are people first participating in a common humanity before they are individuals distorted by prejudice based on ignorance, by fear, or by social conditions which create a spiritual and psychological malaise, sometimes crippling in its effect.

"Little Dog"

"Little Dog" tells the story of a white and gaunt middle-aged woman, head bookkeeper of a coal and coke firm for twenty-one years, who, because of her own sense of prudence, responsibility, and concern, sublimates her own desires to care for her mother, and then, after her mother's death, is left alone and lonely. Although she keeps busy, is comfortably situated, and does not think too much of what she may be missing, she occasionally wonders why she knows no one whom she can appreciate as a friend. One day she inexplicably stops the taxicab in which she is riding in front of a pet shop featuring in its window "fuzzy little white dogs," and she purchases for herself a puppy at a very steep price. She arranges with the janitor of her apartment building, "a tow-headed young Swede," to provide food for her dog, which she names Flips, and soon her life revolves around activities centering on Flips.

One day the janitor does not show up to feed the dog; several days pass until Miss Briggs decides she needs to go down to the basement to search out the janitor. With her dog by her side, she knocks at a door behind which she hears sounds of "happy laughter, and kids squalling, and people moving." The door is opened by a small black boy and soon Miss Briggs discovers that the "tall broad-shouldered Negro" standing amidst the children is the new janitor.

The image patterns and juxtapositions in the story now begin to form meaningful patterns. The white woman, living "upstairs" with the "fuzzy white dog," is contrasted with the black man and his "pretty little brown-black" children who live "downstairs." The gentle and kind black man begins to service Miss Briggs's needs, bringing more food than is good for the dog because he believes the woman desires it and because he is being paid for it; Miss Briggs, however, never tells him that meat every few days is sufficient. Soon Miss Briggs finds herself hurrying home, never realizing that it is no longer the dog but rather the nightly visits of the janitor that compel her to hurry. One evening her words inadvertently reveal her subconscious needs. The black janitor has just left after delivering Flips's food and she can hear him humming as he returns to his family. Suddenly Miss Briggs says to Flips: "Oh, Flips . . . I'm so hungry."

Now, although she never consciously knows why, Miss Briggs decides she needs to move; " . . . she could not bear to have this janitor come upstairs with a package of bones for Flips again. . . . Let him stay in the basement, where he belonged." The accumulation of references to bones, meat, and services provides for the reader, if not for Miss Briggs, a moment of epiphany: "He almost keeps me broke buying bones," Miss Briggs says to the tall and broad-shouldered black janitor. "True," the janitor answers her. The sustenance the black man provides for the dog is no sustenance for the gaunt and bony woman, nor is the dog, like children, sufficient to keep memory of the departed alive. Miss Briggs moves and shortly is completely forgotten by the people in the neighborhood in which she had lived.

"Thank You M'am"

If Miss Briggs seems a portrait of a woman dead before she is buried, Mrs. Luella Bates Washington Jones of "Thank You M'am" is a picture of middle-aged woman still vital and vigorous, although she, too, lives alone; and although it appears she has no children of her own, she is still potent, giving new life to a young black boy who attempts to mug her. The child is no match for the woman, who is identified with her purse so large "that it had everything in it but a hammer and nails." She drags him home with her, sees that he washes, and shares with him her frugal meal. Her presence is so overpowering that the boy is more fearful of trying to get away than of staying, but she breaks down his resistance when she speaks to him of common problems. "I was young once and I wanted things I could not get." The boy waits expecting the "but" to follow. The woman anticipates: "You thought I was going to say, *but I didn't snatch people's pocketbooks. Well, I wasn't going to say that. . . . I have done things, too, which I would not tell you, son. . . . Everybody's got something in common."* The woman's actions, however, tell the boy more than her words do, and at the end of the story the boy is unable to use words, although his lips try to phrase more than "Thank you M'am."

"Professor"

One of Hughes's most-frequently praised stories is "Professor." Focused through the point of view of its protagonist Dr. T. Walton Brown (*T* for Tom, Uncle Tom?), the story examines how a black professor of sociology "bows" and "bobs" like a puppet on a string to members of the wealthy white establishment, doing only those things of which they approve, saying what they want to hear, and, although at times he knows the lies diminish him, still allowing his own needs to determine his behavior patterns.

Bitterly ironic in tone, the story begins with the juxtaposition of Brown in dinner dress against the lobby of a run-down segregated hotel and Brown cared for by a white chauffeur who tucks the professor carefully into the luxury of a limousine to carry him through the black ghetto to a private house as large as a hotel. Brown's posture and attire are carefully contrasted with the "two or three ash-colored children" who run across the street in front of the limousine, "their skinny legs and poor clothes plain in the glare of the headlights." So also are the streets and buildings contrasted—"the Negro streets": "pig's knuckle joints, pawnshops, beer parlors—and houses of vice, no doubt—save that these latter, at least, did not hang out their signs" with the "wide lawns and fine homes that lined the beautiful well-lighted boulevard where white people lived."

Brown has bought entry into the white establishment by prostituting himself, by accepting the degradation of the constant diminishing of his selfhood and his race. He listens to his white counterpart say: "Why, at our city college here we've been conducting some fine interracial experiments. I have had some colored ministers and high school teachers visit my classes. We found them most intelligent." Although at times Brown is moved to make slight and subtle protest, in the end he agrees with the biased white people, saying "You are right."

Brown's behavior is dictated by his desire for the money the white people offer him as long as he conforms to their expectation. Money will buy Brown prestige, will enable his college to survive, and will further his career. Money will also "take his family to South America in the summer where for three months they wouldn't feel like Negroes." Thus, he dances to the "tune of Jim Crow education," diminishing both himself and his race. Although carefully constructed, the story offers no subtleties beyond the ironies present; image patterns are at a minimum, complex symbolism nonexistent. Characterization, too, is sparse. The reader learns only enough about the professor to make his behavior immediately credible, but a traditional plot line moves with careful pacing to climax and pointed resolution, and the theme overshadows technique.

"Fine Accommodations"

Similar in theme and technique to "Professor" is "Fine Accommodations." In this story, a young black porter learns that the Dr. Jenkins, booked into sleeping car accommodations, is not the leader of his race and "fine man" the naïve porter expects but rather another Uncle Tom who keeps on "being a big man" by "bowing to Southern white customs," by helping to keep poor black people just where they have always been "all the time— poor and black." At the end of the story, the porter makes the point of the story: "The last Negro passenger I had in that drawing room was a pimp from Birmingham. Now I got a professor. I guess both of them have to have ways of paying for such fine accommodations."

"Big Meeting"

From the perspective of complexity, subtlety, and power, "Big Meeting" is a considerably better story. Told in the first person by a young black boy who with a companion is observing a church revival meeting held in the woods, the story recounts the boy's moment of epiphany when he realizes, if only subconsciously, that as a cynical observer rather than a participant in the ritual he is more akin to the white folks gathered to watch than to his own people. Making use of dialect and gospel songs, Hughes builds the story to a powerful sermon where the preacher recounts the betrayal of Christ to the accompaniment of echoing refrains and then moves the sermon to the cadences of poetry:

> They brought four long nails
> And put one in the palm of His left hand.
> The hammer said . . . Bam!
> They put one in the palm of His right hand.
> The hammer said . . . Bam!
> They put one through His left foot . . . Bam!
> And one through His right foot . . . Bam!
> . . . "Don't drive it!" a woman screamed. "Don't drive them nails!
> For Christ's sake! Oh! Don't drive 'em!"

In the woods observing the action, the narrator and his companion are near enough to a car full of white people to overhear what they are saying as they comment in ways showing their biases, limitations, and prejudices. As the narrator hears these comments, he begins to respond, but not enough to cause him to identify with the participants in the service. Rather, both he and his companion seem more concerned with the behavior of their mothers who are taking part in the church rituals.

At the climax of the story, the narrator hears his mother's voice: "Were you there when they crucified my Lord?/ Were you there when they nailed Him to the tree?" At the same time as the mother cries out the questions, the preacher opens his arms wide against the white canvas tent, and his body reflects a crosslike shadow. As the mother asks the question again, the white people in the car suddenly drive away creating a swirl of dust, and the narrator cries after them, "Don't go. . . . They're about to call for sinners. . . . Don't go!"

The boy's cry to the white people reflects his understanding of the parallel setup between the white people and the betrayers of Christ. Hughes goes further than this, however, and provides in the last sentence of the story an epiphanic moment: "I didn't realize I was crying until I tasted my tears in my mouth." The epiphany projects a revelation dimly understood by the narrator but clearly present—that as bad as the white people's behavior seemed, his own rejection of his people and heritage was worse.

Analysis: Poetry

Langston Hughes often referred to three poets as his major influences: Paul Laurence Dunbar, Carl Sandburg, and Walt Whitman. If one were to assay which qualities of Hughes's poetry show the influence of which poet, one might say that Hughes got his love of the folk and his lyric simplicity from Dunbar, his attraction to the power of the people—especially urban dwellers—and his straightforward descriptive power from Sandburg, and his fascination with sensual people—people of the body rather than the mind—and his clear sense of rhythm from Whitman. No one would draw such a clear delineation, but the elements described are essential elements of Hughes's poetry. His work explores the humor and the pathos, the exhilaration and the despair, of black American life in ways that are sometimes conventional and sometimes unique. He explored the blues as a poetic form, and he peopled his poems with Harlem dancers, as well as with a black mother trying to explain her life to her son. He worked with images of dreams and of "dreams deferred"; he looked at life in the middle of America's busiest black city and at the life of the sea and of exploration and discovery. Always, too, Hughes examined the paradox of being black in mostly white America, of being not quite free in the land of freedom.

The poetry of Langston Hughes is charged with life and love, even when it cries out against the injustice of the world. He was a poet who loved life and loved his heritage. More than any other black American writer, he captured the essence of the complexity of a life that mixes laughter and tears, joy and frustration, and still manages to sing and dance with the spirit of humanity.

The Weary Blues

Hughes's first collection of poetry, *The Weary Blues*, contains samples of many of the poetic styles and themes of his poetry in general. The collection begins with a celebration of blackness ("Proem") and ends with an affirmation of the black American's growing sense of purpose and equality "Epilogue" ("I, Too, Sing America"). In between, there are poems that sing of Harlem cabaret life and poems that sing the blues. Some of the non-blues poems also sing of a troubled life, as well as expressing an occasional burst of joy. Here, too, are the sea poems drawn from Hughes's traveling experiences. All in all, the sparkle of a love of life in these poems was that which caught the attention of many early reviewers.

The titles of some of the poems about cabaret life suggest their subject: "Jazzonia," "Negro Dancers," "The Cat and the Saxaphone," and "Harlem Night Club." "The Cat and the Saxaphone" is especially intriguing because it intersperses a conversation between two "jive" lovers with the first chorus of "Everybody Loves My Baby," producing the effect of a jazz chorus within the song's rhythmic framework.

Part of the controversy which flared in the black community during the Harlem Renaissance involved whether an artist should present the "low-life" elements or the more conventional middle-class elements in black American life. Hughes definitely leaned toward the former as the richer, more exciting to portray in his poetry.

Because the blues tradition is more tied to the common folk than to the middle-class, Hughes's interest in the possibilities of using the blues style in his poetry is not surprising. He took the standard three-line blues stanza and made it a six-line stanza to develop a more familiar poetic form; the repetition common in the first and second lines in the blues becomes a repetition of the first/second and third/fourth lines in Hughes's poems. As in the traditional blues, Hughes varies the wording in the repeated lines—adding, deleting, or changing words. For example, here is a stanza from "Blues Fantasy":

> My man's done left me,
> Chile, he's gone away.
> My good man's left me,
> Babe, he's gone away.
> Now the cryin' blues
> Haunts me night and day.

Often exclamation points are added to suggest more nearly the effect of the sung blues.

There are not as many blues poems in this first collection as there are in later ones such as *Fine Clothes to the Jew* and *Shakespeare in Harlem*. (The latter contains a marvelous seven-poem effort titled "Seven Moments of Love," which Hughes subtitled "An Un-Sonnet Sequence in Blues.") The title poem of his first collection, "The Weary Blues," is an interesting variation because it has a frame for the blues which sets up the song sung by a blues artist. The poet recalls the performance of a blues singer/pianist "on Lenox Avenue the other night" and describes the man's playing and singing. Later, the singer goes home to bed, "while the Weary Blues echoed through his head." Over the years, Hughes wrote a substantial number of blues poems and poems dealing with jazz, reflecting clearly his love for the music that is at the heart of the black American experience.

Some of the poems in *The Weary Blues* are simple lyrics. They are tinged with sadness ("A Black Pierrot") and with traditional poetic declarations of the beauty of a loved one ("Ardella"). The sea poems are also, by and large, more traditional than experimental. Again, their titles reflect their subject matter: "Water-Front Streets," "Port Town," "Sea Calm," "Caribbean Sunset," and "Seascape."

A few of these early poems reflect the gentle but insistent protest that runs through Hughes's poems; they question the treatment of black Americans and search for a connection with the motherland, Africa. The last section of the book is titled "Our Land," and the first poem in the section, "Our Land: Poem for a Decorative Panel," explores the idea that the black American should live in a land of warmth and joy instead of in a land where "life is cold" and "birds are grey." Other poems in the section include "Lament for Dark Peoples," "Disillusion," and "Danse Africaine." Perhaps the most poignant poem in the book is also in this last section: "Mother to Son." The poem is a monologue in dialect in which a mother encourages her son to continue the struggle she has carried on, which she likens to climbing a rough, twisting staircase: "Life for me ain't been no crystal stair./ It's had tacks in it . . . And places with no carpet on the floor—/ Bare." The collection's final poem, "Epilogue" ("I, Too, Sing America"), raises the hope that some day equality will truly be reached in America for the "darker brother" who is forced "to eat in the kitchen/ When company comes." Taken together, the poems of *The Weary Blues* make an extraordinary first volume of poetry and reveal the range of Hughes's style and subject matter.

The next two principal volumes of poetry, *Fine Clothes to the Jew* and *The Dream Keeper, and Other Poems*, present more of Hughes's blues poems (the latter volume is primarily in that genre) and more poems centering on Harlem's nightlife. The final two volumes, *Ask your Mama* and *The Panther and the Lash*, continue the experiment of combining musical elements with poetry and offer some of Hughes's strongest protest poetry.

Ask Your Mama

Ask Your Mama is dedicated to "Louis Armstrong—the greatest horn blower of them all." In an introductory note, Hughes explains that "the traditional folk melody of the 'Hesitation Blues' is the leitmotif for this poem." The collection was designed to be read or sung with jazz accompaniment, "with room for spontaneous jazz improvisation, particularly between verses, when the voice pauses." Hughes includes suggestions for music to accompany the poetry. Sometimes the instructions are open ("delicate lieder on piano"), and sometimes they are more direct ("suddenly the drums roll like thunder as the music ends sonorously"). There are also suggestions for specific songs to be used, including "Dixie" ("impishly"), "When the Saints Go Marchin' In" and "The Battle Hymn of the Republic." As a final aid, Hughes includes at the end of his collection "Liner Notes" for, as he says, "the Poetically Unhep."

Throughout, the poems in *Ask Your Mama* run the current of protest against "the shadow" of racism that falls over the lives of the earth's darker peoples. Shadows frequently occur as images and symbols, suggesting the fear and the sense of vague existence created by living in oppression. "Show Fare, Please" summarizes the essence of the poet's feeling of being left out because he does not have "show fare," but it also suggests that "the show" may be all illusion anyway. Not all the poems are so stark; the humor of Hughes's earlier work is still very much in evidence. In "Is It True," for example, Hughes notes that "everybody thinks that Negroes have the *most* fun, but, of course, secretly hopes they do not—although curious to find out if they do."

The Panther and the Lash

The Panther and the Lash, the final collection of Hughes's new poetry, published the year he died, also contains some of his most direct protest poetry, although he never gives vent to the anger which permeated the work of his younger contemporaries. The collection is dedicated "To Rosa Parks of Montgomery who started it all . . . " in 1955 by refusing to move to the back of a bus. The panther of the title refers to a "Black Panther" who "in his boldness/ Wears no disguise,/ Motivated by the truest/ Of the oldest/ Lies"; the lash refers to the white backlash of the times (in "The Backlash Blues").

The book has seven sections, each dealing with a particular part of the subject. "Words on Fire" has poems on the coming of the Third World revolution, while "American Heartbreak" deals with the consequences of "the great mistake/ That Jamestown made/ Long ago"; that is, slavery. The final section, "Daybreak in Alabama," does, however, offer hope. In spite of past and existing conditions, the poet hopes for a time when he can compose a song about "daybreak in Alabama" that will touch everybody "with kind fingers."

Other Literary Forms

Although perhaps best known for his poetry, Langston Hughes explored almost every literary genre. His prose fiction includes novels, humorous books, historical, biographical, autobiographical, and cultural works, translations, lyrics, librettos, plays, and scripts. His total output includes more than seventy volumes, as well as numerous articles, poems, and stories that have not yet been collected. Hughes wrote, translated, edited and/or collaborated on works in a number of other genres. He was productive as a playwright, although his plays did not enjoy much critical or financial success. They include *Mulatto, Little Ham, Simply Heavenly* (based on the characters in his Simple stories), and *Tambourines to Glory* (adapted from his novel). The last play was billed as a "gospel song-play," and Hughes created other plays in that category, including *Black Nativity, Jerico-Jim Crow,* and *The Prodigal Son.* These productions are of interest mainly because they underscore Hughes's heartfelt sympathy with the black folk life of America, a love affair he carried on throughout his works.

Hughes wrote the libretti for several operas, a screenplay—*Way Down South,* with Clarence Muse—radio scripts, and song lyrics. His most famous contribution to musical theater, however, was the lyrics he wrote for Kurt Weill and Elmer Rice's musical adaptation of Rice's *Street Scene.*

Over the years, Hughes also wrote several nonfiction articles, mainly focused on his role as a poet and his love of black American music—jazz, gospel, and the blues. Perhaps his most important article was his first: "The Negro Artist and the Racial Mountain," published in *The Nation* on June 23, 1926, in defense of the idea of a black American literary style, voice, and subject matter.

Bibliography

Banks, Kimberly. "'Like a Violin for the Wind to Play': Lyrical Approaches to Lynching by Hughes, Du Bois, and Toomer." *African American Review* 38, no. 3 (Fall, 2004): 451-466. Contrasts the cruelty of lynching with the poetic way in which it has been described by the three authors and draws conclusions on lynching's effects.

Baxter Miller, R. "Reinvention and Globalization in Hughes's Stories." *MELUS* 30, no. 1 (Spring, 2005): 65-84. Discusses the creation of a new African American identity by Hughes in "The Little Virgin" as well as Hughes's importance in the light of now-ubiquitous ideas about globalization.

Berry, Faith. *Langston Hughes: Before and Beyond Harlem.* New York: Wings Books, 1995. The first biography based on primary sources and interviews, which sets out to re-create the historical context in which Hughes lived and worked. Berry quotes an unusual number of poems in their entirety and includes extensive discussions of Hughes's poetry throughout the biography.

Bloom, Harold, ed. *Langston Hughes.* New York: Chelsea House, 1989. An up-to-date collection of some of the best literary criticism of Hughes's works, with several articles on his poetry. Unfortunately, these reprinted essays do not have notes. Bloom's introduction is perfunctory. Supplemented by a useful bibliography and an index.

Borden, Anne. "Heroic 'Hussies' and 'Brilliant Queers': Genderracial Resistance in the Works of Langston Hughes." *African American Review* 28 (Fall, 1994): 333-345. Discusses Hughes's focus on the interrelationship between gender and racial issues, as well as his treatment of gender issues within the black community—particularly the ways in which gender affects the struggle to maintain community in racist society.

Chinitz, David. "Rejuvenation Through Joy: Langston Hughes, Primitivism, and Jazz." *American Literary History* 9 (Spring, 1997): 60-78. Argues that in freeing himself from the primitivist movement, Hughes struggled to undo ideas long fused in primitivist discourse and attempted to rescue elements of primitivism that he continued to find meaningful, especially those pertaining to African American jazz.

Cooper, Floyd. *Coming Home: From the Life of Langston Hughes.* New York: Philomel Books, 1994. A thoughtful look at Hughes's life and works.

Dickinson, Donald C. *A Bio-Bibliography of Langston Hughes, 1902-1967.* 2d ed. Hamden, Conn.: Archon Books, 1972. With its preface by Arna Bontemps, a major scholar and critic of the Harlem Renaissance and a contemporary of Hughes, the reader has both older and updated assessments of Hughes's achievement. Part 1 is the biography, which incorporates information throughout Hughes's life; part 2 includes all of his work through 1965, except short newspaper articles, song lyrics, and phonographic records. Even a glance at the bibliography gives an indication of the range of Hughes's imaginative achievement.

Emanuel, James A. *Langston Hughes.* New York: Twayne, 1967. This survey of Hughes's work as a poet and fiction writer emphasizes the reflection of African American speech patterns, rhythms, and idiomatic expressions in Hughes's work, as well as the folk culture behind these, which he turned into literary devices. The book also points out pan-African themes and the peculiar struggle of a writer with Hughes's background in both the sociological and literary contexts.

Harper, Donna Sullivan. *Not So Simple: The "Simple" Stories by Langston Hughes.* Columbia: University of Missouri Press, 1995. Harper analyzes Hughes's development of the satirical stories with the character Jesse B. Simple. Covering the changes in the character from 1943 to 1965 starting in Hughes's column in the *Chicago Defender* and ending in the *New York Post,* Harper searches for the deeper meanings behind the stories. With a bibliography of the columns from 1942 to 1949, and the contents of the first collection of stories.

Haskins, James. *Always Movin' On: The Life of Langston Hughes.* Trenton, N.J.: Africa World Press, 1993. A good, updated biography of Hughes.

Hokanson, Robert O'Brien. "Jazzing It Up: The Be-bop Modernism of Langston Hughes." *Mosaic* 31 (December, 1998): 61-82. Examines how Hughes uses be-bop jazz to challenge both the boundaries between music and poetry and the distinctions between popular and high culture; argues that Hughes's work constitutes a distinctively "popular" modernism that uses jazz to ground its poetic experimentation in the vernacular tradition of African American culture.

Jemie, Onwuchekwa. *Langston Hughes: An Introduction to the Poetry.* New York: Columbia University Press, 1976. This study of the collected poems omits a number of later works but provides an important focus on the poetic techniques and themes of Hughes. Jemie defends Hughes against charges of being merely popular and emotional, pointing out the African oral tradition as well as African American music as influences on Hughes's poetry and Hughes's role in the development of a black consciousness in American poetry.

Leach, Laurie F. *Langston Hughes: A Biography.* Westport, Conn.: Greenwood Press, 2004. An overview of Hughes's life and development as a playwright, poet, and journalist.

Miller, R. Baxter. *The Art and Imagination of Langston Hughes.* Lexington: University Press of Kentucky, 1989. Divides Hughes's imagination into the "autobiographical," the "apocalyptic," the "lyrical," the "political," and the "tragicomic." Miller carefully examines Hughes's technique and style, and each chapter focuses on a poem or other work central to an appreciation and understanding of Hughes's imagination.

Miyakawa, Felicia M. "'Jazz at Night and the Classics in the Morning': Musical Double-Consciousness in Short Fiction by Langston Hughes." *Popular Music* 24, no. 2 (May, 2005): 273-279. Examines the importance of music in Hughes's life and work. Places particular focus on the development of Hughes's interest in incorporating musical elements into literature.

Mullen, Edward J., ed. *Critical Essays on Langston Hughes.* Boston: G. K. Hall, 1986. Very useful for its generous selection of contemporary reviews of the poet's work. Separate sections are devoted to articles and essays on Hughes's poetry, prose, and drama. An extensive and well-documented introduction surveys and analyzes the critical reception of the poet's work. The index is especially useful in sorting through this heterogenous material.

Rampersad, Arnold. *The Life of Langston Hughes.* 2 vols. New York: Oxford University Press, 1986-1988. This major critical biography illustrates not only the triumphs but also the struggles of the man and the writer. The importance of Hughes in the Harlem Renaissance and his symbolic significance in the developing artistic and imaginative consciousness of African American writers come alive in concrete examples in volume 1, *I, Too, Sing America,* and volume 2, *I Dream a World.* These titles, drawn from Hughes's poetry, reveal the themes illustrating the writer's life and the points in his own characterization of his struggle.

Schwarz, A. B. Christa. *Gay Voices of the Harlem Renaissance.* Bloomington: Indiana University Press, 2003. Schwarz examines the work of four leading writers from the Harlem Renaissance—Countée Cullen, Langston Hughes, Claude McKay, and Richard Bruce Nugent—and their sexually nonconformist or gay literary voices.

Tracy, Steven C. *Langston Hughes and the Blues.* Urbana: University of Illinois Press, 1988. This book uses the folk traditions of African and African American culture as background but concentrates primarily on the blues tradition within that culture as a way of interpreting Hughes's work. The intellectualizing of this tradition and the deliberate incorporation of the blues dimension in imaginative literature is a major emphasis, along with the oral tradition in African culture. This historical survey of the blues as an art form and its application in criticism seeks to counteract the dismissal of some of Hughes's more popular works by critics such as Donald C. Dickinson.

— *Emma Coburn Norris; Mary Rohrberger; Edward E. Waldron*

Zora Neale Hurston

Novelist and folklorist

Born: Eatonville, Florida; January 7, 1891
Died: Fort Pierce, Florida; January 28, 1960

LONG FICTION: *Jonah's Gourd Vine*, 1934; *Their Eyes Were Watching God*, 1937; *Moses, Man of the Mountain*, 1939; *Seraph on the Suwanee*, 1948.

SHORT FICTION: *Spunk: The Selected Short Stories of Zora Neale Hurston*, 1985; *The Complete Stories*, 1995.

DRAMA: *Color Struck*, pb. 1926; *The First One*, pb. 1927; *Mule Bone*, pb. 1931 (with Langston Hughes); *Polk County*, pb. 1944, pr. 2002.

NONFICTION: *Mules and Men*, 1935; *Tell My Horse*, 1938; *Dust Tracks on a Road*, 1942; *The Sanctified Church*, 1981; *Folklore, Memoirs, and Other Writings*, 1995; *Go Gator and Muddy the Water: Writings*, 1999 (Pamela Bordelon, editor); *Every Tongue Got to Confess: Negro Folktales from the Gulf States*, 2001; *Zora Neale Hurston: A Life in Letters*, 2002 (Carla Kaplan, editor).

MISCELLANEOUS: *I Love Myself When I Am Laughing . . . and Then Again When I Am Looking Mean and Impressive: A Zora Neale Hurston Reader*, 1979.

Achievements

Zora Neale Hurston is best known as a major contributor to the Harlem Renaissance literature of the 1920's. Not only was she a major contributor, but she also did much to characterize the style and temperament of the period; indeed, she is often referred to as the most colorful figure of the Harlem Renaissance. Though the short stories and short plays that she generated during the 1920's are fine works in their own right, they are nevertheless apprentice works when compared with her most productive period, the 1930's. During the 1930's, Hurston produced three novels, all telling examples of her creative genius, as well as two collections of folklore, the fruits of her training in anthropology and her many years of fieldwork. It is Hurston's interest in preserving the culture of the black South that remains among her most valuable contributions. Not only did she collect and preserve folklore outright, but she also used folklore, native drama, and the black idiom and dialect in most of her fiction.

Hurston achieved recognition at a time when, as Langston Hughes declared, "the Negro was in vogue." The Harlem Renaissance, the black literary and cultural movement of the 1920's, created an interracial audience for her stories and plays. Enthusiasm for her work extended through the 1930's, although that decade also marked the beginning of critical attacks. Hurston did not portray blacks as victims stunted by a racist society. Such a view, she believed, implies that black life is only a defensive reaction to white racism. Black and left-wing critics, however, complained that her unwillingness to represent the oppression of blacks and her focus, instead, on an autonomous, unresentful black folk culture served to perpetuate minstrel stereotypes and thus fueled white racism. The radical, racial protest literature of Richard Wright, one of Hurston's strongest critics, became the model for black literature in the 1940's, and publishers on the lookout for protest works showed less and less interest in Hurston's manuscripts. Yet, when she did speak out against American racism and imperialism, her work was often censored. Her autobiography, published in 1942, as well as a number of her stories and articles were tailored by editors to please white audiences. Caught between the attacks of black critics and the censorship of the white publishing industry, Hurston floundered, struggling through the 1940's and 1950's to find other subjects. She largely dropped out of public view in the 1950's, though she continued to publish magazine and newspaper articles.

The African American and feminist political and cultural movements of the 1960's and 1970's provided the impetus for Hurston's rediscovery. The publication of Robert Hemenway's excellent book, *Zora Neale Hurston: A Literary Biography* (1977), and the reissue of her novels, her autobiography, and her folklore collections seem to promise the sustained critical recognition Hurston deserves. Her popularity has never been greater, as her works are considered mainstays in any number of canons, among them African American literature, folklore, southern literature, feminist studies, and anthropology.

Biography

Zora Neale Hurston was born on January 7, 1891. Her family lived in the all-black Florida town of Eatonville in an eight-room house with a five-acre garden. Her father, the Reverend John Hurston, mayor of Eatonville for three terms and moderator of the South Florida Baptist Association, wanted to temper his daughter's high spirits, but her intelligent and forceful mother, Lucy Potts Hurston, encouraged her to "jump at de sun." When Hurston was about nine, her mother died. That event and her father's rapid remarriage to a woman his daughter did not like prematurely ended Hurston's childhood. In the next few years, she lived only intermittently at home, spending some time at a school in Jacksonville and some time with relatives. Her father withdrew all financial support during this period, forcing her to commence what was to be a lifelong struggle to make her own living.

When Hurston was fourteen, she took a job as a wardrobe girl to a repertory company touring the South. Hurston left the troupe in Baltimore eighteen months later and finished high school there at Morgan Academy. She went on to study part-time at Howard University in 1918, taking jobs as a manicurist, a waitress, and a maid in order to support herself. At Howard, her literary talents began to emerge. She was admitted to a campus literary club, formed by Alain Locke, a Howard professor and one of the forces behind the Harlem Renaissance. Locke brought Hurston to the attention of Charles S. Johnson, another key promoter of the Harlem Renaissance. Editor of *Opportunity: A Journal of Negro Life*, he published one of her stories and encouraged her to enter the literary contest sponsored by his magazine.

With several manuscripts but little money, Hurston moved to

(Library of Congress)

New York City in 1925, hoping to make a career of her writing. Her success in that year's *Opportunity* contest—she received prizes for a play and a story—won her the patronage of Fanny Hurst and a scholarship to complete her education at Barnard College. She studied anthropology there under Franz Boas, leading a seemingly schizophrenic life in the next two years as an eccentric, iconoclastic artist of the Harlem Renaissance on one hand and a budding, scholarly social scientist on the other.

The common ground linking these seemingly disparate parts of Hurston's life was her interest in black folk culture. Beginning in 1927 and extending through the 1930's, she made several trips to collect black folklore in the South and in the Bahamas, Haiti, and Jamaica. Collecting trips were costly, however, as was the time to write up their results. Charlotte Osgood Mason, a wealthy, domineering white patron to a number of African American artists, supported some of that work, as did the Association for the Study of Negro Life and History and the Guggenheim Foundation. Hurston also worked intermittently during the 1930's as a drama teacher at Bethune Cookman College in Florida and at North Carolina College, as a drama coach for the WPA Federal Theatre Project in New York, and as an editor for the Federal Writers' Project in Florida.

In 1930, Hurston and Langston Hughes collaborated on a black folk play, *Mule Bone*, an undertaking that severed the personal and professional relationship between Hurston and Hughes; the break was never mended and kept the play from being published in its entirety until 1991, long after the deaths of both authors. The dispute, precipitated by the question of principal authorship, while certainly unfortunate, nevertheless illustrates the fiercely independent temperament that Hurston maintained throughout her lifetime.

Though the 1930's got off to a rough start with the controversy with Hughes, the decade proved to be Hurston's most productive. Hurston published her first novel, *Jonah's Gourd Vine*, in 1934, followed in rapid succession by the folklore collection *Mules and Men* in 1935; another novel, the now classic *Their Eyes Were Watching God* in 1937; another folklore collection, *Tell My Horse*, in 1938; and another novel, *Moses, Man of the Mountain*, in 1939. In addition, Hurston wrote several short stories and several essays, notably those on black culture, published in Nancy Cunard's massive collection, *Negro*, in 1934.

Mules and Men and several scholarly and popular articles on folklore were the products of Hurston's collecting trips in the late 1920's and early 1930's. In 1938, she published *Tell My Horse*, the result of trips to Haiti and Jamaica to study hoodoo. As a creative writer, Hurston devised other outlets for her folk materials. Her plays, short stories, and three of her novels, *Jonah's Gourd Vine*, *Their Eyes Were Watching God*, and *Moses, Man of the Mountain*, make use of folklore. She also presented folk materials in theatrical revues, but even though the productions were enthusiastically received, she could never generate enough backing to finance commercially successful long-term showings.

Hurston's intense interest in black folklore prevented her from sustaining either of her two marriages. She could not reconcile the competing claims of love and work. She married Herbert Sheen, a medical student, in 1927 but separated from him a few months later. They were divorced in 1931. She married Albert Price III in 1939, and they too parted less than one year later. Other romantic relationships ended for the same reason.

In 1942, Hurston published her autobiography, *Dust Tracks on a Road*. While the book won the *Saturday Review*'s Ainsfield-Wolf Award for race relations, it proved to be the last significant work of Hurston's career, although she did publish another novel, *Seraph on the Suwanee*, in 1948. There are several reasons for the decline in Hurston's popularity, the most important among them being that her folk-based literature did not fit into protest literature, the dominant literary trend of the 1940's, coupled with Hurston's growing conservatism. Further, in September, 1948, shortly before the publication of *Seraph on the Suwanee*, Hurston was falsely charged with seducing a minor, but before the charges could be dismissed as unfounded, the black press, in particular the *Baltimore Afro-American*, had spread the story to its readers and had severely, almost irreparably, damaged Hurston's reputation. Disillusioned and outraged at her treatment by the court and the black press, Hurston moved back to the South, where she lived for the remainder of her life.

The 1950's was a tragic decade for Hurston. Her career was stagnant, and although she kept writing, she received rejection after rejection. She did, however, do some reporting for the *Pittsburgh Courier*, a black paper with a national circulation; published several essays; and accepted several speaking engagements. She supported herself with occasional work, including substitute teaching and writing freelance articles for various papers.

Toward the end of the 1950's, Hurston's health became increasingly fragile. She suffered from obesity, hypertension, poor diet, gallbladder trouble, ulcers, and various stomach ailments. In 1959, she suffered a stroke, and in October of that year was placed in the Saint Lucie County welfare home, where, alone and penniless, she died on January 28, 1960. She was buried by subscription a week later in Fort Pierce's segregated cemetery, the Garden of the Heavenly Rest.

Analysis: Long Fiction

For much of her career, Zora Neale Hurston was dedicated to the presentation of black folk culture. She introduced readers to hoodoo, folktales, lying contests, spirituals, the blues, sermons, children's games, riddles, playing the dozens, and, in general, a highly metaphoric folk idiom. Although she represented black folk culture in several genres, Hurston was drawn to the novel form because it could convey folklore as communal behavior. Hurston knew that much of the unconscious artistry of folklore appears in the gestures and tones in which it is expressed and that it gains much of its meaning in performance. Even *Mules and Men*, the folklore collection she completed just before embarking on her first novel (although it was published after *Jonah's Gourd Vine*), "novelizes" what could have been an anthology of disconnected folk materials. By inventing a narrator who witnesses, even participates in, the performance of folk traditions, she combated the inevitable distortion of an oral culture by its textual documentation.

Hurston's motives for presenting black folklore were, in part, political. She wanted to refute contemporary claims that African Americans lacked a distinct culture of their own. Her novels depict the unconscious creativity of the African American proletariat or folk. They represent community members participating in a highly expressive communication system which taught them to survive racial oppression and, moreover, to respect themselves and their community. At the beginning of Hurston's second novel, for example, the community's members are sitting on porches. "Mules and other brutes had occupied their skins" all day, but now it is night, work is over, and they can talk and feel "powerful and human" again: "They became lords of sounds and lesser things. They passed nations through their mouths. They sat in judgment." By showing the richness and the healthy influence of black folk culture, Hurston hoped not only to defeat racist attitudes but also to encourage racial pride among blacks. Why should African Americans wish to imitate a white bourgeoisie? The "Negro lowest down" had a richer culture.

Hurston also had a psychological motive for presenting black folk culture. She drew the folk materials for her novels from the rural, southern black life she knew as a child and subsequently recorded in folklore-collecting trips in the late 1920's and 1930's. She had fond memories of her childhood in the all-black town of Eatonville, where she did not experience poverty or racism. In her autobiographical writings, she suggests that she did not even know that she was "black" until she left Eatonville. Finally, in Eatonville, she had a close relationship with and a strong advocate in her mother. In representing the rich culture of black rural southerners, she was also evoking a happier personal past.

Although the novel's witnessing narrator provided Hurston with the means to dramatize folklore, she also needed meaningful fictional contexts for its presentation. Her novels are a series of attempts to develop such contexts. Initially, she maintained the southern rural setting for black folk traditions. In her first novel, *Jonah's Gourd Vine*, she re-created Eatonville and neighboring Florida towns. Hurston also loosely re-created her parents' lives with the central characters, John and Lucy Pearson. Though Hurston claimed that an unhappy love affair she had had with a man she met in New York was the catalyst for her second novel, *Their Eyes Were Watching God*, the feeling rather than the details of that affair appear in the novel. The work takes the reader back to Eatonville again and to the porch-sitting storytellers Hurston knew as a child.

Moses, Man of the Mountain

With her third novel, *Moses, Man of the Mountain*, however, Hurston turned in a new direction, leaving the Eatonville milieu behind. The novel retells the biblical story of Moses via the folk idiom and traditions of southern rural blacks. Hurston leaves much of the plot of the biblical story intact—Moses does lead the Hebrews out of Egypt—but, for example, she shows Moses to be a great hoodoo doctor as well as a leader and lawgiver. In effect, Hurston simulated the creative processes of folk culture, transforming the story of Moses for modern African Americans just as slaves had adapted biblical stories in spirituals. Hurston may have reenacted an oral and communal process as a solitary writer, but she gave an imaginative rendering of the cultural process all the same.

Seraph on the Suwanee

Seraph on the Suwanee, Hurston's last novel, marks another dramatic shift in her writing. With this novel, however, she did not create a new context for the representation of folk culture. Rather, she turned away from the effort to present black folklore. *Seraph on the Suwanee* is set in the rural South, but its central characters are white. Hurston apparently wanted to prove that she could write about whites as well as blacks, a desire which surfaced, no doubt, in response to the criticism and disinterest her work increasingly faced in the 1940's. Yet, even when writing of upwardly mobile southern "crackers," Hurston could not entirely leave her previous mission behind. Her white characters, perhaps unintentionally, often use the black folk idiom.

Although Hurston's novels, with the exception of the last, create contexts or develop other strategies for the presentation of folklore, they are not simply showcases for folk traditions; black folk culture defines the novels' themes. The most interesting of these thematic renderings appear in Hurston's first two novels. Hurston knew that black folk culture was composed of brilliant adaptations of African culture to American life. She admired the ingenuity of these adaptations but worried about their preservation. Would a sterile, materialistic white world ultimately absorb blacks, destroying the folk culture they had developed? Her first two novels demonstrate the disturbing influence of white America on black folkways.

Jonah's Gourd Vine

Jonah's Gourd Vine, Hurston's first novel, portrays the tragic experience of a black preacher caught between black cultural values and the values imposed by his white-influenced church. The novel charts the life of John Pearson, laborer, foreman, and carpenter, who discovers that he has an extraordinary talent for preaching. With his linguistic skills and his wife Lucy's wise counsel, he becomes pastor of the large church Zion Hope and ultimately moderator of a Florida Baptist convention. His sexual promiscuity, however, eventually destroys his marriage and his career.

Though his verbal skills make him a success while his promiscuity ruins him, the novel shows that both his linguistic gifts and his sexual vitality are part of the same cultural heritage. His sexual conduct is pagan and so is his preaching. In praying, according to the narrator, it was as if he "rolled his African drum up to the altar, and called his Congo Gods by Christian names." Both aspects of his cultural heritage speak through him. Indeed, they speak through all members of the African American community, if most intensely through John. A key moment early in the novel, when John crosses over Big Creek, marks the symbolic beginning of his life and shows the double cultural heritage he brings to it. John heads down to the Creek, "singing a new song and stomping the beats." He makes up "some words to go with the drums of the Creek," with the animal noises in the woods, and with the hound dog's cry. He begins to think about the girls living on the other side of Big Creek: "John almost trumpeted exultantly at the new sun. He breathed lustily. He stripped and carried his clothes across, then recrossed and plunged into the swift water and breasted strongly over."

To understand why two expressions of the same heritage have such different effects on John's life, one has to turn to the community to which he belongs. Members of his congregation subscribe to differing views of the spiritual life. The view most often endorsed by the novel emerges from the folk culture. As Larry Neal, one of Hurston's best critics, explains in his introduction to the 1971 reprint of the novel, that view belongs to "a formerly enslaved communal society, non-Christian in background," which does not strictly dichotomize body and soul. The other view comes out of a white culture. It is "more rigid, being a blend of Puritan concepts and the fire-and-brimstone imagery of the white evangelical tradition." That view insists that John, as a preacher, exercise self-restraint. The cultural conflict over spirituality pervades his congregation. While the deacons, whom Hurston often portrays satirically, pressure him to stop preaching, he still has some loyal supporters among his parishioners.

White America's cultural styles and perceptions invade Pearson's community in other ways as well. By means of a kind of preaching competition, the deacons attempt to replace Pearson with the pompous Reverend Felton Cozy, whose preaching style is white. Cozy's style, however, fails to captivate most members of the congregation. Pearson is a great preacher in the folk tradition, moving his congregation to a frenzy with "barbaric thunder-poems." By contrast, Cozy, as one of the parishioners complains, does not give a sermon; he lectures. In an essay Hurston wrote on "The Sanctified Church," she explains this reaction: "The real, singing Negro derides the Negro who adopts the white man's religious ways. . . . They say of that type of preacher, 'Why he don't preach at all. He just lectures.'"

If Pearson triumphs over Cozy, he nevertheless ultimately falls. His sexual conduct destroys his marriage and leads to an unhappy remarriage with one of his mistresses, Hattie Tyson. He is finally forced to stop preaching at Zion Hope. Divorced from Hattie, he moves to another town, where he meets and marries Sally Lovelace, a woman much like Lucy. With her support, he returns to preaching. On a visit to a friend, however, he is tempted by a young prostitute and, to his dismay, succumbs. Although he has wanted to be faithful to his new wife, he will always be a pagan preacher, spirit *and* flesh. Fleeing back to Sally, he is killed when a train strikes his car.

In its presentation of folklore and its complex representation of cultural conflict, *Jonah's Gourd Vine* is a brilliant first novel, although Hurston does not always make her argument sufficiently clear. The novel lacks a consistent point of view. Though she endorses Pearson's African heritage and ridicules representatives of white cultural views, she also creates an admirable and very sympathetic character in Lucy Pearson, who is ruined by her husband's pagan behavior. Nor did Hurston seem to know how to resolve the cultural conflict she portrayed—hence, the deus ex machina ending. It was not until she wrote her next novel, *Their Eyes Were Watching God*, that Hurston learned to control point of view and presented a solution to the problem of white influences on black culture.

Their Eyes Were Watching God

The life of Janie Crawford, the heroine of *Their Eyes Were Watching God*, is shaped by bourgeois values—white in origin. She finds love and self-identity only by rejecting that life and becoming a wholehearted participant in black folk culture. Her grandmother directs Janie's entrance into adulthood. Born into slavery, the older woman hopes to find protection and materialistic comforts for Janie in a marriage to the property-owning Logan Killicks. Janie, who has grown up in a different generation, does not share her grandmother's values. When she finds she cannot love her husband, she runs off with Jody Stark, who is on his way to Eatonville, where he hopes to become a "big voice," an appropriate phrase for life in a community that highly values verbal ability. Jody becomes that "big voice" as mayor of the town, owner of the general store, and head of the post office. He lives both a bourgeois and a folk life in Eatonville. He constructs a big house—the kind white people have—but he wanders out to the porch of the general store whenever he wants to enjoy the perpetual storytelling which takes place there. Even though Janie has demonstrated a talent for oratory, he will not let her join these sessions or participate in the mock funeral for a mule which has become a popular character in the townspeople's stories. "He didn't," the narrator suggests, "want her talking after such trashy people." As Janie tells a friend years later, Jody "classed me off." He does so by silencing her.

For several years, Janie has no voice in the community or in her private life. Her life begins to seem unreal: "She sat and watched the shadow of herself going about tending store and prostrating itself before Jody." One day, after Stark insults her in front of customers in the store, however, she speaks out and, playing the dozens, insults his manhood. The insult causes an irreconcilable break between them.

After Jody's death, Janie is courted by Tea Cake Woods, a laborer with little money. Though many of her neighbors disapprove of the match, Janie marries him. "Dis ain't no business proposition," she tells her friend Pheoby, "and no race after property and titles. Dis is uh love game. Ah done lived Grandma's way, now Ah mens tuh live mine." Marriage to Tea Cake lowers her social status but frees her from her submissive female role, from her shadow existence. Refusing to use her money, Tea Cake takes her down to the Everglades, where they become migrant workers. She picks beans with him in the fields, and he helps her prepare their dinners. With Tea Cake, she also enters into the folk culture of the Everglades, and that more than anything else enables her to shed her former submissive identity. Workers show up at their house every night to sing, dance, gamble, and, above all, to talk, like the folks in Eatonville on the front porch of the general store. Janie learns how to tell "big stories" from listening to the others, and she is encouraged to do so.

This happy phase of Janie's life ends tragically as she and Tea Cake attempt to escape a hurricane and the ensuing flood. Tea Cake saves Janie from drowning but, in the process, is bitten by a rabid dog. Sick and crazed, he tries to shoot Janie. She is forced to kill him in self-defense. Not everything she has gained during her relationship with Tea Cake, however, dies with him. The strong self-identity she has achieved while living in the Everglades enables her to withstand the unjust resentment of their black friends as well as her trial for murder in a white court. Most important, she is able to endure her own loss and returns to Eatonville, self-reliant and wise. Tea Cake, she knows, will live on in her thoughts and feelings—and in her words. She tells her story to her friend Pheoby—that storytelling event frames the novel—and allows Pheoby to bring it to the other members of the community. As the story enters the community's oral culture, it will influence it. Indeed, as the novel closes, Janie's story has already affected Pheoby. "Ah done growed ten feet higher from jus' listenin' tuh you," she tells Janie. "Ah ain't satisfied wid mahself no mo'."

In her novels, Hurston did not represent the oppression of

blacks because she refused to view African American life as impoverished. If she would not focus on white racism, however, her novels do oppose white culture. In *Their Eyes Were Watching God,* Janie does not find happiness until she gives up a life governed by white values and enters into the verbal ceremonies of black folk culture. Loving celebrations of a separate black folk life were Hurston's effective political weapon; racial pride was one of her great gifts to American literature. "Sometimes, I feel discriminated against," she once told her readers, "but it does not make me angry. It merely astonishes me. How *can* any deny themselves the pleasure of my company? It's beyond me."

Analysis: Short Fiction
The bulk of Zora Neale Hurston's short fiction is set in her native Florida, as are most of her novels. Even when the setting is not Florida, however, the stories are informed by the life, habits, beliefs, and idioms of the people whom Hurston knew so well, the inhabitants of Eatonville primarily. One criticism often leveled at Hurston was that she frequently masqueraded folklore as fiction, or, in other cases, imposed folklore on the fictive narrative. Whatever the merits of such criticism may be, Hurston's short stories abound with an energy and zest for life that Hurston considered instructive for her readers.

"John Redding Goes to Sea"
Hurston's first published short story is entitled "John Redding Goes to Sea." It was published in the May, 1921, issue of the *Stylus,* the literary magazine of Howard University, and was reprinted in the January, 1926, issue of *Opportunity.* While the story is obviously the work of a novice writer, with its highly contrived plot, excessive sentimentality, and shallow characterizations, its strengths are many, strengths upon which Hurston would continue to draw and develop throughout her career.

The plot is a simple one: Young John Redding, the titular character, wants to leave his hometown to see and explore parts and things unknown. Several circumstances conspire, however, to keep him from realizing his dream. First, John's mother, the pitifully possessive, obsessive, and superstitious Matty Redding, is determined not to let John pursue his ambitions; in fact, she pleads illness and threatens to disown him if he leaves. Second, John's marriage to Stella Kanty seems to tie him permanently to his surroundings, as his new wife joins forces with his mother to discourage John's desire to travel. Further, his mother's tantrums keep John from even joining the Navy when that opportunity comes his way. Later, when John is killed in a tempest while working with a crew to build a bridge on the St. John's River, his father forbids his body to be retrieved from the river as it floats toward the ocean. At last, John will get his wish to travel and see the world, although in death.

If the plot seems overdone and the sentimentality overwhelming, "John Redding Goes to Sea" does provide the reader with the first of many glimpses of life among black Floridians—their habits, superstitions, strengths, and shortcomings. For example, one of the more telling aspects of the story is that Matty believes that her son was cursed with "travel dust" at his birth; thus, John's desire to travel is Matty's punishment for having married his father away from a rival suitor. Hurston suspends judgment on Matty's beliefs; rather, she shows that these and other beliefs are integral parts of the life of the folk.

Another strength that is easily discernible in Hurston's first short story is her detailed rendering of setting. Hurston has a keen eye for detail, and nowhere is this more evident than in her descriptions of the lushness of Florida. This adeptness is especially present in "John Redding Goes to Sea" and in most of Hurston's other work as well.

By far the most important aspect of "John Redding Goes to Sea" is its theme that people must be free to develop and pursue their own dreams, a recurring theme in the Hurston canon. John Redding is deprived of self-expression and self-determination because the wishes and interpretations of others are imposed upon him. Hurston clearly has no sympathy with those who would deprive another of freedom and independence; indeed, she would adamantly oppose all such restrictive efforts throughout her career as a writer and folklorist.

"Spunk"

Another early short story that treats a variation of this theme is "Spunk," published in the June, 1925, issue of *Opportunity*. The central character, Spunk Banks, has the spunk to live his life as he chooses, which includes taking another man's wife and parading openly around town with her. While Hurston passes no moral judgment on Banks, she makes it clear that she appreciates and admires his brassiness and his will to live his life according to his own terms.

When the story opens, Spunk Banks and Lena Kanty are openly flaunting their affair in front of the Eatonville townspeople, including Lena's husband, Joe Kanty. The other town residents make fun of Joe's weakness, his refusal to confront Spunk Banks. Later, when Joe desperately attacks Spunk with a razor, Spunk shoots and kills him. Spunk is tried and acquitted but is killed in a work-related accident, cut to death by a circular saw.

Again, superstition plays an important role here, for Spunk claims that he has been haunted by Joe Kanty's ghost. In fact, Spunk is convinced that Joe's ghost pushed him into the circular saw, and at least one other townsman agrees. As is customary in Hurston's stories, however, she makes no judgment of the rightness or wrongness of such beliefs but points out that these beliefs are very much a part of the cultural milieu of Eatonville.

"Sweat"

Another early Eatonville story is "Sweat," published in 1926 in the only issue of the ill-fated literary magazine *Fire!*, founded by Hurston, Hughes, and Wallace Thurman. "Sweat" shows Hurston's power as a fiction writer and as a master of the short-story form. Again, the story line is a simple one. Delia Jones is a hardworking, temperate Christian woman being tormented by her arrogant, mean-spirited, and cruel husband of fifteen years, Sykes Jones, who has become tired of her and desires a new wife. Rather than simply leaving her, though, he wants to drive her away by making her life miserable. At stake is the house for which Delia's "sweat" has paid: Sykes wants it for his new mistress, but Delia refuses to leave the fruit of her labor.

Sykes uses both physical and mental cruelty to antagonize Delia, the most far-reaching of which exploits Delia's intense fear of snakes. When Delia's fear of the caged rattlesnake that Sykes places outside her back door subsides, Sykes places the rattlesnake in the dirty clothes hamper, hoping that it will bite and kill Delia. In an ironic twist, however, Delia escapes, and the rattlesnake bites Sykes as he fumbles for a match in the dark house. Delia listens and watches as Sykes dies a painful, agonizing death.

While "Sweat" makes use of the same superstitious beliefs as Hurston's other stories, a more complex characterization and an elaborate system of symbols are central to the story's development. In Delia, for example, readers are presented with an essentially good Christian woman who is capable of great compassion and long suffering and who discovers the capacity to hate as intensely as she loves; in Sykes, readers are shown unadulterated evil reduced to one at once pitiful and horrible in his suffering. In addition, the Christian symbolism, including the snake and the beast of burden, adds considerable interest and texture to the story. It is this texture that makes "Sweat" Hurston's most rewarding work of short fiction, for it shows her at her best as literary artist and cultural articulator.

"The Gilded Six-Bits"

Although Hurston turned to the longer narrative as the preferred genre during the 1930's, she continued writing short stories throughout the remainder of her career. One such story is "The Gilded Six-Bits," published in 1933, which also examines relationships between men and women. In this story, the marriage bed of a happy couple, Joe and Missie May Banks, is defiled by a city slicker, Otis D. Slemmons. Missie May has been attracted by Slemmons's gold money, which she desires to get for her husband. The gold pieces, however, turn out to be gold-plated. Hurston's message is nearly cliché—"all that glitters is not gold"—but she goes a step further to establish the idea that true love transcends all things. Joe and Missie May are reconciled at the end of the story.

"Cock Robin, Beale Street"

Hurston's last stories are fables that seem to have only comic value but do, however, advance serious thoughts, such as the ridiculousness of the idea of race purity in "Cock Robin, Beale Street" or the equal ridiculousness of the idea that the North was better for blacks, in "Story in Harlem Slang." While these stories are not artistic achievements, they do provide interesting aspects of the Hurston canon.

In many ways, Hurston's short stories are apprentice works to her novels. In these stories, she introduced most of the themes, character types, settings, techniques, and concerns upon which she later elaborated during her most productive and artistic period, the 1930's. This observation, however, does not suggest that her short stories are inferior works. On the contrary, much of the best of Hurston can be found in these early stories.

Other Literary Forms

In addition to her four novels, Zora Neale Hurston produced two collections of folklore, *Mules and Men* and *Tell My Horse*, and an autobiography, *Dust Tracks on a Road*. Hurston also published plays, short stories, and essays in anthologies and in magazines as diverse as *Opportunity*, the *Journal of Negro History*, the *Saturday Evening Post*, the *Journal of American Folklore*, and the *American Legion Magazine*. Finally, she wrote several articles and reviews for such newspapers as the *New York Herald Tribune* and the *Pittsburgh Courier*. Hurston's major works were reissued only in the late twentieth century. Some of her essays and stories have also been collected and reprinted. Although the anthologies *I Love Myself When I Am Laughing...* and *The Sanctified Church* helped to bring her writing back into critical focus, some of her works ceased to be readily available, and her numerous unpublished manuscripts can be seen only at university archives and the Library of Congress.

Bibliography

Awkward, Michael, ed. *New Essays on "Their Eyes Were Watching God."* Cambridge, England: Cambridge University Press,

1990. Essays by Robert Hemenway and Nellie McKay on the biographical roots of the novel, and by Hazel Carey on Hurston's use of anthropology. Rachel Blau DuPlessis provides a feminist perspective in "Power, Judgment, and Narrative in a Work of Zora Neale Hurston." Includes an introduction and bibliography.

Boyd, Valerie. *Wrapped in Rainbows: The Life of Zora Neale Hurston.* New York: Scribner, 2002. A very well-written and researched biography that focuses special attention on Hurston's spirituality and travels.

Chinn, Nancy, and Elizabeth E. Dunn. "'The Ring of Singing Metal on Wood': Zora Neale Hurston's Artistry in 'The Gilded Six-Bits.'" *The Mississippi Quarterly* 49 (Fall, 1996): 775-790. Discusses how Hurston uses setting, ritual, dialect, and the nature of human relationships in the story; argues that the story provides a solution to the problem of reconciling her rural Florida childhood with her liberal arts education and training.

Cobb-Moore, Geneva. "Zora Neale Hurston as Local Colorist." *The Southern Literary Journal* 26 (Spring, 1994): 25-34. Discusses how Hurston's creation of folk characters enlarges the meaning of local color; shows how Hurston proves that while physical bodies can be restricted, the imagination is always free.

Cooper, Jan. "Zora Neale Hurston Was Always a Southerner Too." In *The Female Tradition in Southern Literature*, edited by Carol S. Manning. Urbana: University of Illinois Press, 1993. Examines the hitherto neglected role that Hurston played in the Southern Renaissance between 1920 and 1950. Argues that Hurston's fiction is informed by a modern southern agrarian sense of community. Suggests that the Southern Renaissance was a transracial, cross-cultural product of the South.

Donlon, Jocelyn Hazelwood. "Porches: Stories: Power: Spatial and Racial Intersections in Faulkner and Hurston." *Journal of American Culture* 19 (Winter, 1996): 95-110. Comments on the role of the porch in Faulkner and Hurston's fiction as a transitional space between the public and the private where the individual can negotiate an identity through telling stories.

Fitch, Elizabeth. "Hurston on Hurston." *Amsterdam News*, December 23, 2004, p. 25-27. This article discusses the book *Speak So You Can Speak Again.* An exuberant introduction to Hurston's work.

Gates, Henry Louis, Jr. *The Signifying Monkey: A Theory of Afro-American Literary Criticism.* New York: Oxford University Press, 1988. The chapter on Hurston discusses her best-known novel, *Their Eyes Were Watching God,* as a conscious attempt to rebut the naturalistic view of blacks as "animalistic" that Gates claims she saw in Richard Wright's fiction.

Glassman, Steve, and Kathryn Lee Siedel, eds. *Zora in Florida.* Orlando: University of Central Florida Press, 1991. This collection of essays by seventeen Hurston scholars explores the overall presence and influence of Florida in and on the works of Hurston. This collection grew out of a Hurston symposium held in Daytona Beach, Florida, in November, 1989, and includes an excellent introduction to the importance of Florida in the study of Hurston.

Hemenway, Robert E. *Zora Neale Hurston: A Literary Biography.* Urbana: University of Illinois Press, 1977. Perhaps the best extant work on Hurston. Hemenway's painstakingly researched study of Hurston's life and literary career was crucial in rescuing Hurston from neglect and establishing her as a major American writer. Although some of the facts of Hurston's chronology have been corrected by later scholarship, Hemenway's study is the most valuable introduction to Hurston's work available. Includes a bibliography of published and unpublished works by Hurston.

Hill, Lynda Marion. *Social Rituals and the Verbal Art of Zora Neale Hurston.* Washington, D.C.: Howard University Press, 1996. Chapters on Hurston's treatment of everyday life, science and humanism, folklore, and color, race, and class. Hill also considers dramatic reenactments of Hurston's writing. Includes notes, bibliography, and an appendix on "characteristics of Negro expression."

Howard, Lillie P. *Zora Neale Hurston.* Boston: Twayne, 1980. A good general introduction to the life and works of Hurston. Contains valuable plot summaries and commentaries on Hurston's works. Supplemented by a chronology and a bibliography.

Hurston, Lucy Anne. *Speak, So You Can Speak Again: The Life of Zora Neale Hurston.* New York: Doubleday, 2004. A brief biography written by Hurston's niece. Most notable for the inclusion of rare photographs, writings, and other multimedia personal artifacts. Also contains an audio CD of Hurston reading and singing.

Hurston, Zora Neale. *Zora Neale Hurston: A Life in Letters.* Edited by Carla Kaplan. New York: Doubleday, 2002. A collection of more than five hundred letters, annotated and arranged in chronological order.

Johnson, Barbara. *A World of Difference.* Baltimore: Johns Hopkins University Press, 1987. The two essays on Hurston examine how her fiction addresses the problem of the social construction of self.

Kanthak, John F. "Legacy of Dysfunction: Family Systems in Zora Neale Hurston's *Jonah's Gourd Vine.*" *Journal of Modern Literature* 28, no. 4 (Summer, 2005): 113-130. Views Hurston's novel as a critique of the family and family relations, one that is not race-specific.

Lyons, Mary E. *Sorrow's Kitchen: The Life and Folklore of Zora Neale Hurston.* New York: Charles Scribner's Sons, 1990. Perhaps the only straightforward biography of Hurston, written with the younger reader in mind. Especially useful for those who need a primer in Hurston's background in all-black Eatonville.

Newsom, Adele S. *Zora Neale Hurston: A Reference Guide.* Boston: G. K. Hall, 1987. A catalog of Hurston criticism spanning the years 1931-1986, arranged chronologically with annotations. This source is an invaluable aid to serious scholars of Hurston. Also contains an introduction to the criticism on Hurston. An especially useful resource for all inquiries.

Patterson, Tiffany Ruby. *Zora Neale Hurston and a History of Southern Life.* Philadelphia: Temple University Press, 2005. Using Hurston's texts and the few official documents available, the author presents an interesting interpretation on what day-to-day life was like for African American southerners, particularly in Florida.

Pierpont, Claudia Roth. *Passionate Minds: Women Rewriting the World.* New York: Alfred A. Knopf, 2000. Evocative, interpretive essays on the life paths and works of twelve women, including Hurston, connecting the circumstances of their lives with the shapes, styles, subjects, and situations of their art.

Thompson, Mark Christian. "National Socialism and Blood-Sacrifice in Zora Neale Hurston's *Moses, Man of the Mountain.*" *American Review* 38, no. 3 (Fall, 2004): 395-416. Studies the roles of power and dominance in *Moses, Man of the Mountain,* comparing it to Niccolo Machiavelli's *Il principe* (wr. 1513, pb. 1532; *The Prince,* 1640).

Walker, Pierre A. "Zora Neale Hurston and the Post-modern Self in *Dust Tracks on a Road.*" *African American Review* 32 (Fall, 1998): 387-399. Uses post-structuralist theory to discuss Hurston's autobiography, showing how she avoids certain autobiographical conventions; argues that Hurston focuses on the life of her imagination, on the psychological dynamics of her family, on retelling community stories, on portraying the character of certain friends, and on her ambiguous pronouncements about race.

— Warren J. Carson; Deborah Kaplan

Charles Johnson

Novelist and short-story writer

Born: Evanston, Illinois; April 23, 1948

LONG FICTION: *Faith and the Good Thing,* 1974; *Oxherding Tale,* 1982; *Middle Passage,* 1990; *Dreamer,* 1998.

SHORT FICTION: *The Sorcerer's Apprentice,* 1986; *Soulcatcher, and Other Stories: Twelve Powerful Tales About Slavery,* 2001; *Dr. King's Refrigerator, and Other Bedtime Stories,* 2005.

TELEPLAYS: *Charlie Smith and the Fritter Tree,* 1978; *Booker,* 1984; *The Green Belt,* 1996.

NONFICTION: *Black Humor,* 1970 (cartoons and drawings); *Half-Past Nation Time,* 1972 (cartoons and drawings); *Being and Race: Black Writing Since 1970,* 1988; *Africans in America: America's Journey Through Slavery,* 1998 (with Patricia Smith); *I Call Myself an Artist: Writings By and About Charles Johnson,* 1999 (Rudolph P. Byrd, editor); *King: The Photobiography of Martin Luther King, Jr.,* 2000 (photographs by Bob Adelman); *Turning the Wheel: Essays on Buddhism and Writing,* 2003; *Passing the Three Gates: Interviews with Charles Johnson,* 2004 (Jim McWilliams, editor).

EDITED TEXTS: *Black Men Speaking,* 1997 (with John McCluskey, Jr.).

Achievements

Charles Johnson has internationally propounded his belief that the process of fiction must have a vital, nonideological philosophical infrastructure. With several international editions of his novels as well as more than twenty grants and awards and professional and public recognition of Johnson's affirmative philosophical approach to the chaotic dualities of the Western world, his profound belief in the inexhaustible capacities of humankind is unquestionable.

Johnson has been the recipient of a 1977 Rockefeller Foundation grant, a 1979 National Endowment for the Arts Creative Writing Fellowship, and a 1988 Guggenheim Fellowship. His teleplay *Booker* alone received four awards: against strong network competition, the 1985 Writers Guild Award for outstanding children's show script; the distinguished 1985-1987 Prix Jeunesse (International Youth Prize); the 1984 Black Film Maker's Festival Award; and the 1984 National Education Film Festival Award for Best Film in the social studies category. In addition, *Oxherding Tale* was given the 1982 Washington State Governor's Writers Award, and *The Sorcerer's Apprentice* was one of the 1987 final nominees for the prestigious PEN/Faulkner Award. In 1989, Johnson was named by a University of California study as one of the ten best American short-story writers. In 1990, his *Middle Passage* was honored with a National Book Award, making him the first male African American writer to receive this prize since Ralph Ellison won for *Invisible Man* (1952). Johnson, who received the Journalism Alumnus of the Year Award from Southern Illinois University in 1981, was again honored in 1994 when the university established the Charles Johnson Award for Fiction and Poetry. In 1998, he was awarded a coveted "genius grant" from the John D. and Catherine T. MacArthur Foundation in recognition of his entire body of work.

Biography

In 1948, Charles Richard Johnson was born to Ruby Elizabeth (Jackson) and Benjamin Lee Johnson of Evanston, Illinois. Both parents had immigrated from the South, specifically Georgia and North Carolina. Johnson's mother, an only child (as is Johnson himself), had wanted to be a schoolteacher but could not because of severe asthma. Instead, she fulfilled her artistic and aesthetic passions in the Johnson home. His father's education was cut short by the Depression, a time when all able-bodied males worked in the fields. Later, he worked with his brother, who was a general contractor in Evanston.

Johnson describes his early years as a "benign upbringing" in a progressive town of unlocked doors and around-the-clock safety, similar to the television neighborhood of *Leave It to Beaver.* Schools had been integrated by the time Johnson became a student; therefore, he did not encounter serious racism during his childhood or adolescence. His first two short stories, "Man Beneath Rags" and "50 Cards 50" (which he also illustrated), as well as many cartoons (one award-winning), were published at Evanston Township High School, then one of the best high schools in the country. While in high school, Johnson began to work with Laurence Lariar, a cartoonist and mystery writer. In 1965, he sold his first drawing to a Chicago magazine's catalog for illustrated magic tricks. From 1965 to 1973, Johnson sold more than one thousand drawings to major magazines.

After high school graduation, Johnson had planned to attend a small art school rather than a four-year college. Nevertheless, as the first person in his extended family to attend college, he felt some obligation to fulfill his parents' hopes. This concern, combined with his art teacher's recommendation that he attend a four-year college for practical reasons, was enough to motivate Johnson to register at Southern Illinois University at Carbondale as a journalism major (with a compelling interest in philosophy). His continuing study of martial arts and Buddhism began in 1967. A cartoonist for the *Chicago Tribune* from 1969 to 1970, Johnson wrote and aired fifty-two fifteen-minute PBS episodes of *Charlie's Pad,* a how-to show on cartooning in 1970.

During his senior year in college, Johnson began writing novels. With his journalistic background (B.S., 1971), he saw no problem with allotting two or three months for each novel. Consequently, from 1970 to 1972, Johnson wrote six novels; three are naturalistic, while three are in the style of the Black Arts movement. Although his fourth novel was accepted for publication, Johnson withdrew it after talking with John Gardner about the implications of precipitate first publication. All six apprentice novels have been filed, unread, in a drawer. Johnson credits Gardner's tutelage on *Faith and the Good Thing* with saving him six additional years of mistakes.

In 1973, Johnson was awarded his master's degree in philosophy from Southern Illinois University with the thesis "Wilhelm

Reich and the Creation of a Marxist Psychology." Following three years of doctoral work at the State University of New York at Stony Brook, Johnson began teaching at the University of Washington as well as serving as fiction editor of the *Seattle Review.* Under a 1977-1978 Rockefeller Foundation grant, he joined the WGBH New Television Workshop as writer-in-residence. In 1982, he became a staff writer and producer for the last ten episodes of KQED's *Up and Coming* series and wrote the second season's premiere episode "Bad Business." A thirty-minute script for KCET's *Y.E.S. Inc.* aired in 1983.

From 1985 to 1987, Johnson worked on the text for *Being and Race: Black Writing Since 1970,* a project he had begun while guest lecturing for the University of Delaware. His 1983 draft of the first two chapters in *Middle Passage* came quickly, but Johnson worked on the novel sporadically from 1983 to 1987 before finally giving it his full attention for nine months. In addition to his continuing projects, he was a 1988 National Book Award judge and received the Lifting Up the World Award and medallion presented to seventeen University of Washington faculty by Sri Chinmoy.

Beginning in 1975, Johnson practiced meditation seriously and studied many Eastern religions, including Hinduism and Daoism. Although his upbringing was Episcopalian, he became an "on-again-off-again Buddhist" in 1980. As part of his lifelong involvement with the martial arts, particularly karate and kung fu, Johnson codirected the Blue Phoenix Club, a martial arts club in Seattle. This interest is also reflected in his writing, as in the short stories "China," which appeared in *The Sorcerer's Apprentice,* "kwoon" (a training hall for students of kung fu), which was included in the O. Henry *Prize Stories* of 1993; and the teleplay *The Green Belt,* published in 1996.

He continued to teach at the University of Washington and to serve as fiction editor for the *Seattle Review.* In addition, his monthly reviews have been published in the *Los Angeles Times* and *The New York Times.* He also revisited his first love, political cartooning, and his gentle satires on racial factionalism in America appear regularly in the *Quarterly Black Review.* Johnson was director of the University of Washington's creative writing program for three years (1987-1990). In 1990, he was awarded an endowed chair, the first Pollock Professorship in Creative Writing at the University of Washington. He assumed the lifetime position in the fall of 1991.

Johnson was married to Joan New in 1970. The couple have two children: Malik, a son born in 1975, and a daughter, Elizabeth, born in 1981. His life is chronicled in Joan Walkinshaw's PBS documentary *Spirit of Place*, which aired in Seattle.

Analysis: Long Fiction

Because Charles Johnson believes implicitly in the power of language, he examines his writing line by line, word by word, to eliminate plot superfluities and to ensure verbal precision. (His drafts of *Oxherding Tale* totaled more than twenty-five hundred pages.) Token characterization to this author is "fundamentally immoral"; rather, he insists, a writer must expend the same energy with his fictional characters that he would in understanding and loving those in his physical world. Even further, Johnson identifies the committed writer as someone who cares enough about his work that it "is something he would do if a gun was held to his head and somebody was going to pull the trigger as soon as the last word of the last sentence of the last paragraph of the last page was finished." For Johnson, who thinks of himself as an artist rather than as an author, writing is a nonvolitional necessity.

A phenomenologist and metaphysician, Johnson constructs fictional universes that not only adhere to the Aristotelian concepts of coherence, consistency, and completeness but also elucidate integral life experiences in the universal search for personal identity. Moreover, the multiplicity of consciousness embodied by his characters seeks to strip the preconceptions from his readers so that they may "reexperience the world with unsealed vision." Consequently, the unrelenting integrity of his fictional vision resolutely reaffirms humanity's potential to live in a world without duality and in the process also reveals Johnson's own indefatigable regard for the unfathomable, moment-by-moment mystery of humankind.

Even though Johnson has dedicated himself to the evolution of "a genuinely systematic philosophical black American literature" and most frequently creates his *Lebenswelt* (lifeworld) within a black context, he sees the racial details as qualifiers of more universal questions. The nonlinear fictional progressions, the proliferations of synaesthetic imagery, the delicate counterbalances of comic (and cosmic) incongruities, and the philosophical underpinnings viscerally reinforced lend a Zen fluidity to the consequent shifting levels of awareness. Thus, the characters' movements toward or away from self-identity, action without ulterior motivation, and mind-body integration assume universal relevance.

Faith and the Good Thing
Written from the fall of 1972 to the early summer of 1973 under the tutelage of John Gardner, *Faith and the Good Thing* is the metaphysical journey of eighteen-year-old Faith Cross, who believes that she is following her mother's deathbed instructions and the werewitch Swamp Woman's advice by searching the external world for the "Good Thing." This quest for the key that will release her and everyone else from servitude leads from Hatten County, Georgia, to Chicago, Illinois, and home again. Despite limitations inherent in the narrative form itself, occasional lapses in viewpoint, and infrequent verbal artifice, Johnson has created a magical novel of legendary characters and metaphysical import.

The diverse characters who people Faith's life enrich her explorations on both ordinary and extraordinary levels of existence, yet none can lead her to her Good Thing. Asthmatic, stuttering, alcoholic Isaac Maxwell insists that the real power is in money. Dr. Leon Lynch, who treats her mother, believes that the purpose of human life is death and fulfills his self-prophecy by committing suicide on Christmas Eve. Nervous Arnold Tippis, a former dentist (who lost his license because of malpractice), theater usher, and male nurse, rapes her physically and spiritually. His adaptations, like Faith's initial search, are external. Richard M. Barrett, former Princeton University professor, husband, and father, is now a homeless robber who dies on a Soldiers' Field park bench. An existentialist, he believes enough in her search to will her his blank Doomsday Book and to haunt her after his death on Friday nights at midnight until her marriage. Each character shares his path to his Good Thing with Faith, thereby allowing her to choose pieces for her own.

Faith's mystical odyssey, remembered with relish by a third-person narrator addressing his listeners "children," commits every individual to his own search and, through reflection, to the potential alteration of individual consciousness. Despite identifiable elements of naturalism, romanticism, allegory, the *Bildungsroman*, and black folktales, of far greater importance is that *Faith and the Good Thing* creates its own genre of philosophical fiction in which the metaphysical and the real are integrated into a healing totality of being.

Until her return to Swamp Woman, Faith's choices for survival thrust her upon a path of intensifying alienation from herself and from her world. Her feelings of estrangement and depersonalization escalate to an existential fragmentation during her rape and subsequent periods of prostitution, chemical abuse, and marriage. With her decision to forsake her quest for the Good Thing, to manipulate the eminently unsuitable Isaac Maxwell into marriage, and to settle for a loveless middle-class existence, Faith cripples her sense of metaphysical purpose and sees herself as one of the "dead living," an "IT," her soul severed, "still as stone."

The advent of Alpha Omega Holmes, her hometown first love, enables Faith to recover vitality, but her dependence upon others since childhood for self-definition has been consistently destructive to Faith, who has lived in the past or the future and denied her present being. Holmes continues the pattern by deserting her when she announces that she is five months pregnant with his child. Rejected by Holmes and Maxwell, Faith turns to Mrs. Beasley, her former madam, who cares for her, delivers her baby daughter, and leaves the burning candle that is responsible for the fire that kills Faith's child and critically maims Faith. Repeatedly, psychic abandonment and betrayal have been the consequences of a failure to respect her own and others' process of becoming.

Nevertheless, at the summons of Swamp Woman's white cat, Faith returns to the werewitch's holy ground. Now near death, she is finally prepared to devote her total being to the search. Accepting Swamp Woman's revelations that everyone has a path and a "truth," Faith understands that all humans are the sum of their experiences and that she, as well as they, has no beginning and no end. Thus, she has the power to exchange existence with the esoteric, iconoclastic, witty magician Swamp Woman or to become anyone she wishes, thereby personifying Barrett's premise that thinking directs being. The Good Thing is the dynamic, nonpossessive, fluid freedom of the search itself.

Oxherding Tale

After *Faith and the Good Thing*, Johnson began thinking differently about the storyteller voice. He sought a means by which he could more fully and naturally embody philosophical issues within his characters. In *Oxherding Tale*, he has realized that voice, an intriguing first-person fusion of slave narrative, picaresque, and parable. In the first of two authorial intrusions, chapters 8 and 11, Johnson explains the three existing types of slave narrative. In the second, the author defines his new voice as first-person "universal," not a "narrator who falteringly interprets the world, but a narrator who *is* that world."

Yet the eight years that Johnson worked on his second novel, a novel he believes he was born to create, were fraught with frustration as he wrote and discarded draft after draft until, in 1979, he considered never writing again. Nevertheless, his passion for writing conquered the obstructions. Following a period of extended meditation, Johnson experienced a profound catharsis and eliminated the problematic static quality of the earlier drafts by refashioning the narrator-protagonist from black to mulatto and his second master from male to female.

Oxherding Tale, inspired by Eastern artist Kakuan-Shien's "Ten Oxherding Pictures," describes Andrew Hawkins's rite of passage, an often-humorous, metaphysical search for self through encounters that culminate in his nondualistic understanding of himself and the world. The narrator, born to the master's wife and the master's butler as the fruit of a comic one-night adventure, sees himself as belonging to neither the fields nor the house. Although Andrew lives with his stepmother and his father (recently demoted to herder), George and Mattie Hawkins, Master Polkinghorne arranges his classical education with an eccentric Eastern scholar. An excellent student, Andrew nevertheless expresses his recognition of the dualism when he protests that he can speak in Latin more effectively than in his own dialect. As Andrew opens his mind to the learning of the ages, George Hawkins becomes progressively more paranoid and nationalistic. This delicate counterbalance is sustained throughout the novel until, at the end, the assimilated Andrew learns from Soulcatcher that his father was shot to death as an escaped slave.

At twenty, Andrew wishes to marry the Cripplegate plantation seamstress, Minty. Instead, he is sold to Flo Hatfield, a lonely woman who considers her eleven former husbands subhuman and who has the reputation of sexually using each male slave until, discarding him to the mines or through his death, she replaces him with another. Believing that he is earning the funds for his own, his family's, and Minty's manumission, Andrew cooperates. He finds himself quickly satiated, however, with the orgiastic physical pleasures Flo demands to conceal her psychic lifelessness. Thus, neither his father's intensifying spiritual separatism nor his mistress's concupiscence is a path Andrew can accept.

Andrew proceeds to seek out Reb, the Allmuseri coffinmaker in whose Buddhist voice he finds comfort, friendship, and enlightenment. Flo's opposite, Reb (neither detached nor attached) operates not from pleasure but from duty, acting without ulterior motives simply because something needs to be done. Together, the two escape Flo's sentence to her mines as well as Bannon the Soulcatcher, a bounty hunter, with Andrew posing as William Harris, a white teacher, and Reb posing as his gentleman's gentleman. When Reb decides to leave Spartanburg for Chicago because of Bannon, Andrew, emotionally attached to the daughter of the town doctor, decides that Reb's path is not appropriate for him to follow. Instead, his dharma (Eastern soul-sustaining law of conduct) is to be a homemaker married to Peggy. During their wedding ceremony, Andrew surrenders himself to his timeless vision of all that humanity has the potential to become.

The final chapter, "Moksha," like the last of Kakuan-Shien's ten pictures, reveals the absolute integration between self and universe. "Moksha" is the Hindu concept of ultimate realization, perpetual liberation beyond dualities, of self with the Great Spirit. In an illegal slave auction, the mulatto Andrew discovers and buys his dying first love, Minty. He, Peggy, and Dr. Undercliff unite to ease her transition from this world. Thus, the three move beyond self to *arete*, "doing beautifully what needs to be done," and begin the process of healing their world.

In *Oxherding Tale,* Johnson once again offers the experience of affirmation and renewal. Through the first-person universal voice of Andrew Hawkins, he constructs a tightly interwoven, well-honed portrait of actualization. Minute details, vivid visual imagery, and delicate polarities within and among the characters achieve an exacting balance between portrayal of the process and the process itself. Once again, the search does not belong solely to Johnson's characters; the search belongs to everyone who chooses to be free of "self-inflicted segregation from the Whole."

Middle Passage

Johnson deliberately depersonalized his third novel's working title, "Rutherford's Travels," to *Middle Passage,* a multiple literary allusion, to "emphasize the historical event rather than the character" and to enhance the novel's provocative content. Visual characteristics of Johnson's screenplay writing are sometimes evident in *Oxherding Tale;* however, in *Middle Passage* scenic effect and synaesthetic detail purposefully dominate, with the narrative sections intended as scenic bridges. Johnson had already used members of the Allmuseri, a mystical African tribe reputed to be the origin of the human race, in *Oxherding Tale,* as well as in two short stories, "The Sorcerer's Apprentice" and "The Education of Mingo"; yet never before had he so masterfully drawn the portrait of this compelling tribe of Zen sorcerers.

Recently manumitted Rutherford Calhoun, a landlubbing twenty-three-year-old picaro, stows away aboard the slave ship *Republic* in order to avoid a marriage forced by his prospective bride. Discovered but allowed to remain as chef's helper by the dwarflike captain, Ebenezer Falcon, the first-person universal narrator candidly records the brutality people unleash on one another during the forty-one-day voyage to Bangalang for forty captive Allmuseri and their living god. Later revealed as a duty assigned by the suicidal Falcon, Calhoun's log becomes a primary tool by which he processes his responses to his shipmates and to the ship's adventures.

Following an eerie storm in which the stars themselves shift in the heavens, the Allmuseri revolt and capture the ship less than one week after being confined in the *Republic*'s hold. Yet, this tribe believes that each individual is responsible for the creation of his own universe and that even the most minute action has eternal repercussions, echoing beyond this world. Therefore, that human death was involved in their freedom is a source of great sorrow, particularly for their leader, Ngonyama. Despite ceremonies of atonement, the *Republic* sinks, aided by a storm and the Allmuseri renegade Diamelo, who ignites a cannon pointed in the wrong direction.

Of captors and captives, only five survive until the *Juno*, a floating pleasure palace, rescues them: Rutherford Calhoun, his friend Josiah Squibb, and three Allmuseri children including Rutherford's female tribal ward, Baleka. On board *Juno* is Isadora Bailey, Rutherford's forceful fiancée, now scheduled to marry an underworld figure who profits by betraying his race. Instead, a transformed Rutherford, who understands that the way to deal effectively with dangerous people is to become even more dangerous than they, convinces the Créole gangster that marrying Isadora would not be in his best interest; now Rutherford can marry Isadora himself.

Against a backdrop of sea adventure, the poignancy of the characters' startling self-revelations becomes even more deeply moving. Falcon, the remorseless captain to whom human life has no value other than the price he can pocket, collects his treasures to fulfill his dead mother's dream. The first mate Peter

Cringle, who responds from his heart to others' victimization, escapes his wealthy family's mistreatment of him by offering his body as food for the *Republic*'s last survivors. Nathaniel Meadows, who murdered his own family, is so fiercely loyal to Falcon that he conditions the ships' dogs to attack those persons he believes most likely to lead a mutiny. Conversely, Diamelo, the Allmuseri insurrectionist, is so spiritually consumed by his own anger that he blinds himself to the good of his people and destroys them. Yet Ngonyama, grieving over the loss of his tribe's metaphysical connectedness to the Whole, is able to heal Rutherford before lashing himself to the helm in propitiation for the deaths that his tribe's freedom has cost.

Rutherford, self-proclaimed liar and petty thief, finds that instead of hungering for new sensory experiences, he is finally content to experience the present with acceptance and gratitude. Faced with material choices, such as those having to do with food or bed linens, he can no longer comprehend their relevance. Instead of taking, he seeks opportunities for sharing himself without expectations and in universal love. He has taken full possession of his life. He no longer needs; he simply responds.

Middle Passage employs intricately interwoven scenes appropriate to the multiplicity of levels upon which the characters exist. The Allmuseri god, a shape-shifter, is the individual personification of the living truth most fear to face. Furthermore, the anguish of each "middle passage" is uniquely reflected internally by the character and externally by all those whom the character encounters. Recognition without preconception of humanity's magnificent complexity is a significant step toward universal communion.

Dreamer

Johnson's fourth novel, *Dreamer*, begins during the summer of 1966—in the midst of the Chicago riots, the Civil Rights movement, and the Vietnam War—and continues to the fateful 1968 sanitation workers' strike in Memphis, Tennessee. The book is narrated by an observer, Matthew Bishop, a young civil rights worker in the entourage of Dr. Martin Luther King, Jr., but

King's thoughts and emotions are offered indirectly in italicized sections of the narrative.

Johnson, a clear admirer of King, has re-created a time when the civil rights leader is endangered by death threats and a bounty of thirty thousand dollars on his head, and the U.S. government fears the outbreak of a race war. Even though the character of King is at the center of the novel, he is not *the* center. He shares that position with Chaym (pronounced as if spelled "Cain") Smith, a maimed Korean War veteran and heroin addict who volunteers as King's stand-in to confuse potential assassins. King is presented as an exhausted and selfless man who adheres to Gandhian nonviolence and longs for the chance to rest and renew himself. Johnson researched minute details of King's personal life, even to the brand of lye-based depilatory powder he used on his sensitive face.

Smith, King's physical double, admires and envies the minister. A spiritual enigma, Smith dreams of becoming a great preacher, yet he sets fire to his apartment building after he is evicted. He is a scholar who studied Zen Buddhism in a Japanese temple and mastered Sanskrit in three days, a practical cynic, and a wanderer. He is a descendant of the Allmuseri through Baleka Calhoun of *Middle Passage.* "I don't believe in a blessed thing, including me," he says; "[w]ork is all I got to offer."

After being wounded by a bullet meant for King, Smith moves away from his unhappy dualism, from alternating good and evil deeds, to a more inclusive unity that embraces the best of Eastern philosophy and Western *agape.* He has sacrificed himself for others, but he is not completely unselfish; rather, he is a troubled and imperfect man who grows stronger, then apparently weakens when he seems ready to betray King. He is likened to the brilliant and rebellious Lucifer; he serves as the outcast Cain to King's obedient brother Abel, but the question of whether Smith-Cain is an evil or heroic figure is posed by the novel but never directly answered. Perhaps, true to his own ambiguity, he is neither.

Once again, Johnson is writing on multiple levels. His title *Dreamer* is found in an epigraph alluding to the Old Testament betrayal of Joseph by his brothers, but it also alludes to King's famous "I have a dream" speech. In addition to the obvious biblical symbolism, Chaym Smith's eclecticism in many respects suggests an ideal metaphysical wholeness that the figure of Dr. King, with his faith and his dreams of India, is able to embody more perfectly.

Charles Johnson's innate belief in the essential goodness of humankind and his intuitive grasp of the metaphysical empower him to create living fiction with the potential to alter human consciousness. His mastery of the English language, as well as the tight word-by-word control he exercises, heightens his characters' credibility and consequently his readers' empathic sensitivity. Employing a precise awareness of human motivation, Johnson structures his writing nonlinearly to evince tantalizing pieces of the human mystery, but he withholds consummate revelation until the metaphysical world of philosophical fiction surrounding his characters is fully realized.

Analysis: Short Fiction

From the beginning of his writing life, Charles Johnson sought to combine a deep interest in the dominant aesthetic and philosophical concerns of the Western intellectual tradition with the specific issues and historical consequences of three centuries of chattel slavery and economic discrimination. In response to the numerous stereotypes and misconceptions about African American life that have accumulated in American culture, Johnson observed, "Good fiction sharpens our perception; great fiction *changes* it." Assuming that pioneering black writers like Richard Wright, Ralph Ellison, and Zora Neale Hurston have shattered the silence surrounding the black experience, Johnson has attempted to open the field, further asserting, "We know, of course, more than oppression and discrimination." Describing his objective as "whole sight," Johnson has worked toward a "cross-cultural fertilization" in his fiction, which draws on the full range of technical strategies, which he calls "our inheritance as writers."

One of the most influential people in Johnson's development was the writer and theorist John Gardner, who stressed the

importance of what Johnson calls "imaginative storytelling reinforced by massive technique." In his short fiction collection, *The
Sorcerer's Apprentice,* Johnson's technical facility is evident in stories that range from straight realism to fable, fantasy, folktale, allegory, and quasi-autobiographical confession, mingling modes
within stories, while establishing an authentic, convincing narrative voice that reflects the psychological condition of his protagonists. Six of the eight short stories in *The Sorcerer's Apprentice*
were written as psychic releases from the difficulty Johnson experienced in creating a draft of *Oxherding Tale.* Two of the eight
are award winners: "Popper's Disease" (receiving the 1983 *Callaloo* Creative Writing Award) and "China" (receiving the 1984
Pushcart Prize Outstanding Writer citation). The pattern of development in his stories is from what he calls "ignorance to
knowledge, or from a lack of understanding to some greater understanding." This understanding is often an aspect of the character's quest for identity, a kind of progression in which Johnson
resists a fixed notion of the self in favor of what he calls the "expansive." The stories in the collection touch on some of the
most fundamental aspects of African American life to reveal
what Rudolph Byrd calls "the richness of the black world."

"The Education of Mingo"
Each of the stories in *The Sorcerer's Apprentice* has a specific philo-
sophic concept at the core of the narrative. "The Education of
Mingo," which opens the collection, is informed by the argument that humans are ultimately not responsible for their actions if there is an omniscient deity in control of the universe.
The story is grounded in a very down-to-earth situation involv-
ing a white man, Moses Green, who has trained an African slave,
Mingo, to echo all of his desires, attitudes, preferences, and pre-
dilections. As Mingo begins to act beyond the specific instructions of his master, anticipating Green's subconscious and in-
stinctual urges, the servant/master relationship is presented
as a reciprocal form of entrapment, in which neither is truly
free or completely himself. The costs of this arrangement are
Green's permanent connection to his slave and Mingo's restric-
tion to his status as menial, no matter how skilled or accom-

plished he becomes. The story is both a commentary on three centuries of slavery and a vivid expression of the inner conflicts of an essentially good man, whose well-meaning attempt to educate someone he regards as completely ignorant must lead to a disastrous, violent conclusion due to his own massive ignorance of Mingo's mind. The interlocking destiny of Green and Mingo, the secret sharers of each others' lives, points the story toward an indeterminate future, in which the racial clash of American life remains to be resolved. As the writer Michael Ventura has observed, the stories in *The Sorcerer's Apprentice* often "reveal the underside of the last or next," so that Cooter and Loftis, brothers in the succeeding story, "Exchange Value," are also trapped in an interlocking relationship that wrecks their ability to think with moral clarity or any sense of self-preservation.

"China"

Located at the center of the collection, "China" is the most energetically affirmative story in *The Sorcerer's Apprentice*, closer in mood to Johnson's celebrated novels, *Oxherding Tale* or *Middle Passage*, than to his short fiction. Rudolph Lee Jackson, the protagonist, is a middle-aged man whose entire life has been a catastrophe of caution and avoidance. His marriage is devoid of passion or communication, he is physically feeble, psychically terrified, and steadily deteriorating from even this diminished condition. The story is not an open allegory, but Jackson is presented as an emblem of the frightened, semibourgeois, not-quite-middle-class black man, nearly completely emasculated by a retreat from the daily assaults of a racist society and further discouraged by the constant critical sarcasm of his wife Evelyn, whose disappointment and fear is understandable in terms of Jackson's apparent acceptance of defeat.

Johnson has criticized novels in which "portraits of black men . . . are so limited and one-sided" that they seem immoral. The direction of "China" is an opening away from what Johnson calls "an extremely narrow range of human beings"—exemplified by Jackson, who has a "distant, pained expression that asked: *Is this all?*"—toward a kind of self-actualization and fulfillment, which Jackson achieves through a difficult and painful but energizing course in the philosophy and practice of martial arts. In some of his most engaging, vivid writing, Johnson describes the revitalization and growth that leads to Jackson's symbolic rebirth as a man, as he becomes more and more involved in the life of the kwoon. Initially, Evelyn resists everything about Jackson's enthusiastic, disciplined transformation, but at the story's conclusion, she is, despite her reservations and fears, awakened to the possibility of a life without the artificial, self-imposed limits that African Americans have adopted as a kind of protection from the pain of a three-centuries-long legacy of racial oppression. The story "Kwoon" is a further exploration of the mental condition at the heart of true physical power that martial arts can provide, and it illuminates the genuine humility that the strongest people know when they have moved beyond the ego trap of resistance to enlightenment.

"ALĒTHIA"

"ALĒTHIA" is the most explicitly philosophical of Johnson's short stories. It is narrated by a book-ruled professor, whose ordered, intellectually contained life is fractured when a student pulls him into a forest of uncontrolled passion, the necessary complement to his mental fortress. The two sides of human existence are expressed in the contrast between the professor's measured discourse and the raw reality of the netherworld to which his guide takes him. The word "alēthia" is drawn from the philosopher Max Scheler's term concerning a process that "calls forth from concealedness," and it stands for the revelation of an inner essence that has been previously suppressed—the "ugly, lovely black life (so it was to me) I'd fled so long ago in my childhood." Johnson's presentation of the professor is a commentary on the retreat that a preoccupation with the purely mental may produce and a statement about the futility of repressing aspects of the true self.

Other Literary Forms

Believing that a writer should be able to express himself with competence in all forms of the written word, Charles Johnson has successfully published in several genres, including more than one thousand satirical comic drawings and two books of socially relevant cartoons, *Black Humor* and *Half-Past Nation Time*. Among Johnson's screenplays are *Charlie Smith and the Fritter Tree* (which aired on *Visions* in 1978), the adventure-charged story of the oldest living American who arrived on a slaver and became a Texas cowboy; *Booker* (a 1984 *Wonderworks* premiere), a dramatization of the young Booker T. Washington's dogged struggle to learn at a time when education was by law denied to southern black Americans; and the award-winning *Me, Myself, Maybe* (a 1982 Public Broadcasting System *Up and Coming* episode), one of the first scripts to deal with a married black woman's process of self-determination.

A literary aesthetician, Johnson has also published articles and book reviews. *Being and Race: Black Writing Since 1970*, a controversial critical analysis and winner of the 1988 Washington State Governor's Writers Award, is the product of Johnson's twenty-year exploration into the makings of black fiction.

Bibliography

African American Review 30, no. 4 (Winter, 1996). A special issue of the journal devoted to Johnson's work. Most of the essays consider Johnson's novels, but there are some references to the short fiction. The strength of the issue is the variety of viewpoints it presents, ranging from political assessments to philosophical excursions. Uneven but often informative.

Byrd, Rudolph P., ed. *I Call Myself an Artist: Writings by and About Charles Johnson*. Bloomington: Indiana University Press, 1999. An intelligently chosen, eclectic collection of works by Charles Johnson, which includes an autobiographical essay and several essays explaining his aesthetic perspective and theories of literary composition. There are also two interviews with Johnson and an extensive section of critical discussions of Johnson's work, including an essay by the editor on *The Sorcerer's Apprentice*, which explains Johnson's employment of the philosophical perspectives of Alfred North Whitehead.

Gleason, William. "The Liberation of Perception: Charles Johnson's *Oxherding Tale.*" *Black American Literature Forum* 25 (Winter, 1991): 705-728. One of the most perceptive critiques of the spiritual dimension of Johnson's writing, an important component often overlooked by other commentators.

Harris, Norman. "The Black Universe in Contemporary Afro-American Fiction." *CLA (College Language Association) Journal* 30 (September, 1986): 1-13. Harris's discussion of the aesthetic bases in the contemporary fictional universes of Toni Morrison, Johnson, and Ishmael Reed provides a contextual overview of the black movement toward nonlinear, mythical constructions in contrast to the approaches of Richard Wright's *Native Son* (1940) and Ralph Ellison's *Invisible Man* (1952).

Johnson, Charles. "From Narrow Complaint to Broad Celebration: A Conversation with Charles Johnson." Interview by Nibir K. Ghosh. *MELUS* 29, nos. 3/4 (Fall/Winter, 2004): 359-379. An interview with the author that focuses on his philosophy and interests in martial arts, Buddhism, and folklore.

_____. Interview by Nicholas O'Connell. In *At the Field's End: Interviews with Twenty Pacific Northwest Writers.* Seattle: Madrona, 1987. Presenting a superb interview in an excellent collection, O'Connell remains discreetly in the background as Johnson reveals his thoughts about the artistry and the passion inherent in the writing process, the necessary interconnectedness of philosophy and literature, and his own intrinsically caring life view. With erudition, humor, and honesty, Johnson ranges freely over such topics as the victimization of naturalism's universe, Buddhist tenets, phenomenology, and the potency of language.

_____. "An Interview with Charles Johnson." Interview by Charles H. Rowell. *Callaloo* 20 (Summer, 1997): 531-547. An insightful and wide-ranging interview in which Johnson comments on his early years as a political cartoonist and his hope for an emerging body of philosophical African American fiction. He notes the limitations of naturalism and stresses the critical importance of form in fiction, explaining how he deliberately imposes form on a novel or story.

———. "Reflections on Film, Philosophy, and Fiction." Interview by Ken McCullough. *Callaloo* 1 (October, 1978): 118-128. This interview, conducted while Johnson and McCullough were editing *Charlie Smith and the Fritter Tree*, reflects their concentration upon the film as they contrast various literary art processes with an emphasis upon the screenplay and the novel. An interesting, informal, and literate profile of a writer who lives his words.

Little, Jonathan. *Charles Johnson's Spiritual Imagination*. Columbia: University of Missouri Press, 1997. A critical study of Johnson's work, with a chapter on *The Sorcerer's Apprentice*, arguing that the short fiction, in contrast to novels like *Oxherding Tale* and *Middle Passage*, offers a pessimistic view of human existence, dwelling on the "nightmarish and destructive side of his (Johnson's) integrative aesthetic and social vision." The individual stories are approached with insight and are effectively related to Johnson's other work. Little concludes the chapter with an assertion that "the short stories often resonate with more power, depth and ambiguity" than the longer books.

Lock, Helen. "The Paradox of Slave Mutiny in Herman Melville, Charles Johnson, and Frederick Douglass." *Literature* 30, no. 4 (Fall, 2003): 54-71. An interesting article that offers a new interpretation of the relationship between slaves and those against whom they revolt. Explains the textual relationships between the three authors.

Nixon, Will. "Black Male Writers: Endangered Species?" *American Visions* 5, no. 1 (February, 1990): 24-29. An interesting study of the reasons why African American male writers were largely ignored during the 1980's. Also looks at the rise of African American female writers.

Steinberg, Marc. "Charles Johnson's *Middle Passage*: Fictionalizing History and Historicizing Fiction." *Texas Studies in Literature & Language* 45, no. 4 (Winter, 2003): 375-391. Places Johnson's novel in the context of other writings about slavery and its history and examines Johnson's interpretation of slavery.

Ventura, Michael. "Voodoo and Subtler Powers." *The New York Times Book Review,* March 30, 1986, 7. Ventura's thoughtful essay contends that *The Sorcerer's Apprentice* might best be understood as a "good short novel" in that each story works as a commentary or extension of the next or previous one. His sense of central themes and ongoing concerns is illuminating.

— Leon Lewis; Joanne McCarthy; Kathleen Mills

June Jordan

Poet

Born: Harlem, New York; July 9, 1936
Died: Berkeley, California; June 14, 2002

LONG FICTION: *His Own Where,* 1971.

DRAMA: *In the Spirit of Sojourner Truth,* pr. 1979; *For the Arrow That Flies by Day,* pr. 1981; *Bang Bang Über Alles,* pr. 1986 (libretto; music by Adrienne Bo Torf); *I Was Looking at the Ceiling and Then I Saw the Sky,* 1995 (libretto and lyrics; music by John Adams).

POETRY: *Some Changes,* 1971; *New Days: Poems of Exile and Return,* 1974; *Things That I Do in the Dark: Selected Poetry,* 1977; *Passion: New Poems, 1977-1980,* 1980; *Living Room: New Poems,* 1985; *Bobo Goetz a Gun,* 1985; *Lyrical Campaigns: Selected Poems,* 1989; *Naming Our Destiny: New and Selected Poems,* 1989; *Haruko/Love Poems: New and Selected Love Poems,* 1993 (pb. in the U.S. as *Haruko: Love Poems,* 1994); *Kissing God Goodbye: Poems, 1991-1997,* 1997.

NONFICTION: *Civil Wars,* 1981; *On Call: Political Essays,* 1985; *Moving Towards Home: Political Essays,* 1989; *Technical Difficulties: African-American Notes on the State of the Union,* 1992; *Affirmative Acts: Political Essays,* 1998; *Soldier: A Poet's Childhood,* 2000.

CHILDREN'S/YOUNG ADULT LITERATURE: *Who Look at Me,* 1969; *Fannie Lou Hamer,* 1972; *Dry Victories,* 1972; *New Life: New Room,* 1975; *Kimako's Story,* 1981.

Achievements

June Jordan won the Lila Wallace-Reader's Digest Writer's Award (1995), the National Association of Black Journalists Award (1984), and the PEN Center USA West Freedom to Write Award (1991). She was the recipient of grants and fellowships from the Rockefeller Foundation, the National Endowment for the Arts, the New York Foundation for the Arts, and the Massachusetts Council on the Arts. She also won the Prix de Rome in Environmental Design (1970-1971). In 1971, her book *His Own Where* was nominated for a National Book Award. Her poetry is represented in many major anthologies of contemporary American poetry.

Biography

The essence of June Jordan's life reveals itself in her poetry and in her autobiographical writings, in particular in *Civil Wars* and her memoir *Soldier: A Poet's Childhood.* She was born in Harlem, the daughter of her father Granville, a Panamanian immigrant, and Mildred, her Jamaican mother. When she was five years old, her parents moved to Brooklyn, and Jordan began her education by commuting to an all-white school. She later attended Northfield School for Girls, a preparatory school in Massachusetts.

(Jill Posener)

Her introduction to poetry came through her father, who forced her to read, memorize, or recite the plays and sonnets of William Shakespeare, the Bible, the poetry of Paul Laurence Dunbar, and the poetry of Edgar Allan Poe, as well as the novels of Sinclair Lewis and Zane Grey. At the age of seven, she began to write poetry herself. Unfortunately, her father's pedagogical methods also included beatings for unsatisfactory performance, but Jordan never questioned his love for her, affirming that he had the greatest influence on her poetic and personal development, having given her the idea that "to protect yourself, you try to hurt whatever is out there." Jordan's mother, who committed suicide in 1966, did not oppose her father's harsh treatment of her, and Jordan found this passivity harder to forgive than her father's brutality.

Her interest in poetry was developed at Northfield but was limited mainly to white male poets "whose remoteness from my world . . . crippled my trust in my own sensibilities . . . and generally delayed my creative embracing of my own . . . life as the stuff of my art."

In 1953, at Barnard College, Jordan met Michael Meyer, a white student at Columbia University. They were married in 1955 and Jordan followed her husband to the University of Chicago. The strain of their interracial marriage, at a time when such marriages were frowned upon by the dominant society, began to take its toll, and after a prolonged separation the couple eventually divorced in 1965, leaving Jordan to raise her son Christopher, born in 1958, by herself. Supporting herself at first as a technical writer, journalist, and assistant to Frederick Wiseman (producer of *The Cool World*, a film about Harlem), she began her academic career at the City College of New York in 1967. In 1969, she published her first book, *Who Look at Me*, a series of poetic fragments dealing with the problem of black identity in America, in which she tries to imagine what a white person might see when looking at an African American and what effect such a look can have on the person observed.

In 1970 Jordan traveled to Italy with funding from the Prix de Rome in Environmental Design, which she had won with the support of R. Buckminster Fuller. Her reflections on this journey are contained in her collection *New Days: Poems of Exile and Return*. A breakthrough in her career as a poet came with the publication in 1977 of her best-known collection, *Things That I Do in the Dark*, edited by Toni Morrison.

After the publication of *Who Look at Me*, Jordan published more than twenty books in a variety of genres, including books for children and young adults, political essays, long fiction, plays, and even an opera libretto. She taught at Connecticut College, Sarah Lawrence College, Yale University, and the State University of New York at Stony Brook, eventually taking up a professorship in African studies at the University of California, Berkeley. There she became the head of the popular outreach program Poetry for the People. She was a regular contributor to the liberal periodical *The Progressive*, an outspoken critic of American foreign aid policy, and an aggressive proponent of affirmative action. Jordan died in June, 2002, after losing her decade-long fight against breast cancer.

Analysis: Poetry

June Jordan was not an academic, ivory-tower poet given to abstract speculations about the nature of truth and beauty. She was a self-avowed anarchist activist who considered all poems to be political. Indeed, she stated that to her, William Shakespeare's sonnets were examples of status quo politics, mirroring the ideology of an idle leisure class. Her poetic ambition was to be a "people's poet" in the fashion of Pablo Neruda, particularly a black people's poet.

Jordan's early poems are autobiographical and self-reflective, attempting to come to terms with her relationships with her parents and with her son Christopher. Yet even these early poems transcend the purely personal and illustrate her attempt to cope with being both black and a woman in a society that looks upon women of color with indifference, if not with outright hostility. In *Who Look at Me* she withstands the gaze of the white observer and finally even returns the look defiantly. Over the years this defiance became increasingly characteristic of her poetry, even as the causes in which she engaged herself proliferated.

Her poetic output was to a large degree a running commentary on the social and political life in the United States, with allusions to sociopolitical events such as the 1991 Clarence Thomas/Anita Hill hearings, Jesse Jackson's 1984 presidential campaign, the 1991 police beating of Rodney King and subsequent trial, and even the controversial events surrounding boxer Mike Tyson. Poems that deal with personal topics, such as being raped and coping with illness, reach outward and become expressions of anger and sympathy for other sufferers of injustice and violence: homosexuals, victims of police brutality, or the people of sub-Saharan Africa, Nicaragua, Bosnia, Kosovo, and Palestine.

Although Jordan's tone is frequently sarcastic, angry, and strident, in some sense all of her poems are love poems. Her militancy and unwillingness to be conciliatory appear to be guided by her love for the oppressed and marginalized; her denunciation of the oppressors is accompanied by the call to the victims not to capitulate, to gain and to preserve a sense of self-love and self-worth and then put it into action. This political engagement and her stridency in advocating her causes gained for Jordan many admirers in the women's and Civil Rights movements. Yet her militancy, particularly her refusal to embrace violence in the fight against oppression and injustice, also caused her to be met with coldness and even hostility in some circles. This may also explain why she was consistently overlooked in the selection for the Pulitzer Prize and the National Book Award, although her work was nominated for the latter in 1971.

Some Changes

Jordan's first substantial collection of poems is divided into four parts, each dedicated to a particular facet of her life that she felt needed revision and change. These poems were written in the years after the suicide of her mother and the dissolution of her own marriage; as such they are an assertion of her new independence as a woman, mother, poet, sexual person, and politically autonomous citizen; therefore she dedicates the volume to "new peoplelife."

This "new peoplelife" involves making peace with her mother and father in the opening poem. For the former, she has a list of promises; her father she would "regenerate." In "Poem for My Family: Hazel Griffin and Victor Hernando Cruz," Jordan expands the meaning of "family" beyond the traditional nuclear family to include all suffering people of her race.

In several other poems in the first half of the collection, Jordan's role as a single, working mother translates into concern for children in general and for her own son in particular. The tone of many of these early poems is dark. In "Not a Suicide Poem," she asserts that

> no one should feel peculiar living
> as they do
> . . . [in] terrific reeking epidermal
> damage
> marrow rot . . .

Other poems, such as "The Wedding" and "The Reception," assert a married woman's personal autonomy. Most notable of these is "Let Me Live with Marriage," a clever deconstruction of Shakespeare's sonnet beginning "Let me not to the Marriage of True Minds." Jordan's wish is to be allowed "to live with marriage/ as unruly as alive/ or else alone and longing/ not too long alone."

After declaring her independence from family and marriage in the first half and coming to terms with her losses ("I Live in Subtraction"), she indicates her growing sense of racial pride and political empowerment in the later poems of *Some Changes*. "What would I do white?" she asks in the opening poem of the third section, in which she declares herself in solidarity with all black people, whom she has incorporated into her extended family. In the final section she expands this family yet more to include all people living in poverty and oppression ("47,000 Windows") before returning to memories of her father and her family's former home on Hancock Street in Brooklyn, emphasizing the emptiness of the house and the forlorn wandering of her father after her mother's suicide ("Clock on Hancock Street").

In the final poem of the collection, pessimistically titled "Last Poem for a Little While," the speaker is saying grace at a Thanksgiving dinner of 1969, in which she thanks God "for the problems that are mine/ and evidently mine alone" and asks her fellow diners to "Pass the Ham./ And wipe your fingers on the flag."

In *Some Changes* Jordan found her independent poetic identity, acknowledging the influence of Shakespeare, T. S. Eliot, Emily Dickinson, and Walt Whitman but striking out confidently on her own path.

Naming Our Destiny

Naming Our Destiny: New and Selected Poems updates *Things That I Do in the Dark* to include her poetry up to 1989. It therefore gives the reader a good sense of which poems from her previous collections Jordan considered most worthy of attention. The volume's first section presents selections from *Things That I Do in the Dark* (1958-1977); the second contains poems from *Passion* (1977-1980); the third is a selection from *Living Room* (1980-1984); the fourth is composed of new poems written between 1984 and 1989.

Part 2 includes her most anthologized piece, "A Poem About My Rights." Jordan claimed that this poem was written in response to having been raped a few months before and that she intended to express her psychological reaction to this event. She emphatically states that victims of violence must resist the temptation to internalize the blame for the violent act and put it squarely on the shoulders of the perpetrators. She then characteristically extrapolates from her personal tragedy to the situation of violated people everywhere: "I am the history of rape/ I am the history of the rejection of who I am." As the poem indicates and as Jordan stated in interviews, the difference between her rape and the situation in apartheid South Africa was, for her, minimal. Her anger at this violation finds expression in the menacing final lines of the poem: "but I can tell you that from now on my resistance/ my simple and daily and nightly self-determination/ may very well cost you your life."

The new poems in *Naming Our Destiny* are collected in the fourth section under the title "North Star," a reference to the abolitionist newspaper founded by Frederick Douglass in 1847 and to the constellation that served as the navigational guide to Africans making their escape from slavery. Consequently, most of these poems are unabashedly political, taking to task most of Jordan's adversaries: the Israeli occupiers of Palestine; Bernard Goetz, the New York subway vigilante; the white supremacist rulers of South Africa; Ronald Reagan and the Nicaraguan Contras; the Marcos regime in the Philippines; and even Benjamin Franklin for declaring that there could be no lasting peace with Native Americans, "till we have well-drubbed them" ("Poem for Benjamin Franklin"). Other poems pay homage to friends and fellow activists, such as Angela Davis ("Solidarity").

Kissing God Goodbye
This slender collection of poems written between 1991 and 1997 restates many of the themes of Jordan's previous collections, but despite Jordan's battle with breast cancer, the tone of these poems is more optimistic and conciliatory, compared to the anger and stridency of her earlier work. The volume is dedicated to an anonymous lover and to the "Student Poet Revolutionaries" in her Poetry for the People project at Berkeley. Except for a harsh critique of the American air campaign against Iraq ("The Bombing of Baghdad") and the Israeli devastation of Lebanon, the poems are more personal, introspective, and accepting, particularly "First Poem after Serious Surgery" and "merry-go-round poetry."

The majority are intimate haikus and other poems to b.b.L., clearly a treasured lover, but even the lyricism of "Poem #7 for b.b.L.,"

> Baby
> when you reach out
> for me
> I forget everything
> except
> I do remember to breathe . . . .

is tempered in the last lines by a claim to breathing room.

In the title poem, "Kissing God Goodbye," which brings the collection to an end, the kinder and gentler June Jordan gives way once more to the strident activist, pouring sarcasm on what she considers the bigoted rhetoric of the antiabortion movement Operation Rescue:

> You mean to tell me on the 12th day or the 13th
> that the Lord . . .
> decided who could live and who would die? . . .
> You mean to tell me that the planet
> is the brainchild
> of a single
> male
> head of household?

In *Kissing God Goodbye*, then, Jordan reasserts her position as a fearless critic of American society and public policy, reconfirming her reputation as one of today's most gifted American poets. The Kosovo poem, "April 10, 1999," will surely strike a responsive chord in many readers:

> Nothing is more cruel
> than the soldiers who command
> the widow
> to be grateful
> that she's still alive.

Other Literary Forms

June Jordan's literary reputation is based almost equally on her poetry and her political and autobiographical essays, which she considered inextricably connected. Thus her poetry addresses many of the topics she discusses in her major essay collections. In addition she published a novel, books for children and young adults, an illustrated history of the Reconstruction and Civil Rights eras, dramatic pieces, and the prose memoir *Soldier: A Poet's Childhood.*

Bibliography

Brogan, Jacqueline V. "From Warrior to Womanist: The Development of June Jordan's Poetry." In *Speaking the Other Self: American Women Writers*, edited by Jeanne Campbell Reesman. Athens: University of Georgia Press, 1997. Traces Jordan's growth as a poet, concentrating on her life as a political and social activist.

Brown, Kimberly N. "June Jordan." In *Contemporary African American Novelists: A Bio-bibliographical Critical Sourcebook*, edited by Emmanuel S. Nelson. Westport, Conn.: Greenwood Press, 1999. A useful reference entry in a book devoted to African American writers.

Erickson, Peter. "The Love Poetry of June Jordan." *Callaloo* 9, no. 1 (Winter, 1986): 221-234. Discusses the poems in *Passion*, in particular those selected earlier for *Things That I Do in the Dark*. Claims that attention to Jordan's activist, political poetry has unjustly overshadowed her powerful love poetry.

Houtchens, Bobbi Ciriza. "A Great Loss, A Treasured Legacy." *English Journal* 92, no. 3 (January, 2003): 114-116. A tribute to the poet that details her long career as an activist and her influence on contemporary poetry.

MacPhail, Scott. "June Jordan and the New Black Intellectuals." *African American Review* 33, no. 1 (Spring, 1999): 57-72. Provides an analysis of Jordan's influences and works and the trials she has faced as an African American writer. Primarily concerned with the book *From Coming In to Coming Out*.

Metres, Philip. "June Jordan's War Against War." *Peace Review* 15, no. 2 (June, 2003): 171-178. Proposes that Jordan's unwavering antiwar activism be viewed as a model for all poets interested in making similar poetic statements. Lauds the poet's consistent devotion to antiwar causes.

Semitsu, Junichi P. "Defining June Jordan." *The New Crisis* 109, no. 5 (September/October, 2002): 13-15. A remembrance of the poet that describes some aspects of her upbringing, education, career highlights, and her impacts on students.

Sutton, Soraya, and Sheila Sablo Menezes. "In Remembrance of June Jordan, 1963 to 2002." *Social Justice* 29, no. 4 (Winter, 2002): 205-207. A tribute to Jordan's activist work and her impact in the classroom and in the literary community.

— Franz G. Blaha

William Melvin Kelley

Novelist

Born: Bronx, New York; November 1, 1937

LONG FICTION: *A Different Drummer,* 1962; *A Drop of Patience,* 1965; *dem,* 1967; *Dunfords Travels Everywheres,* 1970.
SHORT FICTION: *Dancers on the Shore,* 1964.

Achievements

William Melvin Kelley received several awards in the years in which he was actively publishing: the Dana Reed Prize from Harvard University, a Bread Loaf Scholar residency, the John Hay Whitney Foundation Award, the Rosenthal Foundation Award, the Transatlantic Review Award, and a fiction award from the Black Academy of Arts and Letters. These awards confirmed early recognition of Kelley's talent but have little to do with his enduring prominence as the creator of *A Different Drummer,* his first and most accomplished work, which brought him the accolades of such writers as Archibald MacLeish, Thomas Merton, and Frank Tuohy. As important in its own way as Ralph Ellison's *Invisible Man* (1952), James Baldwin's *Go Tell It on the Mountain* (1953), and William Demby's *Beetlecreek* (1950), *A Different Drummer* broke new ground within the confines of the subject of race in America. Visionary, grounded in myth and American history, it still confounds readers as they try to categorize and label this enduring novel of the civil rights era. Indeed, all Kelley's novels invite readers to consider the simple difference that race makes in America, as well as the complexity of the individual's dilemma and response in respect to this and other aspects of the human condition.

Biography

William Melvin Kelley is the only child of William Melvin Kelley, Sr., and Narcissa Agatha (Garcia) Kelley. His father was a journalist and an editor, for a time, at the *Amsterdam News*. When William was young, the family lived in an Italian American neighborhood in the North Bronx, but later his parents sent him to the Fieldston School, a small, predominantly white preparatory school in New York, where he became captain of the track team and president of the student council. In 1957, the year of his mother's death, Kelley entered Harvard, intending to study law. By the following year, however, the year of his father's death, he was studying fiction writing with author John Hawkes, and later,

(Library of Congress)

Archibald MacLeish. For the rest of his career (which he left unfinished) at Harvard, no other academic subject was relevant to him. Consumed by writing, he said, "I hope only to write fiction until I die, exploring until there is no longer anything to explore . . . [about] the plight of Negroes as individual human beings in America."

In 1962, after the publication of his first novel, Kelley married Karen Isabelle Gibson, a designer, and worked as a writer, photographer, and teacher in New York, France, and the West Indies. He is the father of two children, Jessica and Ciratikaiji. Though he continued to work on a book entitled *Days of Our Lives* and occasionally appear in print and in public life, Kelley, in large part, would maintain a quiet life.

Analysis: Long Fiction

Critics often fix on the interrelatedness of Kelley's four novels (and his short stories), and, indeed, though each novel is different in style, setting, characters, and even language, the ideas that spawned them are related and grow from each other. Critic Jill Weyant sees Kelley's work as a saga, in that the "purpose of writing a serious saga . . . is to depict impressionistically a large, crowded portrait, each individual novel presenting enlarged details of the whole, each complete in itself, yet evoking a more universal picture than is possible in a single volume." Kelley admits to the possible influence of other great writers of sagas, telling Roy Newquist in an interview, "Perhaps I'm trying to follow the Faulknerian pattern—although I guess it's really Balzacian when you connect everything. I'd like to be eighty years old and look up at the shelf and see that all of my books are really one big book."

A Different Drummer

A Different Drummer is Kelley's first and finest work, an enduring classic of African American literature. Kelley took his literary inspiration from American writer Henry David Thoreau's resounding celebration of individuality: "If a man does not keep pace with his companions, perhaps it is because he hears a different drummer. Let him step to the music which he hears, however measured or far away." Kelley then adapted this idea to the plight of African Americans in a fictional narrative built on a foundation of mythic imagination, American history all the way back to the slave trade, and the racial strife of the 1960's. The black experience of being perceived as different, as a despised people with trenchantly stereotyped racial characteristics, has been anything but positive. It is here, on this ground, that Kelley develops his narrative from two basic questions rooted deeply in the history of American race relations: What would whites do without the black people they so abuse and denigrate, but to whom they are so tied? Also, who might white people be without the prison of their own prejudice?

The novel takes place in the small town of Sutton, in a nameless, imaginary southern state, in June, 1957, when, mysteriously for the white citizens, "all the state's Negro inhabitants departed." The exodus is unconsciously led by the child-sized Tucker Caliban, who, like Rosa Parks (a black woman who refused to relinquish her bus seat to a white man in 1955), simply decided one day that he could no longer comply with the way things had always been in the South. The course of history, or at least his own family history, had to be changed. For four generations the Calibans were defined and limited by their service to the Willsons, and Tucker knows that he cannot reach his full human potential living in the template of the southern racial past. Thus he salts his land, kills his farm animals, axes the grandfather clock which symbolizes all the years of his family's servitude, sets fire to his house, and walks off into the sunset with his pregnant wife and his child. This peaceful, though revolutionary, act of individual initiative and vision is a direct outgrowth of and complement to the rebellion and flight of the massive legendary African whose story begins the novel. This African prince, Tucker's great-grandfather, refused to be enslaved, and it is perhaps his spirit that propels Tucker's quiet self-reliance generations later. Ironically, it is old white Mr. Harper who keeps the memory of the African alive for the white men of Sutton, telling the story on the porch of Thomason's store as often as anyone will listen.

Kelley mixes his multiple points of view between first- and third-person narration, using flashbacks to take his readers inside the heads of the southern whites, not the blacks, who occupy the small southern town of Sutton. The whites that interest Kelley are of two classes. Harry Leland and his young son, Mister Leland, represent the poor-white southerners who wish to break with the past, who wish to know black people as individuals and not as a subjugated mass. The Willsons represent the southern aristocracy, bound by the past and the money they made from slavery, but who are also educated and morally conflicted.

Tucker's opposite, a Harvard-educated black religious leader who comes down from the North to investigate the inspiration behind the exodus, becomes the novel's sacrificial lamb. The ultimately self-seeking Reverend Bennett Bradshaw is superfluous in Sutton; the people have led themselves out of their legacy of bondage and have no need of he who is not one of their own. He becomes flotsam of the most violent of southern white rituals, ironically taking up the cross that the people have left behind.

A Different Drummer is, indeed, as critic David Bradley writes, an "elegant" little book, masterful in its balance of scenes of stunning moment, delivered in the language and points of view of the people most in need of understanding them. Within its covers there is much to understand about the nature of freedom as an individual conviction that must be realized; all social change begins with a human being's belief in his or her own equality, and no lasting social change can happen without it.

A Drop of Patience

With *A Drop of Patience*, Kelley returns to the South to uncover the life of a blind black boy, Ludlow Washington, who is deposited in an institution and left to exist among the faceless masses that society, and particularly a segregated society, builds institutions to hide. Ludlow cannot walk away from his circumstances, like Tucker Caliban, because he is a child, and blind, so he must transcend in another way. He finds his means of self-expression and his route to finding a place in southern black society in his musical instrument, which is never identified but is clearly some sort of horn with several keys. Extremely talented, Ludlow is released to a black bandleader, who takes him to the small southern city of New Marsails to play with his group in a local bar. Ludlow is better than the other members of the band, however, and he has to hold his creative compulsion for avant-garde improvisation in check until he is old enough to be free of his contract, which is essentially indenture. Eventually he leaves the South and migrates to the North, becoming a leading jazz musician with his own band and enjoying relative freedom.

Though this is the framework for "one of the finest novels ever written about a jazz musician," according to critic Stanley Crouch, *A Drop of Patience* is not so much a novel about a musician as it is a novel about a blind boy coming to sexual maturity, and a black man who literally cannot see color (and is therefore able to override its coded constraints to discover deeper qualities in people) but who must come to social maturity in a superficial and pervasively race-bound society. It is a society that can drive a sane person mad, and it does this to Ludlow, who must, at bottom, be able to trust his own senses. At novel's end Ludlow chooses a course that will allow him to be a musician and to be a man among people who can see him.

dem

If *A Drop of Patience* is an enlarged detail of the people who left the imaginary southern state in *A Different Drummer,* then *dem* is an enlarged detail of the people who are incapable of seeing Ludlow Washington as a human being beyond his racial categorization. *dem* is the black perspective on American society's "us" and "them" dichotomy, and it makes sense that this novel is both a satire and a comedy. Satire typically employs sarcasm and irony to expose human folly or vice, and not only does comedic writing provide an absurd vehicle (lighthearted treatment) to transport an absurd commodity (pervasive race prejudice), it also provides the opportunity to temporarily "solve" this immense social problem with justice and laughter. In short, it provides catharsis.

Mitchell Pierce and his wife, Tam, are upper-middle-class white New Yorkers who are frank stereotypes. They are shallow, insular, cold, like mannequins or robots—devoid of the redeeming, individual, distinguishing features that human beings possess. Murder cannot move them, and love, to them, is a plot gleaned from soap operas. Tam gets pregnant by both her husband and her maid's black boyfriend and gives birth to twins, one white and one black. The rest of the novel is about Mitchell's ludicrous hunt through Harlem for the father of the black twin, whom he does not recognize when he sees him. For Mitchell, black people are simply a faceless race meant to serve him, and it never occurs to him that the money in his pocket cannot buy them.

Dunfords Travels Everywheres

Often dismissed by critics as "experimental," there is no doubt that *Dunfords Travels Everywheres* is a difficult book to read, but its inspiration is, after all, James Joyce's *Finnegans Wake* (1939). Critic Michael Wood notes that like Joyce, Kelley "as a black American and a writer, is caught in the language and culture of an enemy country," and Kelley's two protagonists in this novel, Chig Dunford and Carlyle Bedlow, might be understood to be acting this out. The hallucinatory dream sequences, which connect the separate adventures of these two characters, are their common ground, their realm of unconscious constructions of language with African retentions, characterized by black idiomatic expressions and dialect, phonetic sounds and spellings, puns and exuberant wordplays. The Harvard-educated Chig Dunford, hanging out in an imaginary country in Europe with what amounts to imaginary white friends, blurts out two words that are revelatory. He changes his course and finds himself making a surreal transatlantic journey to America, which is, perhaps, his own "Middle Passage" to a destination of self-realization. By journey's end, he has encountered the Harriet of Ludlow Washington's healing in *A Drop of Patience* as well as his Harlem counterpart, Carlyle Bedlow, who figures prominently in *dem* and in some of Kelley's short fiction. Further, it might be argued that Chig's voyage to Harlem, to a place where he can be known, is an updated version of Tucker Caliban's journey away from "dem people's" race-based expectations of him.

Other Literary Forms

In addition to his novels, for which he is primarily known, William Melvin Kelley is the author of a collection of short stories, *Dancers on the Shore*. Some of these stories were written before his first novel, and almost all introduce characters, themes, and ideas which appear in later works. A 1997 *New Yorker* story, "Carlyle Tries Polygamy: How Many Are Too Many?," reveals that, despite almost thirty years of nearly complete fiction-publication silence, Kelley maintained interest in creatively pursuing some of the personages and ideas that appeared earlier in his short and long fiction. Anthologized selections of his fiction mostly appeared in late 1960's and 1970's anthologies of African American writers. He has been a nonfiction and fiction contributor to periodicals such as *Accent, Canto, Esquire, Jazz and Pop, Mademoiselle, Negro Digest, The New Yorker, The New York Times Magazine, The Partisan Review, Playboy, Quilt, River Styx, Urbanite,* and *Works in Progress*.

Bibliography

Adams, Charles H. "Imagination and Community in W. M. Kelley's *A Different Drummer.*" *Critique* 26, no. 1 (Fall, 1984): 26-36. A thoughtful article that seeks to understand the notion of community—and the role of the individual in it—as each is created in Kelley's novel.

Babb, Valerie M. "William Melvin Kelley." In *Afro-American Fiction Writers After 1955*. Vol. 33 in *Dictionary of Literary Biography*, edited by Thadious M. Davis. Detroit: Gale, 1984. In the absence of book-length secondary sources, this is a good start to learning about Kelley. The bibliography includes critical essays and an interview.

Bradley, David. Foreword to *A Different Drummer*. New York: Doubleday, 1989. A carefully researched essay that considers Kelley's first novel in the context of its time and in relation to American William Faulkner's novels, particularly *The Reivers* (1962).

Early, Gerald. Introduction to *A Drop of Patience*. Hopewell, N.J.: Ecco Press, 1996. With a short overview of the black writers of the 1950's and a brief introduction to the Black Arts movement, Early positions Kelley's "jazz novel" on the cusp, between the two eras and of neither.

Hogue, W. Lawrence. "Disrupting the White/Black Binary: William Melvin Kelley's *A Different Drummer.*" *CLA Journal* 44, no. 1 (September, 2000): 1-42. Explains the concept of a white/black binary and its use in *A Different Drummer.* Gives a summary of Tucker Caliban's character and actions.

Karrer, Wolfgang. "Romance as Epistemological Design: William Melvin Kelley's *A Different Drummer.*" In *The Afro-American Novel Since 1960,* edited by Peter Bruck and Wolfgang Karrer. Amsterdam: Gainer, 1982. Karrer considers Kelley's novel of exodus as romantic rather than realistic and positions it among other romances by African American writers.

Ro, Sigmund. *Rage and Celebration: Essays on Contemporary Afro-American Writing.* Atlantic Highlands, N.J.: Humanities Press, 1984. Discusses African American literature, focusing on Kelley, John Alfred Williams, and James Baldwin.

Thomas, H. Nigel. "The 'Bad Nigger' Figure in Selected Works of Richard Wright, William Melvin Kelly, and Ernest Gaines" *CLA Journal* 39, no. 2 (December, 1995). Describes the notion of the "Bad Nigger" and its use as a tool for understanding the relationships between African and European Americans.

Weyant, Jill. "The Kelley Saga: Violence in America." *College Language Association Journal* 19, no. 2 (December, 1975): 210-220. Weyant proposes that Kelley's fiction may be the first saga written by a black American; she examines his work in the light of what she sees as his attempt to redefine the "Complete Man."

— *Cynthia Packard Hill*

Adrienne Kennedy

Playwright

Born: Pittsburgh, Pennsylvania; September 13, 1931

DRAMA: *Funnyhouse of a Negro*, pr. 1962, pb. 1969; *The Owl Answers*, pr. 1963, pb. 1969; *A Rat's Mass*, pr. 1966, pb. 1968; *The Lennon Play: In His Own Write*, pr. 1967, pb. 1968 (with John Lennon and Victor Spinetti); *A Lesson in Dead Language*, pr., pb. 1968; *Sun: A Poem for Malcolm X Inspired by His Murder*, pr. 1968, pb. 1971; *A Beast's Story*, pr., pb. 1969; *Boats*, pr. 1969; *Cities in Bezique: Two One Act Plays*, pb. 1969; *An Evening with Dead Essex*, pr. 1973; *A Movie Star Has to Star in Black and White*, pr. 1976, pb. 1984; *A Lancashire Lad*, pr. 1980; *Orestes and Electra*, pr. 1980; *Black Children's Day*, pr. 1980; *Adrienne Kennedy in One Act*, pb. 1988; *The Alexander Plays*, pb. 1992; *The Ohio State Murders*, pr., pb. 1992; *June and Jean in Concert*, pr. 1995; *Sleep Deprivation Chamber*, pr., pb. 1996 (with Adam Patrice Kennedy).

NONFICTION: *People Who Led to My Plays*, 1986.

MISCELLANEOUS: *Deadly Triplets: A Theatre Mystery and Journal*, 1990 (novella and journal); *The Adrienne Kennedy Reader*, 2001.

Achievements

Adrienne Kennedy departs from the theatrical naturalism used by other African American playwrights in favor of a surrealistic and expressionistic form. Her plays capture the irrational quality of dreams while offering insight into the nature of the self and being. Most of her works are complex character studies in which a given figure may have several selves or roles. In this multidimensional presentation lies Kennedy's forte—the unraveling of the individual consciousness.

The playwright received an Obie Award in 1964 for *Funny-*

house of a Negro, her best-known play, and two Obies in 1996 for *June and Jean in Concert* and *Sleep Deprivation Chamber.* She held a Guggenheim Fellowship in 1967 and was given grants from the Rockefeller Foundation, the New England Theatre Conference, the National Endowment for the Arts, and the Creative Artists Public Service. She also received the Third Manhattan Borough President's Award for Excellence, an Award in Literature from the American Academy of Arts and Letters, a Lila Wallace-Reader's Digest Fund Writer's Award, the Pierre LeComte du Nouÿ Foundation Award, and the American Book Award in 1990 for *People Who Led to My Plays.* Kennedy is included in *The Norton Anthology of African American Literature* and is one of a select few playwrights in the third edition of *The Norton Anthology of American Literature.* The Signature Theatre Company in New York dedicated its 1995-1996 season to Kennedy, offering audiences a retrospective of her dramatic works.

She was a lecturer at Yale University from 1972 to 1974 and a Yale Fellow from 1974 to 1975. In addition to lecturing at Yale, Kennedy has taught playwriting at Princeton and Brown universities.

Biography

Adrienne (Lita Hawkins) Kennedy was born on September 13, 1931, in Pittsburgh, Pennsylvania, the daughter of Cornell Wallace Hawkins, a social worker, and the former Etta Haugabook, a teacher. She grew up in Cleveland, Ohio, and attended Ohio State University, where she received a bachelor's degree in education in 1953. A few years later, she moved to New York and enrolled in creative writing classes at Columbia University and the New School for Social Research. In 1962, she joined Edward Albee's Playwrights' Workshop in New York City's Circle in the Square. She wrote *Funnyhouse of a Negro* for Albee's workshop. A decade later, she became a founder of the Women's Theater Council. In 1953, the playwright married Joseph C. Kennedy, whom she divorced in 1966. She has two sons.

Kennedy settled in New York, where she divided her time between writing and teaching. She continued to receive awards

(Library of Congress)

and recognition for her writing. On March 7, 1992, the opening date of her play *The Ohio State Murders*, the mayor of Cleveland proclaimed it Adrienne Kennedy Day.

Analysis: Drama

Adrienne Kennedy dares to be innovative both in her subject matter and in theatrical form. She writes difficult plays that raise questions rather than providing answers. From *Funnyhouse of a Negro* onward, Kennedy chose a subjective form that she has retained throughout her literary career. Her plays grow out of her own experiences as a sensitive and gifted black American who grew up in the Midwest. There may be little plot in Kennedy's plays, but there is, to be sure, a wealth of symbolism concerning the inherent tensions of the African American experience. Kennedy's daring break from a realistic style in theatrical writing, as well as her bold exploration of her own family history, cultural experience, and identity, provides a foundation for contemporary writers such as Suzan-Lori Parks, Ntozake Shange, and Anna Deveare Smith. These writers join Kennedy in expanding theatrical boundaries, creating theater that offers unforgettable images in culturally resonant, historically significant, and deeply personal plays.

Kennedy's plays are consistent in their exploration of the double consciousness of biracial African Americans who are inheritors of both African and European American culture and tradition. Symbolically represented by the split in the head of Patrice Lumumba, one of the selves in *Funnyhouse of a Negro*, this double identity frequently results in a schizophrenic division in which a character's selves or roles are at odds with one another. Typically it is the African identity with which the protagonist—who is often a sensitive, well-read young woman—is unable to come to grips. By using a surrealistic form to treat such a complex subject, Kennedy is able to suggest that truth can be arrived at only through the unraveling of distortion. Indeed, what Kennedy's protagonist knows of Africa and of blacks has come to her filtered through the consciousness of others who are eager to label Africans and their descendants "bestial" or "deranged." This seems to be what theater critic Clive Barnes meant when he said that Kennedy "thinks black, but she remembers white." For this reason, animal imagery, as well as black and white color contrasts, dominates Kennedy's plays.

Kennedy's concerns with isolationism, identity conflict, and consciousness are presented primarily through character. She has called her plays "states of mind," in which she attempts to bring the subconscious to the level of consciousness. She achieves this essentially by decoding her dreams. Indeed, many of the plays were actually dreams that she later translated into theatrical form. This surrealistic or dreamlike quality of her work has been compared to August Strindberg's dream plays, in that both dramatists render reality through the presentation of distortion. Extracting what is real from what is a distortion as one would with a dream is the puzzle Kennedy establishes for her characters, as well as for her audience, to unravel in each of her major plays: *Funnyhouse of a Negro, The Owl Answers, A Rat's Mass,* and *A Movie Star Has to Star in Black and White.*

Funnyhouse of a Negro

As in life, truth in Kennedy's plays is frequently a matter of subjectivity, and one character's version of it is often brought into question by another's. This is the case in *Funnyhouse of a Negro,* Kennedy's most critically acclaimed play. From the moment a somnambulist woman walks across the stage "as if in a dream" at the beginning of the play, the audience is aware that it is not viewing a realistic performance. Such figures onstage as the woman sleepwalker, women with "wild, straight black hair," a "hunchbacked yellow-skinned dwarf," and objects such as the monumental ebony bed, which resembles a tomb, suggest a nightmarish setting. The action of the play takes place in four settings: Queen Victoria's chamber, the Duchess of Hapsburg's chamber, a Harlem hotel room, and the jungle. Nevertheless, it is not implausible to suggest that the real setting of *Funnyhouse of a Negro* is inside the head of Sarah, Kennedy's protagonist. As Sarah tells the theater audience in her opening speech, the four rooms onstage are "[her] rooms."

As with the four sets that are really one room, Sarah has four "selves" who help to reveal the complexity of her character. At first, Sarah appears to be a version of the kindhearted prostitute, or perhaps a reverse Electra who hates rather than loves her father. Kennedy builds on these types to show Sarah's preoccupation with imagination and dreams, as well as her divided consciousness as a partaker of two cultures. Queen Victoria and the Duchess of Hapsburg are identified with Sarah's mother, or with her white European identity. The other two personalities, Jesus and Patrice Lumumba, the Congolese leader and martyr, on the other hand, are identified with Sarah's father, or with her black African heritage. Significantly, Sarah's four personalities tell the story of the parents' marriage and subsequent trip to Africa and the rape of the mother, which results in the conception of Sarah, each of which event can be called into question by the dreamlike atmosphere of the play and by the mother's insanity.

One by one, the four alter egos add details to the story that allow the picture of Sarah's family to build through accretion. Even so, this story is undermined by the final conversation between the landlady and Sarah's boyfriend, Raymond. Doubling as "the Funnyman" to the landlady's "Funnylady," Raymond comes onstage after Sarah's suicide to tell the audience the truth about Sarah's father in the epilogue to the play. Although Sarah claimed to have killed her father, Raymond tells the audience that the father is not dead but rather "liv[ing] in the city in a room with European antiques, photographs of Roman ruins, walls of books and oriental carpets."

The Owl Answers

The same eschewal of linear progression in *Funnyhouse of a Negro* occurs in *The Owl Answers,* the first of two one-act plays appearing with *A Beast's Story* in the collection titled *Cities in Bezique.* Clara Passmore, the protagonist in *The Owl Answers,* like Sarah in *Funnyhouse of a Negro,* is a sensitive, educated young woman torn between the two cultures of which she is a part. Riveted by her fascination for a culture that seems to want no part of her, Clara, a mulatto English teacher from Savannah, Georgia, learns from her mother that her father, "the richest white man in town," is of English ancestry. She comes to London to give him a fitting burial at Saint Paul's Cathedral, among the "lovely English." Once there, she has a breakdown and is imprisoned in the Tower of London by William Shakespeare, Geoffrey Chaucer, and William the Conquerer, who taunt her by denying her English heritage. Clara, who is the daughter of both the deceased William Mattheson and the Reverend Mr. Passmore (who, with his wife, adopted Clara when she was a child), is as firm in her claim to English ancestry as she is in her plans to bury her father in London. Like Sarah in *Funnyhouse of a Negro,* Clara's true prison exists in her mind. Ironically, Clara Passmore, whose name suggests racial passing, passes only from human into animal form. In a final, violent scene in which the third movement of Haydn's Concerto for Horn in D accentuates the mental anguish of Clara and her mother, Clara's mother stabs herself on an altar of owl feathers. Clara, in the meantime, fends off an at-

tack from a man whom she calls "God," who has assumed that
the love she seeks from him is merely sexual. Clara, who has
grown increasingly more owl-like as the play has progressed, ut-
ters a final "Ow . . . oww." In this play, as in *Funnyhouse of a Negro*,
Kennedy leaves the audience with questions about the nature of
spiritual faith in a world in which one calls on God, yet in which
the only answer heard comes from the owl.

A Rat's Mass

Similar preoccupations with the clash of African and European
culture in *Funnyhouse of a Negro* and *The Owl Answers* can be seen
in *A Rat's Mass*, a one-act play set in the time of the marching of
the Nazi armies. Brother and Sister Rat, who have a rat's head
and a rat's belly, respectively, are both in love with Rosemary, a
descendant of "the Pope, Julius Caesar, and the Virgin Mary."
The two rat siblings struggle to atone for the dark, secret sin
they committed when they "went on the slide together," which
has forced them into hiding in the attic of their home. Alone together in their misery, Kay and Blake, the sister and brother, remember a time when they "lived in a Holy Chapel with parents
and Jesus, Joseph, and Mary, our wise men and our shepherd."
Now they can only hear the gnawing of rats in the attic. In des-
peration, they turn to Rosemary to help them atone for their
sins. Rosemary refuses, stating that only through their deaths
will there be a way of atonement. The way comes when Jesus, Joseph, Mary, two wise men, and the shepherd return as the Nazi
army to open fire on the rats, leaving only Rosemary, like the ev-
ergreen shrub for which she is named, to remain standing.

A Movie Star Has to Star in Black and White

The animal motif employed in *The Owl Answers* and *A Rat's Mass*
is less apparent in *A Movie Star Has to Star in Black and White*.
Clara Passmore of *The Owl Answers* returns for a "bit role" in
which she reads from several of Kennedy's plays. The English literary tradition highly esteemed by the protagonist in *Funnyhouse of a Negro* and *The Owl Answers* is replaced by the American
film tradition. Reinforcing the theme of illusion versus reality
begun in *Funnyhouse of a Negro*, *A Movie Star Has to Star in Black*

and White is actually a series of plays-within-a-play in which scenes from the films *Now, Voyager* (1942), *Viva Zapata* (1952), and *A Place in the Sun* (1961) take place in a hospital lobby, Clara's brother's room, and Clara's old room, respectively. As the title of the play indicates—as well as a stage note directing that all the colors be shades of black and white—Kennedy continues her experimentation with black and white color contrasts onstage. As in other plays by Kennedy, linear progression is eschewed and the illusion of cinema merges with the reality of the life of Clara, a writer and daughter to the Mother and Father, the wife of Eddie, the mother of Eddie, Jr., and the alter ego of the film actresses.

Through lines spoken in the first scene by Bette Davis to Paul Henreid, the audience learns of Clara's parents' dream of success in the North, which ends in disappointment when they learn that racial oppression is not confined to the South. The scene takes place simultaneously on an ocean liner from *Now, Voyager* and in a hospital lobby in which Clara and her mother have come to ascertain the condition of Wally, Clara's brother, who lies in a coma.

Scene 2 moves to Wally's room, while Jean Peters and Marlon Brando enact lines from *Viva Zapata.* History repeats itself when it is revealed that Clara, like her mother before her, is having marital problems with her husband, Eddie. In the meantime, Marlon Brando's character changes the bedsheets onto which Jean Peters's character has bled, reminding the audience of Clara's miscarriage while Eddie was away in the armed services.

In the following scene, Shelley Winters and Montgomery Clift appear onstage in a small rowboat from the film *A Place in the Sun.* In this scene, Clara reveals her frustration as a writer who is black and a woman. She says that her husband thinks that her life is "one of my black and white movies that I love so . . . with me playing a bit part." The play ends with the news that Wally will live, but with brain damage. In the interim, Shelley Winters's character drowns as Montgomery Clift's character looks on, suggesting a connection between Clara's fantasy life in motion pictures and the real world, from which she struggles to escape.

Other Plays

Kennedy's other plays deal with themes similar to those in the works discussed. The animal motif, coupled with the theme of sexuality, is continued in *A Beast's Story* and *A Lesson in Dead Language*. In *A Beast's Story*, Beast Girl kills her child with quinine and whiskey and then kills her husband with an ax after he attempts to make love to her. Her parents, Beast Man and Beast Woman, preside over the dark course of events as shamans eager for their daughter to rid the household of the "intruder" whose presence has caused a black sun to hover above them. Animal imagery is paired with the rite-of-passage motif in *A Lesson in Dead Language*. In this play, a schoolteacher who is a white dog "from the waist up" instructs seven young girls about menstruation. Similarly, the dreamlike quality of earlier plays continues in *Sun*, a play-poem written about the death of Malcolm X, and in *An Evening with Dead Essex*, based on the assassination of black sniper Mark James Essex.

With the 1980's, Kennedy branched out into the writing of children's plays on commission. Among these plays are *A Lancashire Lad*, *Orestes and Electra*, and *Black Children's Day*. Kennedy wrote prolifically in the late 1980's and early 1990's, producing her esteemed "scrapbook of memories" *People Who Led to My Plays*, *Deadly Triplets: A Theatre Mystery and Journal*, and *The Alexander Plays*, the latter centering on the protagonist Suzanne Alexander and including such pieces as *The Ohio State Murders*, *She Talks to Beethoven*, *The Dramatic Circle*, and *The Film Club*.

Notable among her later works is her play *The Ohio State Murders*, the source of which was Kennedy's emotionally scarring experience as an undergraduate at Ohio State University. According to dramaturge Scott T. Cummings, "the play reflects [Kennedy's] abiding feeling that 'nothing has changed for American blacks,' that 'American blacks would have been better off leaving this country.'"

Other Literary Forms

In addition to her plays, Adrienne Kennedy has published a wide-ranging memoir, *People Who Led to My Plays*. In 1990, she published *Deadly Triplets: A Theatre Mystery and Journal.* In 2001, the University of Minnesota Press published Kennedy's *The Adrienne Kennedy Reader.* A collection of some of her best plays, the book also includes short stories and other prose works, including both published and previously unpublished material.

Bibliography

Barrios, Olga. "From Seeking One's Voice to Uttering the Scream: The Pioneering Journey of African American Women Playwrights Through the 1960s and 1970s." *African American Review* 37, no. 4 (Winter, 2003): 611-619. An examination of pioneering African American women playwrights. Primarily concerned with the pain these writers have experienced and the voyages of self-discovery they undergo through artistic creation.

Benston, Kimberly W. "*Cities in Bezique*: Adrienne Kennedy's Expressionistic Vision." *College Language Association Journal* 20 (1976): 235-244. In this essay on *The Owl Answers* and *A Beast's Story*, Benston delineates Kennedy's skillful use of expressionism. Sees part of Kennedy's richly symbolic form as having been borrowed from both the folktale and August Strindberg's dream plays.

Blau, Herbert. "The American Dream in American Gothic: The Plays of Sam Shepard and Adrienne Kennedy." *Modern Drama* 27 (1984): 520-539. Blau examines three plays by Shepard and three by Kennedy. Combines personal reflections on his work with Kennedy with sociological, psychological, and thematic approaches to her plays. Sees her as having been "out of place in the emergence of Black Power" and views powerlessness and death as obsessions in her oeuvre.

Bryant-Jackson, Paul, and Lois More Overbeck, eds. *Intersecting Boundaries.* Minneapolis: University of Minnesota Press, 1992. An anthology of essays on Kennedy's work, this volume consists of four parts, including interviews and critical analyses of her work by various scholars. The first of its sort on Kennedy's plays, it makes a substantial contribution to Kennedy scholarship.

Curb, Rosemary. "Fragmented Selves in Adrienne Kennedy's

Funnyhouse of a Negro and *The Owl Answers.*" *Theater Journal* 32 (1980): 180-195. Curb argues that Kennedy eschews linear narrative progression to portray "the fragmented mental states of her characters," with the central conflict occurring inside the main character's mind. Suggests that Kennedy is a "poet-playwright," examines Kennedy's central images alongside her theme of death, and compares her work to that of Ntozake Shange.

Hurley, Erin. "Blackout: Utopian Technologies in Adrienne Kennedy's *Funnyhouse of a Negro.*" *Modern Drama* 47, no. 2 (Summer, 2004): 200-219. An interesting exploration of the techniques Kennedy employs in her play.

Kennedy, Adrienne. "A Growth of Images." *Tulane Drama Review* 21 (1977): 41-47. Kennedy discusses her reasons for selecting autobiographical materials for her plays and states that most of them grow out of her dreams. Provides sources for Clara Passmore in *The Owl Answers.*

McDonough, Carla J. "God and the Owls: The Sacred and the Profane in Adrienne Kennedy's *The Owl Answers.*" *Modern Drama* 40 (1997): 385-402. McDonough explores the recurring motifs, dialogue, and theatrical images in both *The Owl Answers* and Kennedy's other plays, with particular attention to the blending of religious idolatry, colonialism, mixed-race heritage, family history, and female sexuality that *Owl* examines.

Meigs, Susan. "No Place but the Funnyhouse: The Struggle for Identity in Three Adrienne Kennedy Plays." In *Modern Drama: The Female Canon,* edited by June Schlueter. Rutherford, N.J.: Fairleigh Dickinson University Press, 1990. Meigs begins her discussion of *Funnyhouse of a Negro, The Owl Answers,* and *A Movie Star Has to Star in Black and White* by noting the significance of Kennedy's trip to Africa in 1960, which had a substantial impact on her worldview. Believes that the conflict between Western and African tradition and culture undergirds the major theme of Kennedy's "complex, surrealistic psychodramas."

Mickelbury, Penny. "Saluting an Innovative Dramatist: Ahead of Her Time, Playwright Adrienne Kennedy Paved the Way for

Ntozake Shange, George C. Wolfe, and the Rest." *Black Issues Book Review* 5, no. 5 (September/October, 2003): 34-36. Includes a brief biography and description of Kennedy's plays, as well as her primary influences and the awards she has received.

Sollors, Werner. "Owls and Rats in the American Funnyhouse: Adrienne Kennedy's Drama." *American Literature: A Journal of Literary History, Criticism, and Bibliography* 63 (1991): 507-532. States that Kennedy's oeuvre is best seen as "a full-fledged modern American attempt at rewriting family tragedy." Examines seven plays against the background of her autobiography, *People Who Led to My Plays*.

Zinman, Toby Silverman. "'In the Presence of Mine Enemies': Adrienne Kennedy's *An Evening with Dead Essex*." *Studies in American Drama, 1945-Present* 6 (1991): 3-13. Notes that unlike most of Kennedy's plays, this one "is based on a newspaper account, and is mostly male, apparently realistic, and raggedly structured." Concludes that Kennedy has enormous enemies in mind, including the American government and American society.

— Sheila McKenna; P. Jane Splawn

Jamaica Kincaid

(Elaine Potter Richardson)

Novelist and memoirist

Born: Saint Johns, Antigua; May 25, 1949

LONG FICTION: *Annie John*, 1985; *Lucy*, 1990; *The Autobiography of My Mother*, 1996; *Mr. Potter*, 2002.

SHORT FICTION: *At the Bottom of the River*, 1983.

NONFICTION: *A Small Place*, 1988; *My Brother*, 1997; *My Garden (Book)*, 1999; *Talk Stories*, 2001; *Among Flowers: A Walk in the Himalaya*, 2005.

CHILDREN'S/YOUNG ADULT LITERATURE: *Annie, Gwen, Lilly, Pam, and Tulip*, 1986 (with illustrations by Eric Fischl).

EDITED TEXTS: *The Best American Essays 1995*, 1995; *My Favorite Plant: Writers and Gardeners on the Plants They Love*, 1998.

Achievements

Jamaica Kincaid's short-story collection *At the Bottom of the River* received the Morton Dauwen Zabel Award from the American Academy of Arts and Letters in 1983. Her novel *Annie John* was one of three finalists for the international Ritz Paris Hemingway Award in 1985. Her short story "Xuela" was included in *The Best American Short Stories 1995*; "In Roseau" was included in *The Best American Short Stories 1996*.

Jamaica Kincaid made writing about her life her life's work. She developed a finely honed style that highlights personal impressions and feelings over plot development. Though she allows a political dimension to emerge from her use of Caribbean settings, her fiction does not strain to be political. Rather, the political issues relating to her colonial background are used to intensify the most important issue of her fiction: the intense bond between mother and daughter. Her spare, personal style simultaneously invites readers to enter her world and, by its

634

toughness, challenges them to do so. Although she made no specific effort to align herself with any ideology, her first book, *At the Bottom of the River,* quickly established her as a favorite among feminist and postcolonial critics, who lauded her personal but unsentimental presentation of the world of women and of the Caribbean.

Biography

Jamaica Kincaid was born Elaine Potter Richardson in Saint John's, Antigua, the daughter of Annie Richardson and Roderick Potter, a taxi driver. Her father was not a significant presence in her life. The man she considered her father was David Drew, a cabinetmaker and carpenter whom her mother married shortly after Elaine's birth. Elaine learned to read at the age of three, and when she turned seven, her mother gave her a copy of the *Concise Oxford Dictionary* as a birthday gift. The family was impoverished: Their house had no running water or electricity. The young girl's chores included drawing water from a community faucet and registering with the public works so that the "night soil men" would dispose of the family's waste. Even so, her childhood was idyllic. She was surrounded by the extraordinary beauty of the island, was accepted by her community, and was loved and protected by her mother.

The birth of her three brothers, Joseph in 1958, Dalma in 1959, and Devon in 1961 (whose death from AIDS in 1996 would provide the focus for *My Brother*), changed her life, not only because it meant that she was no longer an only child but also because she began to realize that her education would never be taken as seriously as her brothers' would be. While Elaine's parents made plans for their sons' university training, Elaine was sent to study with a seamstress twice a week. The closeness that Kincaid had enjoyed was at first disturbed and then destroyed. She credits the lies that she began to tell her mother as the catalyst for her fiction writing: "I wasn't really lying. I was protecting my privacy or protecting a feeling I had about something. But lying is the beginning of fiction. It was the beginning of my writing life." Also at this time, she began to

(Sigrid Estrada)

comprehend the insidious impact of colonialism. (Antigua was a British colony until 1967, and only in 1981 did it receive full independence.) The Antiguans' docile acceptance of their inferior status enraged her. Thus the serenity she had known as a child was displaced by loneliness and anger.

In 1966, Kincaid, seeking to disassociate herself from her mother, left Antigua not to return for nineteen years and then only after she was a naturalized citizen of the United States and an established writer. Arriving in Scarsdale, New York, the seventeen-year-old Kincaid worked as a live-in babysitter. She did not open letters from her mother, and when, after a few months, she took an au pair position in New York City, she did not send her mother her new address. For the next three years, she cared for the four young girls of Michael Arlen, a writer for *The New Yorker* and a future colleague when she herself would become a staff writer for the magazine. Her childhood and early New York experiences are fictionalized in *At the Bottom of the River, Annie John*, and *Lucy*.

Over the course of the next few years, she would study photography at the New School for Social Research and at Franconia College in New Hampshire before returning to New York to work briefly for the magazine *Art Direction*. In 1973 she sold her first professional publication, an interview with Gloria Steinem published in *Ingenue* on what life was like for the well-known feminist at the age of seventeen. In 1973 she also changed her name to Jamaica Kincaid, a move probably inspired by her need to create an anonymous, authorial identity; significantly, her adopted pen name marks her as Caribbean to the American reading audience, something her birth name does not. Also in 1973, George Trow, a writer for the "Talk of the Town" column in *The New Yorker*, started incorporating quotations by her in his writing (she was his "sassy black friend"), and her writing career was started. She worked as a freelance writer until she became a staff writer for *The New Yorker* in 1976 (a position she held until a 1995 disagreement with then-editor Tina Brown over the direction of the magazine led to her resignation). In 1979, she married Allen Shawn, son of William Shawn, the editor of *The New Yorker* at the time, and the couple moved to North Bennington, Vermont, where Shawn was on the faculty of Bennington College. The couple had two children, Annie (born in 1985) and Harold (born in 1989). Aside from being a novelist, Kincaid became a passionate gardener; she wrote on gardening for *The New Yorker* and edited a book of garden writing, *My Favorite Plant*, published in 1998.

Analysis: Long Fiction

Jamaica Kincaid is known for her impressionistic prose, which is rich with detail presented in a poetic style, her continual treatment of mother-daughter issues, and her relentless pursuit of honesty. More so than many fiction writers, she is an autobiographical writer whose life and art are inextricably woven together. She began her career by mastering the short story, the form from which her longer fiction grew. Most of the pieces that constitute *At the Bottom of the River* and *Annie John* were first published in *The New Yorker*, as were the chapters of *Lucy*. Though the individual pieces in each work have a self-contained unity, *Annie John* and *Lucy* also have a clear continuity from story to story, something less true of the impressionistic writing of *At the Bottom of the River*; thus, it is often considered a collection of short stories, while *Annie John* and *Lucy* are clearly novels. Nonetheless, it was *At the Bottom of the River* that won for Kincaid the Morton Dauwen Zabel Award for short fiction and that contained "Girl," a story written as a stream of instructions from a mother to a daughter, which is her best-known piece.

Kincaid's native Antigua is central in her writing. This colonial setting strongly relates to her mother-daughter subject matter, because the narrators Annie and Lucy of her first two novels both seem to make a connection between their Anglophile mothers and the colonial English, and also because the childhood experiences of both narrators have been shaped by a colonial background that limits their options and makes their relationships with their mothers that much more intense.

Beginning with *Lucy*, Kincaid cultivates a detachment with which she explores issues of anger and loss, carefully disallowing any easy resolution. Kincaid seems less interested in solving fictional problems than in exploring contrary states of mind that perceive problems. Admittedly, this style is not to everyone's taste, and quite a few readers who were seduced by Kincaid's earlier works were less pleased with *Lucy* and *The Autobiography of My Mother*. However, even if her incantatory rhythms and her tight focus on bleak, emotional situations in her post-*Annie John* works are not universally appreciated, few readers deny her eye for poetic detail and her ability to achieve a shimmering honesty in her prose.

Annie John

Kincaid's first novel, *Annie John*, is about a talented young girl in Antigua who, while growing into early womanhood, must separate herself from her mother. Fittingly, the book begins with a story of her recognition of mortality at the age of ten. Fascinated by the knowledge that she or anyone could die at any time, she begins to attend the funerals of people she does not know. At one point, she imagines herself dead and her father, who makes coffins, so overcome with grief that he cannot build one for her, a complex image suggesting her growing separation from her family. When, after attending a funeral for a child she did know, Annie neglects to bring home fish, as her mother demanded, Annie's mother punishes her before kissing her good-night. Though this ending kiss suggests a continued bond between mother and daughter, the next chapter places it in a different context. The title "The Circling Hand" refers to her mother's hand on her father's back when Annie accidentally spies her parents making love. Almost as if in contradiction to the reassuring maternal kiss of the earlier story, this chapter offers the rising specter of sexuality as a threat that will separate mother and daughter. Annie learns not only that she must stop dressing exactly like her mother but also that she must someday be married and have a house of her own. This is beyond Annie's comprehension.

Though Annie never fully understands this growing distance from her mother, she contributes to it. For instance, when she becomes friends with a girl at school named Gwen, she does not tell her mother. In part, she is transferring her affections to friends as a natural process of growing up, but as the chapters "Gwen" and "The Red Girl" make clear, she is also seeking comfort to ease the disapproval of her mother. Gwen becomes her best friend, and Annie imagines living with her, but Gwen is replaced briefly in Annie's affections by the Red Girl, who is a friend and cohort with whom Annie plays marbles, against the wishes of her mother.

The growing separation from her mother comes to a crisis in the chapter "The Long Rain," when Annie lapses into an extended depression and takes to her bed. When medicine and the cures of a local conjure woman do nothing to help, Annie's grandmother, Ma Chess, also a conjure woman, moves in with her. The weather remains damp the entire time Annie remains bedridden, and she feels herself physically cut off from other people. When she is finally well enough to return to school, she discovers she has grown so much that she needs a new uniform;

symbolically, she has become a new person. Thus it is that the last chapter, "The Long Jetty," begins with Annie thinking, "My name is Annie John," an act of self-naming that is also an act of self-possession. The chapter tells of Annie's last day in Antigua as she prepares to meet the ship that will take her to England, where she plans to study to become a nurse. A sensitive, detailed portrayal of a leave-taking, this chapter serves as a poignant farewell to childhood and to the intimacy with her mother that only a child can know. This last chapter captures perfectly Kincaid's ability to tell a story sensitively without sentimentality.

Lucy

Kincaid's third novel, *Lucy*, is a thematic sequel to her first. Lucy is seventeen when the novel begins, newly arrived in the United States from Antigua to work as an au pair, watching the four girls of Lewis and Mariah, an upper-middle-class New York couple. Although the novel is set entirely outside Antigua and Lucy's mother never appears in it, Lucy's attempt to separate herself from her mother constitutes the main theme of the novel.

Mariah is presented as a loving but thoroughly ethnocentric white woman. A recurring example of this is her attempt to make Lucy appreciate the Wordsworthian beauty of daffodils, unaware that it is precisely because Lucy had to study Wordsworth's poetry about a flower that does not grow in Antigua that this flower represents the world of the colonizer to her. In fact, Mariah's unselfconscious, patronizing goodwill is exactly what Lucy loves most and yet cannot tolerate about her employer, because it reminds her of her mother.

When Lucy learns that Lewis is having an affair with Mariah's best friend, Dinah, she understands that this idyllic marriage is falling apart. When a letter from home informs her that her father has died, she is unable to explain to Mariah that her anger toward her mother is based on mourning the perfect love she had once felt between them. At the same time, her own sexuality begins to emerge, and she develops interests in young men. Wanting more space, she moves in with her friend Peggy, a young woman who represents a more exciting world to Lucy, cutting short her one-year au pair agreement. The novel ends with Lucy writing her name, Lucy Josephine Potter, in a book and wishing that she could love someone enough to die for that love. This ending clearly signals an act of self-possession (much like the self-naming at the end of *Annie John*), but it also signifies the loneliness of breaking away from others, even to assert oneself. Though *Lucy* is a much angrier novel than *Annie John*, Lucy's anger is best understood in terms of the writer's earlier autobiographical surrogate in *Annie John*; the melancholy that debilitates Annie at the end of her novel is turned into anger by Lucy.

The Autobiography of My Mother

The Autobiography of My Mother is a tough, bleakly ironic novel written by a writer at the full height of her powers. It follows Xuela Claudette Richardson, a Caribbean woman who aborted her only pregnancy. If this fact seems to imply that Kincaid has taken a step away from the style of autobiographical fiction, the self-contradictory title and the main character's last name, Richardson, a name she shares with Jamaica Kincaid, both suggest that this story is not very far removed from the facts of Kincaid's own family.

The novel begins with the narrator proclaiming that her mother died the moment she was born, "and so for my whole life there was nothing standing between myself and eternity." This interesting statement reveals as much about the importance of mothers in Kincaid's writing as about the character Xuela. She lives with her father and a stepmother, who hates her and may have tried to kill her with a poisoned necklace, until she is sent at fifteen to live with a wealthy couple. Ostensibly, she is to be a student, but in fact she is to be the man's mistress.

Though the relationship between the colonizer and the colonized is important in all of Kincaid's writing, *The Autobiography of My Mother* brings it to the foreground in different ways. The first words Xuela learns to read are the words "the British Empire," written across a map. Meanwhile, her stepmother refuses to speak to Xuela in anything other than a patois, or provincial dialect, as if to reduce Xuela to the status of an illegitimate subject of the empire. When Xuela eventually marries (after many affairs with men), it is to a man she identifies as "of the victors"— the British. She takes a cruel satisfaction in refusing to love him, even though, according to her, he lived for the sound of her footsteps. Though it is never a relationship based on love, she lives with him for many years, and he becomes for her "all the children I did not allow to be born." While this is hardly an ideal relationship, it is not a completely empty one.

Toward the end, Xuela declares that her mother's death at the moment of her birth was the central facet of her life. Her ironic detachment from life seems to have been based on this, as if, devoid of the only buffer between herself and the hardship of life that she can imagine—a mother—she further rejects all other comforts and answers that people wish to propose. If Xuela is the least likable of Kincaid's main characters, her tough-as-nails approach to the world nonetheless makes her among the most compelling.

Analysis: Short Fiction

Jamaica Kincaid is noted for her lyrical use of language. Her short stories and novels have a hypnotic, poetic quality that results from her utilization of rhythm and repetition. Her images, drawn from her West Indian childhood, recall Antigua, with its tropical climate, Caribbean food, local customs, and folklore laced with superstitions. Many of her stories move easily from realism to surrealistic fantasy, as would a Caribbean folktale. She is also praised for her exploration of the strong but ambiguous bond between mother and daughter and her portrayal of the transformation of a girl into a woman. Thus her work touches upon the loss of innocence that comes when one moves out of the Eden that is childhood. These are the features that are found not only in her short fiction but also in her novels, the chapters of which *The New Yorker* originally published as short stories, and in *Annie, Gwen, Lilly, Pam, and Tulip*, a children's book that was part of a project designed by the Whitney Museum of American Art, the original publisher, who sought to bring together contemporary authors and artists for a series of limited editions aimed primarily at collectors.

Kincaid's concern with racism, colonialism, classicism, and sexism is rooted in her history: "I never give up thinking about the way I came into the world, how my ancestors came from Africa to the West Indies as slaves. I just could never forget it. Or forgive it." She does not hesitate to tackle these issues in her writing. In her nonfictional *A Small Place*, she directs the force of her language toward an examination of her native island of Antigua, presenting the beauty as well as the racism and corruption rooted in its colonial past. In her fiction, these same issues are not slighted; for example, *Annie John* and *Lucy* address various forms of oppression and exploitation.

Jamaica Kincaid's short stories, strongly autobiographical, are often set in the West Indies or incorporate images from the islands and include many events from her youth and young adulthood. In general, her stories chronicle the coming-of-age of a young girl. Because the mother-daughter relationship is central to the process, Kincaid often examines the powerful bond between them, a bond that the child must eventually weaken, if not break, in order to create her own identity. Kincaid has been accurately called "the poet of girlhood and place."

"Girl"

The first of the ten stories in *At the Bottom of the River* is the often praised and quoted "Girl." Barely two pages in length, the story outlines the future life of a young girl growing up on a small Caribbean island. The voice heard belongs to the girl's mother as she instructs her daughter in the duties that a woman is expected to fulfill in a culture with limited opportunities for girls. Twice the girl interrupts to offer a feeble protest, but her mother persists.

The girl is told how to wash, iron, and mend clothes; how to cook fritters and pepper pot; how to grow okra; and how to set the table—in short, everything that will enable her to care for a future husband. She is told how to smile, how to love a man, and how to get rid of an unborn baby should it be necessary. Most important, however, her mother warns her about losing her reputation because then the girl (and this is unsaid) loses her value as a potential wife. Almost as a refrain, the mother cautions, "On

Sundays try to walk like a lady and not like the slut you are so bent on becoming" or "This is how to behave in the presence of men who don't know you very well, and this way they won't recognize immediately the slut I have warned you against becoming." On the island, the girl's most important asset is her virginity.

The language is a prime example of Kincaid's ability to work a hypnotic spell. The story consists of a series of variations on particular instruction: "This is how to sew on a button; this is how to make a buttonhole for the button you have just sewed on; this is how to hem a dress when you see the hem coming down and so to prevent yourself from looking like the slut I know you are so bent on becoming." The rhythm and repetition create a lyric poetic quality that is present to some degree in all Kincaid's fiction. Her prose demands to be read out loud.

"Girl" suggests the child's future life on the island, but several stories in the collection re-create the atmosphere of her present existence. The story "In the Night" recounts her daily experiences. Thus, details such as crickets or flowers that would be important to her are recorded, often in the form of lists or catalogs: "The hibiscus flowers, the flamboyant flowers, the bachelor's buttons, the irises, the marigolds, the whiteheadbush flowers, lilies, the flowers on the daggerbush," continuing for a full paragraph. Here cataloging, a familiar feature of Kincaid's prose, represents a child's attempt to impose an order on her surroundings. The young narrator does not question her world but only reports what she observes. Thus witchcraft exists side by side with more mundane activities: "Someone is making a basket, someone is making a girl a dress or a boy a shirt . . . someone is sprinkling a colorless powder outside a closed door so that someone else's child will be stillborn." This melding of the commonplace with the supernatural occurs frequently in Kincaid's fiction. The narrator's troubles, such as wetting the bed, are those of a child and are easily resolved by her mother. Her plans for the future, marrying a woman who will tell her stories, also are typical of a child. This is an idyllic world before the fall from innocence, a world in which everything is ordered, listed, and cataloged. Nothing is threatening, since the all-powerful mother protects and shields.

"Holidays"

In several other stories, including "Wingless" and "Holidays," the girl is again shown to be occupied by the usually pleasant sensations of living: walking barefoot, scratching her scalp, or stretching, but sometimes, as illustrated in "Holidays," experiencing pain: "spraining a finger while trying to catch a cricket ball; straining a finger while trying to catch a softball; stepping on dry brambles while walking on the newly cut hayfields." The trauma, however, is clearly limited to physical sensations. When the child thinks of the future, the images are those of wishful thinking, similar to daydreams. This tranquil state of youth, however, is only temporary, as "Wingless" implies. The narrator, wingless, is still in the "pupa stage."

"The Letter from Home"

In "The Letter from Home," the narrator's growing awareness makes it impossible for her to maintain the comforting simplicity of her child's world. Questions about life and death intrude: "Is the Heaven to be above? Is the Hell below?" These inquiries, however, are set aside in favor of the present physical reality—a cat scratching a chair or a car breaking down. Even love and conception are reduced to the simplest terms: "There was a bed, it held sleep; there was movement, it was quick, there was a being." She is not ready to confront the idea of death, so when death beckons, she "turned and rowed away."

"What I Have Been Doing Lately"

Just as the philosophical questions about life and death disrupt the bliss of childhood, so does the journey toward selfhood, which Kincaid symbolically represents as a journey over rough or impassable terrain or water. In "What I Have Been Doing Lately," the obstacle is water: "I walked for I don't know how long before I came to a big body of water. I wanted to get across it but I couldn't swim. I wanted to get across it but it would take me years to build a boat. . . . I didn't know how long to build a bridge." Because the journey is difficult, as any passage to adult-hood would be, the narrator is hesitant, afraid of finding the world not beautiful, afraid of missing her parents, so she goes back to bed: She is not ready yet. Soon, however, she will not have the option of retreating and waiting.

"My Mother"

The journey toward selfhood necessitates a separation from the mother, as is suggested in the story "My Mother." The protection that was vital during childhood becomes stifling in adolescence: "Placing her arms around me, she drew my head closer and closer to her bosom, until finally I suffocated." Furthermore, the girl's feelings are ambiguous. Realizing that she has hurt her mother, she cries, but then she utilizes those tears to create a pond, "thick and black and poisonous," to form a barrier over which they "watched each other carefully." The all-protecting mother of the earlier stories transforms herself into a mythic monster and thus threatens the emerging selfhood of the daughter. The daughter, however, also grows "invincible" like her mother, and she, too, metamorphoses into a similar beast. Strong as the daughter has become, however, she can never vanquish her mother: "I had grown big, but my mother was bigger, and that would always be so." Only after the daughter completes her own journey toward selfhood is her mother no longer a threat: "As we walked along, our steps became one, and as we talked, our voices became one voice, and we were in complete union in every way. What peace came over me then, for I could not see where she left off and I began, or where I left off and she began."

"At the Bottom of the River"

The concluding and title story is also the longest in the collection, at about twenty pages. "At the Bottom of the River" suggests answers to the questions raised in the other stories. Again, Kincaid employs the symbol of a journey through forbidding terrain to suggest traveling through life. What is the purpose of the journey, for what does one ultimately face but death? One man, overwhelmed, does nothing. Another discovers meaning in his family, his work, and the beauty of a sunrise, but still he struggles and "feels the futility." How can one live with the paralyzing knowledge that "dead lay everything that had lived and dead also lay everything that would live. All had had or would have its season. And what should it matter that its season lasted five billion years or five minutes?" One possible response is suggested in the life of "a small creature" that lives in the moment, aware only of the sensation of grass underfoot or of the sting of a honeybee.

The narrator, who at first knew only the love of her mother, suffers from its necessary withdrawal. Adrift, she embarks on a symbolic journey in which she submerges herself in a river-fed sea. Discovering a solution at the bottom of the river, she emerges with a commitment to the present. Death, because it is natural, cannot be destroyed, but the joys derived from the commonplace—books, chairs, fruit—can provide meaning, and she "grow[s] solid and complete."

"Xuela"

Kincaid's story "Xuela" became the first chapter of her novel *The Autobiography of My Mother.* Like many of her other stories, it is set against a rich description of the botany and geography of tropical Dominica, and it continues Kincaid's meditation on the theme of mothers and daughters. Xuela, the daughter who shares her mother's name, also shares with many Kincaid women an anger at the mother who has rejected her and a fury at the world which little understands—and little cares—about her needs.

In the story's first sentence, the reader learns that Xuela's mother died in giving her birth, and the rest of the story is the record of the first seven years of Xuela's life. Her father places the infant in the care of Eunice, his laundry woman, and visits her every two weeks when he delivers the dirty clothes. He is physically and emotionally incapable of caring for his daughter, and is oblivious to his laundrywoman's lack of affection for her foster child.

The child, however, knows very well that her foster mother has no use for her, and she grows ever more bitter and withdrawn. When she breaks Eunice's treasured china plate, she cannot bring herself to utter the words "I'm sorry." Like the turtles she captures and carelessly kills, Xuela has withdrawn into a shell which threatens to destroy her with enforced isolation.

At that point her father sends Xuela to school. The few other students are all boys; like their teacher they are "of the African people" and unable to respond to the powerful element of Carib Indian in Xuela's ancestry. The teacher wears her own African heritage like a penance and is quick to label Xuela's intelligence as a sign of her innate evil. When the child is found writing letters to her father, he removes her from the school and takes her to live with him and his new wife, another woman who has no love for the child. Like her insensitive teacher, her father's power as a jailer seems to suggest the destructive powers of colonialism, another Kincaid theme.

Through all these trials, the child is sustained by a vision of her mother, who appears to her in sleep. In the dream, she sees her true mother descending a ladder to her, but always the dream fades before she can see more than her mother's heels and the hem of her robe. Frustrating as it is, the dream also comes to represent the presence of the only person outside herself that Xuela can identify with unreserved love.

The story's themes of the mother who, from the child's point of view, has willfully withdrawn her love joins with the theme of the child's wakening to the use of sexuality to replace her lost mother's love, linking this story to the rest of Kincaid's work.

Kincaid's stories are praised for their strong images, poetic language, and challenging themes, and they are criticized for their lack of plot and sometimes obscure symbolism. Any reader, however, who, without reservations, enters Kincaid's fictive world will be well rewarded.

Other Literary Forms

In addition to her short stories and novels, Jamaica Kincaid has written a book-length essay concerning her native island Antigua entitled *A Small Place*; a children's book, *Annie, Gwen, Lilly, Pam, and Tulip*, with illustrations by Eric Fischl, and the nonfiction works *My Brother* and *My Garden (Book)*. In 1998, she edited *My Favorite Plant: Writers and Gardeners on the Plants They Love.* Additionally, as a staff writer for *The New Yorker* for twenty years, she wrote numerous "Talk of the Town" pieces and frequent articles on gardening.

Bibliography

Als, Hilton. "Don't Worry, Be Happy." Review of *Lucy*, by Jamaica Kincaid. *The Nation* 252 (February 18, 1991): 207-209. Als compares the novel with *A Small Place*, since both are concerned with oppression. Als emphasizes Kincaid's importance as a Caribbean writer who is not afraid to tackle the issues of racism and colonialism at the risk of alienating readers.

Bloom, Harold, ed. *Jamaica Kincaid.* Philadelphia: Chelsea House, 1998. A collection of some of the best essays about the author, geared primarily to an audience of graduate students and scholars.

Davies, Carole Boyce. *Black Women, Writing, and Identity: Migrations of the Subject.* New York: Routledge, 1994. Focuses on the importance of migration in the construction of identity in black women's fiction in the United States, Africa, and the Caribbean. Especially insightful regarding Kincaid's *Lucy.*

De Abruna, Laura Nielsen. "Jamaica Kincaid's Writing and the Maternal-Colonial Matrix." In *Caribbean Women Writers*, edited by Mary Condé and Thorunn Lonsdale. New York: St. Martin's Press, 1999. Discusses Kincaid's presentation of women's experience, her use of postmodern narrative strategies, and her focus on the absence of the once-affirming mother or mother country that causes dislocation and alienation.

Ellsberg, Peggy. "Rage Laced with Lyricism." Review of *A Small Place*, by Jamaica Kincaid. *Commonweal* 115 (November 4, 1988): 602-604. In her review of *A Small Place*, with references to *At the Bottom of the River* and *Annie John*, Ellsberg justifies the anger that is present in *A Small Place*, anger that is occasioned by exploitation.

Emery, Mary Lou. "Refiguring the Postcolonial Imagination: Tropes of Visuality in Writing by Rhys, Kincaid, and Cliff."

Tulsa Studies in Women's Literature 16 (Fall, 1997): 259-280. Emery uses one of Jean Rhys's novels to illustrate a dialectical relationship between the European means of visualization and image-making in postcolonial literatures as something not just of the eye. Argues that the use of the rhetorical trope of ekphrasis (an artistic hybrid) reflects the cultural hybrid nature of postcolonial literature.

Ferguson, Moira. *Jamaica Kincaid: Where the Land Meets the Body.* Charlottesville: University Press of Virginia, 1994. In a book clearly oriented to scholars and graduate students, Ferguson provides a politically informed interpretation of Kincaid's writing that emphasizes the importance of the colonial setting in her works.

Garis, Leslie. "Through West Indian Eyes." *The New York Times Magazine* 140 (October, 7, 1990): 42. Based on an interview with Kincaid, this six-page article is the best source of information about Kincaid's life. Contains details about her childhood in Antigua, her relationship with her mother, her early interest in books, her early years in New York, and her marriage to Allen Shawn. Includes illustrations.

Holcomb, Gary E. "Travels of a Transnational Slut: Sexual Migration in Kincaid's *Lucy.*" *Critique* 44, no. 3 (Spring, 2003): 295-313. Examines the role of migration and diasporas and their relationship to imperialism in the novel.

Hoving, Isabel. "Remaining Where You Are: Kincaid and Glissant on Space and Knowledge." *Thamyris/Intersecting: Place, Sex & Race* 9, no. 1 (May, 2003): 125-141. A discussion of the importance of travel and migration in Kincaid's work, and in postcolonial literature in general. The author considers the relationship between ideas of home and the pursuit of knowledge and experience.

Kincaid, Jamaica. "An Interview with Jamaica Kincaid." Interview by Kay Bonetti. *Missouri Review* 15, no. 2 (Winter, 1992): 124-142. An interview in which the author talks at great length about her mother's influence on her and about her deeply ambivalent feelings about her homeland.

_____. "A Lot of Memory: An Interview with Jamaica Kincaid." Interview by Moira Ferguson. *The Kenyon Review,* n.s. 16 (Winter, 1994): 163-188. Kincaid discusses the inspiration for her writing and the reasons she wrote her first book in an experimental style; describes the influence of the English tradition on fiction in the Caribbean; comments on the nature of colonial conquest as a theme she explores through the metaphor of gardening.

Milton, Edith. "Making a Virtue of Diversity." Review of *At the Bottom of the River*, by Jamaica Kincaid. *The New York Times Book Review*, January 15, 1984, 22. Milton presents the major criticism of Kincaid's fiction—that the stories are obscure, plotless, and too visionary. Milton also discusses the strong Caribbean folktale influence evident in Kincaid's stories.

Onwordi, Iki. "Wising Up." Review of *At the Bottom of the River* and *Annie John*, by Jamaica Kincaid. *The Times Literary Supplement*, November 29, 1985, 1374. A brief review in which Onwordi discusses the works' similarities, especially in language and themes.

Rejouis, Rose-Myriam. "Caribbean Writers and Language: The Autobiographical Poetics of Jamaica Kincaid and Patrick Chamoiseau." *Massachusetts Review* 44, nos. 1/2 (Spring/Summer, 2003): 213-233. Explores the different ways in which the two authors have referenced Caribbean and Creole literature and places their works in autobiographical contexts.

Simmons, Diane. *Jamaica Kincaid*. New York: Twayne, 1994. A clear, lucid critical overview of Kincaid's life and work. A good introduction to her work for nonspecialist readers.

— *Thomas Cassidy; Ann Davison Garbett; Barbara Wiedemann*

Martin Luther King, Jr.

Activist, essayist, and orator

Born: Atlanta, Georgia; January 15, 1929
Died: Memphis, Tennessee; April 4, 1968

NONFICTION: *Stride Toward Freedom: The Montgomery Story*, 1958; *The Measure of a Man*, 1959; *Letter from Birmingham City Jail*, 1963; *Strength to Love*, 1963; *A Martin Luther King Treasury*, 1964; *Why We Can't Wait*, 1964; *The Trumpet of Conscience*, 1967; *Where Do We Go from Here?*, 1967; *The Words of Martin Luther King, Jr.*, 1983, 1987; *A Testament of Hope: The Essential Writings and Speeches of Martin Luther King, Jr.*, 1986, 1991; *The Papers of Martin Luther King, Jr.*, 1992-2000 (4 volumes; Clayborne Carson, editor); *The Autobiography of Martin Luther King*, 1998 (Carson, editor); *A Knock at Midnight: Inspiration from the Great Sermons of Reverend Martin Luther King, Jr.*, 1998 (Carson and Peter Halloran, editors); *A Call to Conscience: The Landmark Speeches of Dr. Martin Luther King, Jr.*, 2001 (Carson, editor).

Achievements

The life of Martin Luther King, Jr., ended by an assassin's bullet nine months short of his fortieth birthday, was filled with achievements. He did so well in school that he was admitted to Morehouse College at the age of fifteen. After graduation, King continued his education at Crozier Theological Seminary and at Boston University, where he received a Ph.D. in 1955. His first preaching assignment was in Montgomery, Alabama, in 1954. The following year, Rosa Parks, a black woman, refused to yield her bus seat to a white man and was arrested. Local blacks organized the Montgomery Improvement Association (MIA) to protest Parks's arrest, and they elected King president. In this capacity, he spearheaded a yearlong boycott by black residents against Montgomery's public transportation system and white merchants, crippling them financially.

This act brought national and international attention to King's efforts and resulted in a ruling from the Supreme Court of the United States declaring racial segregation on public conveyances illegal. King became a dynamic and nonviolent civil rights activist who organized other protests against racial discrimination in Birmingham and Selma, Alabama. He was named *Time* magazine's Person of the Year in 1963 and received the Nobel Peace Prize in 1964. King is one of only three Americans whose birthday is a national holiday.

Biography

Martin Luther King, Jr., was the son of a Baptist minister, Martin Luther King, Sr., and his wife, Alberta Christine Williams King, a teacher. The elder King was pastor of Ebenezer Baptist Church in Atlanta. After completing his undergraduate education, King continued his studies in the Philadelphia area and then in Boston, as a doctoral student at Boston University. Here he met Coretta Scott, a concert singer, whom he married in 1953.

In 1959, the Kings traveled to India to pursue Martin's interest in Mahatma Gandhi's means of changing society through nonviolent means. Gandhi's philosophy impressed King. He visited the places where Gandhi had struggled against the British and met people who had known Gandhi, who was clearly one of King's heroes.

This trip convinced King that nonviolence was the only justifiable form of protest and that he must become fully engaged in the Civil Rights movement. His trip to India resulted in his resigning his Montgomery, Alabama, pastorate at the Dexter Avenue Baptist Church, where he had served from 1954 until 1960, and moving to Atlanta, where he served with his father as co-pastor of Ebenezer Baptist Church from 1960 until his death eight years later. In Atlanta, he was close to the headquarters of the Southern Christian Leadership Conference (SCLC), whose stated goals were to increase black voter registration in the South and to bring an end to segregation.

King was exposed to activism and its potential for change through his position as president of the Montgomery Improve-

(Library of Congress)

ment Association. During the Montgomery boycott, he received
frequent death threats and, at one point, his home was bombed.
Nevertheless, the MIA's support of Rosa Parks's right to a seat
on a municipal bus led to a Supreme Court decision outlawing
segregation on public conveyances.

In 1962, King turned his attention to Alabama's largest city,
Birmingham, which was considered the most segregated city in
the United States. His assault on this bastion of segregation was
well-planned. He recruited and schooled participants in nonviolent tactics, employing socio-dramas as training vehicles.

When a thousand youths were arrested because they had
skipped school to attend the civil rights protests, King made the
agonizing decision to allow the children actively to join the pro-

test. The police fire-hosed these young people and allowed snarling dogs to attack them. Pictures of these atrocities, beamed around the world, brought international disdain upon Birmingham and upon white America.

King's demands from the city of Birmingham were simple: desegregation of rest rooms, lunch counters, fitting rooms, and drinking fountains throughout the city. King was arrested for his efforts, placed in a musty cell with no bedding, and held for several days, during which he wrote one of his most celebrated documents, *Letter from Birmingham City Jail*. He was finally bailed out through the efforts of Harry Belafonte, who persuaded other prominent people in show business to contribute bail money.

Because he was not a resident of the city, King was widely criticized for meddling in Birmingham's affairs. He responded by saying that Birmingham was where injustices were occurring, so he felt compelled to intervene. He reminded his critics that injustice anywhere is injustice everywhere.

In 1963, King's civil rights march on Washington attracted over 250,000 protesters. It was at this gathering that King made his famous "I Have a Dream" speech. *Time* magazine declared King its Person of the Year, and, in December, 1964, King received the Nobel Peace Prize.

After his success in Birmingham, King vowed to clear the way for southern blacks to register to vote. His efforts met incredible resistance, but King led his protesters from Selma to Montgomery, Alabama, to place their demands before Governor George Wallace. Some five hundred school children were arrested and charged with juvenile delinquency when they cut classes to attend the protests, and more than a hundred adults were arrested for picketing Selma's courthouse. Police beat a clergyman, who died two days later.

President Lyndon Johnson, a strong civil rights advocate who had signed the Civil Rights Act of 1964 into law, sent federal troops to Alabama, demanding voter registration rights for blacks. The Selma march drew five hundred protesters, who made the five-day trek with federal troops guarding their route. The following year, President Johnson signed the Voter Rights Act.

King next turned his attention to racial discrimination in Chicago, but his efforts were less successful there than in the South. He also became a strident voice in opposition to the War in Vietnam. In April, 1968, King went to Memphis, Tennessee to support garbage workers who wanted to form a union. He was also preparing for a second march on Washington at this time. On the evening of April 4, he stepped out of his room at the Lorraine Motel and was fatally shot by an assassin. His assassination only heightened his influence.

Analysis: Nonfiction

Martin Luther King, Jr., was most persuasive as an orator. His writing was often oratorical, and it captured the cadences of black spirituals. He had an instinctive ability to use conceits such as rhythm, pause, and emphasis to dramatize his speech and to reach out to his listeners. King's extraordinary speaking skills drew in audiences, making every member feel as though he were addressing each person as an individual. He spoke in riveting cadences that consistently held his audiences' attention.

Stride Toward Freedom: The Montgomery Story

Published in 1958, King's first major publication grew out of a speech he had made in San Francisco in 1956 about the Rosa Parks incident and its aftermath, which included the bombing of King's home and frequent death threats directed at him and at members of his family. This book provides a blueprint for the ways in which a repressed populace can resist oppression nonviolently by creating a unified front against their oppressors. In the Montgomery case, this was accomplished through the boycott of public transportation and of white merchants who depended on Montgomery's black population for much of their income.

The tactics King outlines in this book are foolproof. Merchants cannot force people to patronize them, so when an oppressed group shuns them, they must eventually yield to the demands of those staging the boycott. The only rub is that a boycott like that in Montgomery places difficult demands upon those supporting it.

Many Montgomery blacks depended on public transportation to get to their jobs. Arrangements had to be made to get them to those jobs by other means. Not patronizing local stores meant obtaining food and other necessities elsewhere. Survival under such conditions demanded planning and coordination. King became an expert in creating the master plans necessary to implement his followers' actions.

Stride Toward Freedom had considerable influence among black leaders associated with such organizations as the SCLC. It outlined the effectiveness of nonviolence. It cast the oppressed as victims of an unjust society rather than as aggressors pitted against the dominant society. When Mahatma Ghandi challenged the British Empire, he and his followers were greatly outnumbered, but through employment of Ghandi's nonviolent tactics, they appealed to the morality of their oppressors and, in the long term, achieved their ends against odds that initially seemed insurmountable. King devoutly believed that American blacks could succeed by employing similar tactics.

Letter from Birmingham City Jail

Probably the single most memorable piece of writing produced by Martin Luther King, Jr., was written during the few days that he languished in Birmingham's city jail. This book, published in 1964, includes the full text of King's letter and outlines in considerable detail how the elaborate plans for the Birmingham protests evolved.

King, painfully aware of the injustices visited upon blacks in Birmingham, came to the city because of these injustices. He was publicly denounced as an interloper. Newspaper articles about his interference and an open letter by six local clergymen contended that, since King wasn't a citizen of Birmingham, he had no right to intervene in what they considered a local matter.

King took the high moral ground, asserting his need to seek out injustice where it existed and to regard people in towns in which he did not reside as brothers. He considered it a moral imperative to concern himself with their welfare, particularly when they were clearly the victims of an established policy of racial discrimination imposed upon them by the white society. The changes King demanded in Birmingham were reasonable. He wanted blacks to be served at the city's lunch counters and to be permitted to use drinking fountains then available to whites only. He sought to desegregate public restrooms and fitting rooms in stores.

The crux of this book is its detailed account of how the SCLC's training committee used simulations to replicate what protesters might expect to experience at the hands of bigoted police officers and enraged white citizens. Rather than fighting back, protesters were advised to be quiet and to let their bodies go limp. They were urged to resist without bitterness, to receive verbal abuse and not reply, and to be beaten without retaliating.

Arrested for his participation in the Birmingham protest, King wrote *Letter from Birmingham City Jail* on paper smuggled to him and then smuggled out of the jail. Although he spent only a few days in confinement before being bailed out through Harry Belafonte's efforts, this incarceration shaped King's future in many ways.

Why We Can't Wait
The hundredth anniversary of Abraham Lincoln's signing of the Emancipation Proclamation occurred in 1963. To commemorate that anniversary, Martin Luther King, Jr., wrote *Why We Can't Wait*. The book, published the following year, discussed the irony of celebrating this anniversary while blacks in many parts of the United States were still segregated, discriminated against, and oppressed. In most southern states, interracial marriage was still banned by outmoded and clearly unconstitutional miscegenation laws. And, though Lincoln's pen theoretically freed America's slaves, their grandchildren and great-grandchildren were, in much of the United States, denied the right to vote, to attend the schools of their choice, to eat in restaurants of their choosing, and to stay in hotels that, throughout the South, were designated "White Only."

In 1939, world-acclaimed singer Marian Anderson was denied the right to sing in Constitution Hall in the nation's capital, and forbidden from staying in any of Washington's major hotels, simply because of the color of her skin. Blacks were similarly humiliated throughout the South and in much of the North. They were underemployed and underpaid for the work they did.

School segregation, although perhaps not specifically mandated as it was in the South, was a fact of life in most northern cities largely because blacks could not rent or buy homes in the parts of town with the best schools. Many secondary schools in the inner cities had black enrollments of 97 percent or more.

In *Why We Can't Wait*, King deplored segregation, discrimination, and gradualism. Many southern political leaders, realizing that racial integration would inevitably be thrust upon them, devised plans to integrate the schools so gradually that they would in effect remain segregated far into the future. Making his case with impeccable logic and considerable factual evidence, King developed an airtight argument for immediate and decisive action. Before the decade was out, substantial progress had been made, largely because of King's pioneering and persistent efforts.

Other Literary Forms

During King's lifetime, he published *Where Do We Go from Here: Chaos or Community?*, which had a considerable impact. This book provided a blueprint for future civil rights activists. A collection of King's letters originally published in *Liberation, Unwise and Untimely?*, was published in 1963, as was *Strength to Love*, a collection of his sermons. *The Trumpet of Conscience* is a selection of transcripts from his many radio broadcasts.

Bibliography
Bowling, Lawson. *Shapers of the Great Debate on the Great Society: A Biographical Dictionary.* Westport, Conn.: Greenwood Press, 2005. The eighteen-page section that deals with Martin Luther King, Jr., is valuable for considering him in the context of a score of others involved, either positively or negatively, in shaping the Great Society. Entries range from opponents

such as Strom Thurmond to supporters, including Lyndon B. Johnson.

Dickerson, Dennis C. "African American Religious Intellectuals and the Theological Foundations of the Civil Rights Movement, 1930-55." *Church History* 74, no. 2 (June, 2005): 217-235. Explores King's qualifications as a preacher and his contributions to the Civil Rights movement, comparing him with the founder of African American theology, James H. Cone.

Garrow, David J. *Bearing the Cross: Martin Luther King, Jr., and the Southern Christian Leadership Conference.* New York: Morrow, 1986. One of the most incisive discussions in print of King's activism.

January, Brendan. *Martin Luther King, Jr.: Minister and Civil Rights Activist.* Chicago: Ferguson, 2000. Aimed primarily at adolescent readers, January presents an overview of King's life and work. Easily accessible to most readers.

King, Coretta Scott. *My Life with Martin Luther King, Jr.* New York: Henry Holt, 1969. An important book for King scholars because it offers his wife's view of what was going on during King's crusade for racial equality.

Nall, Jeff. "Will the Real Martin Luther King Please Stand Up?" *Humanist* 65, no. 3 (May/June, 2005): 4-5. Discusses King's thoughts on the separation of church and state, as well as his views on the Supreme Court's decision against prayer in schools.

Peck, Ira. *The Life and Works of Martin Luther King, Jr.* New York: Scholastic, 2000. Peck presents a detailed biography of King. Although aimed at adolescent readers, the book will prove informative to adult readers as well.

Walker, Martin. *America Reborn: A Twentieth Century Narrative in Twenty-six Lives.* New York: Alfred A. Knopf, 2000. Walker examines closely the lives and work of twenty-six notable Americans who have helped to reshape the United States. Chapter 23, "Martin Luther King, Jr., and American Sainthood," presents a seventeen-page summary of King's contributions to America's rebirth.

— *R. Baird Shuman*

Etheridge Knight

Poet

Born: Corinth, Mississippi; April 19, 1931
Died: Indianapolis, Indiana; March 10, 1991

POETRY: "For Malcolm, a Year After," 1967 (a contribution to *For Malcolm: Poems on the Life and Death of Malcolm X*, 1967); *Poems from Prison*, 1968; *Black Voices from Prison*, 1970 (with others); *A Poem for Brother/Man (After His Recovery from an O.D.)*, 1972; *Belly Song, and Other Poems*, 1973; *Born of a Woman: New and Selected Poems*, 1980; *The Essential Etheridge Knight*, 1986.

Achievements

Etheridge Knight opened the eyes of a nation to the views and experiences of prisoners, a previously ignored population. The initial acclaim lavished on *Poems from Prison*, published in 1968, and the praise of honored authors such as Gwendolyn Brooks and Robert Bly, opened the door to a 1972 grant from the National Endowment for the Arts. His third collection, *Belly Song, and Other Poems*, earned 1973 Pulitzer Prize and National Book Award nominations. He received a Guggenheim Fellowship in 1974 and won the Shelley Memorial Award in 1984. His last book, *The Essential Etheridge Knight*, earned the Before Columbus Foundation's 1987 American Book Award.

Biography

Etheridge Knight, one of Bushie and Belzora (Cozart) Knight's seven children, came into the world on April 19, 1931, near Corinth, Mississippi. During this time the United States was gripped by one of history's most sensational racial battles, the Scottsboro Boys trial. Nine black males, ages twelve to nineteen, were taken off a train near Scottsboro, Alabama, and charged with the rape of two Huntsville, Alabama, white women, Ruby Bates, eighteen, and Victoria Price, twenty-one. The incident seeded a cloud of white fear and rage that shadowed black men throughout the South for more than thirty years.

Angered by the racial segregation and disgusted by the back-breaking work of sharecropping, Knight dropped out of school after the eighth grade and left home. He wandered for about five years, then enlisted in the Army in 1947.

Knight was a medic, stationed in Guam, Hawaii, and at the battlefront in the Korean War until 1951, when he was wounded by a piece of shrapnel. In 1957, the now drug-addicted soldier

(Judy Ray)

was discharged. Drugs dominated his life. In 1960, Knight was sentenced to prison for a robbery in Indianapolis, Indiana, motivated by his need to buy drugs. Doing time at Indiana State Prison in Michigan City, Indiana, led Knight to self-discovery and an increased desire to be more than an outcast in America. Those yearnings prompted him to write.

Poems from Prison, his first collection, was published by Broadside Press in 1968, with an introduction by Pulitzer Prize-winning poet Gwendolyn Brooks. She mentored Knight, who eventually gained support from members of the Black Arts movement, which gave artistic voice to African Americans' struggles for social rights and political freedom. One of those members, poet Dudley Randall, was the founder and editor of Broadside Press. Another poet, Sonia Sanchez, married Knight. By year's end, Knight had gained a career, a wife, and three stepchildren: Morani, Mungu, and Anita Sanchez. His fame peaked between 1969 and 1975, when the movement waned. An anthology of prison writings, *Voce Negre dal Carcere* (1968), first published in Laterza, Italy, broadened the popularity of Knight's work. Two years later, Pathfinders Press released *Black Voices from Prison* in the United States. Doors opened. The poet was writer-in-residence at the University of Pittsburgh (1968-1969), the University of Hartford (1969-1970), and Lincoln University (1972) in Jefferson City, Missouri. He received a 1972 National Endowment for the Arts grant and a 1974 Guggenheim Fellowship.

Knight's career was going well, but his personal life was in a downward slide. Drugs kept him in and out of Veterans Administration hospitals. The marriage to Sanchez crumbled into a 1972 divorce. On June 11, 1973, Knight married Mary Ann McAnally. The couple had two children: Mary Tandiwe and Etheridge Bambata. That same year, Broadside published the first collection of his poems written outside prison, *Belly Song, and Other Poems*. In 1978, he married Charlene Blackburn. The relationship is celebrated in *Born of a Woman*, and with her he had a son, Issac Bushie Knight.

Knight continued to write. *The Essential Etheridge Knight*, was released in 1986, but Knight never regained prominence. He died of lung cancer in 1991 in Indianapolis, Indiana.

Analysis: Poetry

As black writers and artists in the late 1960's reached for words to politicize their expressions, Etheridge Knight's voice proved perfect. Like the works of LeRoi Jones (Amiri Baraka), Don L. Lee (Haki R. Madhubuti), Dudley Randall, and Sonia Sanchez, Knight's poems celebrate black heritage and criticize injustices. What readers will find in Knight's poetry is an attempt to understand belonging and racial isolation in U.S. society. As Cassie Premo wrote in *The Oxford Companion to African American Literature,* even dead, Knight "continues to testify to the power of freedom, and human capacity to envision it even when in prison."

He talked about life behind bars, unveiling a humanity in prisoners that most Americans, black or white, never knew existed. At the same time, his poetry revealed links between the ways black people survived on both sides of the wall.

Poems such as "Hard Rock Returns to Prison from the Hospital for the Criminal Insane" epitomized the standard for what in the early 1960's was still called Negro literature. A New York City poet then named LeRoi Jones (now Amiri Baraka of Newark, New Jersey) wrote in a 1962 essay, "The Myth of a Negro Literature":

> Negro Literature, to be a legitimate product of the Negro experience in America, must get at that experience in exactly the terms America has proposed for it in its most ruthless identity.

As Patricia Liggins Hill wrote in "The Violent Space: The Function of the New Black Aesthetic in Etheridge Knight's Prison Poetry," Knight's prison poems interweave temporal and spatial elements that "allow him to merge his personal consciousness with the consciousness of Black people." The poet himself once said:

> . . . a major part of discovering an aesthetic is coming to grips with oneself. The "true" artist is supposed to examine his own experience of this process as a reflection of his self, his ego.

Like many of the writers and painters during the Black Arts movement that surfaced in major urban centers between 1965 and 1975, Knight believed that a black artist's main duty was to expose the lies of the white-dominated society. In *Contemporary Authors*, he is quoted as saying that the traditional idea of the aesthetic drawn from Western European history demands that the artist speak only of the beautiful: "His task is to edify the listener, to make him see beauty of the world." That aesthetic definition was a problem because African Americans were identified in the traditional European mind as not beautiful. In fact, the broader society saw everything in African American life as ugly. Black artists hoped to erase that mindset. They saw art as a force through which they could move people of all races toward understanding and respect. In *Contemporary Authors*, Knight is quoted as saying that the African American writer has to

> perceive and conceptualize the collective aspirations, the collective vision of black people, and through his art form give back to the people the truth that he has gotten from them. He must sing to them of their own deeds, and misdeeds.

Knight began to write poetry in prison, but he did not come to the task cold. Scholar Shirley Lumpkin states that Knight was "an accomplished reciter" before he entered prison. She explains that "reciters" in the African American tradition made "toasts," which were long, memorized, narrative poems, often in rhymed couplets, in which "sexual exploits, drug activities, and violent aggressive conflicts [involved] a cast of familiar folk." Like later rap and hip-hop artists, reciters wove the stories in typically gritty, sometimes pornographic street language. Indiana State Prison toasts honed Knight's skill in the art form and opened his eyes to poetry's potential.

In *The Dictionary of Literary Biography*, Lumpkin wrote:

> Since toast-telling brought him into genuine communion with others, he felt that poetry could simultaneously show him who he was and connect him with other people.

Poetry was what brought him into contact with Gwendolyn Brooks and Dudley Randall, who exposed Knight to the world.

In *Broadside Memories: Poets I Have Known* (1975), Randall states, "Knight sees himself as being one with Black people." As in the toasts, in rap and hip-hop, rhyme becomes the glue in the black community. "Knight does not abjure rime like many contemporary poets," Randall wrote. "He says the average Black man in the streets defines poetry as something that rimes, and Knight appeals to the folk by riming." Knight's view of the world and himself was forged in the anguish that comes from trying to make it as an outsider. His writings show that he saw African Americans as outcasts everywhere outside their culture, finding roots only in family connections.

"Hard Rock Returns to Prison from the Hospital for the Criminal Insane"

In "Hard Rock Returns to Prison from the Hospital for the Criminal Insane," Knight turns an uncontrollable prisoner into a new-day folk hero. Hard Rock is a Paul Bunyan without a pretty fate. The author understood that most African American lives, even mythic ones, do not have happy endings. The poem also shows that sometimes heroes are not what most people (meaning whites) see as nice or pretty. In the language of the incarcerated, Knight laid out the heroic stature:

> "Ol Hard Rock! Man, that's one crazy nigger."
> And then the jewel of a myth that Hard Rock once bit
> A screw on the thumb and poisoned him with syphilitic spit.

To many, those details are as alienating as the description:

> Hard Rock was "known not to take no shit
> From nobody," and he had the scars to prove it:
> Split purple lips, lumped ears, welts above
> His yellow eyes, and one long scar that cut
> Across his temple and plowed through a thick
> Canopy of kinky hair.

The prisoner, Knight recognized, is an archetype of all black Americans, only nominally "free" but really imprisoned. In prison, the prisoner stays in a hole, a tiny cell devoid of light.

The guards' intimidation cannot break the man's spirit, so the prison doctors give him a lobotomy. They take his ability to think. Knight saw that scenario as identical to the experience of the descendants of Africans in America. In Mississippi and other places, he had seen black people who tried to stand tall against the onslaught of racial oppression either killed or, like the fictional Hard Rock, tamed:

> A screw who knew Hard Rock
> From before shook him down and barked in his face
> And Hard Rock did *nothing*. Just grinned and looked silly.
> His eyes empty like knot holes in a fence.

The poem captures the disappointment and defeat Knight saw in black men on both sides of the walls:

> We turned away our eyes to the ground. Crushed.
> He had been our Destroyer, the doer of things
> We dreamed of doing but could not bring ourselves to do.

"The Idea of Ancestry"

Knight reflects on those connections in both "A Poem for Myself (Or Blues for a Mississippi Black Boy)" and "The Idea of Ancestry," in his *Poems from Prison*. In the first part of "The Idea of Ancestry," he wrote:

> Taped to the wall of my cell are 47 pictures: 47 black
> faces: my father, mother, grandmothers (1 dead), grandfathers
>   (both dead), brothers,
> sisters, uncles, aunts, cousins (1st & 2nd), nieces, and nephews.
>   They stare
> across the space at me sprawling on my bunk. I know
> their dark eyes, they know mine. I know their style,
> they know mine. I am all of them, they are all of me;
> they are farmers, I am a thief, I am me, they are thee.

After exploring the variety of their individualism, he concludes differences cannot break family ties:

> I have the same name as 1 grandfather, 3 cousins, 3 nephews,
>   and 1 uncle. The uncle disappeared when he was 15, just took

667

off and caught a freight (they say). He's discussed each year
when the family has a reunion, he causes uneasiness in
the clan, he is an empty space. My father's mother, who is 93
and who keeps the Family Bible with everybody's birth dates
(and death dates) in it, always mentions him. There is
no place in her Bible for "whereabouts unknown."

Works written after prison extended Knight's reflections on connections. When considered to its fullest extent, what binds people is love. Knight's reflection on ancestry in "The Idea of Ancestry" reveals an understanding of a family, the accidental space where one shares traits and foibles with loved ones. Accidental refers to things outside a person's control. In the 1980 essay "The Violent Space," Hill acknowledged that "the form of the poem as well as the idea of ancestry in the poem also represents the problem of ancestral lineage for the Black race as a whole." The power to direct family lines was stripped from African Americans for generations. The practice of selling slaves without regard for emotional ties also made it hard to keep track of the existing linkages.

"A Poem for Myself"
Born of a Woman, Poems from Prison, Black Voices from Prison and *Belly Song, and Other Poems* have pieces that openly grapple with questions of belonging. Those themes and styles resonate with legendary black poets such as Langston Hughes and Sterling Brown. This is particularly clear in the blues poem "A Poem for Myself (Or Blues for a Mississippi Black Boy)":

> I was born in Mississippi;
> I walked barefooted thru the mud.
> Born black in Mississippi,
> Walked barefooted thru the mud.
> But when I reached the age of twelve
> I left that place for good.

The narrative stanza sounds no different from the lines of a traditional Mississippi blues ballad. Many black poets, particularly during the Harlem Renaissance in the early twentieth century, used the style and meter of the music. Sung ballads usually have three iambic pentameter lines with the second line repeated. Knight slightly varies the meter, echoing the first line in the third and the second line in the fourth to create a more accessible feel and slightly disguise the poem's basic blues flavor.

In a review of *Born of a Woman*, Hill described Knight as a blues singer, "whose life has been 'full of trouble' and thus whose songs resound a variety of blues moods, feelings, and experiences and later take on the specific form of a blues musical composition." In *Obsidian: Black Literature in Review*, Craig Werner states that Knight "merges musical rhythms with traditional metrical devices, reflecting the assertion of an Afro-American cultural identity within a Euro-American context." If the blues form bodes defiance of established norms, it becomes as rebellious as the use of rhyme. It becomes yet another way to identify with the masses, which is clearly more of Knight's interest than meeting Western European standards. Lumpkin states that some critics find Knight's language objectionable and "unpoetic." They judged his use of verse forms to be poor. In 1980, she wrote, "Some believe that he 'maintains an outmoded, strident black power rhetoric from the 1960's.'" She concludes: "Those with reservations and those who admire his work all agree . . . upon his vital language and the range of his subject matter. They all agree that he brings a needed freshness to poetry, particularly in his extraordinary ability to move an audience."

Knight died without ever finding the answers to the ties that bind people to something larger than themselves. However, as Premo wrote, "Knight's poetry expresses our freedom of consciousness and attests to our capacity for connections with others."

Other Literary Forms

Etheridge Knight almost exclusively wrote poetry. A few of his articles appeared in African American magazines such as *Black Digest* (with a format similar to *Reader's Digest*), *Emerge* (similar to *Time* magazine), and *Essence*, the foremost black women's periodical publication.

Bibliography

Anaporte-Easton, Jean. "Etheridge Knight: Poet and Prisoner." *Callaloo* 19, no. 4 (Fall, 1996): 940-947. Chronicles Knight's life, from his time in prison through his development as a poet under the tutelage of Gwendolyn Brooks.

Andrews, William L., Frances Smith Fuller, and Trudier Harris, eds. *The Oxford Companion to African American Literature.* New York: Oxford University Press, 1997. In this reference work, Cassie Premo briefly profiles the author, assessing his poetry's contribution to American writing. She concludes that his poetry expresses "our freedom of consciousness and attests to our capacity for connection to others."

Ford, Karen. "These Old Writing Paper Blues: The Blues Stanza and Literary Poetry." *College Literature* 24, no. 3 (October, 1997): 84-103. Ford weighs Knight's use of written and oral form in "For Malcolm, a Year After." She says that the "reciprocal, mutually informing and accommodating relationship" between them "dramatizes playful adaptation and rich potential."

Hill, Patricia Liggins. "The Violent Space: The Function of the New Black Aesthetic in Etheridge Knight's Prison Poetry." *Black American Literature Forum* 14, no. 3 (1980). The scholar analyzes how Knight's perspective, as seen in "Hard Rock Returns to Prison from the Hospital for the Criminal Insane" and other prison poems, fits within the aesthetic that often treats writing as a political act.

Knight, Etheridge. "An Interview with Etheridge Knight." Interview by Charles H. Rowell. *Callaloo* 19, no. 4 (Fall, 1996): 968-984. A discussion centered on the form of African American art.

Lifson, Amy. "Knight." *Humanities* 19, no. 1 (January/February, 1998): 36-37. A brief profile of the poet, including his conviction for robbery and work in prison. Also discusses several of his poems and his relationship with Gwendolyn Brooks.

Randall, Dudley. *Broadside Memories: Poets I Have Known.* Detroit: Broadside Press, 1975. The poet is one of several authors Randall discusses. The publisher saw Knight's work as closer to the pulse of the African American masses than that of most members of the Black Arts movement in the late 1960's.

Vendler, Helen Hennessy, ed. *Part of Nature, Part of Us: Modern American Poets*. Cambridge, Mass.: Harvard University Press, 1980. Shirley Lumpkin writes about "Hard Rock Returns to Prison from the Hospital for the Criminal Insane," tying the themes in the works that appear in *Poems from Prison* and *Born of a Woman* to his writings about Malcolm X and family. She highlights the work's sense of community and observes, "What renders the picture of 'Hard Rock' even more powerful is the first person plural's persona's voice, which uses black, prison, and standard vocabulary to explain what Hard Rock's destruction means to the 'we' speaking in the poem."

— *Vincent F. A. Golphin*

Yusef Komunyakaa

(James Willie Brown)

Poet

Born: Bogalusa, Louisiana; April 29, 1947

POETRY: *Dedications and Other Darkhorses*, 1977; *Lost in the Bonewheel Factory*, 1979; *Copacetic*, 1984; *I Apologize for the Eyes in My Head*, 1986; *Toys in the Field*, 1986; *Dien Cai Dau*, 1988; *February in Sydney*, 1989; *Magic City*, 1992; *Neon Vernacular: New and Selected Poems*, 1993; *Thieves of Paradise*, 1998; *Talking Dirty to the Gods*, 2000; *Pleasure Dome: New and Collected Poems*, 2001; *Taboo: The Wishbone Trilogy, Part One*, 2004.

NONFICTION: *Blue Notes: Essays, Interviews, and Commentaries*, 1999 (Radiclani Clytus, editor).

EDITED TEXTS: *The Jazz Poetry Anthology*, 1991 (with Sascha Feinstein); *The Second Set: The Jazz Poetry Anthology, Volume 2*, 1996 (with Feinstein).

TRANSLATIONS: *The Insomnia of Fire*, 1995 (with Martha Collins, of poetry by Nguyen Quang Thieu).

Achievements

Many readers, critics, and fellow poets have long recognized Yusef Komunyakaa as a major poet of his generation. His poems about the Vietnam War place him among the finest writers who have explored this difficult terrain. His use of jazz and blues rhythms places him in the tradition of poet Langston Hughes and the best Southern writers. Of his many awards and honors, perhaps the most impressive is the 1994 Pulitzer Prize in poetry for *Neon Vernacular*, which also won the Kingsley Tufts Award and the William Faulkner Prize. *Thieves of Paradise* was a finalist for the National Book Critics Circle Award. Komunyakaa has also won the Thomas Forcade Award and the Hanes Poetry Prize. In 1999, he was elected a chancellor of the Academy of American Poets.

He has been awarded creative writing fellowships from the National Endowment for the Arts, the Fine Arts Center in Provincetown, Massachusetts, and the Louisiana Arts Council. He has served as a judge for numerous poetry competitions and has been on the advisory board for the *Encyclopedia of American Poetry* (1998, 2001). His work has appeared in all the major poetry journals, as well as national magazines such as *The Atlantic Monthly* and *The New Republic.* One indication of Komunyakaa's appeal is the number of diverse anthologies that include his work. He appears repeatedly in the annual *The Best American Poetry*, collections of verse about Vietnam, and numerous periodicals.

Biography

The oldest of five children, Yusef Komunyakaa had a strained relationship with his father, which he vividly chronicled years later in a fourteen-sonnet sequence titled "Songs for My Father," which appears in *Neon Vernacular.* The Bogalusa of Komunyakaa's childhood was a rural community in southern Louisiana that held few opportunities economically or culturally, especially for a young black man. The main industry was the single paper mill, one that turned "workers into pulp," according to one poem. There was a racially charged atmosphere. The public library admitted only whites; the Ku Klux Klan was still active. In "Fog Galleon," Komunyakaa writes of these difficulties:

> I press against the taxicab
> Window. I'm black here, interfaced
> With a dead phosphorescence;
> The whole town smells
> Like the world's oldest anger.

Daydreaming and reading were ways of escaping and coping with a slow life. Daydreaming, which Komunyakaa now sees as an important creative act of his youth, is evident in his early identification with his grandfather's West Indian heritage. He took the name Komunyakaa from his grandfather, who, according to family legend, came to America as a stowaway from Trinidad. In the poem "Mismatched Shoes," Komunyakaa writes of this identification:

> The island swelled in his throat
> & calypso leapt into the air,
>
> . . . .
>
> I picked up those mismatched shoes
> & slipped into his skin. Komunyakaa.
> His blues, African fruit on my tongue.

The Bible and a set of supermarket encyclopedias were his first books. He has noted the influence of the Bible's "hypnotic cadence," sensitizing him to the importance of music and metaphor. James Baldwin's *Nobody Knows My Name* (1961), discovered in a church library when Komunyakaa was sixteen, inspired him to become a writer. Jazz and blues radio programs from New Orleans, heard on the family radio, formed a third important influence. Komunyakaa speaks fondly of those early days of listening to jazz and acknowledges its importance in his work.

After graduation from high school in 1965, Komunyakaa traveled briefly and in 1969 enlisted in the army. He was sent to Vietnam. He served as a reporter on the front lines and later as editor of *The Southern Cross*, a military newspaper. The experience of being flown in by helicopter to observe and then report on the war effort laid the groundwork for the powerful fusion of passion and detached observation that is a hallmark of his war poems, written years later. He was awarded the Bronze Star for his service in Vietnam.

Upon being discharged, Komunyakaa enrolled at the University of Colorado, where he majored in English and sociology, earning a bachelor's degree in 1975. A creative writing course there inspired him to pursue a master's degree in creative writing at Colorado State University, which he earned in 1978. He received his master of fine arts degree from the University of California, Irvine, in 1980. During this period he published limited editions of his first two short books of poems, *Dedications and Other Darkhorses* and *Lost in the Bonewheel Factory*.

Komunyakaa taught poetry briefly in public school before

joining the creative writing faculty at the University of New Orleans, where he met Mandy Sayer, whom he married in 1985. That year he became an associate professor at Indiana University at Bloomington, where in 1989 he was named Lilly Professor of Poetry. He later became a professor in the Council of Humanities and Creative Writing Program at Princeton University.

Analysis: Poetry

Because Yusef Komunyakaa's poetry is so rich in imagery, allusion, metaphor, musical rhythms, and ironic twists, it possesses a freshness and a bittersweet bite whether the subject is the raw beauty of nature or the passions and follies of human nature. He has said that poetry does not work for him without "surprises." His poetry surprises both in its technique—the juxtaposition of disparate images and sudden shifts in perspective—and in its subjects. Generally his poems have a sensual quality even though the subject matter varies greatly: childhood memories, family feuds, race, war, sex, nature, jazz. Scholar Radiclani Clytus commented early in Komunyakaa's career that the poet's interpretation of popular mythology and legend gave readers "alternative access to cultural lore. Epic human imperfections, ancient psychological profiles, and the haunting resonance of the South are now explained by those who slow drag to Little Willie John and rendezvous at MOMA." Komunyakaa's comment that "a poem is both confrontation and celebration" aptly captures the essence of his own work.

Copacetic

Two early books, the first ones published by a major university press, introduce many of Komunyakaa's subjects and techniques and were the first to win him critical acclaim. *Copacetic* focuses primarily on memories of childhood and the persuasive influence of music. The narrator speaks of "a heavy love for jazz," and in fact musical motifs run throughout Komunyakaa's poetry. He has compared poetry to jazz and blues in its emphasis on feeling and tone, its sense of surprise and discovery, and its diversity within a general structure. Poems such as "Copacetic Mingus," "Elegy for Thelonious," and "Untitled Blues" convey the power of this kind of music, in which "Art & life bleed into each other." Depending on the poem, music can serve as escape, therapy, or analogy. Often it is combined with richly sensual images, as in "Woman, I Got the Blues."

I Apologize for the Eyes in My Head and Dien Cai Dau
I Apologize for the Eyes in My Head continues this motif while adding new subjects and themes. The ugly side of race relations in the United States is suggested in several poems. Komunyakaa also begins to explore the pain of the Vietnam War. "For the Walking Dead" is a moving account of "boyish soldiers on their way to the front" who seek respite with Veronica in a local bar.

The past wounds and present scars of the Vietnam War are the subjects of *Dien Cai Dau*, whose title means "crazy" in Vietnamese. The powerful yet exquisitely sensitive—and sensual—way in which Komunyakaa conveys the pain, loss, and psychic confusion of his experience in Vietnam found a receptive audience. Most present a moment or a reflection in a richly nuanced but undogmatic way. In "We Never Know" he juxtaposes a delicate image of dancing with a woman with the reality of an enemy in the field, whom he kills and whose body he then approaches. The moral ambiguity of the moment is highlighted by the tenderness with which the soldier regards the body:

> When I got to him,
> a blue halo
> of flies had already claimed him.
> I pulled the crumbled photograph
> from his fingers.
> There's no other way
> to say this: I fell in love.
> The morning cleared again,
> except for a distant mortar
> & somewhere choppers taking off.
> I slid the wallet into his pocket
> & turned him over, so he wouldn't be
> kissing the ground.

Poems such as "Tu Du Street" and "Thanks" are even more complex in their multiple, often conflicting, images. The former presents the bizarre reality of racial prejudice even in Vietnam, "where only machine gun fire bring us together." The women with whom the soldiers seek solace provide one common denominator:

> There's more than a nation
> inside us, as black & white
> soldiers touch the same lovers
> minutes apart, tasting
> each other's breath,
> without knowing these rooms
> run into each other like tunnels
> leading to the underworld.

In "Thanks" the narrator gives thanks to an unspecified being for the myriad coincidences that saved him one day in the jungle as he "played some deadly/ game for blind gods." The poet provides no resolution or closure, just a series of powerful, haunting images:

> Again, thanks for the dud
> hand grenade tossed at my feet
> outside Chu Lai. I'm still
> falling through its silence.

Thieves of Paradise

Komunyakaa won an Academy of Arts and Letters Award given to writers with "progressive and experimental tendencies." This book is an example of this artist's ability to experiment with form and ease the reader into accepting poetry that is unfamiliar. Much of the subject matter is familiar—the grim reality of war and its psychological aftermath, the body's hungers and betrayals, the allure of memory and imagination—but the presentation is fresh and intriguing. "Palimpsest" is a seemingly random, kaleidoscopic series of four-quatrain poems that move from "slavecatchers" to tanks in Beijing's Tiananmen Square to the backwoods to jazz musician Count Basie. By confronting uncomfortable truths, the poet writes, "I am going to teach Mr. Pain/ to sway, to bop."

Several, such as "Nude Interrogation," "Phantasmagoria," and "Frontispiece," are prose poems that force one to rethink the nature of the form, while Komunyakaa's images work on the emotions. "The Glass Ark" is a five-page dialogue between two paleontologists.

This collection includes the libretto "Testimony," about Charlie Parker, written in twenty-eight fourteen-line stanzas. It captures the reckless allure of the man and the time:

> Yardbird
> could blow a woman's strut
> across the room . . . pushed moans through brass. . . . High
> heels clicking like a high hat.
> Black-beaded flapper. Blue satin
> Yardbird, he'd blow pain & glitter.

Talking Dirty to the Gods

This volume stands apart from earlier works in its adherence to a strict, traditional form. Each of its 132 poems consists of sixteen lines, in four unrhymed quatrains. Much of the appeal of this collection stems from the freedom and friction Komunyakaa creates by presenting his unusual images and bizarre juxtapositions in a tightly controlled format. The gods he discusses are taken from the ancient and the modern worlds, the exotic and the commonplace. Whether discussing the maggot ("Little/ Master of earth"), Bellerophon, or Joseph Stalin, he is able to humanize his subject enough to win at least some sympathy from the reader.

Neon Vernacular

Neon Vernacular won considerable critical acclaim as well as the Pulitzer Prize. In addition to culling the best from earlier books, it adds gems of its own, including the unrhymed sonnet sequence "Songs for My Father," fourteen powerful poems that chronicle the poet's complicated relationship with his dad. In "At the Screen Door," in which a former soldier murders because he cannot separate the past from the present, Komunyakaa returns to the psychological aftermath of Vietnam.

Pleasure Dome
The publication of *Pleasure Dome* led to laudatory reviews not only for its poetic achievement but also for its high purpose: "Nearly every page of these collected poems will pull you from your expectations, tell you something you did not know, and leave you better off than you were," said the reviewer for *Library Journal*, while *Booklist* praised Komunyakaa's "fluent creative energy, and his passion for living the examined life." *Pleasure Dome* is an extraordinarily rich collection of more than 350 poems. All earlier books except *Talking Dirty to the Gods* are represented. There is also a section titled "New Poems" and another, "Early Uncollected." Among the new poems is "Tenebrae," a moving meditation on Richard Johnson, the black Indiana University music professor who committed suicide. The lines "You try to beat loneliness/ out of a drum" are woven throughout the poem with a cumulative, haunting effect.

Other Literary Forms
Despite his impressive poetic output—a book of poems every few years since 1977 and publication in all the major poetry journals—Yusef Komunyakaa has not been content to stay within these traditional confines. He has made a number of sound and video recordings of his readings of his work. One of the more interesting of these is *Love Notes from the Madhouse*, a live reading performed with a jazz ensemble led by John Tchicai. He has written two libretti, "Slip Knot," with T. J. Anderson, about an eighteenth century slave, and "Testimony," about jazz great Charlie Parker. In *Thirteen Kinds of Desire*, vocalist Pamela Knowles sings lyrics by Komunyakaa. Of his fight against traditional poetic boundaries, he notes: "I am always pushing against the walls [that categories] create. I will always do this.... Theater and song won't be the last of me."

Blue Notes: Essays, Interviews, and Commentaries, edited by Radiclani Clytus, is an eclectic mix of seven interviews with the poet from 1990 to 2000, as well as twelve short impressionistic essays by him and five new poems with commentary by the author. With Sascha Feinstein, he edited *The Jazz Poetry Anthology*. Together with Martha Collins, Komunyakaa translated the work of Vietnamese poet Nguyen Quang Thieu. His own poetry has been translated into Vietnamese as well as Russian, Korean, Czech, French, and Italian.

Bibliography

Conley, Susan. "About Yusef Komunyakaa: A Profile." *Ploughshares* 23, no. 1 (Spring, 1997): 202-207. Conley gives a concise overview of the poet's career, his central themes and motifs, his views on race relations in America, and his usual method of writing poetry.

Gordon, Fran. "Yusef Komunyakaa: Blue Note in a Lyrical Landscape." *Poets & Writers* 28, no. 6 (November/December, 2000): 26-33. Gordon terms Komunyakaa "one of America's most receptive minds" and "one of its most original voices." This interview provides a glimpse into the poet's thoughts on his background and early reading, his interest in nature and mythology, and his use of imagery and music in his poetry.

Gotera, Vincente. "Depending on the Light: Yusef Komunyakaa's *Dien Cai Dau*." In *America Rediscovered: Critical Essays on Literature and Film of the Vietnam War*, edited by Owen Gilman. New York: Garland, 1990. Komunyakaa differs from other war poets in his "devotion to highly textured language"; he refuses "to present Vietnam to the reader as exotica," but rather "underline[s] the existential reality" of his experience. That same year Gotera published an interview with the poet in *Callaloo*; he includes Komunyakaa's poetry in his 1994 *Radical Visions: Poetry by Vietnam Veterans*, published by the University of Georgia Press.

Hedges, Chris. "A Poet of Suffering, Endurance and Healing." *The New York Times*, July 8, 2004, p. B2. An article that focuses on Komunyakaa's childhood and path to his current position at Princeton University.

Komunyakaa, Yusef. "Still Negotiating with the Images: An Interview with Yusef Komunyakaa." Interview by William Baer.

Kenyon Review 20, nos. 3/4 (Summer/Fall, 1998): 5-21. A conversation with the author that delves into his experiences in Vietnam during the war and again in 1990. Also discusses Komunyakaa's relationship to his hometown, Bogalusa, Louisiana.

Ringnalda, Don. *Fighting and Writing the Vietnam War.* Jackson: University Press of Mississippi, 1994. As he does in "Rejecting 'Sweet Geometry'" (*Journal of American Culture* 16, no. 3, Fall, 1993), Ringnalda suggests that much of the poetry about Vietnam is too safe in both form and content. Because Komunyakaa realizes that the old paradigms are shattered, he "gains the freedom to explore subterranean, prerational landscapes. This results in a poetry of rich, disturbing associations."

Salas, Angela M. "Race, Human Empathy, and Negative Capability: The Poetry of Yusef Komunyakaa." *College Literature* 30, no. 4 (Fall, 2003): 32-54. Deconstructs the notion of a single African American perspective and explains the ways in which Komunyakaa's work seeks to avoid this oversimplification.

Stein, Kevin. "Vietnam and the 'Voice Within': Public and Private History in Yusef Komunyakaa's *Dien Cai Dau.*" *Massachusetts Review* 36, no. 4 (Winter, 1995/1996): 541-562. Attempts to place Komunyakaa's work in an autobiographical context while simultaneously keeping it open to public interpretation.

Weber, Bruce. "A Poet's Values: It's the Words Over the Man." *The New York Times Biographical Service* 25 (May, 1994): 666-667. Written three weeks after Komunyakaa won the Pulitzer Prize, this brief account adds several new and interesting anecdotes about the poet's early years and his views on his craft.

— *Danny Robinson*

Nella Larsen

Novelist

Born: Chicago, Illinois; April 13, 1891
Died: New York, New York; March 30, 1964

LONG FICTION: *Quicksand*, 1928; *Passing*, 1929.
SHORT FICTION: "Sanctuary," 1930.
MISCELLANEOUS: *An Intimation of Things Distant: The Collected Fiction of Nella Larsen*, 1992 (also as *The Complete Fiction of Nella Larsen*, 2001).

Achievements

Nella Larsen's greatest formal honor was the Guggenheim Fellowship she received in 1930, which was the first ever awarded to an African American woman. In addition, *Passing* received the Harmon Foundation's bronze medal for literature. However, these two important distinctions aside, Larsen's work has been largely neglected until very recently. Her books began to reappear in print in the late 1990's and have been of particular interest to feminist scholars. Larsen's reputation—and that of other African American women writers such as Zora Neale Hurston—has been almost completely resurrected, and academics and students alike have noted that her consistent exploration of her own identity has done much to inform concepts of race and gender in twentieth century America.

Biography

Nella Larsen, born Nellie Walker, was the daughter of Peter Walker, a cook who Larsen later described as a "colored" man from the West Indies, and Mary Hanson, who was originally from Denmark. Larsen's parents were, it appears, never actually married, though they applied for a marriage license in 1890.

Walker died in 1892 or 1893, and Hanson later had a child with a Danish man named Peter Larson, whom she married in 1894. Larson moved his new wife and daughter to Chicago's suburbs, where Larsen attended private schools with her half sister and other white children. She adopted her stepfather's name (with a spelling change) but felt that he looked down on her because of her biracial heritage. In 1907, Peter Larson sent Larsen to Fisk University's Normal School in Nashville. Later, Mary Larson would tell the Census Bureau that she had only one child, and this sense of rejection would become an important theme in Nella Larsen's writing.

(Department of State)

Larsen scholars generally agree that this version of the writer's early life is correct. Still, Larsen sometimes contradicted herself when recounting her history, leaving room for speculation. An alternate scenario has been proposed by her biographer Thadious M. Davis, who argues that Peter Walker, who was light-skinned, may not have died but instead changed his name and created a new identity so that he could live with Mary Larson and their light-skinned daughter.

After attending Fisk, Larsen traveled to Copenhagen, Denmark, where she probably lived with her mother's family. She may have audited courses at the University of Copenhagen, but no hard evidence exists on Larsen's whereabouts from 1909 to 1912. She did, however, settle in New York City in 1912, and she graduated from Lincoln Hospital's nursing program in 1915. She went to Tuskegee, Alabama, to work for a year at the John A. Andrew Hospital and Nurse Training School. Disappointed with the school (which would later serve as the model for Naxos in *Quicksand*) and with her position as superintendent of nurses, Larsen returned to New York and found a job at the city's health department.

By the middle of 1919, she had met and married Dr. Elmer Samuel Imes, a well-known African American physicist. Her nursing career started to take a backseat to her interest in writing, and in 1920 she began to publish pieces in a children's journal called *The Brownies' Book*, created by the literary editor of *The Crisis*, Jessie Redmon Fauset. Larsen took a job at the 135th Street branch of the New York Public Library in 1921 and graduated from the New York Public Library's Library School in 1923. She resigned from her position as librarian in 1926, but by this point she had become firmly ensconced in the Harlem Renaissance and was working on *Quicksand*. Her relationship with Fauset, Imes, and the white author Carl Van Vechten only strengthened her growing reputation in the African American literary community; she had already sparked some interest with her *Brownies' Book* stories, which she published under the name Nella Larsen Imes, and with two pulp-fiction stories featured in *Young's Magazine* under the pseudonym Allen Semi.

Quicksand, published in 1928 by Knopf, was immediately

praised by critics. W. E. B. Du Bois called it "the best piece of fiction that Negro America has produced since the heydey of [Charles] Chesnutt" in his review in *The Crisis*. *Passing* met with similar success, but Larsen's professional accomplishments were somewhat muted by the dissolution of her marriage in 1929. Imes followed his own career to Fisk University in Nashville, where he established the school's physics department. Larsen's Guggenheim Fellowship allowed her to go to Spain rather than rejoin the restrictive atmosphere that she had earlier encountered in academia. In Spain she began two other novels, but they were never published.

The trip to Spain was conveniently timed for another reason: In 1930, Larsen was accused of plagiarism in her short story "Sanctuary," and the trip offered her a much-needed respite from the scandal. Though an investigation ensued and she was eventually exonerated, the charge always haunted her and is likely to have been a major factor in the early termination of her career. Larsen's discovery of her husband's extramarital affairs is also likely to have contributed. After a brief attempt to live together in Nashville, the pair were divorced in 1933. Larsen again settled in New York City, but this time she chose Greenwich Village over Harlem. For a while she seems to have been an active figure in the Village's intellectual circles, but by the late-1930's, she had become quite elusive, and is even reported to have feigned voyages to other countries in order to avoid contact with people.

Imes paid alimony until he died in 1941, an event that prompted Larsen to return to nursing. From 1944 to 1961, she was a supervisor at Governeur Hospital. When it was absorbed by Beth Israel Medical Center and Hospital, she moved on to Metropolis Hospital, where she worked until her death in 1964. Her final years were troubled, and she became increasingly depressed, perhaps as a result of a visit to her half sister, Anna Gardner, in Santa Monica, California. The two had not seen each other for thirty years, and Gardner would later assert that they were not related at all. Larsen died of heart failure while reading in bed, but her body was not discovered until a week after her death, when colleagues from work noticed that she was missing.

Analysis: Long Fiction

Both of Larsen's major works have important autobiographical elements, and both deal with similar themes. *Quicksand*, though, is probably more heavily based on Larsen's life, and it focuses more closely on the complex notion of African American women's sexuality as perceived both by the individual and by others. Like *Passing*, *Quicksand* also delves into questions of biracial identity, which was clearly a subject to which Larsen had strong personal connection. These two weighty issues might even be viewed as the ingredients that erupt in the violence and passion of *Passing*'s most climactic scene, in which Larsen vividly illustrates the overwhelming difficulties inherent in any attempt to reconcile an individual's black and white heritages with twentieth century American culture.

Quicksand

In many respects, *Quicksand* is a highly autobiographical work. Larsen's protagonist, Helga Crane, is, like Larsen, a biracial woman whose mother is Danish and whose father is from the West Indies. Seeking a firmer grasp on her complex personal, cultural, and sexual identity, Crane moves to the southern United States, becomes an instructor at an all-black college called Naxos, and travels to Chicago, New York City, and Denmark. Literary critics have theorized that Crane's frequent relocation is, in some ways, a manifestation of an inner urge to better understand and to pinpoint her fragile emotional and physical center. If nothing else, Crane's transitory nature points to her hope of locating an external source of emotional peace and stability.

Naxos, unsurprisingly, bears a strong resemblance to the Tuskegee Institute, where Larsen worked. Crane gradually becomes disillusioned with the school's attempts to follow a Booker T. Washington-type philosophy (in which African Americans attempt to elevate their position in society by imitating whites and by maintaining what is effectively a "separate but equal" position within society). She soon abandons Naxos and moves to Chicago, but there her misfortune continues: She is rejected by her maternal uncle, Poul, who was also her teacher for many years. Rebuffed in much the same way that Larsen was in her own life, Crane escapes to New York, where the vibrance and excitement of the Harlem Renaissance strike a chord with Crane's own emerging energy and sexuality.

Crane is ill-equipped to deal with her emotions, however, and refuses to tackle them head-on. Instead, she runs away to Copenhagen after accepting money from her uncle. The Danish city is comparatively free from prejudice, but Crane still stands out as a foreigner, and she longs to be part of an African American community. She leaves Denmark and the offer of marriage that she received there and returns to New York, where the Harlem Renaissance is in full swing. In New York, though, the tables of romance turn on Crane, and she is rejected by a one-time colleague from Naxos. Distracted by the strength of her sexuality and struggling to find an outlet for it, Crane finally marries a Revivalist minister, Reverend Green, and follows him back to the South. As the novel concludes, Crane is in labor with her fifth child, a process that consumes her mentally, emotionally, and physically and results in the emotional paralysis to which the title refers.

Passing

Like *Quicksand*, *Passing* centers on the marginalization of African American women. Some literary critics have maintained that Larsen's choice of title—and, indeed, the book's main theme—only strengthens the effect of the characters' isolation. However, most scholars consider the novel to be the finest treatment of the concept of hidden racial identity in modern American literature.

The novel's protagonist, Clare Kendry, escaped from cruel, racist aunts by "passing"—that is, by using her light skin color to join the white community and to adopt a white identity. Her childhood friend, Irene Redfield, lives her life in fear and carefully avoids any hint of danger. Seeking a safe lifystyle, she has married, but her marriage hangs by a thread. She does, however, take an active role in Harlem's middle-class black society, and it is through her friendship with Redfield that Kendry begins to rediscover her identity as an African American. The women are able to maintain their friendship despite Kendry's absorption into white society, and Redfield does not chastise her friend for her decision. In fact, the women are first reunited at a party at which Irene herself has "passed" as white in order to seek refuge from the tumult of Chicago's rough neighborhoods.

Larsen is careful to point out that Kendry's life as a white woman is far from idyllic. In some ways, any advantage Kendry might have had as a white person is replaced in her mind by the disadvantages created by her lack of money (compared to her relatively prosperous white acquaintances). She seeks comfort in Redfield's Harlem, but her period of self-exploration comes to an abrupt halt when her husband, John Bellew, discovers Kendry's real identity and rejects her entirely. Much hinges on the novel's climax, in which Kendry attends a Christmas party with Redfield and her husband Brian. Redfield has become increasingly jealous of the affection between her husband and her friend, and begins to feel that Kendry may be trying to dissolve her marriage. As the party continues, Kendry falls from a sixth-floor window and is killed. Several critics, though, have argued that she was pushed by Redfield.

In many ways, the success of this scene (and the novel as a whole) rests on Larsen's depiction of the relationship between the two women. When Kendry's husband storms into the party, calling his wife a "damned nigger," Redfield rushes to her friend's side in a gesture that seems, on its surface, to be a loving act of defense. However, Larsen reveals Redfield's thoughts: "One thought possessed her. She couldn't have Clare Kendry cast aside by Bellew. She couldn't have her free." Redfield's well-being is dependent on her friend's entrapment; Redfield is unable to draw any kind of distinction between her desire for and her desire to be Kendry, nor is she able to reconcile these desires. The complex web that Larsen constructs around and between these four characters (but most especially between the two women) is further tangled by the novel's lack of resolution. It never becomes clear whether Kendry was killed or whether she killed herself. The reader is left unsatisfied, unless he or she can be satisfied with ambiguity, as, Larsen had to be in her own life.

Other Literary Forms

In January, 1930, Larsen published the short story "Sanctuary" in *Forum* magazine. Several readers commented that the story bore a striking resemblance to Sheila Kaye-Smith's "Mrs. Adis," published in 1922 in *Century* magazine. Larsen's editor had seen many drafts of the story and defended Larsen in a supplement to *Forum* published in April, 1930. Larsen insisted that she had heard the story from a patient at Lincoln Hospital, but that the story was widely known and its many variations were parts of the African American oral tradition. Larsen's editors studied the matter and eventually dismissed all accusations against the author, but Larsen remained deeply wounded by the charge.

Bibliography

Davis, Thadious M. *Nella Larsen, Novelist of the Harlem Renaissance: A Woman's Life Unveiled.* Baton Rouge: Louisiana State University Press, 1994. Davis is a well-respected scholar of African American history and literature, and she is arguably the best-known Larsen scholar. This volume examines Larsen's life thoroughly and is a crucial starting point for any serious research.

Defalco, Amelia. "Jungle Creatures and Dancing Apes: Modern Primitivism and Nella Larsen's *Quicksand.*" *Mosaic: A Journal for the Interdisciplinary Study of Literature* 38, no. 2 (June, 2005): 19-25. Helga Crane's physical body often wields more influence than the character's ideas, argues Defalco. She goes on to assert that much of Crane's unhappy life is the product of societal tendencies to fetishize the African American female body.

Knadler, Stephen. "Domestic Violence in the Harlem Renaissance: Remaking the Record in Nella Larsen's *Passing* and Toni Morrison's *Jazz.*" *African American Review* 38, no. 1 (Spring, 2004): 99-118. This interesting article cites decades of reporting on domestic violence in the *Amsterdam News*, New York City's flagship African American periodical, and studies the relationship between reality and Larsen's and Morrison's fiction. Knadler argues that women's use of violence only strengthened their subservient relationships to men.

Larson, Charles R. *Invisible Darkness: Jean Toomer and Nella Larsen.* Iowa City: University of Iowa Press, 1993. This volume treats the authors separately, devoting two sections to each. Larson focuses on the impact of Larsen's adolescence on her later writing and on her relationship to the Harlem Renaissance. Contains a bibliography and an index.

Rottenberg, Catherine. "*Passing*: Race, Identification, and Desire." *Criticism* 45, no. 4 (Fall, 2003): 435-452. Focuses on *Passing*'s presentation of passing as a way of combating, rather than conforming to, racial prejudices and stereotypes. Argues that *Passing* is the most important work of literature on the subject.

Sato, Hiroko. "Under the Harlem Shadow: A Study of Jessie Fauset and Nella Larsen." In *The Harlem Renaissance Remembered*, edited by Arna Bontemps. New York: Dodd, Mead, 1972. Sato examines Fauset's influence on Larsen and her career and asserts that race is a fundamental feature of both authors' works.

Sherrard-Johnson, Cherene. "A Plea For Color: Nella Larsen's Iconography of the Mulatta." *American Literature* 76, no. 4 (December, 2004): 833-869. Combining art and literature, this article studies the role of the multiracial female protagonist. The author delves into the psychological complexity of the portrait painted by Larsen's fiction.

Thaggert, Miriam. "Racial Etiquette." *Meridians: Feminism, Race, Transnationalism* 5, no. 2 (April, 2005): 1-29. This article centers on *Passing*, which Thaggert sees as a work of complex meanings, in which characters communicate their thoughts through glances as much as they do through speech. Thaggert persuasively argues that Larsen's use of this subtle technique keeps the reader in suspense.

Watson, Reginald. "The Tragic Mulatto Image in Charles Chesnutt's *The House Behind the Cedars* and Nella Larsen's *Passing*." *CLA Journal* 46, no. 1 (September, 2002): 48-71. This article discusses the representation of multiracial characters in works by these two important authors.

Young, John K. "The Ends of Nella Larsen's *Passing.*" *College English* 66, no. 6 (July, 2004): 632-651. Young argues that literature written by racial minorities and women deserves especially careful study, both because these texts have been overlooked in the past and because they provide unique insights into the nature of female and minority cultures.

— Anna A. Moore

Audre Lorde

Poet and essayist

Born: Harlem, New York; February 18, 1934
Died: Christiansted, St. Croix, Virgin Islands;
November 17, 1992

POETRY: *The First Cities,* 1968; *Cables to Rage,* 1970; *From a Land Where Other People Live,* 1973; *New York Head Shop and Museum,* 1974; *Between Our Selves,* 1976; *Coal,* 1976; *The Black Unicorn,* 1978; *Chosen Poems, Old and New,* 1982 (revised as *Undersong: Chosen Poems, Old and New,* 1992); *A Comrade Is as Precious as a Rice Seedling,* 1984; *Our Dead Behind Us,* 1986; *Need: A Chorale for Black Woman Voices,* 1990; *The Marvelous Arithmetics of Distance: Poems, 1987-1992,* 1993; *The Collected Poems of Audre Lorde,* 1997.

NONFICTION: *Uses of the Erotic: The Erotic as Power,* 1978; *The Cancer Journals,* 1980; *Zami: A New Spelling of My Name: A Biomythography,* 1982; *Sister Outsider: Essays and Speeches,* 1984; *I Am Your Sister: Black Women Organizing Across Sexualities,* 1985; *Apartheid U.S.A.,* 1986; *A Burst of Light: Essays,* 1988; *The Audre Lorde Compendium: Essays, Speeches, and Journals,* 1996.

Achievements

Audre Lorde received a National Endowment for the Arts grant and was a poet in residence at Tougaloo College in Jackson, Mississippi, in 1968. She also won the Creative Artists Public Service grant (1972 and 1976) and the Broadside Poets Award (1975). In 1975 she was named Woman of the Year by Staten Island Community College. She received the Borough of Manhattan President's Award for literary excellence (1987), the American Book Award from the Before Columbus Foundation for *A Burst of Light,* a Walt Whitman Citation of Merit, and two Lambda Literary Awards for Lesbian Poetry: in 1993 for *Undersong* and in

1994 for *The Marvelous Arithmetics of Distance*. She was named poet laureate of New York in 1991.

Biography

Audre Lorde's parents emigrated from Grenada to New York City in 1924. Lorde, the youngest of three girls, was born in 1934. She recounted many of her childhood memories in *Zami*, identifying particular incidents that had an influence or effect on her developing sexuality and her later work as a poet. She attended the University of Mexico (1954-1955) and received a B.A. from Hunter College (1959) and an M.L.S. from Columbia University (1961). In 1962, she was married to Edwin Rollins, with whom she had two children before they were divorced in 1970.

Prior to 1968, when she gained public recognition for her poetry, Lorde supported herself through a variety of jobs, including low-paying factory work. She also served as a librarian in several institutions. After her first publication, *The First Cities*, Lorde worked primarily within American colleges and free presses. She was an instructor at City College of New York (1968-1970), an instructor and then lecturer at Lehman College (1969-1971), and a professor of English at John Jay College of Criminal Justice (1972-1981). From 1981 to 1987, she was a professor of English at Hunter College at CUNY, and she became a Thomas Hunter Professor for one year there (1987-1988). She also served as poetry editor of the magazine *Chrysalis* and was a contributing editor of the journal *Black Scholar*.

In the early 1980's, she helped start Kitchen Table: Women of Color Press, a multicultural effort publishing Asian American and Latina as well as African American women writers. In the late 1980's Lorde became increasingly concerned over the plight of black women in South Africa under apartheid, creating Sisterhood in Support of Sisters in South Africa and remaining an active voice on behalf of these women throughout the remainder of her life. She also served on the board of the National Coalition of Black Lesbians and Gays. With the companion of her last years, the writer and black feminist scholar Gloria I. Jo-

(Ingmar Schullz)

seph, she made a home on St. Croix in the U.S. Virgin Islands. Shortly before her death in 1992 she completed her tenth book of poems, *The Marvelous Arithmetics of Distance.*

Analysis: Poetry

Audre Lorde called herself a "black lesbian feminist warrior poet." At the heart of her work as poet, essayist, teacher, and lecturer lies an intense and relentless exploration of personal identity. Beyond the stunning portrayals of her deepest insights and emotions, her work is filled with powerful evocations of universal survival. The substance of her poetry and essays always reaches beyond the individual self into deep concerns for all humanity. Progressively, her work reveals an increasing awareness of her West Indian heritage in relation to her place in American society and its values.

All Audre Lorde's poems, essays, and speeches are deeply personal renditions of a compassionate writer, thinker, and human being. Indeed, she drew much of her material from individual and multifaceted experience; she rendered it in writing that sought to reveal the complexity of being a black feminist lesbian poet. She expressed the feelings of being marginalized in an American society that is predominantly white, male, heterosexual, and middle class. Her writings reflected the changing constitution and perspective of American life, but she never relented to an easy optimism, nor did she make uninformed dismissals of society's ills. Her personal experiences made her compassionate toward those who suffer under oppressive regimes all over the world. By drawing from the history and mythology of the West Indies, she was able to refer to the racism and sexism that exist in other cultures.

The title of one of her essays is especially appropriate to inform her work as a poet, "The Transformation of Silence into Language and Action." In a self-characterization when she was a poet in residence at Tougaloo College, Lorde said, "I became convinced, anti-academic though I am, that all poets must teach what they know, in order to continue being." Her insistent drive to exist according to the terms of her individual desires and powers was the focal point of many of her speeches and essays. Lorde was also active on the lecture circuit, and she was invited to speak to women writers in the Soviet Union and in Berlin. She documented many of her insights into various cultures and places in essays and poems.

The various forms of her writing provided many pieces to the whole picture that made up Lorde's life and work. She was unsentimental in naming the people who have been a part of her life and in evaluating the events that make up her experiences. Her parents and her sisters are addressed with some frequency in her poems. A girlhood friend, Genevieve, appears in *Zami*, and Lorde eulogizes her death in a poem titled "Memorial II."

Many women are treated in several different poems, sometimes in cycles—for example, Martha and Eudora. In these ways, Lorde documented the people and the course of her life as she charted the changes and the progress that occur; at each turn, she sought to understand more deeply the situation and to learn which detours to take next.

When she was in her forties, Lorde was diagnosed with breast cancer. *The Cancer Journals* and the essay "A Burst of Light: Living with Cancer" are important pieces of personal writing that recorded her uncertainties, fears, and doubts about her mortality. Writing mostly in the form of a diary, Lorde allowed the reader to enter into her most private thoughts and emotions, with the hope that others may be encouraged to fight cancer. From her determination to survive, Lorde converted her struggles with cancer into energy for battling on behalf of other humanitarian concerns.

She set out rigorously to combat racism, sexism, heterosexism, and homophobia in her work. At times she dealt with the issues separately, but more frequently she spoke of the whole gamut, since she perceived that each stems from human blindness about the differences among people. What was remarkable about Lorde's insight is the balance that she sought in presenting her views. Overtly political in intent and social in content, the essays and speeches ask all individuals to understand more deeply the ways in which human lives are organized. She then beckoned people to take charge of their lives, to confront the tasks at hand, and to take responsibility for making changes.

Much of Lorde's mature work evolved from her identity as a black feminist lesbian poet. These terms are essential conjunctions that expressed her existence and her vision. In the essay "The Master's Tools Will Never Dismantle the Master's House," Lorde made no apologies or defenses for her choices. She wrote, "For women, the need and desire to nurture each other is not pathological but redemptive, and it is within that knowledge that our real power is rediscovered." For Lorde, the power to exist and be alive came from her love—in all senses of the word—for women.

In her most-often cited essay, "The Uses of the Erotic: The Erotic as Power," Lorde dislodged some of the negative assumptions that have sprung up around the terms "erotic" and "power," and offered new perspectives on how an individual must use her power and ability to love. For Lorde, the erotic was "a resource within each of us that lies in a deeply female and spiritual plane, firmly rooted in the power of our unexpressed or unrecognized feeling." Through a redefinition of the terms, Lorde showed how societal oppression numbs a woman's ability to feel and act deeply. Often the two—emotion and action—are in conflict with the values of a "racist, patriarchal, and anti-erotic society." Before individual human beings can come together as one society, each person must be in touch with his or her own feelings and be willing to express and share with others. These are the necessary first steps to effecting real political change.

Lorde contended that the need to share is a fundamental one that all people feel. Unfortunately, the prevailing attitudes of American society preclude true expression of individualism: If people do not fit into the norms or expectations of the dominant system of values, they are deemed "not normal" or deviant. Lorde argued against the hypocrisy of American values: Where is freedom if any forms of expression considered "unfit" are excluded? How might one such as herself, who is on the margins of all that is "normal," empower herself to take effective action?

These are the kinds of difficult questions Lorde raised from the beginning of her work as a writer and poet. She made efforts to answer them anew in much of what she produced. She emphasized the necessity of listening to others and teaching what she herself had learned in the course of her work. Always receptive to the notion of difference that exists among all people, Lorde set out to consider the meaning of her own experiences first, before she attempted to convey to others what those experiences might mean in the larger context of existence. On the one hand, her work was intensely personal; it may even be considered self-absorbed at times. Yet on the other, she managed to transform her deeply private pains and joys into universal and timeless concerns.

The First Cities and Cables to Rage

In her early collections of poetry, *The First Cities* and *Cables to Rage*, Lorde expressed a keen political disillusionment, noting the failure of American ideals of equality and justice for all. When Lorde used the pronoun "we" in her poetry, she spoke for all who have been dispossessed. In "Anniversary," for example, she wrote, "Our tears/ water an alien grass," expressing the separation between those who belong and those who do not. In poems such as "Sowing," the poet revealed the land's betrayal of its inhabitants by showing images of destruction juxtaposed to personal rage: "I have been to this place before/ where blood seething commanded/ my fingers fresh from the earth."

She also demonstrated a concern for the children of this earth in "Blood-birth": Casting about to understand what it is in her that is raging to be born, she wondered how an opening will come "to show the true face of me/ lying exposed and together/ my children your children their children/ bent on our conjugating business." The image of the warrior, the one who must be prepared to go about the business of existing in an unjust world, signifies the need to take care of those not yet aware of unfulfilled promises.

If the rage in her early poems appears "unladylike," Lorde was setting out to explode sexual typecasting. Certainly, there was nothing dainty about her sharp images and powerful assessments of social conditions. As she confronted harsh realities, the portrayals were necessarily clamorous. Yet the poet's rage did not lead to a blind rampage. In "Conversation in Crisis," the poet hoped to speak to her friend "for a clear meeting/ of self upon self/ in sight of our hearth/ but without fire." The poet must speak honestly and not out of false assumptions and pretenses so that real communication can occur. The reader and listener must heed the words as well as the tone in order to receive the meaning of the words. Communication, then, is a kind of contractual relationship between people.

From a Land Where Other People Live and Between Our Selves

In the collections *From a Land Where Other People Live* and *Between Our Selves*, Lorde used a compassionate tone to tell people about the devastation of white racism upon African Americans. She mixes historical fact with political reality, emphasizing the disjunction that sometimes occurs between the two. In "Equinox," Lorde observed her daughter's birth by remembering a series of events that also occurred that year: She had "marched into Washington/ to a death knell of dreaming/ which 250,000 others mistook for a hope," for few at that time understood the victimization of children that was occurring not only in the American South but also in the Vietnam War. After she heard that Malcolm X had been shot, she reread all of his writings: "the dark mangled children/ came streaming out of the atlas/ Hanoi Angola Guinea-Bissau . . . / merged into Bedford-Stuyvesant and Hazelhurst Mississippi."

From the multiplicity of world horrors, the poet returned to her hometown in New York, exhausted but profoundly moved by the confrontation of history and the facts of her own existence. In "The Day They Eulogized Mahalia," another event is present in the background as the great singer Mahalia Jackson is memorialized: Six black children died in a fire at a day care center on the South Side; "firemen found their bodies/ like huddled lumps of charcoal/ with silent mouths and eyes wide open." Even as she mourned the dead in her poems, the poet seems aware of both the power and the powerlessness of words to effect real changes. In the poem, "Power," Lorde writes,

> The difference between poetry and rhetoric
> is being ready to kill
> yourself
> instead of your children.

Once the event has occurred, one can write about it or one can try to prevent a similar event from occurring; in either case, it is not possible to undo the first event. Therefore, as a society, people must learn from their errors and their failures to care for other people. Lorde even warned herself that she must discern and employ this crucial difference between poetry and rhetoric; if she did not, "my power too will run corrupt as poisonous mold/ or lie limp and useless as an unconnected wire."

Coal, The Black Unicorn, and Our Dead Behind Us

For Lorde, the process of learning all over again how to transform thought into action began with the awareness of her personal reality. In the collections *Coal*, *The Black Unicorn*, and *Our Dead Behind Us*, the poet addressed more specifically the individual human beings in her life, creating vignettes of her relationships with other people. In particular, she returned again and again to images of her mother, Linda Belmar Lorde, whose relatively light-colored skin is mentioned in many of the poems. In "Outside," she links her mother's lightness to the brutal faces of racism: "Nobody lynched my momma/ but what she'd never been/ had bleached her face of everything." When Lorde questioned, "Who shall I curse that I grew up/ believing in my mother's face," she echoed the anger that also appears in the poem "Sequelae." There she stated explicitly the rage that evolved from the mother's lies, white lies: "I battle the shapes of you/ wearing old ghosts of me/ hating you for being/ black and not woman/ hating you for being white." (*Zami* elaborates many of the specific events to which Lorde referred in her poems about her mother.)

The return to childhood allowed the poet to come to new terms with her mother. In several of her poems, she also returned to even deeper roots constituting her identity. In "Dahomey," she referred to the African goddess Seboulisa, "the Mother of us all" or the creator of the world. In embracing the mother goddess, the poet was able "to sharpen the knives of my tongue." Because the subjects of her poetry are painful ones, Lorde empowered her own speech by always calling attention to the dangers of remaining silent. In "A Song for Many Movements," she stated simply and precisely the project of her poetry: "Our labor has become/ more important/ than our silence."

Undersong

Three decades of production and the work from Lorde's first five published collections form her 1992 collection titled *Undersong: Chosen Poems, Old and New*, a reworking of her 1982 work, *Chosen Poems, Old and New*. It is not a "selected poems" in the usual meaning of the term, because it contains no work from her centrally important *The Black Unicorn*, which she considered too complex and too much of a unit to be dismembered by excerpting, and holds little of *Our Dead Behind Us*. Thus a large chunk of her strongest work is missing—including most of the poems in which she conjured and confronted "the worlds of Africa."

As she stated in an introduction, her revisions of *Chosen Poems, Old and New* were undertaken to clarify but not to recast the work—necessitating that she "propel [herself] back into the original poem-creating process and the poet who wrote it." Lorde returned to her work of *Chosen Poems, Old and New* after Hurricane Hugo wrecked her home in the Virgin Islands and she found "a waterlogged but readable copy of [the book], one of the few salvageable books from [her] library." The drama of the incident seemed to take an allegorical cast and inspired her to treat the anchoring of her poems in truth with the same fierce honesty she had devoted to confronting her childhood, her blackness, and her sexual identity. She thus seemed determined to keep her poetry under spiritual review with the same intensity that she devoted to the infinite difficulties of being an African American woman and lesbian in late twentieth century America. The changes she made in this collection seem limited to the excising of a handful of early poems, substituting others previously unpublished, and reworking line breaks and punctuation to give more space and deliberate stress to each stanza and image.

The themes of the book largely circulate on two central axes: The notion of changeable selves—the broken journey toward self—is a recurrent motif, as is her consuming involvement with issues of survival. In examining changeable selves, she juxtaposes the longing for completion with the awareness of change as a paradoxical condition of identity. In "October," Lorde appeals to the goddess Seboulisa, elsewhere described as the "Mother of us all":

> Carry my heart to some shore
> my feet will not shatter

> do not let me pass away
> before I have a name
> for this tree
> under which I am lying
> Do not let me die still
> needing to be stranger.

As the final couplet hints, the counterpoint to the search for self is the search for connection, and to that end, dialogue is used as a structuring device, creating a sense of companionship won in the face of a proudly borne singularity.

Poems with images of destruction also abound: the dead friend Genevieve; the father who "died in silence"; the "lovers processed/ through the corridors of Bellevue Mattewan/ Brooklyn State the Women's House of D./ St. Vincent's and the Tombs"; "a black boy (Emmett Till) hacked into a murderous lesson"; the lost sisters and daughters of Africa and its diaspora, whose "bones whiten/ in secret." Lorde's dual themes of the unending search for identity and a struggle for survival heightens the impact of the word "nightmare," which cycles endlessly throughout Lorde's work. The word represents her expression for history as glimpsed in surreal previsions and "Afterimages" (the title of a poem linking her memories of Emmett Till's lynching to television pictures of a Mississippi flood). One looks in vain for a "positive" counterweight, before realizing that the nightmare, for Lorde, is not a token of negativity but rather symbolizes the denied and feared aspects of experience that must be recalled and accepted for change to occur.

The Marvelous Arithmetics of Distance: Poems, 1987-1992

In her final collection of poems, published posthumously, Lorde displays a personal, moving, bare, and striking set of work that strives for poignant reckonings with her family. "Legacy—Hers" is about her mother, "bred for endurance/ for battle." "Inheritance—His" is about her father. She also has farewells to her sister, whom she forgives ("both you and I/ are free to go"), and to her son, whom she challenges ("In what do you believe?") She has many bouquets for Gloria, her partner.

She also visits her characteristic theme of politics in this collection. For example, she writes cinematically about the destruction wrought by U.S. foreign policy in a ferocious "Peace on Earth: Christmas, 1989":

> the rockets red glare where
> all these brown children
> running scrambling around the globe
> flames through the rubble
> bombs bursting in air
> Panama Nablus Gaza
> tear gas clouding the Natal sun.
> THIS IS A GIFT FROM THE PEOPLE OF THE UNITED
> STATES OF AMERICA
> quick cut
> the crackling Yule log
> in an iron grate.

In "Jesse Helms," which begins "I am a Black woman/ writing my way to the future," she takes on the bigotry of the senator from North Carolina with intentional crudeness:

> Your turn now jessehelms
> come on its time
> to lick the handwriting
> off the walls.

In this sparse and commanding book, perhaps the most arresting lines are those in which she wrestles with the nearness of her own death. In "Today is not the day," she writes:

> I am dying
> but I do not want to do it
> looking the other way.
> Audre Lorde never looked the other way.

Other Literary Forms

The Cancer Journals is a personal account of Audre Lorde's struggles with breast cancer. *Zami: A New Spelling of My Name*, which Lorde called a "biomythography," is a retrospective narrative of her emerging sexuality. *Sister Outsider: Essays and Speeches* and *A*

Burst of Light: Essays are collections of essays and speeches on poetry, feminism, lesbianism, and racism.

Bibliography
Avi-Ram, Amitai F. "*Apo Koinou* in Lorde and the Moderns: Defining the Differences." *Callaloo* 9 (Winter, 1986): 193-208. *Apo koinou* comes from a Greek phrase meaning "in common." This original and ambitious essay discusses the uses of eroticism and the importance of a political consciousness in Lorde's work. The author situates Lorde's work in the context of other modernist poets. The argument is sophisticated and learned; its stimulating premise derives from a familiarity with literary history and Western philosophical thought.

Bowen, Angela. "Diving into Audre Lorde's 'Blackstudies.'" *Meridians: Feminism, Race, Transnationalism* 4, no. 1 (October, 2003): 109-130. Explores the use of code and hidden messages in Lorde's 1974 poem "Blackstudies."

Brooks, Jerome. "In the Name of the Father: The Poetry of Audre Lorde." In *Black Women Writers, 1950-1980: A Critical Evaluation*, edited by Mari Evans. Garden City, N.Y.: Doubleday, 1984. This brief chapter deals with a topic to which Lorde gives little direct attention in her own essays—the death of her father. It is a useful analysis of a focused topic that clarifies the meaning of some of the poems in which the figure of the father appears.

De Veaux, Alexis. *Warrior Poet: A Biography of Audre Lorde.* New York: W. W. Norton, 2004. Lorde's childhood in Harlem, literary career, and her battle with breast cancer are detailed in this first biography of the renowned poet. De Veaux's material is gleaned from personal journals, private archives, and interviews with Lorde's family and friends.

Dilworth, Thomas. "Lorde's 'Power.'" *The Explicator* 57, no. 1 (Fall, 1998): 54-57. Examines the complex imagery in Audre Lorde's poem "Power," found in her collection titled *The Black Unicorn.* He argues that the poem is more than an expressive, rhetorical piece—it is a work of art.

Field, Susan. "Open to Influence: Ralph Waldo Emerson and Audre Lorde on Loss." *ATQ* 19, no. 1 (March, 2005). Draws interesting parallels between writings by Audre Lorde on her experiences with breast cancer and Ralph Waldo Emerson's treatment of his son's death. Both writers, Field says, see their grief as a force that detracts from their individual identity.

Hull, Gloria T. "Living on the Line: Audre Lorde and *Our Dead Behind Us.*" In *Changing Our Own Words: Essays on Criticism, Theory, and Writing by Black Women,* edited by Cheryl A. Wall. New Brunswick, N.J.: Rutgers University Press, 1989. This is a thoughtful essay on one of Lorde's collections of poetry. While it refers to some contemporary critical theory, it is an engaging and accessible study that traces the trajectory of Lorde's work. Hull also assesses various critical reviews of the collection.

Lewis, Gail. "Audre Lorde: Vignettes and Mental Conversations." *Feminist Review* 19, no. 80 (2005): 130-146. An article concerned with Lorde's contributions to left-wing feminism and to African American freedom. Also provides biographical highlights and descriptions of Lorde's works.

Lorde, Audre. *The Cancer Journals.* San Francisco: Aunt Lute Books, 1997. A new edition with posthumous tributes from other writers and poets added to Lorde's autobiographical exploration of her breast cancer and mastectomy.

————. "Sadomasochism: Not About Condemnation." Interview by Susan Leigh Star. In *A Burst of Light.* Ithaca, N.Y.: Firebrand Books, 1988. Lorde talks energetically about her sexuality, setting the discussion in the context of her life's work. This interview is the first in a series of private meditations centered on her bouts with cancer.

Lorde, Audre, and Adrienne Rich. "An Interview: Audre Lorde and Adrienne Rich." In *Sister Outsider: Essays and Speeches.* Trumansburg, N.Y.: Crossing Press, 1984. The two poets speak about a wide range of topics such as power, knowledge, and eroticism. Lorde also discusses her views on the uses of prose and poetry, focusing on the process of perception.

Martin, Joan. "The Unicorn Is Black: Audre Lorde in Retrospect." In *Black Women Writers, 1950-1980: A Critical Evaluation,* edited by Mari Evans. Garden City, N.Y.: Doubleday,

1984. This is a useful compendium of Lorde's work up to 1984, focusing on the collection titled *The Black Unicorn*.

Olson, Lester C. "Liabilities of Language: Audre Lorde Reclaiming Difference." *Quarterly Journal of Speech* 84, no. 4 (November, 1998): 448-470. Distortions around the naming and the misnaming of human differences are the central foci of Audre Lorde's speech "Age, Race, Class, Sex: Women Redefining Difference," which she delivered at Amherst College in Massachusetts on April 3, 1980. Here she exemplifies her deep understanding of what she refers to in an earlier speech as "that language which has been made to work against us."

Walk, Lori L. "Audre Lorde's Life Writing: The Politics of Location." *Women's Studies* 32, no. 7 (December, 2003): 815-835. Takes a closer look at the ways in which Lorde deals with her anger and her cancer through poetry.

— Sarah Hilbert; Cynthia Wong

Claude McKay

Poet, novelist, and short-story writer

Born: Sunny Ville, Jamaica; September 15, 1889
Died: Chicago, Illinois; May 22, 1948

LONG FICTION: *Home to Harlem*, 1928; *Banjo*, 1929; *Banana Bottom*, 1933.

SHORT FICTION: *Gingertown*, 1932.

POETRY: *Songs of Jamaica*, 1912; *Constab Ballads*, 1912; *Spring in New Hampshire, and Other Poems*, 1920; *Harlem Shadows*, 1922; *Selected Poems of Claude McKay*, 1953.

NONFICTION: *A Long Way from Home*, 1937 (autobiography); *Harlem: Negro Metropolis*, 1940.

MISCELLANEOUS: *The Passion of Claude McKay: Selected Poetry and Prose, 1912-1948*, 1973 (Wayne F. Cooper, editor; contains social and literary criticism, letters, prose, fiction, and poetry).

Achievements

Claude McKay received a medal from the Jamaican Institute of Arts and Sciences (1912), the National Association for the Advancement of Colored People's Harmon Foundation Award (1929) for *Harlem Shadows* and *Home to Harlem*, an award from the James Weldon Johnson Literary Guild (1937), and the Order of Jamaica. He was named that country's national poet in 1977. McKay's contribution to American poetry cannot, however, be measured in awards and citations alone. His peculiar pilgrimage took him from Jamaica to Moscow, from communism to Catholicism, from Harlem to Marseilles. He lived and worked among common laborers most of his life, and developed a respect for them worthy of Walt Whitman. He rejected the critical pronouncements of his black contemporaries and, as poet and critic Melvin Tolson points out, he "was unaffected by the New Poetry and Criticism." His singular blend of modern political and social radicalism with the timeworn cadences of the sonnet won for him, at best, mixed reviews from many critics, black and white.

In any attempt to calculate his poetic achievement, however, one must realize that, with the exception of his early Jamaican dialect verse (certainly an important contribution in its own right to the little-studied literature of the British West Indies) and some rather disappointing poetry composed late in his life, his poetic career spanned little more than a decade. At the publication in 1922 of *Harlem Shadows,* the furthest extent of his poetic development, he was only thirty-three. McKay should be read as a poet on the way up.

Surely there is no more ludicrous task than to criticize a writer on the basis of his potential, and so one should take McKay as one finds him, and indeed, in those terms, he does not fare badly. His was the first notable voice of anger in modern black American poetry. Writing when he did, he had to struggle against the enormous pressure, not of white censure, but of a racial responsibility that was his, whether he wanted it or not. He could not be merely a poet—he had to be a "black poet," had to speak, to some extent, for countless others; such a position is difficult for any poet. Through it all, however, he strove for individuality and fought to keep from being bought by any interest, black or white, right- or left-wing.

Largely through the work of McKay, and of such Harlem Renaissance contemporaries as Countée Cullen and Langston Hughes, the task of being a black poet in America was made easier. *Harlem Shadows* marked a decisive beginning toward improving the predicament so concisely recorded by Cullen, who wondered aloud in the sonnet "Yet Do I Marvel" how a well-intentioned God could in his wisdom do "this curious thing:/ To make a poet black and bid him sing."

Biography

Festus Claudius McKay was born in 1889 on a small farm in Clarendon Parish, Jamaica. His parents were well-respected members of the community and of the local Baptist church. He received his early education from his older brother, a school-teacher near Montego Bay. In 1907, he was apprenticed to a wheelwright and cabinetmaker in Brown's Town; this apprenticeship was short-lived, but it was in Brown's Town that McKay entered into a far more fruitful apprenticeship of another sort. Walter Jekyll, an English aristocrat and student of Jamaican culture, came to know young Claude and undertook the boy's literary education. As McKay recalled years later in his autobiography, *A Long Way from Home,* Jekyll opened a whole new world to him:

> I read poetry: *Childe Harold, The Duncaid, Essay on Man, Paradise Lost,* the Elizabethan lyrics, *Leaves of Grass,* the lyrics of Shelley and Keats and of the late Victorian poets, and . . . we read together pieces out of Dante, Leopardi, and Goethe, Villon and Baudelaire.

It was Jekyll who first recognized and nurtured McKay's gift for writing poetry, and who encouraged him to put that gift to work in the service of his own Jamaican dialect. The result was the publication of *Songs of Jamaica* and *Constab Ballads.* The first is a celebration of peasant life, somewhat after the manner of Robert Burns; *Constab Ballads* is more like Rudyard Kipling, drawing as it does upon McKay's brief stint as a constable in Kingston, Jamaica.

Kingston gave McKay his first taste of city life, and his first real taste of racism. The contempt of the city's white and mulatto upper classes for rural and lower-class blacks was an unpleasant revelation. The most blatant racism that McKay witnessed in Kingston, however, was not Jamaican in origin—it was imported in the form of American tourists. He would come to know this brand of racism much more intimately in the next few years, for, after only eight months in the Kingston constabulary, he resigned his post and left for the United States. In 1912 he enrolled as an agronomy student, first at Tuskegee Institute and then at Kansas State College. His plan was to return to Jamaica to help modernize the island's agriculture. The plan might have succeeded but for a gift of several thousand dollars from an unidentified patron—most likely Walter Jekyll—that paid McKay's way to New York, where he invested his money in a restaurant and married Eulalie Imelda Edwards, an old Jamaican sweetheart. Neither marriage nor restaurant survived long, but McKay found a certain consolation in the bustle and energy of the city. One part of town in particular seemed to reach out to him: Harlem.

In the next five years or so he worked at a variety of jobs—bar boy, longshoreman, fireman, and finally porter, then waiter, on the Pennsylvania Railroad. This was yet another apprenticeship, one in which he further developed the sympathy for the working class that remained with him all his life. Since his youth he had leaned politically toward socialism, and his years among the

(Library of Congress)

proletariat solidified his beliefs. His race consciousness developed hand-in-hand with his class consciousness. During this period of apprenticeship and developing awareness, he wrote. In 1918, he began a long association with Max Eastman, editor of the communist magazine *The Liberator.* McKay began publishing poems and essays in this revolutionary journal, and eventually became an associate editor. In 1919, in response to that year's bloody postwar race riots, McKay published in *The Liberator* what would become his most famous poem, "If We Must Die." The defiant tone and the open outrage of the poem caught the attention of the black community, and practically overnight McKay was at the forefront of black American poets.

Then came another of the abrupt turns that were so much a part of McKay's life and work. Before his newly won reputation had a chance to flourish, he left for England and stayed for more than a year, writing and editing for a communist newspaper, *Workers' Dreadnought.*

In 1920, he published his first book of poetry since the Jamaican volumes, *Spring in New Hampshire, and Other Poems.* He returned to New York early in 1921 and spent the next two years with *The Liberator,* publishing a good bit of prose and verse and working on his principal book of poems, *Harlem Shadows.* Upon its publication in 1922, observes biographer Wayne F. Cooper, McKay "was immediately acclaimed the best Negro poet since Paul Laurence Dunbar." Once again, however, he did not linger long over success. He was tired and in need of a change, especially after a chance meeting with his former wife reopened old wounds. Late in 1922, he traveled to Moscow for the Fourth Congress of the Third International. He quickly became a great favorite with Muscovites, and was allowed to address the Congress on the plight of American blacks and on the problem of racism within the Communist Party. As McKay described it, he was greeted "like a black ikon in the flesh." He was, it seemed, on the verge of a promising career as a political activist; but despite his successes in Russia, he still saw himself primarily as a writer. When he left Russia, he was "eager to resume what he considered the modern writer's proper function—namely, to record as best he could the truths of his own experience."

The 1920's were the decade of the expatriate artist, but though he spent most of his time in France until settling in Tangiers in 1931, McKay had very little to do with such writers as Ernest Hemingway and F. Scott Fitzgerald; his exile was too different from theirs. During his stay in Europe and North Africa, McKay published all his major fiction, along with a number of magazine articles. His first two novels, *Home to Harlem* and *Banjo*, were financially successful, in spite of the outraged reaction they drew from most black American critics. *Gingertown*, a collection of short stories, was not nearly so successful, and McKay's third novel, *Banana Bottom*, was a critical and financial disaster. Financially ruined, McKay was forced to end his expatriate existence.

With the help of some American friends, McKay returned to New York in 1934. He hoped to be of service to the black community, but upon his return, observes Cooper, "he found a wrecked economy, almost universal black poverty, and little sense of unity among those black writers and intellectuals he had hoped to work with in years ahead." As for his literary ambitions, the Harlem Renaissance was finished; black writers were no longer in vogue. Not only could he not find a publisher, he was unable to find any sort of a job, and wound up in Camp Greycourt, a government welfare camp outside New York City. Fortunately, Eastman was able to rescue him from the camp and help him to get a job with the Federal Writers' Project. In 1937 he was able to publish his autobiography, *A Long Way from Home*. Once again, he was publishing articles in magazines, but his views isolated him from the mainstream black leaders; he felt, again in Cooper's words, that "their single-minded opposition to racial segregation was detrimental to any effective black community organization and to the development of a positive group spirit among blacks." McKay's thought at this time also shows a drift away from communism, and a growing disillusionment with the fate of the "Grand Experiment" at the hands of the Soviets.

A Long Way from Home was neither a critical nor a financial success. Neither was his next and last book, *Harlem: Negro Metropolis*, a historical study published in 1940. By then, in spite of the steady work provided him by the Federal Writers' Project, his literary reputation was declining steadily. Despite his final acceptance of American citizenship in 1940, he could still not bring himself to regard America as home. His exile from both the black leadership and the left-wing establishment was becoming more and more total; worse still, his health began to deteriorate rapidly. Once again, like Jekyll and Eastman in earlier years, a friend offered a hand. Ellen Terry, a Catholic writer, rescued McKay from a Harlem rooming house, and McKay's life took one last unexpected turn. As a young man he had rejected the fundamentalist Christianity of his father, and during his varied career had had little use for religion. Through his friendship with Terry, and later with the progressive Chicago bishop, Bernard Scheil, McKay experienced a change of mind and heart. In the spring of 1944 he moved to Chicago, and by fall of that year he was baptized into the Roman Catholic Church.

At last he seemed to have found a refuge, though his letters reveal a lingering bitterness over his lot. With his newfound faith, however, came a satisfying involvement in Chicago's Catholic Youth Organization and the opportunity to go on writing. His health continued to decline, and on May 22, 1948, McKay died of heart failure. He had recently finished preparing his *Selected Poems of Claude McKay* for publication. It is probably just as well that the volume appeared posthumously, as it took five years to find a publisher; at the time of his death, all of his works were out of print. After a requiem mass in Chicago, McKay was brought back to Harlem for a memorial service. He was buried in Queens, "a long way from home."

Analysis: Poetry

At the conclusion of his essay "The Renaissance Re-examined," which appears as the final chapter of Arna Bontemps's 1972 book, *The Harlem Renaissance Remembered*, Warrington Hudlin insists that any true appreciation of the Harlem Renaissance hinges on the realization that this celebrated literary phenomenon "opened the door" for the black writing of today: "The Harlem Renaissance will always be remembered for this reason. It will be valued for its merits. It will come again to importance because of its idea." The poetry of Claude McKay must be read in much the same light. Though it is easy enough to find fault with much of his verse, he did help to establish a precedent for those who would follow; as such, he deserves to be valued for his merits, judged by his strengths.

"Invocation"
Though progressive enough in thought, McKay never felt compelled to experiment much with the form of his poetry. In content he is a black man of the twentieth century; in form he is more an English lyricist of the nineteenth, with, here and there, Miltonic echoes. The effect is, at times, a little peculiar, as in "Invocation," a sonnet in which the poet beseeches his muse to

> Let fall the light upon my sable face
> That once gleamed upon the Ethiopian's art;
> Lift me to thee out of this alien place
> So I may be, thine exiled counterpart,
> The worthy singer of my world and race.

Archaic trappings aside, there is a kind of majesty here, not bad work for a young man in his twenties. The Miltonic ring is probably no accident; McKay, it must be remembered, received something of an English gentleman's education. As the work of a black man pursuing what had been to that time primarily a white man's vocation, McKay's "Invocation" bears comparison with John Milton's "Hail native Language." One of the young Milton's ambitions was to vindicate English as poetic language, deserving of the same respect as Homer's Greek, Vergil's Latin, or Dante's Italian. McKay found himself in the position of vindicating a black man's experience of a white culture as a worthy subject for poetry.

"The Tropics in New York"
Not all of McKay's verse concerns itself specifically with the theme of interracial tension. Among his poems are love lyrics, idyllic songs of country life, and harsher poems of the city, where "the old milk carts go rumbling by,/ Under the same old stars," where "Out of the tenements, cold as stone,/ Dark figures start for work." A recurring theme in McKay's work is the yearn-

ing for the lost world of childhood, which for him meant memories of Jamaica. This sense of loss is the occasion for one of his finest poems, "The Tropics in New York":

> Bananas ripe and green, and ginger-root,
> Cocoa in pods and alligator pears,
> And tangerines and mangoes and grape fruit,
> Fit for the highest prize at parish fairs.

The diction here is simple; one can almost hear Ernest Hemingway in the loving list of fruits. The speaker's memory stirs at the sight of a shop window. In the midst of the city his thoughts turn to images of "fruit-trees laden by low-singing rills,/ And dewy dawns, and mystical blue skies/ In benediction over nun-like hills." Here, in three straightforward quatrains, is the mechanism of nostalgia. From a physical reality placed by chance before him, the observer turns his eyes inward, visualizing a happy scene of which he is no longer a part. In the final stanza his eyes are still involved in the experience, only now they have grown dim, "and I could no more gaze;/ A wave of longing through my body swept." All of the narrator's senses tune themselves to grief as the quickening of smell and taste turns to a poignant hunger for "the old, familiar ways." Finally, the poem closes on a line as classically simple and tersely musical as anything in the poems of A. E. Housman: "I turned aside and bowed my head and wept."

Indeed, the poem is reminiscent of "Poem XL" in Housman's *A Shropshire Lad* (1896):

> Into my heart an air that kills
> From yon far country blows:
> What are those blue remembered hills,
> What spires, what farms are those?

It is a long way, to be sure, from Shropshire to Clarendon Parish, Jamaica, but the issue here is the long road back to lost experience, to that "land of lost content" that shines so plain, "The happy highways where I went/ And cannot come again." Any fair assessment of McKay's verse must affirm that he knew that land, those highways, all too well.

715

Protest Poems

That same fair assessment, however, must give a prominent place to those poems upon which McKay's reputation was made—his poems of protest. McKay, in the estimation of Bontemps, was black poetry's "strongest voice since [Paul Laurence] Dunbar." Dunbar's "racial" verse is a good indication of the point to which black American poetry had progressed by World War I. His plantation-style dialect verse tries, with a certain ironic cheerfulness, to make the best of a bad situation. At their best, these poems exhibit a stinging wit. At their worst, they are about as dignified as a minstrel show. In his poems in literary English, Dunbar is more assertive of his racial pride, but with an emphasis on suffering and forbearance, as in "We Wear the Mask." This poem, which could be read in retrospect as an answer to those critics and poets who would later disown Dunbar for not being "black" enough, speaks of the great cost at which pain and anger are contained:

> We smile, but O great Christ, our cries
> To Thee from tortured souls arise.
> We sing, but oh, the clay is vile
> Beneath our feet, and long the mile;
> But let the world dream otherwise,
> We wear the mask.

The anguish is plain enough, yet the poem, couched in a prayer, seems to view this "wearing of the mask" as an ennobling act, as a virtuous sacrifice. McKay was not inclined to view things in quite that way.

"If We Must Die"

From the spring through the fall of 1919, numerous American cities were wracked by bloody race conflicts, the worst of which was a July riot in Chicago that left dozens dead and hundreds injured or homeless. While he was never the object of such violence, McKay and his fellow railroad waiters and porters walked to and from their trains with loaded revolvers in their pockets. Not unexpectedly, his reaction to the riots was far from mild; his concern was not with turning the other cheek, but with returning the offending slap. When the sonnet "If We Must Die" appeared in *The Liberator* it marked the emergence of a new rage in black American poetry:

> If we must die, let it not be like hogs,
> Hunted and penned in an inglorious spot,
> While round us bark the mad and hungry dogs,
> Making their mock at our accursed lot.

Again, the form is of another century, the language dated, even by late nineteenth century standards—"O kinsmen! We must meet the common foe! . . . What though before us lies the open grave?" The message, however, is ageless, avoiding as the poem does any direct reference to race.

On the heels of much-publicized violence against black neighborhoods, the implications were clear enough, but the universality of the poem became more obvious with time. A Jewish friend of McKay's wrote him in 1939, "proclaiming that . . . ["If We Must Die"] must have been written about the European Jews persecuted by Hitler." In a more celebrated instance, Winston Churchill read the poem before the House of Commons, as if, in the words of Tolson, "it were the talismanic uniform of His Majesty's field marshal." The message reaches back to Thermopylae and Masada, and forward to Warsaw, Bastogne, and beyond. In its coverage of the bloodbath at the New York State Prison at Attica, *Time* (September 27, 1971) quoted the first four lines of McKay's sonnet as the "would-be heroic" effort of an anonymous, rebellious inmate. McKay might not have minded; he stated in his autobiography that "If We Must Die" was "the only poem I ever read to the members of my [railroad] crew." A poem that touches prisoners, railroad workers, and prime ministers alike must be termed a considerable success, despite any technical flaws it may exhibit.

Even so, one must not altogether avoid the question of just how successful McKay's poems are as poems. James Giles, in his 1976 study, *Claude McKay*, remarks on the disparity "between McKay's passionate resentment of racist oppression and his Victorianism in form and diction," finding in this conflict "a

unique kind of tension in many of his poems, which weakens
their ultimate success." Giles is probably correct to a point. In
many cases McKay's art might have found fuller expression had
he experimented more, let content more often shape form; he
had shown abilities in this direction in his early Jamaican poems, and he was certainly open to experimentation in his later
prose. The simple fact, however, is that he consistently chose to
use traditional forms, and it would be unfair to say that it was a
wholly unsuccessful strategy.

"The Lynching"
Indeed, the very civility of his favorite form, the sonnet, sometimes adds an ironic tension that heightens, rather than dimin-
ishes, the effect of the poem. For example, one could imagine
any number of grisly, graphic effects to be achieved in a *vers libre*,
expressionistic poem about a lynching. In McKay's "The Lynching," though, one cannot help feeling the pull of an under-
stated horror at seeing the act translated to quatrains and couplets: "and little lads, lynchers that were to be,/ Danced round
the dreadful thing in fiendish glee." No further description of
the "dreadful thing" is necessary. When McKay uses his poems
to focus on real or imagined experience—a lynching, a cor-
nered fight to the death, an unexpected remembrance of things
past—his formal restraint probably works most often in his
favor.

Angry Sonnets
In poems that set out to convey a self-conscious message, however, he tends to be less successful, not so much because the
form does not fit the content as because poetry and causes are
dangerous bedfellows. Some of McKay's other angry sonnets—
"The White House," "To the White Fiends," "Baptism"—may
leave readers disappointed because they preach too much.
McKay's specifically sociological, political, and, later, religious
views receive better expression elsewhere, in his prose. Perhaps
that is why he did not devote so much of his time to poetry after
the publication of *Harlem Shadows*. In any case, his position in
black American poetry is secure. Perhaps he should be judged

more by that which was new in his poems, and that which inspired other black writers to carry on the task, as later generations have judged the Harlem Renaissance—as a bold and determined beginning, a rolling up of the sleeves for the hard work ahead.

Other Literary Forms

Even though he is probably best known as a poet, Claude McKay's verse makes up a relatively small portion of his literary output. While his novels, *Home to Harlem, Banjo,* and *Banana Bottom,* do not place him at the forefront of American novelists, they were remarkable at the time for their frankness and slice-of-life realism. *Home to Harlem* was the first best-selling novel of the Harlem Renaissance, yet it was condemned by the majority of black critics, who felt that the black American art and literature emerging in the 1920's and 1930's should present an uplifting image of the African American. McKay, however, went on in his next two novels to express his admiration for the earthy ways of uneducated lower-class blacks, somewhat at the expense of black intellectuals. The remainder of McKay's published fiction appears in *Gingertown,* a volume of short stories.

McKay also produced a substantial body of literary and social criticism, a revealing selection of which appears, along with a number of his letters and selections from his fiction and poetry, in *The Passion of Claude McKay: Selected Poetry and Prose, 1912-1948,* edited by Wayne F. Cooper. An autobiography, *A Long Way from Home,* and an important social history, *Harlem: Negro Metropolis,* round out the list of his principal works.

Bibliography

Cooper, Wayne F. *Claude McKay: Rebel Sojourner in the Harlem Renaissance.* Baton Rouge: Louisiana State University Press, 1987. This first full-length biography of McKay is a fascinating and very readable book. Special attention is paid to McKay's early life in Jamaica and the complex influences of his family. Includes nine photographs and a useful index.

Gayle, Addison, Jr. *Claude McKay: The Black Poet at War.* Detroit:

Broadside Press, 1972. This brief study looks closely at four poems—"Flame-Heart," *Harlem Shadows*, "To the White Fiends," and "If We Must Die"—as they demonstrate McKay's growing skill and militancy throughout his career. Gayle argues that McKay was an important revolutionary poet.

Giles, James R. *Claude McKay.* Boston: Twayne, 1976. This study examines McKay's work as it was influenced by his homeland of Jamaica, the Harlem Renaissance, the Communist Party, and the Roman Catholic Church. Giles asserts that McKay's fiction represents his major achievement. The book includes a chronology and a briefly annotated bibliography.

Hathaway, Heather. *Caribbean Waves: Relocating Claude McKay and Paule Marshall.* Bloomington: Indiana University Press, 1999. A biographical and critical study of the lives and works of two writers and the way that their works have been shaped by their Caribbean heritage.

Holcomb, Gary E. "Diaspora Cruises: Queer Black Proletarianism in Claude McKay's *A Long Way from Home.*" *Modern Fiction Studies* 49, no. 4 (Winter, 2003): 714-746. Views McKay's work in the light of his participation in extremist political movements and in the light of his association with gay groups during the Harlem Renaissance.

James, Winston. "Becoming the People's Poet: Claude McKay's Jamaican Years, 1889-1912." *Small Axe: A Caribbean Journal of Criticism,* no. 13 (March, 2003): 17-46. Explores the roles of women in McKay's poetry and places them in an autobiographical context. Also takes a close look at McKay's rise to fame in Jamaica.

_____. *A Fierce Hatred of Injustice: Claude McKay's Jamaica and His Poetry of Rebellion.* New York: Verso, 2001. A critical study of McKay's early writing with a focus on the poet's use of Jamaican creole in two early collections, *Songs of Jamaica* and *Constab Ballads,* and in his previously uncollected poems for the Jamaican press. An anthology of the latter is provided together with McKay's comic sketch about Jamaican peasant life and his autobiographical essay.

LeSeur, Geta. "Claude McKay's Marxism." In *The Harlem Renaissance: Revaluations,* edited by Amritjit Singh, William S. Shiver, and Stanley Brodwin. New York: Garland, 1989. This article examines McKay's struggle to find in Marxism the solution to the "Negro question" and looks at his trip to Russia to assess Marxism in action firsthand in 1922 and 1923.

Rosenberg, Leah. "Caribbean Models for Modernism in the Work of Claude McKay and Jean Rhys." *Modernism/Modernity* 11, no. 2 (April, 2004): 219-239. A persuasive argument for viewing McKay's work as critiquing modernism from within a modernist framework. Examines McKay's challenges to the European tendency to see African American women in purely sexual terms.

Schwarz, A. B. Christa. *Gay Voices of the Harlem Renaissance.* Bloomington: Indiana University Press, 2003. Schwarz examines the work of four leading writers from the Harlem Renaissance—Countée Cullen, Langston Hughes, Claude McKay, and Richard Bruce Nugent—and their sexually nonconformist or gay literary voices.

— Richard A. Eichwald

Reginald McKnight

Novelist and short-story writer

Born: Fürstenfeldbruck, Germany;
February 26, 1956

LONG FICTION: *I Get on the Bus*, 1990; *He Sleeps*, 2001.
SHORT FICTION: *Moustapha's Eclipse*, 1988; *The Kind of Light That Shines on Texas*, 1992; *White Boys*, 1998.
EDITED TEXTS: *African American Wisdom*, 1994; *Wisdom of the African World*, 1996.

Achievements

Reginald McKnight is the recipient of a National Endowment for the Arts Fellowship, an O. Henry Award, the Kenyon Review Award for excellence (which he received twice), a PEN/Hemingway Special Citation, a Pushcart Prize, the Drue Heinz Literature Prize, the Watson Foundation Fellowship, the Whiting Writers' Award, and the Bernice M. Slote Award.

Biography

Reginald McKnight was born in Fürstenfeldbruck, Germany, to military parents in 1956. His father Frank was a U.S. Air Force noncommissioned officer, and his mother Pearl was a dietician. Because of his military background, McKnight has lived all over the world, moving a total of forty-three times. After a brief stint in the U.S. Marine Corps, McKnight earned an associate degree in anthropology (1978) from Pikes Peak Community College and a B.A. in African literature (1981) from Colorado College. He received the Thomas J. Watson Fellowship to study folklore and literature in West Africa, so he spent a year teaching and writing in Senegal. In 1987, he earned an M.A. in English with an emphasis in creative writing from the University of Denver. McKnight has taught at Arapahoe Community College, the University of Denver, and the University of Maryland at College Park. He married Michele Davis in 1985 and has two daughters.

Analysis: Short Fiction

Reginald McKnight's work is a refreshing change from much of the black protest literature of the 1970's and 1980's. While white people are often presented as unpleasant, annoying, and mean-spirited, they are seldom presented as outrightly diabolical. McKnight deliberately refrains from political statement in his fiction, believing that art has the higher purpose of bringing a sense of joy to the reader, the type of joy that makes one think that "life is deep, limitless, and meaningful." Yet he does not believe that art should be harmless. "It should get under your skin," he says. McKnight refuses to accept or to promote any singular concept of black identity; instead, he respects the diversity of black experience found in the United States and elsewhere.

Like many writers, McKnight draws heavily on personal experience to find subject matter for his stories. For example, several stories found in his collections are set in West Africa with an anthropologist as the narrator. Other stories include the painful experience of being one of a handful of black children in a school. His experience in the military is also woven into several stories. His stories, however, are no mere transcription of personal experience. He is equally successful in portraying the experiences of black working-class males.

Many of McKnight's stories are boldly experimental in point of view, tone, style, and concept. His stories set in West Africa are particularly notable for their non-Western philosophical views and the incorporation of the fantastic. For example, in "The Homunculus: A Novel in One Chapter" (found in *The Kind of Light That Shines on Texas*), the protagonist is a young writer in a fairy-tale-like place who becomes so consumed with his writing that it becomes a flesh and blood likeness of himself. Mc-

Knight's work is characterized by his successful, convincing use of multiple voices.

"Uncle Moustapha's Eclipse"

"Uncle Moustapha's Eclipse," the title story of McKnight's first collection, is narrated in the broken English of a Senegalese interpreter working for an American anthropologist living in Africa. This story has the feel of a folktale; that is, it is clearly meant to teach a lesson. Uncle Moustapha is a successful peanut farmer, who lives in a small African village with his three wives and seven children. His only problem is that he constantly thinks of death; he would not have this problem if he had not adopted the white man's tradition of celebrating his birthday.

On the eve of his sixtieth birthday (or at least what he has designated as his birthday), he goes to bed anticipating an eclipse of the sun, which has been predicted for the next day. On the following morning, a white scientist arrives to set up his viewing equipment on Uncle Moustapha's land. The scientist warns Moustapha not to view the eclipse directly with naked eyes. At first, Moustapha complies and views the eclipse properly through the scientific equipment. However, he quickly becomes overjoyed with the eclipse, believing that it was sent to him as a gift from Allah and his ancestors. Moustapha runs to fetch his favorite wife, Fatima. They rush together to the baobab tree, which is believed to house the spirits of their ancestors. After a brief prayer, Moustapha experiences a rush of heightened sensory perceptions. He turns to stare at the eclipse with his eyes wide open, so that he can see "it all in supreme detail." As he returns home, the world seems more beautiful to him than ever before, except for a black shape that begins to flicker on and off in his left eye.

The ending of the story is ambiguous. It is not clear whether he goes blind or it is death that is finally coming to Uncle Moustapha. However, he has no regrets because he has seen "what no other living soul has seen today." Clearly, he does not believe that going blind or even dying is too great a price to pay for such a magnificent experience.

"The Kind of Light That Shines on Texas"

In this O. Henry Award-winning story, McKnight explores the ambivalence of friendship, not just between blacks and whites but also between blacks and blacks. Clinton Oates, the narrator, is one of three black children in his sixth-grade class in Waco, Texas. Oates, who is eager to prove himself inoffensive to whites, feels embarrassed by the presence of Marvin Pruitt, a black boy who fulfills most negative black stereotypes. Pruitt "smelled bad, was at least two grades behind, was hostile, dark skinned, homely, close-mouthed." Pruitt sleeps away most of the school day; the other black child is a large, passive girl who refuses to speak.

This class is full of older children, including a sixteen-year-old white bully, Kevin Oakley, who is just looking for a reason to fight with Oates. One day, their coach (who probably wants to see Oates get hurt) singles out the two boys for a game of "murder ball," using two hard-pumped volleyballs instead of the usual red rubber balls. Completely in fair play, Oates hits Oakley square in the face, causing a nosebleed and the boy's humiliation. Shortly afterward, in the locker room, Oakley threatens to attack Oates after school. Oates sees Pruitt, an innocent bystander, and asks, "How come you after me and not him?" Oates escapes from Oakley that afternoon by getting on the bus early, but he cannot escape the implications of what he had said in the locker room. Clearly, Oates meant that Pruitt deserved to be picked on or beaten up because he so neatly fit all the negative stereotypes of blacks.

The next morning, Oakley predictably picks a fight with Oates. Surprisingly, Pruitt intervenes on Oates's behalf, with a disdainful "git out of my way, boy." This action shows that Pruitt is, without a doubt, morally superior to Oates, the nice young black who is only too eager to do his "tom-thing." The reader is left to believe that Pruitt knows exactly what Oates had meant in the locker room, but he still rises above this black-on-black racial insult. While never exactly friends, the black boys' relationship proves that blood is, indeed, thicker than water.

"Quitting Smoking"

This story, also found in *The Kind of Light That Shines on Texas*, is narrated by a working-class black man, Scott Winters, who lives with his white lover, Anna. Their relationship does not work, partly because Scott cannot stop smoking, partly because race becomes a barrier, and partly because Scott cannot bring himself to share his deepest secret with her. Scott began smoking in his late teens to hide the smell of reefer from his parents. He discovers that he likes the buzz from cigarettes better than any other "high." When he meets Anna—a vegetarian, health nut, and feminist—he naturally and easily loses his desire to smoke and to eat meat. One night, Anna confides to him an incident of acquaintance rape. This confidence immediately reminds him of a time in his teens that he and three other males witnessed the abduction of a woman into a car. The woman struggled and screamed for help, but none of the young men intervened on her behalf. Nagged by this memory, Scott goes out and buys a pack of cigarettes.

What follows is a story of cigarette addiction that anyone who has ever smoked will find familiar. He continues to sneak out for smokes in the middle of the night. He begins to keep an arsenal of cover-up supplies in his truck—gum, toothpaste, mouthwash, deodorant, and air freshener. Cigarettes become his secret infidelity. When Anna confronts him with a cigarette she has found, Scott vows to quit but does not. Scott's deeper problem is that he cannot bring himself to confess to Anna what he had allowed to happen to the woman who had been abducted and perhaps raped or killed.

One night, he makes elaborate preparations for this confession; he cleans the house, makes dinner, and buys wine and flowers. Scott tentatively approaches the subject by saying, "I wouldn't be surprised if you hated men." Anna, who has grown distant for other reasons, counters, "I'm surprised I don't hate black men. The guy who raped me was black." Scott, who feels this racial insult as an almost physical injury, immediately packs his bags and walks out the door. Both partners are guilty of erecting barriers that destroy the relationship, but only Anna chose to use race as a weapon.

"The White Boys"

This story opens with yet another move for a black military family. The Oates are, in many ways, a typical black middle-class family. Both parents are strict, even to the point of violence. Two particularly nasty beatings of the young protagonist Derrick are recounted in this narrative. His two siblings Dean and Alva are spared similar beatings, mostly because they are less conspicuous or odd than Derrick. Both parents greatly fear that one of their children will bring shame or trouble to their home. They know, only too well, that white people will conjure up the worst possible racial stereotypes at the slightest provocation.

The day after they move in, Derrick provides this type of provocation by innocently scooping snow off of his neighbor's car. The neighbor, Sergeant Hooker, vehemently hates blacks, following his childhood experience of growing up in a predominantly black neighborhood in Baltimore. His mother, with whom he no longer communicates, even married a black man. Ironically, Hooker's best friend from childhood was also black. Furious over the Oates's moving next door, Hooker sets out to instill racial hatred equal to his own in his three sons. The youngest son Garrett is determined to hate Derrick, but a friendship begins to grow between the two boys. When Hooker discovers this friendship, he devises a diabolical scheme to scare Derrick away permanently. He plans to take Derrick and his three sons on a fishing trip, during which time the four whites will stage a mock lynching of Derrick. Garrett, unable to confront his father or to warn Derrick, comes up with his own scheme to save his friend. On the Friday before this fateful weekend, he calls Derrick a nigger, not just once but repeatedly. His act destroys their friendship (exactly what his father wanted) but saves Derrick from a far more horrific experience.

In an interview, McKnight has said that the stories in *White Boys* should produce this response: "It's too bad that blacks and whites don't get along very well today." This response is exactly what this story produces. There is every reason except race that the Hookers and Oateses should have been good friends and neighbors.

Other Literary Forms

Reginald McKnight has written two novels, *I Get on the Bus* and *He Sleeps*. He has also edited two collections of folk wisdom, *African American Wisdom* and *Wisdom of the African World*.

Bibliography

Brailsford, Karen. Review of *I Get on the Bus,* by Reginald McKnight. *The New York Times Book Review,* September 16, 1990, 22-27. A valuable and in-depth analysis of McKnight's novel.

McKnight, Reginald. "An Interview with Reginald McKnight." Interview by Renée Olander. *The Writer's Chronicle* 3 (February, 2000): 5-14. McKnight discusses literary influences, his writing philosophies, the use of the word "nigger," and two of his works: *I Get on the Bus* and *White Boys.*

_____. "Reginald McKnight." Interview by P. Giddings. *Essence* 21, no. 11 (March, 1991): 40-42. A conversation with the author that centers on the role of Africa in his novel and on McKnight's various achievements, as well as the important roles that women in his family have played in his life.

_____. "'Under the Umbrella of Black Civilization': A Conversation with Reginald McKnight." Interview by Bertram D. Ashe. *African American Review* 35, no. 3 (Fall, 2001): 427-438. A discussion with McKnight that focuses on his ability to make persuasive presentations of vastly different voices and the effect of the writing process on the author's beliefs.

_____. "We Are, in Fact, a Civilization." Interview by William Walsh. *Kenyon Review* 16, no. 2 (Spring, 1994): 27-42. McKnight discusses his background, writing style, and use of first- and third-person narrative.

Megan, Carolyn. "New Perceptions on Rhythm in Reginald McKnight's Fiction." *Kenyon Review* 16, no. 2 (Spring, 1994): 56-62. Megan discusses the importance of sound and rhythm in McKnight's writing process. Her discussion includes the emotional responses evoked by this rhythm.

Murray, Rolland. "Diaspora by Bus: Reginald McKnight, Postmodernism, and Transatlantic Subjectivity." *Contemporary Literature* 46, no. 1 (Spring, 2005): 46-78. Examines the role of movement in McKnight's *I Get on the Bus.* Argues that the changes undergone by the main character, Evan Norris, are so drastic that they transform him into an almost-objective observer of African American identity and the ways in which African Americans navigate complex social systems.

Nixon, Will. "Black Male Writers: Endangered Species?" *American Visions* 5, no. 1 (February, 1990): 24-29. An interesting study of the reasons why African American male writers were largely ignored during the 1980's. Also looks at the rise of African American female writers.

— Nancy Sherrod

Terry McMillan

Novelist

Born: Port Huron, Michigan; October 18, 1951

LONG FICTION: *Mama*, 1987; *Disappearing Acts*, 1989; *Waiting to Exhale*, 1992; *How Stella Got Her Groove Back*, 1996; *A Day Late and a Dollar Short*, 2001; *The Interruption of Everything*, 2005.

SCREENPLAYS: *Waiting to Exhale*, 1995 (adaptation of her novel; with Ronald Bass); *How Stella Got Her Groove Back*, 1998 (adaptation of her novel; with Bass).

NONFICTION: *The Writer as Publicist*, 1993 (with Marcia Biederman and Gary Aspenberg).

EDITED TEXTS: *Breaking Ice: An Anthology of Contemporary African-American Fiction*, 1990.

Achievements

Terry McMillan's novels became best-sellers in the 1990's because the author so accurately described the lives of contemporary, upwardly mobile African American women. The success of her works, two of which became popular films, inspired a number of other writers to try writing fiction like hers. Thus, she is credited for founding a new genre and for creating a large, new reading audience. However, McMillan's skill in blending humor with honesty and her gift for capturing the cadences of African American speech have made her novels truly inimitable. McMillan received a New York Foundation for the Arts Award for fiction in 1986, a Before Columbus Foundation National Book Award for *Mama* in 1987, and a Women in Communication Matrix Award for Career Achievement in Books in 1993. Her very popularity may account for the skepticism of critics; for almost a decade her works received very little critical attention. However, the fact that in 1999 both a biography and the first book-length study of her works appeared suggests that in the twenty-first century her fiction will be given the scholarly attention it deserves.

Biography

Terry McMillan was born on October 18, 1951, in Port Huron, Michigan, the oldest child of Edward Lewis McMillan and Madeline Tillman McMillan. Her mother, an uneducated, hard-working woman, divorced her alcoholic, abusive husband when Terry was thirteen. He died three years later, at the age of thirty-nine.

At sixteen, Terry found a job shelving books in the local library for $1.25 an hour. Her contact with books opened her eyes to new possibilities, including the existence of African American writers. At that point, she still had no notion of becoming a writer herself, but she did resolve to escape from Port Huron.

After finishing high school, McMillan moved to Los Angeles. There she supported herself by working as a typist during the day and taking courses at Los Angeles City College at night. She also wrote her first literary work, a poem. In 1973, McMillan transferred to the University of California at Berkeley, where she majored in journalism. One of her courses was a creative writing workshop taught by the poet and novelist Ishmael Reed. He was impressed by the young woman and encouraged her to write fiction.

After graduating from Berkeley in 1979, McMillan moved to New York City, intending to get an M.F.A. in film from Columbia University. However, she dropped out of graduate school and started working in an administrative position at a law firm. In her spare time, she drank and took drugs with her boyfriend, Leonard Welch. However, just before her thirtieth birthday, McMillan decided to conquer her addictions. After her son Solomon was born in 1984, McMillan was even more determined to make a success of her life.

At the urging of friends in the Harlem Writers Guild, McMillan had turned one of her short stories into a novel, *Mama.* Though Houghton Mifflin accepted it for publication, they did not intend to do much in the way of publicity. McMillan organized her own promotional campaign, and the success of her efforts made publishing history.

From 1987 to 1990, McMillan was a visiting writer at the University of Wyoming in Laramie. In 1990, she became associate

(Marion Ettlinger)

professor at the University of Arizona in Tucson, but she made her permanent home in Danville, California.

In 1993, while McMillan was hard at work on a novel to be titled *A Day Late and a Dollar Short*, her beloved mother died. The next year McMillan lost her best friend. Putting the manuscript aside, she went on a vacation trip to Negril, Jamaica. There she met Jonathan Plummer, a resort worker some twenty years her junior. He followed her to the United States, moved in with her, and enrolled in college. McMillan wrote about their romance in *How Stella Got Her Groove Back*, which was dedicated to Plummer. On September 5, 1998, McMillan and Plummer were married in a small, private service on the beach in Maui, Hawaii.

In 2001, McMillan finally finished *A Day Late and a Dollar*

Short. In 2005, after Plummer admitted that he was gay, Mc-Millan filed for divorce. Her sixth novel, *The Interruption of Everything*, appeared that same year.

Analysis: Long Fiction

Terry McMillan's two major themes are the changing nature of the African American family structure and the obstacles that educated, ambitious African American women encounter in their attempts to find worthy male partners. In all of her novels, McMillan draws heavily from her own experiences.

Mama

Mama is set in a town called Point Haven, Michigan, not far from Detroit. The book is dedicated to McMillan's mother. Like her, the book's protagonist, Mildred Peacock, is a poor, uneducated black woman who has remained with her abusive husband in the hope that he will help support their five children. As the novel begins, however, Crook Peacock has beaten Mildred one time too many. She kicks him out and divorces him. As the title suggests, Mildred sees motherhood as her primary role in life. McMillan shows her dealing with unscrupulous employers, scheming to outwit rent collectors and welfare workers, and even prostituting herself in order to feed her family.

Mildred's efforts to be a good mother are stymied by her addiction to alcohol and her inability to resist attractive men. Ironically, she gets married a second time to a man she does not love, or even like, simply because she needs his income. Her third marriage is no better. That husband, who is a much younger man, walks out on Mildred when he finds family responsibilities too burdensome.

Though education gives most of McMillan's other heroines many more options than Mildred has, their experiences with men are not very different from hers. Like her, they come to depend not on men but on other women, either family members or close friends. In Mildred's case, it is her eldest daughter, Freda, who both inspires her to keep going and, on occasion, offers the wise counsel that Mildred desperately needs.

Disappearing Acts

McMillan's second novel is a romantic comedy set in New York. The main characters in *Disappearing Acts* are Zora Banks, a musician and teacher, and Franklin Swift, a construction worker. One of their problems is that Franklin does not seem motivated to better himself. Another is that Zora and Franklin are not honest with each other. When he loses his job, he does not tell Zora; when she terminates a pregnancy, she does not even consult him. The next time she becomes pregnant, she decides to have the baby. Franklin gets furious and Zora puts him out. Franklin takes refuge in alcohol and cocaine. However, he finally returns to her with his addictions conquered and some solid plans for the future.

McMillan undoubtedly drew the inspiration for *Disappearing Acts* from her life in New York, but, like any other artist, she invented her characters and changed details. Nevertheless, in 1990, McMillan's ex-boyfriend, Leonard Welch, sued McMillan and her publishers, alleging that the character of Swift presented an unflattering portrait of Welch. Ironically, critics agree that Swift is presented as a basically good person. At any rate, the case was decided in McMillan's favor.

McMillan's artistic integrity is also illustrated by her insistence on using alternating monologues in *Disappearing Acts*, telling the story first through Zora's eyes and then from Franklin's perspective. When her publisher insisted that she rewrite the book, making Franklin the sole narrator, McMillan changed publishers.

Waiting to Exhale

In several respects, *Waiting to Exhale* differs from McMillan's earlier works. It has four major characters, it moves often between first- and third-person narration, and each chapter resembles a short story that builds steadily toward a definite ending. The setting, too, is different; this time the action takes place in Phoenix, Arizona. However, this novel, like the others, is about the African American women's quest for men who are responsible, decent, loyal, and available.

Having given up on finding a good man in Denver, Colorado,

Savannah Jackson quits her public relations job and moves to Phoenix. However, the man who offered to drive her there turns out to be a drug addict; a doctor who reappears in her life is married, he says unhappily; and the San Franciscan who seems so taken with her cuts off communications without an explanation.

Bernadine Harris's situation is even worse. Her husband has left her for a young, white woman, taking his assets with him. Bernadine's friend Robin Stokes still has her man, but she has to support him, and he is consistently unfaithful to her. When she becomes pregnant, she has to face the fact that he will never take any responsibility either for her or for their baby. The fourth protagonist, Gloria Matthews, has built her life around her promising son, Tarik. However, she still yearns for love and companionship. Her answer to loneliness is hard work, and she very nearly works herself to death.

Waiting to Exhale ends as it begins, with each of the four women hoping that the next man will turn out to be the right one. The only certainty in the book is that whatever happens, the women will be sustained by their friendship.

How Stella Got Her Groove Back
Like *Disappearing Acts, How Stella Got Her Groove Back*, is a love story. However, this time her novel is unabashedly autobiographical. McMillan's alter ego, Stella Payne, is a successful forty-two-year-old woman with a wonderful son much like McMillan's own, Solomon Welch. In a breathless, first-person narrative, Stella explains how she happened to choose Jamaica for a vacation and describes her chance encounter with Winston Shakespeare, a handsome young man half her age. What begins as attraction turns out to be true love. Nevertheless, Stella cannot forget the difference in their ages, though it seems not to trouble Winston.

Back in California, Stella discovers that she has lost her job. However, she has invested so wisely over the years that money is not a real problem. She even sees this development as an opportunity to take her life in a new direction. This uncharacteristic optimism, she realizes, is the result of her involvement with

Winston. Stella does not waste any time. She makes a second trip to Jamaica, this time taking her son and her niece with her. They get along famously with Winston. As the book ends, Winston is in California with Stella, and they are planning to marry. McMillan dedicated the novel to Jonathan Plummer, her own Jamaican husband.

Reviewers felt that *How Stella Got Her Groove Back* lacked both the craftsmanship and the realism of McMillan's other novels. With its happily-ever-after ending, it was generally dismissed as a romance.

A Day Late and a Dollar Short

Of the six major characters in *A Day Late and a Dollar Short*, Viola Price is the most important. Viola is a matriarch much like McMillan's own mother. She still feels responsible for her children, her grandchildren, and even her ex-husband Cecil. Viola knows that her hard-working, well-to-do oldest daughter, Paris, is addicted to pills; that her second daughter, Charlotte, is possessed by her jealous hatred of Paris; and that her youngest child, Janelle, is too afraid of her second husband to admit that he has raped her daughter. Viola's son, Lewis, is an alcoholic whose hot temper keeps landing him in jail. Viola also has one grandson who is gay and another who was headed for college until his girlfriend got pregnant. Even Cecil is a worry; he has a young girlfriend who Viola believes takes advantage of him.

A Day Late and a Dollar Short begins with Viola lying in a hospital bed worrying about her family. It ends with her reaching out to them from beyond the grave in a final attempt to set them straight and to bring the family closer together. Although the use of six narrative voices sometimes leads to confusion, *A Day Late and a Dollar Short* is considered one of McMillan's most appealing novels.

The Interruption of Everything

McMillan began by writing about young, ambitious women like herself. As she has grown older, however, so have her characters. *The Interruption of Everything* is about middle age. Marilyn Grimes, the heroine of the novel, is a forty-four-year-old woman whose children have gone off to college, leaving her with a live-in mother-in-law, a mother showing signs of Alzheimer's, a sister too addicted to drugs to care for her own children, and a husband who seems to be having his own midlife crisis. Fortunately, Marilyn has two girlfriends to provide the support she desperately needs.

One reason for McMillan's broad appeal is that, though she never pretends that life is easy, she assures women that they have the inherent strength to handle whatever comes their way. In *The Interruption of Everything*, McMillan holds the attention of her readers with one plot complication after another. Marilyn becomes pregnant; her husband goes to Costa Rica to find himself; her son brings a peculiar crew home from college; and her ex-husband reappears, looking better than she remembered. The dialogue is as irreverent and as sparkling as McMillan's readers expect, and *The Interruption of Everything* ends on an optimistic note.

Other Literary Forms

McMillan edited *Breaking Ice: An Anthology of Contemporary African-American Fiction*, which is composed of fifty-seven selections by both established and relatively unknown black writers. She also wrote the screenplays for two of her novels, *Waiting to Exhale*, which was produced by Twentieth Century Fox in 1995, and *How Stella Got Her Groove Back*, produced by the same studio in 1998.

Bibliography

Dandridge, Rita B. "Debunking the Beauty Myth in Terry McMillan's *Waiting to Exhale*. In *Language, Rhythm, and Sound: Black Popular Cultures into the Twenty-first Century*, edited by Joseph K. Adjaye and Adrienne R. Andrews. Pittsburgh: University of Pittsburgh Press, 1997. The four major women characters in the novel all respond differently to the Eurocentric preoccupation with physical beauty. McMillan's message is that women can find fulfillment only by accepting the Afrocentric aesthetic that is the basis of black popular culture.

_____. "Debunking the Motherhood Myth in Terry McMillan's *Mama*." *CLA Journal* 41, no. 4 (1998): 405-416. Shows how the life of the title character in *Mama* is determined by racial history. Therefore, Eurocentric myths of the "saved" mother and ideals of "true womanhood" are not applicable to women like her.

Danford, Natalie. Review of *The Interruption of Everything*, by Terry McMillan. *People*, July 25, 2005, p. 50. The popular weekly magazine reviews McMillan's book.

Ellerby, Janet Mason. "Deposing the Man of the House: Terry McMillan Rewrites the Family." *MELUS* 22, no. 2 (June, 1997): 105-117. McMillan shows how the natural desires of African American women for erotic satisfaction and for children cause them to be trapped into servitude to men. In her fiction she advocates a confuguration of the family unit, in which women derive support from friends and the community, rather than from a father figure who typically proves to be weak and unreliable.

McMillan, Terry. "Author Spotlight: Terry McMillan." Interview. *Ebony* 60, no. 9 (July, 2005): 32-33. The author discusses *The Interruption of Everything* and its characters, and also reveals some of her favorite activities and her feelings about growing older.

_____. "Terry McMillan." http://www.terrymcmillan.com/. Accessed September 1, 2005. The author's Web site contains information about her books and the three movies that have been made from them, as well as a biography and the text of a 1999 interview.

Nunez, Elizabeth, and Brenda M. Greene, eds. *Defining Ourselves: Black Writers in the 90's*. New York: P. Lang, 1999. Based on panel discussions in which a number of major writers, including McMillan, spoke about various issues, including new developments in publishing.

Patrick, Diane. *Terry McMillan: The Unauthorized Biography*. New York: St. Martin's Press, 1999. Even without McMillan's cooperation, Patrick has produced a fair, thoughtful study based on thorough research. Includes perceptive analysis of McMillan's influence on the publishing industry.

Richards, Paulette. *Terry McMillan: A Critical Companion.* Westport, Conn.: Greenwood Press, 1999. Contains a brief biography of McMillan, a chapter placing her in the literary context, and thematic analyses of her first four novels. Bibliography and index.

Smolowe, Jill, and Alison Singh Gee. "A Shakeup for Stella." Review of *The Interruption of Everything,* by Terry McMillan. *People,* July 11, 2005, p. 97-98. A review of McMillan's book. Also includes McMillan's comments on her relationship with and divorce from Jonathan Plummer, as well as the lawsuit in which she accused him of marrying her for his own financial gain.

— *Rosemary M. Canfield Reisman*

James Alan McPherson

Short-story writer and essayist

Born: Savannah, Georgia; September 16, 1943

SHORT FICTION: *Hue and Cry,* 1969; *Elbow Room,* 1977.
NONFICTION: *Crabcakes,* 1998; *A Region Not Home: Reflections from Exile,* 2000; *Hallowed Ground: A Walk at Gettysburg,* 2003.
EDITED TEXTS: *Railroad: Trains and Train People in American Culture,* 1976 (with Miller Williams); *Fathering Daughters: Reflections by Men,* 1998 (with DeWitt Henry).

Achievements

Even though James Alan McPherson has not published many collections of short fiction, his adroit characterizations and his strong sense of place have attracted many readers and influenced a number of writers. His work has been anthologized and has appeared in *The Atlantic Monthly, Playboy, The New York Times Magazine, The Harvard Advocate, Reader's Digest, The Iowa Review, The Massachusetts Review,* and *Ploughshares.* His association with the Writer's Workshop at the University of Iowa and his teaching of courses in fiction writing have given him a forum from which he influences beginning writers across the United States. Though earlier critics noted similarities between McPherson and other African American writers such as James Baldwin and Ralph Ellison, critical attention was later placed on his unique use of language and his ability to create a mythical dimension to his stories. Because of this, his fiction has begun to be examined in a much wider context than previously.

The story "Gold Coast" won the prize for fiction awarded by *The Atlantic Monthly* in 1968. McPherson won the literature award of the National Institute of Arts and Letters in 1970, and he was the recipient of a John Simon Guggenheim Memorial Foundation Fellowship in 1972. *Elbow Room* won the 1978 Pulitzer Prize in fiction and was nominated for the National Book Award. In 1981, his writing achievements earned him a MacArthur Fellowship.

Biography

James Alan McPherson earned degrees from Morris Brown College (B.A., 1965), Harvard Law School (LL.B., 1968), and the Iowa Writers' Workshop (M.F.A., 1971). He has taught at the University of Iowa, the University of California, Harvard University, Morgan State University, and the University of Virginia. Besides being a contributing editor of *The Atlantic Monthly*, he held jobs ranging from stock clerk to newspaper reporter. In the early 1980's, McPherson began teaching fiction writing in the Writers' Workshop at the University of Iowa in Iowa City. After writing *Elbow Room*, McPherson primarily focused on nonfiction essays that center on the need for African Americans to help define the cultural realities of contemporary American life. His first book in twenty years, *Crabcakes*, focuses on his ultimate understanding of what makes people human.

Analysis: Short Fiction

James Alan McPherson is one of the writers of fiction who form the second major phase of modern writing about the African American experience. Indebted, like all of his generation, to the groundbreaking and theme-setting work of Richard Wright, Ellison, and Baldwin, McPherson shies away from doctrinaire argumentation about racial issues. Rather, he uses these issues to give his work a firmly American aura, which includes a preoccupation not only with what it means to be a black person in modern America but also with how the individual responds to a culture that often is plagued by subtle and not-so-subtle racial discriminations. Hence, there are times when blackness becomes for McPherson a metaphor for the alienation experienced by the individual in contemporary society.

This comprehensive concern with American culture informs all of McPherson's work, including those pieces that are in-

cluded in the prose and poetry collection compiled by Mc-
Pherson and Miller Williams, titled *Railroad: Trains and Train
People in American Culture.* A celebration, a lament, and a plea,
this volume deals with the passing of the great era of passenger
railcar service in the United States. To McPherson, the liberating motion integral to the railroad is important, but so is the
sense of place and time that builds for his characters much of
their sense of self. McPherson's characters are often confined by
the conventions of locale, yet McPherson is not a regional writer
in the usual sense of the word; he can bring to life stories set in
Tennessee, Virginia, Boston, Chicago, or London.

Because of the tension in this body of work between the individual and the community, McPherson's people often feel alienated, lonely, and unable fully to reach or to maintain contact
with acquaintances, friends, families, or lovers. Yet such isolation may lead to a character's growth to near-tragic stature. The
integrity of the individual is thus asserted even while a narrator
may worry over the deep inability of any person to penetrate
into the heart and mind of another. Such recognitions contribute to the sympathetic portrayal even of unpromising characters. It should be noted that the reader is not given solutions
in McPherson's fiction, only access to degrees of awareness of
the mysteries of race, sexuality, identity, and love. Reading Mc-
Pherson, a reader may be reminded of Baldwin's presentation
of agonizingly complex racial and sexual problems, of Saul Bellow's portrayal of characters battling absurdity and despair, and
of the struggle of characters, both in Baldwin and in Bellow,
toward the ameliorating but no less mysterious experience of
love.

"Gold Coast"

McPherson's first volume of short fiction, *Hue and Cry,* is an
often-grim affair, containing stories of loneliness, destitution,
defeat, sexual alienation, and racial tension. A prime example
of this early work is "Gold Coast." The narrator of this story is an
"apprentice janitor" in a hotel near Harvard Square in Boston, a
hotel that has seen better days and is now populated with aging
singles or couples who are almost as disengaged from the main-

stream of Boston life as is the superintendent of the building, James Sullivan. Listening to Sullivan and observing the people in the apartments, the narrator, Robert, seeks to gather information for the stories and books he hopes to write. For Robert, being a janitor is in some ways a whim; in addition to gleaning experiential details from rubbish bins, he is constructing his life along romantic lines. Hence, Robert notes that, almost nightly,

> I drifted off to sleep lulled by sweet anticipation of that time when my potential would suddenly be realized and there would be capsule biographies of my life on dust jackets of many books, all proclaiming: "He knew life on many levels. From shoeshine boy, free-lance waiter, 3rd cook, janitor, he rose to. . . ."

Naïve but witty, the narrator humors Sullivan, putting up patiently with the Irishman's redundant reminiscing and opinionated ramblings on society and politics. Sullivan, however, comes to rely on Robert's company; he turns from the horrors of life in the filthy apartment he shares with his obscene, insane wife to interminable conversations with Robert.

Robert's sympathetic tolerance of Sullivan emanates from his sense of the pathetic isolation of Sullivan from human contact and from Robert's recognition for the first time of the terrors of aging. Robert is the archetypal youth coming to awareness of old age as a time of foreshortened expectations and straitened lifestyles, of possible despair and near dehumanization. The apprentice janitor can tolerate Sullivan and his new knowledge while his relationship with the rich, lovely Jean goes well, but Jean and he are soon torn apart by social forces. In fact, they play a game called "Social Forces," in which they try to determine which of them will break first under social disapproval of their interracial relationship. When the game defeats them, Robert first is comforted by and then pulls back from his friendship with the dejected Sullivan, who is especially upset over the loss of his dog.

When Robert finally leaves his briefly held janitorial position, he does so with both relief and guilt over his abandonment of Sullivan. He knows, however, that he is "still young" and not yet doomed to the utter loneliness of the old man. McPherson suggests that the young, nevertheless, will inevitably come to such bleak isolation and that even the temporary freedom of youth is sometimes maintained at the expense of sympathy and kindness. There are dangers in being free, not the least of which are the burden of knowledge, the hardening of the self, and the aching realization of basic, but often unmet, human needs. This theme of loss is picked up in the volume's title story, "Hue and Cry," which includes this interchange between two characters:

"Between my eyes I see three people and they are all unhappy. Why?"

"Perhaps it is because they are alive. Perhaps it is because they once were. Perhaps it is because they have to be. I do not know."

These voices cannot make sense of the losses to which life dooms McPherson's characters, nor does Robert. He simply moves away from the hotel to enjoy, while he can, youth and his sense of potential.

"A Solo Song: For Doc"

The theme of old age and its defeats is further developed in McPherson's well-received "A Solo Song: For Doc," a story which displays well the author's rhythmic and precise control of narration conceived of as speech. McPherson resolves to initiate readers of all races into a facet of their culture that is quickly passing out of sight. The narrator, an aging waiter on a railroad line, tells a young listener about the good old days in the service and about their embodiment, a waiter called Doc Craft. "So do you want to know this business, youngblood?" begins the teller of the tale, and he goes on, "So you want to be a Waiter's Waiter? The Commissary gives you a book with all the rules and tells you to learn them. And you do, and think that is all there is to it." This "Waiter's Waiter" then proceeds to disillusion the "youngblood" by describing the difficult waiter's craft—the finesse, grace, care, and creativity required to make the job into an art and to make that art pay. The grace and dedication displayed by men of Doc Craft's generation is shown to be losing ground to the contemporary world of business in which men such as "Jerry Ewald, the Unexpected Inspector," lie in wait to trap heroes like Doc Craft and to remove them from the service that keeps them alive. The narrator specifies what kept Doc on the road: having power over his car and his customers, hustling tips, enjoying women without being married to them, getting drunk without having to worry about getting home. The shift from passenger to freight service on the railroad, however, begins the company's attempt to fire Doc and also initiates Doc's rise to heroic stature. Older ways of work and life yield to new technology, and, like the old-time railroad, Doc Craft is doomed; Ewald catches Doc on a technicality about iced tea service, and the waiter is fired.

Clearly, McPherson's thematic preoccupations and love of the railroad have coalesced in this story. He captures the complexity, richness, and hardships of the lives of African American traveling men, as well as the initiative and kinship developed by black workers. Movement, adventure, freedom, self-expression, craftsmanship, commitment, exuberance, and endurance—these qualities mark both Doc Craft and the railroad as valuable American entities. Yet the passing of Doc carries McPherson's sense of the epic loss suffered by an America that has allowed the railroad, the metaphoric counterpart of imaginative integration of all kinds, to decay.

"Why I Like Country Music"

Even while remaining faithful to McPherson's characteristic themes, *Elbow Room*, his second volume, includes stories that reach a kind of comic perfection. One example is "Why I Like Country Music." The narrator, a southern-born black, addresses to his northern-born wife an explanation of his love of square-dance music. His wife will not believe or accept this preference, but the narrator quietly insists on it. In one sense, this insistence and the narration that justifies it may be viewed as evidence of the eternal and invincible isolation of the human heart from sympathetic understanding even by loved ones. The forces of memory and of individual development work to isolate human beings from one another. Further, the narrator's insistence that the South Carolina traditions of his youth have given to him preferences and ideas alien to those of the New York-born tends to strengthen this theme of the coherence but separateness of the self.

Such thematic reverberations, however, do not form the main concern of this story. Rather, the narrator tells us of a comic case of childhood puppy love; he explains that he loves country music because it is permanently associated in his mind with a girl in his fourth-grade class whose name was Gweneth Larson. Born in Brooklyn and redolent of lemons, Gweneth is for the narrator an object of first love. The moments when he square danced with her in a school May Day celebration were etched in his mind as moments of surpassing joy and love. Far from exploring alienation, the story celebrates the endurance of such affection.

McPherson's comedy is never heavy-handed, always a matter of a light tone or a moment of incongruity. An example occurs when the narrator describes the calling of the Maypole teams to the playground for their performance:

> "Maypole teams *up!*" called Mr. Henry Lucas, our principal, from his platform by the swings. Beside him stood the white Superintendent of Schools (who said later of the square dance, it was reported to all the classes, "Lord, y'all square dance so *good* it makes me plumb *ashamed* us white folks ain't takin' better care of our art stuff").

"A Loaf of Bread"

A more somber story in *Elbow Room*, "A Loaf of Bread," addresses important issues associated with racism and assimilation by depicting the isolation of the African American middle class. As in many of his other stories, McPherson expresses hope for the evolution of a model of American identity toward which all Americans can proudly gravitate. In "A Loaf of Bread," he explores the difference between exploitation and participation of African Americans in American society.

746

Store owner Harold Green charges higher prices for goods in his store in an African American neighborhood than in the stores he owns in white neighborhoods. Consequently, as an act of restitution for exploiting the black community, Green decides that the best solution is to open his store and give away his merchandise free of charge to members of the exploited black community. The ensuing frenzy leaves Green's store in complete disarray, totally depleted of merchandise.

Nelson Reed, the leader of the community protest against Green, returns to the store later in the day to pay Green one dollar for the loaf of bread that his wife had taken from the store that morning. Reed is evidently seeking the status of a participating consumer versus an exploited one. Characteristic of McPherson's writing, characters in difficult situations struggle for some measure of success. However, Reed's attempt to receive equitable treatment as an American citizen is nullified by Green's response.

Similar to other fiction written by McPherson, the overall plot of "A Loaf of Bread" appears to argue for an American citizenship that eradicates racial boundaries and produces a coherent, color-blind American society. However, McPherson believes that racial exclusion continues to exist like an undeviated line from decades past and that acts of racial prejudice continue to demonstrate the pervasiveness of racial chauvinism. Furthermore, pointing fingers and using the "we/they" phrase in reference to other races only proliferates prejudice and isolation.

In "A Loaf of Bread," the hope for the black community to achieve unified American citizenship seems to be superseded by the lure of participating as a consumer in the marketplace. McPherson suggests that the African American middle class has abandoned the process of discarding some of the traditions of their fathers and embracing a sense of commonality with the white world. Consequently, the African American middle class becomes further isolated from the mainstream of American society. It is notable that in both his comedy "Why I Like Country Music" and his very somber "A Loaf of Bread," McPherson remains firmly focused on the human personality, which is for him the incentive for narration and the core of his art.

Other Literary Forms

With Miller Williams, James Alan McPherson has edited and contributed essays and a short story to a volume of essays, stories, poems, and pictures entitled *Railroad: Trains and Train People in American Culture*. After 1969, McPherson also contributed several essays to *The Atlantic Monthly* and to *Reader's Digest. Crabcakes*, a volume of meditations on many topics, was McPherson's first book after the short-story collection *Elbow Room. Fathering Daughters: Reflections by Men*, edited by McPherson and DeWitt Henry, is a collection of essays on the father-daughter bond.

Bibliography

Beavers, Herman. "I Yam What You Is and You Is What I Yam: Rhetorical Invisibility in James Alan McPherson's 'The Story of a Dead Man.'" *Callaloo* 9 (1986): 565-577. Beavers discusses the linguistic and rhetorical characteristics of McPherson's dialogue and how language shapes perceptions, specifically in "The Story of a Dead Man."

_____. *Wrestling Angels into Song: The Fictions of Ernest J. Gaines and James Alan McPherson*. Philadelphia: University of Pennsylvania Press, 1995. Provides criticism and interpretation of Gaines's and McPherson's works of fiction.

Cox, Joseph T. "James Alan McPherson." In *Contemporary Fiction Writers of the South*, edited by Joseph M. Flora and Robert Bain. Westport, Conn.: Greenwood Press, 1993. A brief introduction to McPherson's art, including a short biographical sketch, a summary and critique of the criticism of his work, and a short discussion of his short-story themes of intolerance and general absence of grace and love in modern society.

Laughlin, Rosemary M. "Attention, American Folklore: Doc Craft Comes Marching In." *Studies in American Fiction* 1 (1973): 221-227. Laughlin discusses McPherson's use of myth and folklore, as well as his ability to create new kinds of folklore in the pages of his story based on his aesthetic use of language and his unique mythical style.

"McPherson, James Alan." *Current Biography* 57 (September, 1996): 34-38. A biographical sketch of McPherson; claims that he sees the United States as a land populated by diverse peoples who are connected by a larger heritage; asserts that his major theme in both fiction and nonfiction has been the common humanity that transcends race.

McPherson, James Alan. "Interview with James Alan McPherson." Interview by Bob Shacochis. *Iowa Journal of Literary Studies* 4 (1983): 6-33. Shacochis focuses on questions relating to McPherson's vision of his literary role and on specific works in his collections. Contains also some discussion of McPherson's obligations as a "black-American" author.

Reid, Calvin. "James Alan McPherson: A Theater of Memory." *Publishers Weekly* 244 (December 15, 1997): 36-37. A biographical profile of McPherson; contends McPherson presents a wonderfully accurate social tableau full of vivid characters and lively, true dialogue, which is delivered within narratives so universal and directly meaningful that the stories aspire to the mythic realm of folklore and legend.

Wallace, Jon. "The Politics of Style in Three Stories by James Alan McPherson." *Modern Fiction Studies* 34 (Spring, 1988): 17-26. Wallace argues that, in three stories by McPherson, "The Story of a Dead Man," "The Story of a Scar," and "Just Enough for the City," characters use language to construct for themselves a defense against human involvement and human communities which often threaten to weaken their sense of self.

_____. *The Politics of Style: Language as Theme in the Fiction of Berger, McGuane, and McPherson.* Durango, Colo.: Hollowbrook, 1992. A study of the importance of language in the fiction of several authors, including McPherson.

_____. "The Story Behind the Story in James Alan McPherson's *Elbow Room.*" *Studies in Short Fiction* 25 (Fall, 1988): 447-452. Wallace argues that McPherson's stories are often attempts to create a new kind of mythology, or mythological space, in which to place the experiences of his characters in the larger context of American society. Because of this, Wallace argues that in McPherson's work it is narrative form that matters much more than either the particulars of the story or the characters.

— *Alvin K. Benson; Cheryl Herr; Edward Huffstetler*

Haki R. Madhubuti

(Don L. Lee)

Poet and editor

Born: Little Rock, Arkansas; February 23, 1942

POETRY: *Think Black,* 1967, revised 1968, revised 1969; *Black Pride,* 1968; *Don't Cry, Scream,* 1969; *We Walk the Way of the New World,* 1970; *Directionscore: Selected and New Poems,* 1971; *Book of Life,* 1973; *Killing Memory, Seeking Ancestors,* 1987; *GroundWork: New and Selected Poems of Don L. Lee/Haki R. Madhubuti from 1966-1996,* 1996; *Heartlove: Wedding and Love Poems,* 1998.

NONFICTION: *Dynamite Voices: Black Poets of the 1960's,* 1971; *From Plan to Planet, Life Studies: The Need for Afrikan Minds and Institutions,* 1973; *Enemies: The Clash of Races,* 1978; *Black Men: Obsolete, Single, Dangerous?,* 1990; *Claiming Earth: Race, Rage, Rape, Redemption—Blacks Seeking a Culture of Enlightened Empowerment,* 1994.

EDITED TEXTS: *To Gwen with Love: An Anthology Dedicated to Gwendolyn Brooks,* 1971 (with Francis Ward and Patricia L. Brown); *Say That the River Turns: The Impact of Gwendolyn Brooks,* 1987; *Confusion by Any Other Name: Essays Exploring the Negative Impact of "The Blackman's Guide to Understanding the Blackwoman,"* 1990; *Why L.A. Happened: Implications of the '92 Los Angeles Rebellion,* 1993; *Black Books Bulletin: The Challenge of the Twenty-first Century,* 1995; *Million Man March, Day of Absence: A Commemorative Anthology—Speeches, Commentary, Photography, Poetry, Illustrations, Documents,* 1996 (with Maulana Karenga); *Releasing the Spirit: A Collection of Literary Works from "Gallery Thirty-seven,"* 1998 (with Gwendolyn Mitchell); *Describe the Moment: A Collection of Literary Works from "Gallery Thirty-seven,"* 2000 (with Mitchell).

MISCELLANEOUS: *Earthquakes and Sunrise Missions: Poetry and Essays of Black Renewal, 1973-1983,* 1984.

Achievements

Perhaps Haki R. Madhubuti's single most impressive accomplishment has been not his success with new forms of poetry, his articulation of new social criticism, his formulation of new aesthetic principles, or his success as a publisher and editor, but his ability to accomplish all of these goals, for which, he asserts, a black poet must struggle. Madhubuti *is* the black poet of his proposed "total dedication" to black liberation and "nationbuilding." In his embodiment of his principles and commitment, Madhubuti has reached into corners of the black community that have been heretofore untouched by black literature or liberation politics. Within four years of the publication of his first book, he had "sold more books of poetry (some 250,000 copies) than probably all of the black poets who came before him combined" (*The Black Collegian*, February/March, 1971). One would be hard-pressed to name *any* American poet who could boast such a large figure in such short time—twenty-five thousand copies, ten percent of Madhubuti's sales, might be considered a phenomenal success. Clearly, Madhubuti's popularity does not rest on library or classroom purchases; it is based on the very "market" he seeks to speak to: the black community. Having defined his audience as exclusively the blacks of America in his social criticism, he has found a quite remarkable response from that desired audience even though he is frequently blunt in his sarcastic ridicule of blacks who aspire to imitate whites. In taking the black community seriously as an audience, Madhubuti has discovered that the audience accepts him seriously. This interaction, then, seems to be the epitome of the "mutual involvement" between artists and community of which he writes in his social criticism.

Madhubuti's popular reception, however, has not diminished his success in a more narrowly defined black literary community. His influence on young black poets and writers of the 1970's is pervasive; one sees imitations of him and dedications to him in many black literary journals. His extensions of Amiri Baraka's theoretical positions in cultural nationalism have forced older black critics to reexamine and reevaluate their criteria for black aesthetic standards. His publishing and editing efforts have enabled many young black writers to reach print, as attested by his numerous introductions and reviews of their work. Most important, however, Madhubuti has succeeded continuously in educating (he would say *reeducating*) ever-increasing numbers of individuals within the black community to participate in that dialogue and to perpetuate it within the community. He has been, and remains, an essential leader in working toward black pride, unity, and power, or as he puts it, in giving "identity, purpose and direction" to black "nationbuilding."

Biography

Haki R. Madhubuti (who changed his name from Don Luther Lee to his Swahili name in 1973), born in Little Rock, Arkansas, moved to Chicago with his parents Jimmy and Maxine Lee midway through his childhood. After graduating from high school, Madhubuti continued his education at Wilson Junior College, Roosevelt University, and the University of Illinois at Chicago Circle. His formal education has been tempered, however, by a wide range of jobs which have increased his rapport with varied classes and individuals within the black community. After serving in the United States Army from 1960 to 1963, Madhubuti returned to Chicago to begin an apprenticeship as curator of the DuSable Museum of African History, which he continued until 1967. Meanwhile, he worked as a stock department clerk for Montgomery Ward (1963 to 1964), a post office clerk (1964 to 1965), and a junior executive for Spiegel's (1965 to 1966). By the end of 1967, Madhubuti's reputation as a poet and as a spokesman for the new black poetry of the 1960's had grown sufficiently to enable him to support himself through publishing and teaching alone.

Madhubuti was writer-in-residence at Cornell University from 1968 to 1969. Similar positions followed at Northeastern Illinois State College (1969-1970) and the University of Illinois at Chicago Circle (1969-1971), where he combined poet-in-residencies with teaching black literature. From 1970 to 1975, Madhubuti taught at Howard University, except for a year at Morgan State College where he was writer-in-residence from 1972 to 1973.

(Courtesy, St. Norbert College)

The extensive popular reception of his poetry and the increasing frequency of his social essays made him a favorite (if controversial) reader and lecturer with black college students across the country. His influence and popularity also enabled him to found, in Chicago, the Institute of Positive Education in 1971, which publishes *Black Books Bulletin*, edited by Madhubuti, and for which he served as director from 1971 to 1991. He is also the publisher and editor of Third World Press, one of the largest and most successful independent African American book publishers, since 1971. In conjunction with his publishing roles, Madhubuti is also a professor of English and director emeritus of the Gwendolyn Brooks Center at Chicago State University.

Madhubuti has also held important executive positions with a number of Pan-African organizations such as the Congress of African People. Madhubuti's publishing, editing, teaching, and writing continue to maintain his stature within the Black Nationalist movement.

Analysis: Poetry

Much of Haki R. Madhubuti's poetry was initially greeted by outright condemnation on the part of white critics whose standards of aesthetic judgment were antagonistic, to say the least, toward the nationalist assumptions inherent in much of the new black poetry of the 1960's. Jascha Kessler, for example, in a review in *Poetry* (February, 1973), said that in "Lee all is converted to rant/ . . . / [he] is outside poetry somewhere, exhorting, hectoring, cursing, making a lot of noise/ . . . you don't have to be black for that/ . . . / it's hardly an excuse." Madhubuti's sociopolitical concerns, in short, were viewed as unfit for poetic rendering, and his urban, rap-style jazz rhythms and phrases in his poems were dismissed as simply disgruntled, militant ravings. Ironically, that sort of reception—and inability to move beyond the parameters of the New Criticism—supported exactly what the new black poets were claiming: White critical standards forced blacks to write as if they were white themselves and thereby denied them their own cultural heritage and suppressed their experience of oppression. Indeed, this is the dilemma in which the young Lee found himself; if he were to "succeed," he would need (even as a poet) to obliterate his own identity as a black man.

The writings of Amiri Baraka, probably more than any other poet's, as well as his independent studies in African culture (probably begun at the DuSable Museum), violently ruptured the assumption that accommodation to the dominant culture was the sole means by which blacks could survive in America. With the break from accommodationist thought, as Marlene Mosher suggests in *New Directions from Don L. Lee* (1975), Madhubuti began his struggle to create identity, unity, and power in a neo-African context that would preserve his heritage and experience while creating a possibility for the black community as a whole to free itself from the oppressive constraints of mainstream American culture. Madhubuti progressed from the accommodationist period through a reactive phase, then through a revolutionary program, to a prophetic vision. These four aspects of his poetry are distinct not only in the ideological content of his work, but also in the structure of the poems themselves. Once the prophetic vision had been embraced, it was necessary to begin a pragmatic clarification of that vision; the necessity to describe specifically the new Black Nation led, ironically, to an increasing devotion to prose, and thus Madhubuti's poetry seemed nearly to disappear—at least in publication—after his book of poems, *Book of Life.* That the vision of his poetry should result in the suspension of his poetry writing in favor of concrete description was, for those who laud his poetry, a great loss. It is not, however, incomprehensible, for Madhubuti, in urging the embodiment of his poetic vision and in describing *how* to build that vision in realistic terms, is actually carrying out what he first proposed as the goal of his work: to construct an African mind and to create a Black Nation. One assumes, then, that his activities left little time for him to pursue his poetry. Fortunately, he began again to publish books of poems in 1984.

The period of accommodation in Madhubuti's work is available only through autobiographical references found in the early poems of the reactive phase. This early "pre-poetic" time is, appropriately, marked by a lack of articulation. Without his own voice, there are no poems, no prose, no statements of any kind. To speak as oneself for one's community was to react to that accommodation. Madhubuti's "confession" of that period, therefore, is marked by bitterness, hatred, and condemnation of almost everything he associated with white America, including himself. Several poems in his first book, *Think Black,* are testimonial as well as vengeful; it is clear in these poems that Madhubuti had been "liberating" himself for several years, and only then was testifying to that personal struggle through accommodation. He was to say later, in "Black Sketches" (*Don't Cry, Scream*), that he "became black" in 1963 and "everyone thought it unusual;/ even me."

Think Black

Both the accommodationist period and the reactive phase are seen in *Think Black*, but the point of view is nearly always that of a reaction against accommodation. In "Understanding But Not Forgetting," Madhubuti speaks of his family life and his "early escape/ period, trying to be white." Among his images are those of an intellectual accommodationist who "still ain't hip," an uneducated grandmother "with wisdom that most philosophers would/ envy," misery-filled weekends with "no family/ but money," a twenty-two-year-old sister with "five children," a mother involved in prostitution but "providing for her family," and a cheating white newspaper distributor who kept "telling/ me what a good boy I was." Reexamining his childhood and adolescence in this poem, Madhubuti concludes: "About positive images as a child—NONE," and further that "About negative images as a child—all black." In his attempt to understand his social conditioning and view it in the larger context of American culture, he is forced to conclude that education, democracy, religion, and even the "BLACK MIDDLE CLASS" (to which he has aspired) have failed him because of "the American System." It is, in fact, those very outcasts of the black community itself—the grandmother and the prostitute-mother, who "read Richard Wright and Chester Himes/ . . . / [bad books," that offer examples of survival against overwhelming oppression.

Black Pride

Madhubuti had not, however, accomplished much more at that time than rejection of the value system which had created his anger and despair: The awareness of *how* to "think black" is vague. The last poem in the book, "Awareness," is a chant of only three words: "BLACK PEOPLE THINK." In the variations of syntactical arrangement of these words, however, one is left with the unmistakable impression that he will struggle to learn from those outcasts of mainstream society just what it means to "THINK BLACK." These lessons are the heart of his second book, *Black Pride*, which is still reactive but nevertheless substantial in its discovery of identity. While many of these poems remain confessional, there is an increase in the clarity of Madhubuti's sociopolitical development. In the brief lead poem, "The New Integrationist," he announces his intention to join "negroes/ with/ black/ people." The one-word lines of the poem force the reader to contemplate not only the irony in his use of "integration," but also the implications inherent in the labels "negro" and "black." It is an appropriate keynote for the fulfillment of that vague awareness with which his first book ended.

Perhaps the growth in self-identity that characterizes *Black Pride* begins, paradoxically, most clearly in "The Self-Hatred of Don L. Lee." The confessional stance of the poet first acknowledges a love of "my color" because it allowed him to move upward in the accommodationist period; it "opened sMall/ doors of/ tokenism." After "struggling" through a reading list of the forerunners of cultural nationalism, Madhubuti then describes a breakthrough from "my blindness" to "pitchblack// awareness." His "all/ black// inner/ self" is now his strength, the basis for his self-identity, and he rejects with "vehement/ hatred" his "light/ brown/ outer" self, that appearance which he had previously exploited by accepting the benefits of tokenism. While Madhubuti had escaped accommodation by this time, he had not yet ceased to react to it; instead of having skin too dark, he had skin too light. He was, as black oral tradition puts it, "colorstruck." He had, however, moved much deeper into the problem of establishing an identity based on dignity rather than denigration.

The growth of identity and black pride still remains, then, a function of what is not blackness instead of what is, or will become, Madhubuti's new Black Nation. In several poems such as "The Primitive," Madhubuti describes the loss of black values under American slavery and the subsequent efforts of blacks to imitate their oppressors who "raped our minds" with mainstream images from "T. V. . . ./ Reader's Digest// tarzan & jungle jim," who offered "used cars & used homes/ reefers & napalm/ european history & promises" and who fostered "alien concepts/ of whi-teness." His message here is blunt: "this weapon called/ civilization// [acts] to drive us mad/ (like them)." For all of his vindictive bitterness, however, Madhubuti addresses himself to the black community more than he does to white America—self-reliance for self-preservation emerges as the crucial issue. As he suggests in the final poem "No More Marching Now," nonviolent protest and civil rights legislation have been undermined by white values; thus, "public/ housing" has become a euphemism for "concentration camps." His charge is typically blunt: "you better wake up// before it's too late."

Although the first two volumes of Madhubuti's poems exist in the tension between accommodation and reaction, they do show growth in the use of language as well as in identity and pride. His work, at times, suffers from clichéd rhetoric and easy catchphrases common to exhortation, but it also possesses a genuine delight in the playfulness of language even while it struggles forward in the midst of serious sociopolitical polemic. In his division of "white," for example, where the one-syllable word is frequently cut into the two-syllable "whi-te" or the second syllable is dropped completely to the next line, Madhubuti demonstrates more than typographical scoring for the sound of his poem, for he displays the fragmentation between ideals and the implementation of those ideals in American culture. In contrast, "Black man" appears frequently as one word, "blackman," sometimes capitalized and sometimes not—to emphasize the gradual dissolution of the individual's ego, to suggest the necessity for unity in the community for which he strives. Capitalization, in a similar way, sometimes connotes pride in his use of "BLACK." At other times, he uses derogatory puns, such as when "U.S." becomes "u ass." His models are street language, urban speech patterns, jazz improvisation, the narrative form of the toast, and the general inventiveness of an oral tradition that belongs wholly to black culture.

Don't Cry, Scream

These early poems continue to develop both thematically and technically in Madhubuti's next two books, *Don't Cry, Scream* and *We Walk the Way of the New World*, in which he began to outline his revolutionary program. Mosher suggests that these works are consciously much less antiwhite and much more problack in their sociopolitical commitment. Madhubuti's artistic commitment fused completely with his politics; as he says in the preface to *Don't Cry, Scream,* "there is *no* neutral blackart." Black poetry is seen as "culture building" rather than as a tool to criticize either white society or blacks who seek assimilation. In this programmatic work, the hate, bitterness, and invective of the earlier two books give way to music, humor, and a gentler insistence on change. The poems are more consciously crafted than previously, but they do not compromise their essentially urgent political fervor.

In perhaps the most widely anthologized poem by Madhubuti, "But He Was Cool, or: he even stopped for green lights," he humorously undermines the stance of black radicals who are far more concerned with the appearance of being a revolutionary than with a real commitment to working for change in the black community. His satire here is more implicit than explicit, for the reader views the "supercool/ ultrablack" radical in "a double-natural" hairstyle and "dashikis [that] were tailor made." His imported beads are "triple-hip," and he introduces himself "in swahili" while saying "good-by in yoruba." Madhubuti then becomes more explicit in his satire by dividing and modifying "intelligent" to read "ill tel li gent," but he quickly moves back to implication by a rapidly delivered "bop" hyperbole that describes the radical as "cool cool ultracool . . . / cool so cool cold cool/ . . . him was air conditioned cool" and concludes that he was "so cool him nick-named refrigerator." The dissonance of the last word with the "ice box cool" earlier in the delivery clashes not only in sound, but also in economic and political connotation. This radical is so busy acting the role of a revolutionary that he has been seduced by the very goals of Western culture that Madhubuti is rejecting: money, power, and sex. By his superficial use of gestures, the "radical" has taken himself even farther away from an awareness of the real needs in the black community. In the aftermath of riots in "detroit, newark, [and] chicago," the would-be revolutionary must still be informed that "to be black/ is/ to be/ very-hot." Despite the humor, music, and wordplay in one of Madhubuti's most consciously and carefully "aesthetic" poems, the message is still primarily political. Although the poem does react to the shal-

lowness of the radical, it is worth noting that the poem is no longer essentially reactive in its tone; by the very act of informing
the radical of his ignorance in the closure of the poem, the implication is established that even this caricature has the possibility of redemption in Madhubuti's version of Black Nationalism.

Throughout *Don't Cry, Scream,* Madhubuti begins to embrace
a wider range of sensibilities in the black community while continuing to denounce those who would betray the needs of black
people. In "Black Sketches," he describes Republican Senator
Ed Brooke from Massachusetts (then a self-proclaimed liberal
advocate of civil rights) as "slashing/ his wrist/ because some-
body/ called him/ black," and portrays the conservative (relative to Madhubuti) Roy Wilkins as the token figure on the television show, "the mod squad." He is relentless in his attack on
black leaders who work within mainstream politics. In another
poem, however, "Blackrunners/ blackmen or run into blackness," Madhubuti celebrates the Olympic medal winners Tom-
mie Smith and John Carlos for their Black Power salutes in 1968
during the awards ceremony. One could hardly describe their
gesture as revolutionary, but Madhubuti accepts and praises
their symbolic act as a sign of solidarity with his own sense of
revolutionary change. In other poems, he is equally open to
the role of black women, intellectuals, and Vietnam veterans.
By the final poem of the volume, he is even willing to concede
that the "negroes" whom he has denounced in earlier work
may also be receptive to his political message. In "A Message All
Blackpeople Can Dig (& a few negroes too)," Madhubuti announces that "the realpeople" must "move together/ hands on
weapons & families" in order to bring new meanings "to// the
blackness,/ to US." While not exactly greeting antagonists with
open arms (the parenthetical shift to the lower case in the title is
quite intentional), his emphasis has changed from the coarse
invective found in *Think Black* to a moral, political force that
proceeds in "a righteous direction." Not even whites are specifically attacked here; the enemy is now perceived as "the whi-
timind," attitudes and actions from "unpeople" who perpetuate
racism and oppression. The message, in short, is now much
closer to black humanism than it ever has been before: "black-

people/ are moving, moving to return this earth into the hands of/ human beings."

We Walk the Way of the New World
The seeds for a revolutionary humanism planted at the close of *Don't Cry, Scream* blossom in *We Walk the Way of the New World.* The flowers are armed to be sure, but in signaling this change, the author's introduction, "Louder but Softer," proclaims that the "cultural nihilism" of the 1960's must give way to the "New World of black consciousness" in which education and self-definition (in the context of the community) will create not noisy, pseudorevolutionaries but self-confident leaders who pursue "real" skills—"doctors, lawyers, teachers, historians, writers"—for ensuring the survival and development of African American culture. Madhubuti's scope and purpose in this book is no less committed than it has been before, but it is far more embracing, compassionate, and visionary. His concern is the establishment of "an ongoing process aimed at an ultimate definition of our being." The tone of urgency ("We're talking about our children, a survival of a people") remains constant and clear, but its directions have moved completely "from negative to positive." While the ideas are not new in *We Walk the Way of the New World,* they do form Madhubuti's most consciously articulated and poetically designed program: Of the three sections that shape the book, "Black Woman Poems," "African Poems," and "New World Poems," he says, "Each part is a part of the other: Blackwoman is African and Africa is Blackwoman and they both represent the *New World.*" What is new in the fourth volume, then, is the degree of structural unity and, to a certain extent, a greater clarity in describing the specific meaning of *Nguzo Saba,* a black value system: "design yr own neighborhoods/ . . . teach yr own children/ . . . but/ build yr own loop// feed yr own people// [and] protect yr own communities."

The unifying metaphor for the book is the pilgrimage into the New World. Arming the heroic, everyman figure "blackman" (unnamed because he is potentially any black man in the service of community rather than in pursuit of individual, egotistical goals) with a knowledge of the contrasts between black

761

women who are positive role-models (with their love tied inextricably to black consciousness) and black women who aspire to imitate white middle-class, suburban women, Madhubuti then distinguishes the values of precolonial Africa from those which have become "contaminated" by Western industrialization. Here his emphasis is on rural communalism, loving family life, and conserving natural resources. By the final section, "blackman" has ceased to function as a depersonalized hero and is embodied in the individuality (having derived such from the community) of real black men, women, and children. This section largely recapitulates the themes and messages of earlier work, but it does so in an affirmative tone of self-asserted action within *kawaida*, African reason and tradition. In the long apocalyptic poem "For Black People," Madhubuti dramatically represents a movement of the entire race from a capitalistic state of self-defeating inactivity to a socialistic economy where mutual love and respect result in an ecologically sound, peacefully shared world of all races (although the "few whi-te communities/ . . . were closely watched"). The movement of the poem, symphonic in its structure, is, in fact, the culmination of Madhubuti's sociopolitical growth and artistic vision to this point.

Book of Life
With *Book of Life*, Madhubuti introduces little new thought, but his ideas are expressed in a much more reserved political tone and poetic structure. His role is that of the visionary prophet, the wise sage offering advice to the young children who must inevitably carry on the struggle to build the New World which he has described. Indeed, the book's cover shows a photograph of his own son in the center of a star, and the volume is dedicated to him "and his sons, and their sons." Throughout the book, photographs of Madhubuti sitting or fishing with his son testify to his affirmation of the future. His introduction still affirms "black world unity" and looks to *kawaida* as the source of this new African frame of reference, but only six new poems speak explicitly to the political dimensions of his vision. The second section, captioned after the title of the book, is composed of ninety-two meditations that echo Laozi's *Dao De Jing* (c. third

century B.C.E.). The language is simple but profound; the tone is quiet but urgent; the intended audience seems to be his son, but the community overhears him; the poetics are nearly devoid of device from any cultural context, but the force of the didacticism is sincere and genuine. Madhubuti, thinking of black poets who talk "about going to the Bahamas to write the next book," denounces those "poets [who] have become the traitors." It may well be that his sense of betrayal by black artists whom he had expected to assist him in his struggle for the New World and his own growing quietism combined to bring an end to his poetry—at least since the 1973 publication of this work. He seems to have followed his own proverb in *Book of Life*: "best teachers/ seldom teach/ they be and do."

Madhubuti demonstrated an astonishingly rapid growth in his poetry and thought—in only six years. With that sort of energy and commitment, it is not surprising that he should do what he has asked of others, shunning the success of the "traitors": to be and do whatever is necessary for the building of the New World. For Madhubuti, that necessity has meant a turning away from publishing poetry and a turning toward the education of the future generation. One might quite easily dismiss Madhubuti as a dreamer or a madman, but then one would need to recall such visionaries as William Blake, who was dismissed too much and too soon.

Earthquakes and Sunrise Missions and Killing Memory, Seeking Ancestors

In the 1980's, the growth in Madhubuti's poetry is clearly evident. A sizable portion of his later poems teach through the impact of artful language, rather than sounding merely teacherly. Madhubuti's two poetry collections of the 1980's, *Earthquakes and Sunrise Missions* and *Killing Memory, Seeking Ancestors*, represent some of his strongest writing as he trusts that his keen observation will yield a bold enough political statement.

For example, in "The Shape of Things to Come," written about the earthquake in Naples, Italy, he observes: "quicker than one can pronounce free enterprise/ like well-oiled rumors or elastic lawyers smelling money/ plastic coffins appear and are sold/ at dusk behind the vatican on the white market./ in Italy in the christian month of eighty/ in the bottom of unimaginable catastrophe/ the profit motive endures as children replenish the earth/ in wretched abundance."

Poems from these volumes, such as "Abortion," "Winterman," "The Changing Seasons of Life," "White on Black Crime," and "Killing Memory" all reflect his increased technical control and subtle political commentary. Poems collected here also show that ideologically, Madhubuti no longer continues to fight all the old battles. Christianity gets a break now, as do some white individuals. He has not, however, wavered in his fundamental commitment to black liberation and in his belief that cultural awareness can ignite and help sustain progressive political struggle. The love in him and for his mission has not diminished. If anything it has grown.

Heartlove: Wedding and Love Poems

Ten years after the publication of his previous volume of poetry, Madhubuti produced *Heartlove: Wedding and Love Poems*, an elegant collection drawn solely from Madhubuti's poetry and prose and designed to capture and celebrate the essence of love in marriage, family meditations, caring, commitment, and friendships. Acting as a poetic script for the cast of a wedding—minister, bride and groom, the maid of honor, and the best man—Madhubuti counsels, "rise with the wisdom of grandmothers, rise understanding that creation is on-going, immensely appealing and acceptable to fools and geniuses, and those of us in between."

Each poem offers words of encouragement and advice to new couples or words of tribute to the lives that have influenced Madhubuti's. From "Wedding Poems" to "Quality of Love" to "Extended Families," *Heartlove* addresses crucial questions about building partnerships and the struggle to preserve community.

Other Literary Forms

Madhubuti has consistently used the social essay to espouse and develop the ideals, difficulties, and goals of what has come to be called "cultural nationalism." His book *From Plan to Planet, Life*

Studies: The Need for Afrikan Minds and Institutions perhaps best expresses the emphasis on "social content" in Madhubuti's use of the essay and "Blackpoetry," which, as he says in the preface to *Don't Cry, Scream,* is to "tell what's *to be* & how to *be* it," as vehicles for black liberation. The book, a collection of thirty brief essays organized into four distinct sections, is unified by the underlying premise that black survival, meaning the survival of all peoples of African descent anywhere in the world, including Africa, is threatened both by the political power of European and American governments and by the racism—latent and manifest—in those two Aryan-derived cultures.

In the attempt to unify the diaspora of African culture, Madhubuti begins by examining the individual's situation in an oppressive culture and asserts the necessity to "*create* or *re-create* an Afrikan (or black) mind in a *predominantly* European-American setting." ("Afrikan" here and throughout Madhubuti's writing is so spelled in order to indicate a harder *c* sound indigenous to African languages before the "contamination" of sound and spelling—implying sociopolitical domination—by European colonialism: The change in "standard" spelling is seen as a "revolutionary" act.) This first section, appropriately untitled in recognition of the difficulty involved in establishing a cultural perspective with which to begin a plan of unity, might be called "To See with Afrikan Eyes." The second section, "Life Studies," moves from the concern for the black individual to the problems inherent in the local black community. Here Madhubuti shifts from the necessity of self-esteem, or "positive identity," to the necessity for a black value system, *Nguzo Saba,* that subordinates individual success to the best interests of the black community as a whole. The code of *Nguzo Saba* nurtures self-reliance through cooperative education, business, and industry (urban or rural). To this end, he asserts that widely diverse and geographically scattered communities can form a "psychological unity" that will result in a Black Nation. Madhubuti's synthesis here achieves less theoretical complexity but more pragmatic clarity than similar ideas from his sources: Julius Nyerere's *ujamaa,* African-based socialism; and Ron Ndabetta Karenga's *kawaida,* African tradition and reason.

One further major literary concern for Madhubuti has been literary criticism, especially the definition of "new Blackpoetry" in the light of the concepts of *ujamaa* and *kawaida*. His collection of critical essays, *Dynamite Voices: Black Poets of the 1960's*, is significant in two respects: It established a responsibility for the black critic to evaluate seriously the merits of the emerging "cultural nationalist school" of black poets, and it provided a model for doing so (if sometimes uneven and superficial in its judgments). Here, too, Madhubuti shows a tendency for his social criticism to overrun his literary evaluation, but the book will remain an important contribution to the development of aesthetic standards for black literature. (Some of Madhubuti's insights have already been explored and expanded much more carefully and thoroughly than in his own book by Stephen Henderson and Addison Gayle, Jr.) In this context, it is also necessary to note that Madhubuti regularly contributes a column, "Worldview," and book reviews to his journal *Black Books Bulletin*. Other reviews, short essays, polemical statements, and introductions are widespread in anthologies and journals such as *The Negro Digest* (later *Black World*), *Third World*, and *The Black Scholar*. In addition to his writings, recordings of Madhubuti are also available that add a great deal to the printed poem on the page. Like the work of Dylan Thomas, much of the delight in hearing Madhubuti's poetry—based as it is on the improvisations and unpredictable qualities of jazz and urban black speech patterns—is lost when his voice is absent. More so than for a great many poets, his work becomes more powerful when heard.

Bibliography

Ards, Angela. "Haki Madhubuti: The Measure of a Man." *Black Issues Book Review* 4, no. 2 (March/April, 2002): 42-47. This article provides an introduction to Madhubuti's Third World Press, including a description of Madhubuti's office, books published, and authors signed. Also includes a brief biography.

Jennings, Regina. "Cheikh Anta Diop, Malcolm X, and Haki Madhubuti." *Journal of Black Studies* 33, no. 2 (November, 2002): 126-145. A thought-provoking analysis of the influence of Senegalese physicist Cheikh Anta Diop on the work of poet Haki Madhubuti and activist Malcolm X. Provides the reader with an understanding of Cheikh Anta Diop's contributions to physics and to the African continent, and draws parallels between his work and that of Malcolm X and Madhubuti.

Madhubuti, Haki R. "Hard Words and Clear Songs: The Writing of Black Poetry." In *Tapping Potential: English Language Arts for the Black Learner,* edited by Charlotte K. Brooks et al. Urbana, Ill.: Black Caucus of the National Council of Teachers of English, 1985. In this article, Madhubuti outlines some of his poetic philosophy. He explains why he writes, as a poet, and as an African American. Helpful to understanding Madhubuti's outlook.

Mosher, Marlene. *New Directions from Don L. Lee.* Hicksville, N.Y.: Exposition Press, 1975. This volume is one of the only available book-length studies on Madhubuti, so it is extremely valuable to any student of his work. Mosher provides criticism and interpretation of Madhubuti's important writing up to the mid-1970's. Includes a bibliography and an index.

Thompson, Julius E. "The Public Response to Haki R. Madhubuti, 1968-1988." *The Literary Griot: International Journal of Black Expressive Cultural Studies* 4, nos. 1/2 (Spring/Summer, 1992): 16-37. A study of the critical treatment and public response to the works of Madhubuti.

— Sarah Hilbert; Michael Loudon

Clarence Major

Novelist and poet

Born: Atlanta, Georgia; December 31, 1936

LONG FICTION: *All-Night Visitors*, 1969; *NO*, 1973; *Reflex and Bone Structure*, 1975; *Emergency Exit*, 1979; *My Amputations*, 1986; *Such Was the Season*, 1987; *Painted Turtle: Woman with Guitar*, 1988; *Dirty Bird Blues*, 1996; *One Flesh*, 2003.

SHORT FICTION: *Fun and Games*, 1990.

POETRY: *The Fires That Burn in Heaven*, 1954; *Love Poems of a Black Man*, 1965; *Human Juices*, 1966; *Swallow the Lake*, 1970; *Symptoms and Madness*, 1971; *Private Line*, 1971; *The Cotton Club*, 1972; *The Syncopated Cakewalk*, 1974; *Inside Diameter: The France Poems*, 1985; *Surfaces and Masks: A Poem*, 1988; *Some Observations of a Stranger at Zuni in the Latter Part of the Century*, 1989; *Parking Lots: A Poem*, 1992; *Configurations: New and Selected Poems, 1958-1998*, 1998; *Waiting for Sweet Betty*, 2002.

NONFICTION: *Dictionary of Afro-American Slang*, 1970 (also known as *Juba to Jive: A Dictionary of African-American Slang*, 1994); *The Dark and Feeling: Black American Writers and Their Work*, 1974; *Necessary Distance: Essays and Criticism*, 2001; *Come by Here: My Mother's Life*, 2002; *Conversations with Clarence Major*, 2002 (Nancy Bunge, editor).

EDITED TEXTS: *Writers Workshop Anthology*, 1967; *Man Is Like a Child*, 1968; *The New Black Poetry*, 1969; *Calling the Wind: Twentieth-Century African-American Short Stories*, 1993; *The Garden Thrives: Twentieth-Century African-American Poetry*, 1996.

Achievements

Clarence Major has won numerous awards and grants in his career, including a Pushcart Prize for poetry in 1976 and a Fulbright-Hays Exchange Award in 1981-1983. His novel *My Amputations* (1986) won the Western States Book Award, *Such Was the Season* (1987) was a Literary Guild Selection, *Painted Turtle: Woman with*

Guitar (1988) was a *New York Times* notable book, *Fun and Games* was a finalist for the *Los Angeles Times* Book Critics Award, and his collection *Calling the Wind: Twentieth-Century African-American Short Stories* (1993) was a Book-of-the-Month Club selection.

Biography

Clarence Major was born in Atlanta, Georgia, grew up on the South Side of Chicago, and served in the U.S. Air Force from 1955 to 1957. He studied at the Chicago Art Institute, graduated from the State University of New York at Albany, and earned a Ph.D. from the Union of Experimenting Colleges and Universities. Major taught at a number of universities, both in the United States and abroad, and after 1989 at the University of California at Davis. In addition to his fiction and poetry, Major has exhibited and published paintings and photographs. He has also been an editor and columnist and has lectured widely. He has been married twice and has lived in various parts of the United States and for extended periods in France and Italy.

Analysis: Short Fiction

Clarence Major's short fiction has attracted much less critical attention than his novels, and yet, as critic Doug Bolling has noted, "his short fiction is valuable in its own right and deserves wide reading and critical discussion." Among other strengths, Major is capable of a range of fictional styles, from the conventional to the experimental. Nearly all of his fiction is marked by lyricism and a fascination with language, but even his most realistic short stories (like "My Mother and Mitch" and "Ten Pecan Pies") tend to challenge readers. His antimimetic, experimental fiction, as Bolling argues,

> helps us to see that fiction created within an aesthetic of fluidity and denial of closure, not to mention verbal freedom, can generate an excitement and awareness of great value; the rigidities of plot, characterization, and illusioned depth can be softened and, finally, dropped in favor of new and valid rhythms.

Critic Jerome Klinkowitz has written that the central achievement of Major's career

> has been to show just how concretely we live within the imagination—how our lives are shaped by language and how by a simple act of self-awareness we can seize control of the world and reshape it to our liking and benefit.

Fun and Games

Clarence Major's short-story collection *Fun and Games* was nominated for the *Los Angeles Times* Book Critics Award in 1990. While the volume represents Major's short fiction through the 1980's, it is a good barometer of his continuing fictional interests and forms. The sixteen stories in the volume are divided into five parts: Section 1 contains three stories (including the realistic "My Mother and Mitch" and "Ten Pecan Pies"), section 2 also has three shorter and more surreal stories, section 3 contains six stories, section 4 has three, and section 5 comprises "Mobile Axis: A Triptych," three interconnected short fictions. While Major is capable of one form of social realism (as in "Letters"), he more regularly leans toward a staccato, fragmentary prose fiction in which the links are missing among characters and incidents ("The Horror" and the title story).

"The Exchange," for example, is a fairly realistic and even comic story about a faculty exchange gone horribly wrong. When the narrator and his wife arrive on the opposite coast to begin the year-long exchange, they find a dilapidated house. Worse, when they return to their own home at the end of the year, their exchangees have turned the house into a replica of their own—down to the moldy contents of the refrigerator. Likewise, the collection's title story is a first-person narration about a man's three or four girlfriends, who keep leaving him and returning. The story is comic and at the same an oblique commentary on transience and commitment in contemporary society.

More common in *Fun and Games*, however, are the themes found in "Mother Visiting," a short, three-page story that violates most of the conventions of fictional verisimilitude. While the story touches upon a number of contemporary issues (notably sex and violence), its postmodernist style emphasizes the play of language over sense. Likewise in the short story "Virginia," the dazzling use of language and image have replaced the demands of plot.

"My Mother and Mitch"

This story won the Pushcart Prize for fiction in 1989 and leads off the *Fun and Games* collection. In some ways it does not resemble Major's other short fiction, being a leaner and less experimental coming-of-age story. "My Mother and Mitch" centers on the date that Tommy Anderson's mother had with Mitch Kibbs when Tommy was a teenager in Chicago in 1951. Mitch had dialed a wrong number and then kept calling to talk with Tommy's mother, even after he discovered that she was black. The climax of the story comes when Mitch asks her to meet him in a restaurant, and Tommy watches the white man and his mother talking at the counter of a predominantly black eatery. The story is barely about interracial dating, for the couple never meet again after that night. What is more important is what the young Tommy discovers about his single mother: "I learned for the first time that she did not always know what she was doing. It struck me that she was as helpless as I sometimes felt." That knowledge makes the adolescent Tommy feel closer to his mother: "there she was, just finding her way, step by step, like me. It was something wonderful anyway." The story may remind readers of Sherwood Anderson's "Death in the Woods," for Tommy is retelling the tale many years later and still trying to get it right and discover its meaning through the retelling. In its lean recreation of the spare events here, the story may also remind readers of Raymond Carver and other minimalist short-story writers of the late twentieth century, who forsake long exposition and elaborate descriptions for the psychological revelations of a single voice.

"Ten Pecan Pies"

"Ten Pecan Pies" uses still another fictional style, here a third-person, more traditional narration. The story was first published in *Seattle Review,* is reprinted in the first section of *Fun and Games,* and may remind readers of William Faulkner or Truman

Capote in its rural southern setting and voices. "Ten Pecan Pies" concerns one Christmas in the Flower household, when the patriarch Grady Flower has kept two bags of pecans to himself and will not let his wife make her annual Christmas pies. The other preparations for Christmas—finding and decorating a tree, for example—go on, but Grady hoards the pecans in his room until Christmas Eve, when Thursday finally shames her husband and then, when he gives in, "suddenly kisse [s] the side of his face. The first time in years." The story has other tensions—the drunken son Slick John killing the rabbits in front of his niece, Gal, for example—but the overwhelming feeling of the story is lyrical and nostalgic. Thursday douses the fire in the stove, the story concludes, "Yet the warmth stayed."

"Scat"

"Scat" was the only story of his own that Clarence Major selected for *Calling the Wind,* the collection of twentieth century African American fiction he edited in 1993, so readers can assume he thinks the story is important, but it is also representative of a certain comic-surreal style Major mastered. The story covers a nightmare cab ride the narrator and his white girlfriend take into New York City with a cabdriver who subjects them to a monologue about the dangers of Manhattan, where the couple want to go, and the relative safety of Brooklyn, where the cabdriver lives. In his frustration at the cabdriver's tales of the "superstitious practices" and "voodoo rites" in Manhattan, the narrator counters with his own stories of body snatching in Brooklyn. Readers conclude the story still not knowing who is crazier: the cabdriver, who talks knowingly of the "evil art of capnomancy," or the narrator, who speaks of "the Plot, I mean the Sacrifice" and seems equally deranged. Perhaps, if one pursues the definition of the tale's title, the story is the fictional equivalent of jazz singing with nonsense syllables, each voice trying to outdo the other.

"An Area in the Cerebral Hemisphere"

This story has been collected in Gloria Naylor's *Children of the Night: The Best Short Stories by Black Writers, 1967 to the Present*

(1995) and is the best example of Major's postmodernist style, fragmentary and barely coherent but with a powerful edge to it. The story centers on a young African American woman, a visit by a friend, and the young woman's thoughts about her father and her own life. These events are parceled out in a style that dispels meaning: "The friend lit a cigarette and sat on the sounds of her own voice. Motion. And made a blowing sound," Major writes early in this story, and, a little later on, "And mother's couch was eaten by what might easily have been taxicabs with hooks on them. Anything can happen. (In any case, swift traffic was known to move through her living room.)" This metaphor of motion runs through the story, but it hardly ties together the various fragmented incidents and scraps of dialogue. What readers are left with is Major's brilliant and poetic use of language. Naylor titled the section containing this story "Breaking New Ground," which Major does with his experimental and poetic fictions.

Other Literary Forms

Clarence Major is the author of a number of novels and books of poetry, including *Parking Lots: A Poem* and *Configurations: New and Selected Poems, 1958-1998*. He has also edited a number of collections, like *The New Black Poetry* and *Calling the Wind: Twentieth-Century African-American Short Stories*. In addition, he has written several critical studies, including *The Dark and Feeling: Black American Writers and Their Work*, and *Dictionary of Afro-American Slang* (reprinted as *Juba to Jive: A Dictionary of African-American Slang*).

Bibliography

Bell, Bernard W. "Introduction: Clarence Major's Double Consciousness as a Black Postmodernist Artist." *African American Review* 28 (Spring, 1994): 5-10. Bell introduces this special issue of the journal, which includes eight "Writings by Clarence Major," a section of his artwork, as well as critical analyses of his poetry and fiction.
Bolling, Doug. "A Reading of Clarence Major's Short Fiction."

Black American Literature Forum 13 (1979): 51-56. This early study of Major's short stories recognizes that the artist "works with 'process,' with open forms, with the inconclusive, and with the interplay of formal and informal tensions." One of the best analyses of Major's short fiction, the essay includes discussions of "Ten Pecan Pies," "Fun and Games," and "An Area in the Cerebral Hemisphere."

Fleming, Robert. "Thirty-five Years as a Literary Maverick: Clarence Major Is Revered and Respected for His Literary Achievements. He's Just Not as Widely Known as He Should Be." *Black Issues Book Review* 6, no. 2 (March/April, 2004): 54-58. Gives a good overview of Major's background, awards, and work. Includes a selected bibliography.

Hogue, W. Lawrence. "Postmodernism, Traditional Culture Forms, and the African American Narrative: Major's *Reflex*, Morrison's *Jazz*, and Reed's *Mumbo Jumbo*." *Novel: A Forum on Fiction* 35, nos. 2/3 (Spring/Summer, 2002): 169-193. Takes a closer look at the roles of postmodernism and jazz in works by Major, Toni Morrison, and Ishmael Reed.

Klinkowitz, Jerome. "Clarence Major's Innovative Fiction." *African American Review* 28 (Spring, 1994): 57-63. While dealing primarily with Major's novels, Klinkowitz recognizes the "anti-realistic (and even anti-mimetic)" strain to much of Major's fiction.

_____. *The Life of Fiction*. Urbana: University of Illinois Press, 1977. Chapter 8 of Klinkowitz's early study of a dozen postmodernist American writers focuses on Major and recognizes both the lyricism and the anticonventional strains of Major's fiction.

Major, Clarence. "And an Artist with Paris on His Mind." *The New York Times*, February 18, 1996, Section 2, p. 39. Explores the tendency among certain African American artists and writers to live and work in Paris.

_____. "Clarence Major." http://www.clarencemajor.com/. Accessed September 1, 2005. Major's Web site provides samples of his paintings and literary works.

_____. "'I Follow My Eyes': An Interview with Clarence Major." Interview by Larry McCaffrey and Jerzy Kutnik. *African*

American Review 28, no. 1 (Spring, 1994): 121-138. Discusses the relationship between the history of English and the development of the language as it is spoken by many African Americans. Major also explains the importance of the black aesthetic in his work.

_____. "An Interview with Clarence Major." Interview by Charles H. Rowell. *Callaloo* 20, no. 3 (Summer, 1997): 667-689. Rowell asks Major about his views on technology and about his own writing style.

_____. "Necessary Distance: Afterthoughts on Becoming a Writer." *African American Review* 28, no. 1 (Spring, 1994): 36-47. Major explains some of his thoughts on the process of becoming a writer.

O'Brien, John. "Clarence Major." In *Interviews with Black Writers.* New York: Liveright, 1973. This fourteen-page interview with Major sheds light on the writer's life and work.

Roney, Lisa C. "The Double Vision of Clarence Major, Painter and Writer." *African American Review* 28, no. 1 (Spring, 1994): 65-76. Compares Major's written and visual works and pinpoints African and American influences on them.

Selzer, Linda Furgerson. "Reading the Painterly Text: Clarence Major's 'The Slave Trade: View from the Middle Passage.'" *African American Review* 33, no. 2 (Summer, 1999): 209-230. An analysis of Major's poem centering on the difficult task faced by African Americans who seek freedom from the restrictions and hierarchies inherent in Christianity and economics.

Weixlmann, Joe. "African American Deconstruction of the Novel in the Work of Clarence Major." *MELUS* 17, no. 4 (Winter, 1991/1992): 57-80. A discussion of works by Clarence Major and Ishmael Reed.

_____. "Clarence Major: A Checklist of Criticism." *Obsidian* 4, no. 2 (1978): 101-113. This checklist brings together some of the most important works of literary criticism written about Major's fiction.

— David Peck

Paule Marshall

Novelist and short-story writer

Born: Brooklyn, New York; April 9, 1929

LONG FICTION: *Brown Girl, Brownstones,* 1959; *The Chosen Place, the Timeless People,* 1969; *Praisesong for the Widow,* 1983; *Daughters,* 1991; *The Fisher King,* 2000.

SHORT FICTION: *Soul Clap Hands and Sing,* 1961; *Reena, and Other Stories,* 1983 (also known as *Merle: A Novella and Other Stories,* 1985).

Achievements

Only in the 1990's did Paule Marshall's work begin to receive the critical attention it deserves. While most of her novels received high praise when they were first published, they were not always commercially successful. Marshall nevertheless received the Guggenheim Fellowship (1960), the Linda and Richard Rosenthal Foundation Award (1962), a Ford Foundation grant for poets and fiction writers (1964-1965), and a National Endowment for the Arts Fellowship (1984). She also received the Langston Hughes Medallion Award (1986), the New York State Governor's Award for Literature (1987), the John Dos Passos Award for Literature (1989), and the John D. and Catherine T. MacArthur Fellowship (1992).

Marshall's major contribution to literature is her deep understanding of the human psyche, which allows her to create characters that are movingly sympathetic. She gives careful attention to female characters—especially the black female, whom she feels has been long neglected in literature. She destroys stereotypes, creating black women who are neither "sensual, primitive, pleasure-seeking, or immoral, nor sinner, siren or matriarch (strong, humble, devoutly religious and patient)." Her women are complex, with deep reservoirs of strength that can be called upon when needed.

Biography

Paule Burke Marshall was born in Brooklyn, New York, to Samuel Burke and Ada Clement Burke, who migrated to New York from Barbados shortly after World War I and joined the growing community of West Indian immigrants in Brooklyn. She was born to parents who had brought with them to America a strong sense of pride and tradition that was an integral part of West Indian culture, and she was nourished by a community of people who revered their West Indian heritage, even as they embraced the advantages that America afforded them. Her parents continually returned to their homeland of Barbados, taking their small daughter with them. Thus, from her earliest years, Marshall began to develop an understanding of the two worlds to which she belonged and to appreciate their differences—a fact that is immediately recognizable in her fiction.

She wrote poetry as a child and listened to the talk of women, both preparing her for her career as a powerful and poetic writer. In the opening of *Reena, and Other Stories*, she describes the influence of her mother, woman relatives, and other female friends on her experience in an essay called "From the Poets in the Kitchen":

> They taught me my first lesson in the narrative art. They trained my ear. They set a standard of excellence. This is why the best of my work must be attributed to them; it stands as testimony to the rich legacy of language and culture they so freely passed on to me in the workshop of the kitchen.

Paule Marshall attended Brooklyn College, where she received a bachelor's degree in 1953, graduating magna cum laude and Phi Beta Kappa. After leaving Brooklyn College, Marshall went to work as a researcher and later as a feature writer for *Our World* magazine. In 1955, she enrolled as a graduate student at Hunter College (City University of New York) but continued to write for *Our World*, where her assignments carried her to Brazil and the West Indies. In 1957, she married Kenneth Marshall, with whom she had one son, Evan Keith. Her trips to the Caribbean islands were rewarding in that they provided her an oppor-

777

tunity to return to the land of her ancestors. While there, she immersed herself in the culture, absorbing the nuances of language, customs, and traditions that were to figure so prominently in her novels.

In 1960, Marshall received a Guggenheim Fellowship, which allowed her to complete her second work, a collection of novellas, *Soul Clap Hands and Sing*. Eight years passed, however, before the publication of her second novel. In that interim, she worked for *New World*, a Caribbean magazine, produced several short stories, and continued work on her novel. So committed was she to her craft that she would often obtain a babysitter, over her husband's objections, and go every day to the home of a friend in order to continue her writing. She divorced Kenneth Marshall in 1963.

In 1970, Marshall was married for the second time, to Nourry Menard, a Haitian businessman—a man with whom she said she had an "open and innovative marriage," one that gave her the time and freedom to pursue her work. In the fall of 1970 she took the position of lecturer on creative writing at Yale Univer-

(AP/Wide World Photos)

sity. She also lectured on black literature at several colleges and universities, including the University of Oxford, Columbia University, Michigan State University, Lake Forest College, and Cornell University. Marshall has combined her writing career with teaching and holds a professorship at Virginia Commonwealth University in Richmond, Virginia.

Analysis: Long Fiction

Being of both African American and Caribbean ancestry helped to shape Paule Marshall as a woman and as a writer. She first traveled to Barbados as a nine-year-old child. When she visited the island as a young woman just starting out on a writing career, she began to develop a deeper appreciation for the West Indian culture—its rituals, its customs, its people and language—and a greater sense of pride in her West Indian heritage. She was most impressed with the strength and character she observed in West Indian women, qualities she saw reflected in the women of the Brooklyn community where she had grown up.

The lives of these women, whom she calls her "literary foremothers," were to become the major focus of her novels. They were primarily domestic workers who would sit around her mother's kitchen table in the evenings after a hard day's labor, talking endlessly about everything from the white women for whom they worked to politics to their own husbands and families. Because of their creative use of language, Marshall considered these women poets, though they had never written a line. They had their special cadences and rhythms; they played with syntax; and they introduced certain Africanisms into their speech and sprinkled it with a generous smattering of French Creole expressions, biblical quotations, and colorful proverbs.

Their use of language and their storytelling skills influenced Marshall's style, and their strength and deep sense of pride are the essential qualities of the female characters she creates. The protagonists of Marshall's novels are all women and are products of a dual culture. In her characterization of these women, Marshall explores the ways in which their psyches are affected by their cultural heritage and by the society in which they live.

She also focuses upon the difficulties that they encounter in trying to integrate their two worlds.

Brown Girl, Brownstones

In *Brown Girl, Brownstones,* Marshall begins to develop the self-identity theme through the character of Selina Boyce, a girl moving from childhood into adolescence in Brooklyn and caught between two cultures, the American culture in which she lives and the Barbadian culture of her ancestors, the customs of which are carefully observed in her household.

The novel treats the problems she encounters in trying to reconcile these two disparate parts of herself. She is a "divided self," feeling little connection with either the "bajan" community or the larger white community. She rejects her Barbadian heritage and its "differentness" and yearns to be a part of the white community, which rejects her. The sense of isolation that she feels is the source of all her problems.

At the climax of the novel, the "divided self" is integrated as Selina finally accepts her heritage and discovers that with acceptance comes wholeness. She resolves her conflict with her mother, she makes peace with the Barbadian Association, and she leaves Brooklyn to begin her travels. As she passes through her old neighborhood, she feels psychically connected to all the people who helped create her integrated self. As a final symbolic act, she tosses behind one of her two Barbadian bangle bracelets and retains the other as a reminder of her link with the past. Selina has finally learned that true selfhood begins with the acceptance of one's own history.

The Chosen Place, the Timeless People

This novel is set in the West Indies, specifically Bournehills—a remote part of one of the Caribbean islands. Here, Marshall expands the identity theme, focusing not on the individual self but rather on the collective self of a community of people in search of a common bond. While Merle Kimbona is the protagonist of the novel and a strong female character—a mulatto who has returned to Bournehills to become mistress of a large estate left to her by her white father after spending many adventuresome years in Europe—she is really not the central figure of the novel. At the center of the novel are the people of Bournehills, who, having been oppressed first by slavery, then by their own people, search for some common thread of unity. They discover this in Carnival, an annual ritual in which the people reenact the story of Cuffee Ned, who led a slave revolt against the slaveholder Percy Byram.

The plot turns with a visit by a team from an American philanthropic organization sent to Bournehills to provide aid to this underdeveloped country. The team consists of a Jewish American social scientist, Saul Amron; his wife, Harriet; and two returning natives of Bournehills, Allen Fuso and Vere. During their stay on the island, the outsiders interact with the natives, observing their rituals and customs, and contrasting them with their American experience. As guests at the estate of Merle Kimbona, now a political activist, they also become involved in the political affairs of Bournehills.

The contrasts between the two cultures are apparent throughout the novel. The high-tech white society, represented by the machine—in this case the machines in the sugarcane factory—enslave the people of Bournehills in much the same way they had been enslaved by Percy Byram. Also it is the machine— the American automobile—that takes the life of the Bournehills native Vere.

Marshall brings together characters from many backgrounds and classes—black and white; upper, middle, and lower classes; natives and outsiders—in this "chosen place." The ritual reenactment of their history at Carnival is the common thread that binds all classes of people in Bournehills, and it also connects them to their African ancestry and Western culture.

Praisesong for the Widow

In *Praisesong for the Widow*, Marshall continues the theme of self-discovery through her protagonist, Avey Johnson, a middle-aged, middle-class black woman on a Caribbean cruise with two of her women friends. Avey is haunted by a recurring dream about a story told to her by her great-aunt, with whom she had spent summers in Tatem, South Carolina, of how the African slaves who landed at Tatem had immediately turned back toward the sea, walking across the water back to their home in Africa.

Deciding to leave the ship before the cruise is over and return home, Avey misses her flight to New York and is stranded in Grenada just at the time of the annual excursion to the island of Carriocou. Here, again, Marshall uses ritual to reveal to Avey the importance of connecting to her African ancestry. In a scene that is almost surreal she is transported to Carriocou, where this annual ritual is to take place. Reluctant to participate at first, Avey eventually joins in the ritual and discovers the meaning of her recurring dream. The landing of the Ibos in South Carolina and their return to Africa by the mythic walk on water symbolize the link between Africa and all black people of the diaspora. In participating in this ritual, Avey becomes aware that she can achieve wholeness only if she becomes reconnected to her African roots.

Daughters

Like the protagonists of most of Marshall's other novels, the protagonist of *Daughters*, Ursa MacKensie, is a woman caught between two cultures: the African American culture of her mother, Estelle, and the Caribbean culture of her father, Primus. The action of the novel is divided almost equally between New York City, where Ursa lives, and Triunion, the West Indian island where her parents reside, her father being a leading politician, known from his boyhood as the PM (prime minister). Although firmly rooted in the urban culture of New York, where she is pursuing a career as a young black professional, Ursa keeps one foot planted in the small Caribbean island through her relationship with her doting father, a relationship strengthened by frequent letters and periodic visits.

In this novel, Marshall again explores the themes of identity and the attempt to bridge the gap between two cultures. The novel addresses the integration of the two cultures on several levels, the first being the marriage of Ursa's parents—her African American mother to her West Indian father. The second is the birth of their daughter, Ursa-Mae, who physically integrates the two cultures. Then, the African American and West Indian cultures are geographically and spiritually linked as Ursa's mother moves to Triunion with her husband and becomes integrated into that community.

As in *The Chosen Place, the Timeless People*, much of the novel is devoted to the workings of Triunion politics and their effect upon the Triunion people, the marriage of Primus and Estelle, and Ursa. Its setting and wide array of characters provide Marshall the opportunity to explore the theme of self-discovery from a number of perspectives.

Analysis: Short Fiction

Paule Marshall's work has been concerned from the beginning with a number of major themes: the experience of growing up African American in the United States; the clash of cultures between Westerners and African Americans, West Indians and inhabitants of the American mainland; and the relationships between men and women.

Soul Clap Hands and Sing

Marshall's first collection of shorter works, *Soul Clap Hands and Sing*, contains four longer short stories, almost novellas. They are given the titles of the settings: "Barbados," "Brooklyn," "British Guiana," and "Brazil." In each, the main character is an older man, and the stories explore how that man has failed to live his life fully, for whatever reasons. This failure is indicated by the title of the collection, taken from the William Butler Yeats poem "Sailing to Byzantium," which includes the lines "An aged man is but a paltry thing/ A tattered coat upon a stick, unless/ Soul clap its hands and sing." In each case, the failure of the man to allow his soul to "clap hands" has led to the emptiness or aridity of his life. Thus, he is forced to realize his failure to live truly through the intervention of a woman who, in some way, exposes his inadequacies.

In "Barbados," Mr. Watford, who has returned to his native island after having worked single-mindedly throughout his adult life in the United States just so he can return for this purpose,

lives like a white colonizer. He has built a house, bought plantation land, and planted coconut trees, which he tends faithfully,
despite years of accumulated fatigue. He has never completely
finished his house, however, and he lives in total isolation,
proud of the fact that he needs no one and no one needs him. It
takes a young native woman, foisted on him as a servant, to reveal the paucity of his life, the emptiness of his days. He recognizes that he has not been able to bear the responsibility for the
meaninglessness of his life, but when he goes to confront the
young woman with the hope of some renewal, he is capable only
of attacking her verbally, to which she responds, "you ain't people, Mr. Watford, you ain't people." It is this that destroys him:
He has not been able to be a part of the people who bore him,
and has not found sustenance living the same way as those who
oppressed him.

In "Brooklyn," an aging Jewish professor, who has been
banned from teaching by the Red-baiters of the McCarthy era,
attempts to coerce a young black woman who is taking his class
to spend some time at his summer home. She refuses but in the
end returns to his class for the final and takes him up on his invi-
tation, only to express her outrage as well as the freedom that
she now feels. She has also felt an outcast from her own people,
while unable to trust whites. Now she has the courage to live not
as her parents have taught her but as she chooses. Professor Max
Berman, on the other hand, is forced to recognize that it is his
failure to believe in or stand up for anything that has resulted in
his loneliness and misery. Interestingly, in "Barbados" the female protagonist is not given a name, while here she is named
only in dialogue as Miss Williams.

"British Guiana" explores the present of Gerald Motley, a
man who is indeed a motley collection of races; he could have
been taken for white, because of the British army officer who
was one of his ancestors, or black, for the slave woman that officer had been intimate with, or East Indian, from some Hindu
who also had a part in his creation. He has achieved a certain
amount of success as the head of a radio station, but he knows
that he has failed to live his life fully. Although as a young man
he had shown a great ability and had rejected his middle-class

background to organize a strike, he had been bought off by a job in radio, which forces him to copy the whites who have colonized his country. When he attempts to penetrate the jungle, to prove his worth to himself, he is prevented by another motley person, Sybil, an African Chinese woman with whom he is involved. He is forever conscious of his betrayal of himself and also of Sybil's part in this, which results in a life of cynicism and taking the easy way. At the end of the story, when Sybil, whom he might have married, returns to visit, his last act is to bargain with her for a protégé who despises him but deserves a chance. In the conclusion, he realizes that he is going to die a failure by his own doing.

The final story in the book, "Brazil," reminds the reader of Carson McCullers's *The Ballad of the Sad Café* (1951) in that it is the story of what appears to be a strange love affair between a white woman of epic proportions and a black dwarf. In this story, the dwarf is a performer who goes by the name of O Grande Caliban and has teamed up with a blonde of Germanic appearance to perform a comic and athletic act. He has decided that it is time to retire, but his mistress does not wish to do so. One of the interesting things about the story is the breaking of the traditional white reader's expectations; it is the undersized black man who is trying to end a relationship with the Aryan-looking female. He has become so famous as Caliban, however, that no one, not even his wife, knows him as he had been. He has been living a lie so long that he cannot convince people of the truth anymore, and so he destroys everything.

Reena, and Other Stories

Reena, and Other Stories is a collection of previously printed works gathered together for the first time in 1983 by Feminist Press. It begins with Marshall's autobiographical essay, "From the Poets in the Kitchen," which had originally been published in *The New York Times Book Review*'s series called "The Making of a Writer." This essay celebrates the women in Marshall's life who helped form her thought and shape her voice. The collection includes two of the stories discussed above, "Brooklyn" and "Barbados," previously published in *Soul Clap Hands and Sing*. Also included is a novella, *Merle*, which has been excerpted from her 1969 novel *The Chosen Place, the Timeless People* but was extensively reshaped and rewritten. Marshall wrote autobiographical headnotes to each story, which help to place them in the context of her experience and development as a writer.

The first story in the collection, "The Valley Between," was, as Marshall explained, "my very first published story, written when I could barely crawl, never mind stand up and walk as a writer." In it, the characters are white, a deliberate decision as Marshall herself was at the time married to Kenneth E. Marshall, a marriage she describes as "an early, unwise first marriage," and she wished to disguise the autobiographical elements in it. It is the story of a marriage falling apart because the wife (and mother of a small child) continues to grow, while the husband wishes her to remain the same, to be nothing more than a wife and mother. Published in August, 1954, it is a story well before its time in its depiction of the stifling expectations placed upon a woman of talent and energy.

The title story, "Reena," is unusual in that it was commissioned by *Harper's Magazine* for a special supplement on "The American Female," published in October of 1962. Intended by the editors to be an article on the African American woman, the story instead became a thinly disguised fiction concerning the women whom Marshall knew best: "those from an urban, working-class and lower middle-class, West Indian American background who, like [Marshall herself], had attended the free New York City colleges during the late forties and fifties."

A first-person narrator named Paulie recounts her meeting again after twenty years with a friend from her childhood, Reena, formally named Doreen, who—being a child who shapes her own life as best she can in a world that discriminates against women, African Americans, and particularly African Americans from the West Indies—had transformed herself into Reena, "with two ees!"

The meeting place is at the funeral of Aunt Vi, Reena's aunt, a woman who represents the strong, nurturing, enduring women "from the poets in the kitchen," and who will reappear in Marshall's fiction. Having been out of touch for so long,

Reena and Paulie have much to discuss, and much of the story is Reena's recounting of what has been happening in her life: the struggle for meaningful work; her relationship with her family, particularly her mother; relationships with white men (usually unsuccessful) and with black men, who have to learn how to relate to and accept a strong, educated, ambitious black woman; childbearing; radical politics; and loneliness. In almost essayistic form, this story provides an intimate glimpse into the struggle, suffering, and successes of this group of African American women.

"To Da-duh, in Memoriam" is based on a visit that Marshall made to her maternal grandmother in Barbados when she was nine. Da-duh is another of the ancestor figures who populate Marshall's fiction, like Aunt Vi in the previous story and Merle in the story of that same name; as Marshall says, "Da-duh turns up everywhere."

Merle
Another example of ancestor figures appears in the final selection in the collection, the novella *Merle,* from *Merle: A Novella and Other Stories.* Merle is "Part saint, part revolutionary, part obeah woman," a woman who, wherever she goes, exhorts people to resist oppression, while on a personal level she is "still trying to come to terms with her life and history as a black woman, still seeking to reconcile all the conflicting elements to form a viable self."

Merle is the woman whom Paule Marshall creates in various guises, calling into being a new character for twentieth century American literature. In her compelling portrayal of women in her works, she brings to life for her readers a vision of the direction in which the world should be going by showing readers the people whom the world desperately needs to listen to and perhaps emulate.

Bibliography
Brown, Lloyd W. "The Rhythms of Power in Paule Marshall's Fiction." *Novel: A Forum on Fiction* 7, no. 2 (Winter, 1974): 159-167. This essay focuses on Marshall's short story "To Da-duh,

in Memoriam," tracing Marshall's concern with the problems of African American women, tied to her commitment to feminism and racial equality. Brown argues that Marshall sees power as both a political goal of ethnic and feminist movements and a social and psychological phenomenon that affects racial and sexual roles, shapes cultural traditions, and molds the individual psyche.

Cartwright, Keith. "Notes Toward a Voodoo Hermeneutics: Soul Rhythms, Marvelous Transitions, and Passages to the Creole Saints in *Praisesong for the Widow.*" *Southern Quarterly* 41, no. 4 (Summer, 2003): 127-144. A detailed discussion of the African origin of creole and voodoo traditions, their influences on Caribbean culture, and the importance of music in daily life and in politics.

Christian, Barbara. "Paule Marshall: A Literary Biography." In *Black Feminist Criticism: Perspectives on Black Women Writers.* New York: Pergamon Press, 1985. This essay traces the development of themes in Marshall's fiction from *Brown Girl, Brownstones* through *Praisesong for the Widow.*

Cobb, Michael L. "Irreverent Authority: Religious Apostrophe and the Fiction of Blackness in Paule Marshall's *Brown Girl, Brownstones.*" *University of Toronto Quarterly* 72, no. 2 (Spring, 2003): 631-649. Seeks to understand the role of religion as a catalyst that aids female characters in their pursuit of freedom from racial and social restrictions.

Collier, Eugenia. "The Closing of the Circle: Movement from Division to Wholeness in Paule Marshall's Fiction." In *Black Women Writers, 1950-1980*, edited by Mari Evans. Garden City, N.Y.: Anchor Press/Doubleday, 1984. Collier finds in Marshall's writing a movement from the separated, segmented self to a discovery of wholeness and completion; this healing and wholeness is found within the context of the community. Contains good discussions of the short fiction. The first of two essays on Marshall in Evans's collection, which should be required reading for anyone interested in African American woman writers. Contains a bibliography of criticism on Marshall and an index.

Coser, Stelamaris. *Bridging the Americas: The Literature of Paule*

Marshall, Toni Morrison, and Gayl Jones. Philadelphia: Temple University Press, 1995. Compares and contrasts the fiction of the three authors, taking their cultural heritage into consideration.

DeLamotte, Eugenia C. *Places of Silence, Journeys of Freedom: The Fiction of Paule Marshall.* Philadelphia: University of Pennsylvania Press, 1998. Studies Marshall's oeuvre, focusing on her Caribbean roots.

Demirtürk, Lâle. "Postcolonial Reflections on the Discourse of Whiteness: Paule Marshall's *The Chosen Place, the Timeless People.*" *CLA Journal* 48, no. 1 (September, 2004): 88-103. Explores Marshall's novel and its critique of colonialism, the colonialist legacy, and the privileged status of white Americans.

Denniston, Dorothy Hamer. *The Fiction of Paule Marshall: Reconstructions of History, Culture, and Gender.* Knoxville: University of Tennessee Press, 1995. Reviews Marshall's novels, concentrating on her dominant theme in each. Examines cultural expansion, personal and political liberation, diasporan connections, and transformation of female identity.

Greene Benjamin, Shanna. "Weaving the Web of Reintegration: Locating Aunt Nancy in *Praisesong for the Widow.*" *MELUS* 30, no. 1 (Spring, 2005): 49-68. Provides an in-depth study of Marshall's references to African ways of learning and healing, spiritually, psychologically, and medically. Marshall emphasizes African techniques over their Western counterparts, empowering those who retain their African connections.

Ibironke, Olabode. "The Paradox of Cultural Self-Representation in Paule Marshall's *Praisesong For the Widow.*" *Language & Intercultural Communication* 4, nos. 1/2 (2004): 60-68. An exploration of Marshall's novel in the context of migration, forced exile, and displacement. The author is primarily concerned with how characters reinvent themselves under different circumstances.

Johnson, Beverly A. "Revolutionary Solutions Challenging Colonialist Attitudes in the Works of Paule Marshall." *CLA Journal* 45, no. 4 (June, 2002): 460-457. Examines Marshall's use of the sea as a metaphor and the importance of travel in her books.

Kapai, Leela. "Dominant Themes and Technique in Paule Marshall's Fiction." *College Language Association Journal* 16 (September, 1972): 49-59. Examines Marshall's use of folk tradition in her novels through *The Chosen Place, the Timeless People* and also in the short story "Reena." Kapai claims that Marshall puts being a human being and the universal human experience before racial identity and states that Marshall is aware of her Western heritage, even as she writes out of her personal experience as an African American. Contains some good, close readings.

Lock, Helen. "'Building Up from Fragments': The Oral Memory Process in Some Recent African-American Written Narratives." *College Literature* 22 (October, 1995): 109-120. Discusses Marshall and others as representative of a generation of African American literary artists whose sensibilities do not exclude orally constituted modes of thought; claims she energizes the dialectic between oral and literate conceptions of memory by reasserting—through the medium of the written word—the value of an orally derived perception.

McClusky, John, Jr. "And Called Every Generation Blessed: Theme, Setting, and Ritual in the Works of Paule Marshall." In *Black Women Writers, 1950-1980,* edited by Mari Evans. Garden City, N.Y.: Anchor Press/Doubleday, 1984. This essay, the second on Marshall in Evans's book, gives an overview of Marshall's achievement, evolution, and her future directions in writing.

Macpherson, Heidi Slettedahl. "Perception of Place: Geopolitical and Cultural Positioning in Paule Marshall's Novels." In *Caribbean Women Writers,* edited by Mary Condé and Thorunn Lonsdale. New York: St. Martin's Press, 1999. Although the focus of this article is on Marshall's novels, it is a helpful discussion of her use of fictionalized island backdrops in her fiction generally; argues that while she acknowledges a geopolitical place, her representation of place moves beyond a specific locale.

Washington, Mary Helen. Afterword to *Brown Girl, Brownstones.* New York: Feminist Press, 1981. An excellent critical commentary on the novel.

Waxman, Barbara Frey. "Dancing Out of Form, Dancing into Self: Genre and Metaphor in Marshall, Shange, and Walker." *MELUS* 19 (Fall, 1994): 91-106. Discusses how texts by Paule Marshall, Ntozake Shange, and Alice Walker articulate truths about the multiple selves of African American women by creating new mythopoetic genres and tropes that mediate between the word and the dance.

— *Mary LeDonne Cassidy; Theodore C. Humphrey;*
Gladys J. Washington

Toni Morrison

(Chloe Anthony Wofford)

Novelist

Born: Lorain, Ohio; February 18, 1931

LONG FICTION: *The Bluest Eye,* 1970; *Sula,* 1973; *Song of Solomon,* 1977; *Tar Baby,* 1981; *Beloved,* 1987; *Jazz,* 1992; *Paradise,* 1998; *Love,* 2003.

DRAMA: *Dreaming Emmett,* pr. 1986.

NONFICTION: *Playing in the Dark: Whiteness and the Literary Imagination,* 1992; *Conversations with Toni Morrison,* 1994 (Danille Taylor-Guthrie, editor); *Birth of a Nation'hood: Gaze, Script, and Spectacle in the O. J. Simpson Case,* 1997.

CHILDREN'S/YOUNG ADULT LITERATURE: *The Big Box,* 1999 (with Slade Morrison and Giselle Potter); *The Book of Mean People,* 2002 (with Slade Morrison); *The Lion or the Mouse?,* 2003 (with Slade Morrison); *The Ant or the Grasshopper?,* 2003 (with Slade Morrison); *Remember: The Journey to School Integration,* 2004.

EDITED TEXTS: *To Die for the People: The Writings of Huey P. Newton,* 1972; *The Black Book: 300 Years of African American Life,* 1974; *Race-ing Justice, En-gendering Power: Essays on Anita Hill, Clarence Thomas, and the Construction of Social Reality,* 1992; *Deep Sightings and Rescue Missions: Fiction, Essays, and Conversations,* 1996 (of Toni Cade Bambara).

Achievements

Toni Morrison is widely regarded as one of the most significant African American novelists to have emerged in the 1970's. Her novel *Sula* was nominated for the National Book Award in 1975. In 1977, *Song of Solomon* won the National Book Critics Circle Award. The former was a Book-of-the-Month Club alternate and the latter, a main selection. In 1988, *Beloved* was awarded the Pulitzer Prize, and in 1993 Morrison was the first black woman to win the Nobel Prize in Literature.

Morrison's fiction, especially *Song of Solomon*, has been compared to Ralph Ellison's *Invisible Man* (1952) for its mixture of the literal and the fantastic, the real and the surreal. Morrison has been praised for her use of language and for the sense of voice that emerges not only in her dialogue but also in the movement of her narratives. Morrison's novels are also remarkable for their sense of place, for the detailed, coherent physical worlds she creates. Finally, her fiction is noteworthy for its depiction of the deep psychic realities of women's experience.

(© Maria Mulas)

Biography

Toni Morrison, whose father was a shipyard welder, was born the second of four children. In the first grade, she was the only black student and the only child able to read in her class. Her early literary influences included Leo Tolstoy, Gustave Flaubert, and Jane Austen. At Howard University, Morrison toured the South with the Howard University Players. She was married in 1958 and divorced in 1964. She has two children, Harold Ford and Slade Kevin.

Morrison received her B.A. in English and minored in classics. She taught at the State University of New York at Purchase as a professor of English from 1971 to 1972 and was the Albert Schweitzer Chair in the Humanities at the State University of New York at Albany from 1984 to 1989. Beginning in 1989, Morrison held the position of Robert F. Goheen Professor in the Council of the Humanities at Princeton University. Other positions include trustee of the National Humanities Center, cochair of the Schomberg Commission for the Preservation of Black Culture, and member of the American Academy and Institute of Arts, the American Academy of Arts and Sciences, the National Council on the Arts, the Authors Guild, and the Authors League of America. Morrison became a popular public lecturer, focusing on African American literature.

Analysis: Long Fiction

In all of her fiction, Toni Morrison explores the conflict between society and the individual. She shows how the individual who defies social pressures can forge a self by drawing on the resources of the natural world, on a sense of continuity within the family and within the history of a people, and on dreams and other unaccountable sources of psychic power.

The Bluest Eye

In *The Bluest Eye*, Morrison shows how society inflicts on its members an inappropriate standard of beauty and worth, a standard that mandates that to be loved one must meet the absolute "white" standard of blond hair and blue eyes. Morrison's narrator says that two of the most destructive ideas in history are the idea of romantic love (canceling both lust and caring) and the idea of an absolute, univocal standard of beauty.

In the novel, the most extreme victim of these destructive ideas is Pecola, who finds refuge in madness after she has been thoroughly convinced of her own ugliness (confirmed when she is raped by her own father, Cholly). Mrs. Breedlove, Pecola's mother, is another victim who gets her idea of an unvarying standard of beauty from romantic motion pictures which glorify white film stars. When she realizes the impassible gap between that ideal and her physical self (she has a deformed foot and two missing teeth), she also gives up any hope of maintaining a relationship with Cholly, her husband, except one of complete antagonism and opposition. Mrs. Breedlove even comes to prefer the little white girl she takes care of at work to her own daughter, Pecola, whom she has always perceived as ugly.

The ideal of unattainable physical beauty is reinforced by the sugary, unattainable world of the family depicted in the school readers—of Mother and Father and Dick and Jane and their middle-class, suburban existence. The contrast between that false standard of life and the reality lived by the children makes them ashamed of their reality, of the physical intimacy of families in which the children have seen their fathers naked.

Although Pecola is thoroughly victimized, Freida and Claudia MacTeer, schoolmates of Pecola, do survive with some integrity and richness. Freida seems to accept Shirley Temple as the ideal of cuteness, but her sister Claudia, a center of consciousness in the novel, responds with anger and defiance, dismembering the hard, cold, smirking baby dolls she receives at Christmas. What Claudia really desires at Christmas is simply an experience of family closeness in the kitchen, an experience of flowers, fruit, and music, of security.

Claudia's anger at the white baby dolls springs from a conviction of her own reality and her own worth. In defense of her own individuality, Claudia rejects Shirley Temple and "Meringue Pie," the high yellow princess, Maureen Peal. It is that defense of her own reality that makes Claudia sympathize with Pecola and try to defend her, even to the point of sacrificing Freida's money and her own.

Claudia is especially puzzled and regretful that nobody says "poor baby" to the raped Pecola, that nobody wants to welcome her unborn baby into the world. It would be only natural, "human nature," it seems, for people to sympathize with a victim and rejoice at the creation of a human life. Instead, the springs of human sympathy have been dammed up by social disapproval. Suffering from the self-hatred they have absorbed from the society around them, the black community maintains inflexible social standards and achieves respectability by looking down on Pecola. The two MacTeer sisters appeal to nature to help Pecola and her unborn baby, but nature fails them just as prayer did: No marigolds sprout and grow that year. The earth is unyielding. The baby is stillborn. Eventually, even the two girls become distanced from Pecola, whose only friend is an imaginary one, a part of herself who can see the blue eyes she was promised. Pecola functions as a scapegoat for the society around her, and Claudia's sympathy later grows into an understanding of how the community used Pecola to protect themselves from scorn and insult. What finally flowers in Claudia is insight and a more conscious respect for her own reality.

Sula

Sula also explores the oppressive nature of white society, evident in the very name of the "Bottom," a hillside community which had its origin in the duplicitous white treatment of an emancipated black slave who was promised fertile "bottom land" along with his freedom. In a bitterly ironic twist, the whites take over the hillside again when they want suburban houses that will catch the breeze. In taking back the Bottom, they destroy a place, a community with its own identity. In turn, the black community, corrupted by white society, rejects Sula for her experimenting with her life, for trying to live free like a man instead of accepting the restrictions of the traditional female role.

Sula provokes the reader to question socially accepted concepts of good and evil. As Sula is dying, she asks her girlhood friend Nel, "How do you know that you were the good one?" Al-

796

though considered morally loose and a witch by the townspeople, the unconventional Sula cannot believe herself to be an inferior individual. Contrasting the traditional role of mother and church woman that Nel has embraced, Sula's individuality is refreshing and intriguing. Despite her death, Sula maintains an independence that ultimately stands in proud opposition to the established network of relationships that exist within conventional society.

The novel shows that the Bottom society encompasses both good and evil. The people are accustomed to suffering and enduring evil. In varying degrees, they accept Eva's murder of her drug-addict son, Plum, and Hannah's seduction of their husbands, one after another. The community, nevertheless, cannot encompass Sula, a woman who thinks for herself without conforming to their sensibilities. They have to turn her into a witch, so that they can mobilize themselves against her "evil" and cherish their goodness. Without the witch, their goodness grows faint again. Like Pecola, Sula is made a scapegoat.

Growing up in the Bottom, Sula creates an identity for herself, first from the reality of physical experience. When she sees her mother Hannah burning up in front of her eyes, she feels curiosity. Her curiosity is as honest as Hannah's admission that she loves her daughter Sula the way any mother would, but that she does not like her. Hearing her mother reject her individuality, Sula concludes that there is no one to count on except herself.

In forging a self, Sula also draws on sexual experience as a means of joy, as a means of feeling sadness, and as a means of feeling her own power. Sula does not substitute a romantic dream for the reality of that physical experience. She does finally desire a widening of that sexual experience into a continuing relationship with Ajax, but the role of nurturing and possession is fatal to her. Ajax leaves, and Sula sickens and dies.

A closeness to the elemental processes of nature gives a depth to the lives of the Bottom-dwellers, although nature does not act with benevolence or even with consistency. Plum and Hannah, two of Eva's children, die by fire, one sacrificed by Eva and one ignited by capricious accident. Chicken Little and several of those who follow Shadrack on National Suicide Day drown because acts of play go wrong and inexplicably lead to their destruction. Sula's supposed identity as a witch is connected to the plague of robins that coincides with her return to the Bottom. The people of the Bottom live within Nature and try to make some sense of it, even though their constructions are strained and self-serving.

On one level, Sula refuses any connection with history and family continuity. Her grandmother Eva says that Sula should get a man and make babies, but Sula says that she would rather make herself. On the other hand, Sula is a descendant of the independent women Eva and Hannah, both of whom did what they had to do. It is at least rumored that Eva let her leg be cut off by a train so that she could get insurance money to take care of her three children when BoyBoy, her husband, abandoned her. When her husband died, Hannah needed "manlove," and she got it from her neighbors' husbands, despite community disapproval. In their mold, Sula is independent enough to threaten Eva with fire and to assert her own right to live, even if her grandmother does not like Sula's way of living.

To flourish, Morrison suggests, conventional society needs an opposite pole. A richness comes from the opposition and the balance—from the difference—and an acceptance of that difference would make scapegoats unnecessary. The world of the Bottom is poorer with Sula dead and out of it.

Song of Solomon

In *Song of Solomon*, Morrison again traces the making of a self. The novel is a departure for Morrison in that the protagonist is not female, but a young man, Milkman Dead. Milkman grows up in a comfortable, insulated, middle-class family, the grandson of a doctor on his mother's side and the son of a businessman, whose father owned his own farm. Son of a doting mother, Milkman is nursed a long time, the reason for his nickname, and is sent to school in velvet knickers. Guitar Baines, a Southside black, becomes Milkman's friend and an ally against the other children's teasing.

As the novel progresses, though, and as Milkman discovers the reality of his family and friends as separate people with their own griefs and torments, Milkman comes to feel that everyone wants him dead. Ironically, Milkman's last name actually is "Dead," the result of a drunken clerk's error when Milkman's grandfather was registering with the Freedmen's Bureau.

Milkman learns that his mere existence is extraordinary, since even before his birth, his father tried to kill him. Milkman survived that threat through the intercession of his mother and, especially, of his aunt, Pilate, a woman with no navel. After having been conjured by Pilate into making love to his wife again, years after he had turned against her, Macon Dead wanted the resulting baby aborted. Ruth, the baby's mother, out of fear of her husband, took measures to bring about an abortion, but Pilate intervened again and helped Ruth to find the courage to save the child and bear him.

In the present action of the novel, Hagar, Milkman's cousin, his first love and his first lover, pursues him month after month with whatever weapon she can find to kill him. Hagar wants Milkman's living life, not his dead life, but Milkman has rejected her, out of boredom and fear that he will be maneuvered into marrying her. At this point, he does not want to be tied down: He wants freedom and escape.

Hagar, like Pecola of *The Bluest Eye*, feels unlovely and unloved, rejected because Milkman does not like her black, curly hair. Pilate says that Milkman cannot *not* love her hair without *not* loving himself because it is the same hair that grows from his own body. Hagar is another victim of an absolutely univocal standard of beauty, and she is a character who needs a supporting society, a chorus of aunts and cousins and sisters to surround her with advice and protection. Instead, she has only Pilate and Reba, grandmother and mother, two women so strong and independent that they do not understand her weakness. Unhinged by Milkman's rejection of her, Hagar chases Milkman with various weapons, is repeatedly disarmed, and finally dies in total discouragement.

Trying to find out about his family's past, Milkman travels to Virginia, to Shalimar, a black town, where the men in the general store challenge him to fight, and one attacks him with a knife. Milkman does not understand why these people want his life, but they think he has insulted and denied their masculinity with his powerful northern money and his brusque treatment of them, by not asking their names and not offering his own.

The most serious threat to Milkman's life, however, turns out to be Guitar, Milkman's friend and spiritual brother. When Guitar tries to kill Milkman, he is betraying the reality of their friendship for the idea of revenge against whites and compensation for the personal deprivation he has suffered. Guitar thinks that Milkman has a cache of gold that he is not sharing with him, so he decides to kill him. Guitar rationalizes his decision by saying that the money is for the cause, for the work of the Seven Days, a group of seven black men sworn to avenge the deaths of innocent blacks at the hands of the whites.

Milkman's being alive at all, then, is a triumph, a victory that he slowly comes to appreciate after coming out of his comfortable shell of self-involvement. Unwillingly, Milkman comes to know the suffering and griefs of his mother and father and even his sisters Magdelene and Corinthians. The decisive experience in his self-making, however, is the quest for Pilate's gold on which his father sets him. In the first stage, the men are convinced that Pilate's gold hangs in a green sack from the ceiling of her house, and Guitar and Milkman attempt to steal it. The two friends succeed in taking the sack because the women in the house are simply puzzled, wondering why the men want a sack which is really full of old bones. In leaving the house, though, the two men are arrested, and Pilate must rescue them and the bones by doing an Aunt Jemima act for the white policemen. Milkman's father, Macon, is convinced that the gold still exists somewhere, and Milkman sets out to find it by going back to Pennsylvania, where Macon and Pilate grew up, and later to Virginia, where the previous generation lived.

Milkman's making of a self includes many of the archetypal adventures of the heroes of legend and myth. Like other heroes of legend, Milkman limps, with one leg shorter than the other, a mark of his specialness. Like Oedipus's parents, his parents try to kill him early in his life. There is a wise old lady who gives him help and advice. He goes on a quest for a treasure, and he hopes for gold and the hand of a beautiful princess. He solves a puzzle or riddle to achieve his quest and confirm his identity. He has a transcendent experience and reaches heights of prowess (he can fly). When his people turn against him, he gives his life for them.

Like Sula, too, Milkman creates a self from the reality of physical experience, the processes of nature, a connection to history and family continuity, and springs of human possibility through myth, dreams, legends, and other sources of psychic power. Milkman reaches an understanding of physical experience and the processes of nature in a struggle against the physical environment. As a rich city boy, Milkman was insulated from nature, but in his trip south to try to get the gold, he overcomes a series of physical obstacles to reach the cave where Macon and Pilate in their youth encountered white people and gold. Milkman gets there only after falling into the river and climbing up twenty feet of rock, splitting his shoes and the clothes that mark him as a city man. During the trip, Milkman loses his possessions—trunk, clothes, and whiskey—and he makes it on his own, in a place where his father's name and father's money do not protect him. Milkman succeeds in finding Circe, who years ago sheltered Pilate and Macon when their father was killed, and he reaches the cave where there is no longer any gold.

Milkman also encounters nature as an obstacle to be overcome when, after the knife fight in Shalimar, he is invited to go on a coon hunt into the woods with the older men of Shalimar. Again, Milkman undergoes a test, having to move through the woods in the dark, having to show the courage and physical endurance necessary to be one of the hunters. Milkman also experiences the music of the hunt, the communication between the men and the dogs, the language before language, of a time when people were so close to their physical reality that they were in harmony with all creatures.

Milkman also creates himself in searching for his origins. In searching for his fathers, he discovers himself; like the Telemachus of Greek mythology and James Joyce's Stephen Dedalus, Milkman must find the reality of his fathers to know his own potential. Milkman's original pursuit of the gold seems to be an impulse he gets from his father, the man of business, and even from his father's father, who was a lover of property. The quest, however, changes as Milkman pursues it, finding the thread of his family's history. Stopping in Pennsylvania, Milkman hears the stories of the men who knew his father and grandfather and who rejoice in their successes. The story of the Dead family dramatizes the dream and the failure of that dream for blacks in America. When the older Macon Dead was killed by white men for his flourishing farm, the possibilities of his neighbors were narrowed and their lives scarred. Seeing his father and grandfather through their former neighbor's eyes helps Milkman to understand better the pride that Macon had when he said that his father had let Macon work side by side with him and trusted him to share in his achievements.

In Shalimar, Milkman also learns about his great-grandfather by piecing together the memories of people there and by deciphering the children's game and song, a song about Solomon and Rynah that seems to be interspersed with nonsense words. Milkman matches this song to a song that he had heard Pilate sing about Sugarman. He solves the riddle of the song, and he even figures out what the ghost of Pilate's father meant when he said, "Sing," and when he told Pilate to go get the bones. Finally, he discovers that his grandmother was an American Indian, Singing Bird, and that his great-grandfather, Solomon, was one of the legendary flying Africans, the father of twenty-one sons, a slave who one day flew back to Africa. His grandfather Jake had fallen through the branches of a tree when Solomon dropped him, trying to take his last baby son back with him. Learning about that magic enables Milkman himself to fly when he surrenders to the air and lets himself be upheld.

Milkman creates a self so that he can share it and even sacrifice it for a friend. With Pilate, Milkman buries the bones of Jake, his grandfather, on Solomon's Leap. Guitar, who has continued to stalk Milkman, shoots and kills Pilate, but Milkman, saying to Guitar, "Do you want my life? Take it if it is any good to you," leaps into the air and flies. Guitar is free to kill his friend, but Milkman soars.

The ending of the novel shows the transcendence of the spirit, as the hero achieves his destiny. The satisfaction of the ending, which also soars into legend, comes from the triumph of the human spirit, the triumph that even death cannot destroy. *Song of Solomon* is a beautiful, serious, funny novel that moves beyond the social to the mythic.

Tar Baby

Tar Baby explores three kinds of relationships: the relationship between blacks and whites; the relationships within families, especially between parents and children; and the relationship between the American black man and black woman. In the epigraph to the novel, Saint Paul reproaches the Corinthians for allowing contentions to exist among their ranks; the quote serves to foreshadow the discord that abounds in the novel's relationships.

In *Tar Baby*, Morrison depicts not a self-contained black society, but an onstage interaction between blacks and whites. The novel juxtaposes two families, a white family of masters and a black family of servants. The white family includes a retired candy-maker, Valerian Street, and his wife Margaret, once the "Principal Beauty of Maine," who is now in her fifties. The couple's only son Michael lives abroad; his arrival for Christmas is expected and denied by various characters.

The black family consists of the husband, Sydney Childs, who is Valerian's valet and butler, and the wife, Ondine, who serves as cook and housekeeper. They are childless, but their orphan niece Jadine plays the role of their daughter. (Valerian has acted as Jadine's patron, paying for her education at the Sorbonne.)

The pivotal character, however, who enters and changes the balance of power and the habitual responses of the families, is a black man who rises out of the sea. His true name is Son, although he has gone by other aliases. The veneer of politeness and familiarity between the characters is shaken by Son's abrupt appearance. Uncomfortable racial and personal assumptions are put into words and cannot be retracted. The Principal Beauty is convinced that Son has come to rape her: What else would a black man want? (Jadine is convinced that if Son wants to rape anyone, it is she, not Margaret.) Sydney finds Son a threat to his respectability as a Philadelphia black because when

Son appears, the white people lump all blacks together. Ondine seems less threatened, but most of her energy goes into her running battle with the Principal Beauty. Jadine is apprehensive at Son's wild appearance, and later she is affronted by his direct sexual approach. Only Valerian welcomes Son. He sees him as a vision of his absent son Michael, and he invites him to sit down at the dining table and be a guest.

Son's coming is the catalyst that causes time-worn relationships to explode when Michael does not come for Christmas. His failure to appear leads to the revelation that the Principal Beauty abused her son as a child, pricking him with pins and burning him with cigarettes. Ondine, the black woman, finally hurls this accusation at Margaret, the white woman, and makes explicit what the two women have known mutually since the beginning. Valerian, who has been haunted by the memory of Michael as a lonely child who would hide under the sink and sing to himself, is hit with a reality much harsher than he has known or admitted.

Structured as it is in terms of families, the whole novel revolves around family responsibilities, especially between parents and children. Michael Street does not come home for Christmas, but the abuse he suffered as a child seems to justify his absence. Thus, the undutiful mother Margaret has thrown the whole family off balance. In the black family, later in the novel, attention is drawn to the undutiful daughter Jadine, although it seems implied that she has learned this undutifulness, partly at least, from whites, wanting her individual success to be separate from family ties and responsibilities.

This undutifulness also springs from a question of identity. In Paris, even before she comes to Valerian's island, Jadine feels affronted by a beautiful, proud, contemptuous African woman in yellow, who buys three eggs and carries them on her head. She is herself and embodies her tradition consummately, exhibiting balance and physical grace which symbolize spiritual poise. Jadine feels diminished and threatened by the African woman, who spits at her. The scorn sends Jadine back to her family, Sydney and Ondine.

Jadine is similarly disturbed by her dream of the women with breasts, the mothers, who reproach her for not joining that chain of mothers and daughters who become mothers with daughters. Although Jadine herself is an orphan, reared by Ondine and Sydney and owing much to their care, she refuses to take the self-sacrificing role of the woman who cares for her family. Jadine wants money and the power it brings in the white world. After a little more modeling, she wants to run her own business, perhaps a boutique. Also, she may choose a white husband, like the man who bought her a seductive sealskin coat.

Jadine is the Tar Baby of the novel, and Son is Brer Rabbit from the Uncle Remus stories. As the Tar Baby, Jadine acts as a possible trap for Son set by his enemies, white society. Jadine, who has absorbed many white values, wants money and success. Son wants something purer, something associated with nature (he is associated with the sea and the beauty of the savannahs) and with family tradition. Nature, direct physical experience, and family traditions that are integral to personal identity are all important values in Son's existence. Son has a home—the completely black town of Eloe—and there he abides by the ideas of respectability held by his father and his Aunt Rosa. (He asks Jadine to sleep at Aunt Rosa's, apart from him, and he comes to her secretly only when she threatens to leave if he does not.) To amuse herself in the traditional town, in which she is uncomfortable, Jadine takes photographs of the people and steals their souls, stealing their individual beauty and grace. In the photographs, they seem graceless, poor, and stupid, even to Son, who usually sees them with loving eyes.

Individually, Son and Jadine love each other, but they seem unable to find a world in which they can both thrive. Yet Son is an undaunted lover, unwilling to let Jadine go, even when she flees from him. Son tries to return to Isle de Chevaliers, Valerian's island, to get news of Jadine, but the only way he can get there seems to be through the help of Thérèse, the half-blind, fifty-year-old black woman who says that her breasts still give milk. Thérèse takes him by boat to the island of the horsemen. Son has said that he cannot give up Jadine, but Thérèse tells him to join the fabled black horsemen who see with the mind. At the end of the novel, Son is running toward his destiny, whether that be Jadine and some way to make her part of his world or the black horsemen who ride free through the hills. Readers do not know what Son's fate is to be; they only know that Son is running toward it, just as Brer Rabbit ran from his enemy Brer Fox and from the Tar Baby. Like Milkman Dead at the end of *Song of Solomon*, Son leaps into mythic possibility; like Brer Rabbit, Son, the black man, is a figure with the power to survive.

Beloved

In editing *The Black Book*, a collection of African American historical memorabilia, Toni Morrison discovered an article that would serve as the foundation of her fifth novel. *Beloved* is based on a true account of a runaway slave mother who, rather than allowing her children to be taken back into slavery, murders three of the four. As the novel begins, Sethe's sons, Buglar and Howard, have already run away, while Denver, the youngest child, survived the murder attempt and still lives with her mother in a house beset by her murdered sister Beloved's spirit. Morrison deliberately disorients the reader as she delves into the "interior life" of slavery, creating an experience similar to that of slavery, as the narrative breaks apart, shifts, and confounds. The author personifies 124 Bluestone Road as a tormented being when Beloved returns, emerging from a lake, fully clothed, the same age she would have been had she survived the infanticide. What the spirit wants initially is unclear. Morrison uses metaphorical imagery with tremendous skill, for example when describing Sethe's back, a relief map of scars from savage beatings, as resembling the branches of a chokecherry tree. When Paul D, a former slave whom Sethe once knew, moves in, Beloved wreaks havoc. The spirit behaves like an enraged toddler, but the damage she does is that of a full-grown woman. As the ghost continues to threaten her mother and sister, the characters' thoughts intertwine until one cannot be certain which character is which.

Jazz

Toni Morrison intended *Jazz*, another novel inspired by a news article, to follow *Beloved* as the second of a trilogy, although the narrative does not pick up where *Beloved* ends. Joe Trace, a married man and cosmetics salesman, shoots his teen lover, Dorcas, at a party. She dies refusing to reveal his name. At her funeral, Violet, Joe's wife, a hairdresser, defaces the girl's corpse. Set in 1926, *Jazz* begins after Violet has cut the dead girl's face, twenty years after she and Joe arrived in Harlem from the South, where they scraped out a living as sharecroppers. After Dorcas's funeral, Violet returns home and releases her caged parrot, the only creature in her life who says "I love you" anymore. The deep, unrealized passion for human contact in *Beloved* takes root in *Jazz*, but it too becomes messy, dangerous, and out of control. Violet's mind unravels, and, strangely, she turns to Alice Manfred, Dorcas's aunt, for comfort. *Beloved*'s theme of mother loss, profound and frustrated, continues in *Jazz*: Dorcas's mother burns to death in an intentionally set fire; Violet's mother throws herself down a well from despair over not providing for her children. Years later, Violet longs so achingly for a child she considers stealing one. It is only at the end of *Jazz*, when Violet and Joe reconcile and Violet buys a sick parrot that she nurses back to health by playing jazz for it, that there is some hope of a lasting human connection.

Paradise

Paradise, Morrison's seventh novel, like her previous two, was inspired by a little-known event in African American history, this time the 1870's westward migration of former slaves set on establishing their own all-black utopia, known in the book as Ruby. Shifting back and forth across a century of time, *Paradise* begins in 1976, when a group of the settlers' male descendants attack a mansion-turned-convent of women, convinced it is the women's eschewing of male companionship and their questionable pasts that threaten the town's survival. Ruby is founded as a response not only to white racism but also to other African Americans who turned away settlers for having skin that was "too black." Twin brothers Deacon and Steward, the town's elders, are deeply committed to keeping Ruby as pristine and trouble-free as possible. Together, they symbolize Ruby's twin identity and conscience.

Initially, the town has no crime and therefore needs no police. There is no hunger; everyone assists those in need. However, such total isolation from the outside world proves to be the town's undoing, as the rebellion of the 1960's youth movement seeps into Ruby. A ragtag group of women, most escaping either abusive relationships or responsibilities of motherhood, settle outside Ruby. Among others, there is Consolata, the maternal leader; Seneca, abandoned as a child by her teen mother; and Pallas, a white woman fleeing from her wealthy but negligent parents. The violent confrontation between the men of Ruby and the self-exiled women is, in part, brought on by the black men's anger at women who have willfully chosen a life without them. *Paradise* is a significant addition to Morrison's body of work.

Other Literary Forms

Toni Morrison, primarily a novelist, edited *The Black Book*, a collection of documents and articles on African American history compiled by Middleton Harris. She also published a short story, "Big Box," in *Ms.* magazine in 1980. Morrison's first play, *Dreaming Emmett*, was commissioned by the New York State Writers Institute of the State University of New York. Morrison has written many essays, some of the most notable of which are "The Site of Memory" in *Inventing the Truth: The Art and Craft of Memoir* (1987), edited by William Zinsser, and "Unspeakable Things Unspoken: The Afro-American Presence in American Literature" in *Michigan Quarterly Review* 28 (Winter, 1989). "Honey and Rue," with lyrics by Toni Morrison and music by André Previn, was commissioned by Carnegie Hall for soprano Kathleen Battle and premiered in January, 1992. Another collection of essays, *Birth of a Nation'hood: Gaze, Script, and Spectacle in the O. J. Simpson Case*, was published in 1997.

Bibliography

Bloom, Harold, ed. *Toni Morrison*. New York: Chelsea House, 1990. A fine selection of criticism on Morrison, with an excellent introduction by Bloom and an extensive bibliography.

Beloved is discussed in three essays by Margaret Atwood, Margaret Sale, and M. S. Mobley. The real gem, however, is an essay by Morrison herself in which she argues for inclusion of black literature in the canon of American literature.

Bruck, Peter, and Wolfgange Karrer, eds. *The Afro-American Novel Since 1960.* Amsterdam: B. R. Gruener, 1982. This compilation of essays on black authors includes a chapter on Morrison by Bruck, entitled "Returning to One's Roots: The Motif of Searching and Flying in Toni Morrison's *Song of Solomon*" (originally printed in 1977).

Conner, Marc C., ed. *The Aesthetics of Toni Morrison: Speaking the Unspeakable.* Jackson: University Press of Mississippi, 2000. A collection of essays concentrating on the imagery and stylistics of Morrison's writings and her ability to convey the "unspeakable" aspects of African American experience.

Fultz, Lucille P. *Toni Morrison: Playing with Difference.* Urbana: University of Illinois Press, 2003. An examination of Morrison's approach to differences (for example, black and white, male and female, wealth and poverty) in her intricate narratives.

Furman, Jan. *Toni Morrison's Fiction.* Columbia: University of South Carolina Press, 1996. Part of the Understanding Contemporary American Literature series, this book addresses such topics as black womanhood, male consciousness, and community and cultural identity in Morrison's novels. Includes a bibliography and an index.

Harris, Trudier. *Fiction and Folklore: The Novels of Toni Morrison.* Knoxville: University of Tennessee Press, 1991. A collection of essays that examine Morrison's novels from an African and African American mythological and folkloric perspective and examine the archetypes and antiheroes that pervade her stories. An important scholarly guide to understanding the subtext of Morrison's work.

Hayes, Elizabeth T. "The Named and the Nameless: Morrison's 124 and Naylor's 'The Other Place' as Semiotic 'Chorae.'" *African American Review* 38, no. 4 (Winter, 2004): 669-682. An interesting article that explores the role of houses as physical manifestations of their inhabitants' personalities.

Hogue, W. Lawrence. "Postmodernism, Traditional Culture Forms, and the African American Narrative: Major's *Reflex*, Morrison's *Jazz*, and Reed's *Mumbo Jumbo*." *Novel: A Forum on Fiction* 35, nos. 2/3 (Spring/Summer, 2002): 169-193. Takes a closer look at the roles of postmodernism and jazz in works by Morrison, Clarence Major, and Ishmael Reed.

Holloway, Karen F. C., and Stephanie A. Demetrakopoulos. *New Dimensions of Spirituality: The Novels of Toni Morrison*. New York: Greenwood Press, 1987. In this study, each author contributes individually with a common theme of spiritual development in Morrison's first four novels. Demetrakopoulos has a Jungian background and examines the archetypal feminine images of Morrison's heroines. The notes are themselves excellent secondary resources. The chapter "A Critical Perspective" provides valuable views on the criticism available on Morrison.

Kubitschek, Missy Dehn. *Toni Morrison: A Critical Companion*. Westport, Conn.: Greenwood Press, 1998. An excellent source of literary criticism. Contains a bibliography and an index.

McKay, Nellie Y., ed. *Critical Essays on Toni Morrison*. Boston: G. K. Hall, 1988. This volume, which is part of a series on American literature, firmly places Morrison on the list as one of the "most important writers in America." A compilation of reprinted essays by various authors, nine of which are original and written specifically for this publication. Also includes reviews, interviews, and literary criticism of Morrison's first four novels. A diverse and comprehensive work on Morrison. No bibliography.

Middleton, David L. *Toni Morrison: An Annotated Bibliography*. New York: Garland, 1987. The articles and essays by Morrison and the interviews with her listed here are arranged chronologically to present clearly the evolution of her ideas. Includes critical reviews of her fiction and a listing of honors and awards. Subject index provided. An indispensable guide.

Otten, Terry. *The Crime of Innocence in the Fiction of Toni Morrison*. Columbia: University of Missouri Press, 1989. In this groundbreaking study of Morrison's first five novels, Otten explores the mythic substance in her writings by tracing the motif of the biblical fall. Insightful readings and unflagging attention to the historical and literary backdrop. A valuable guide to the increasing scholarship on Morrison.

Peach, Linden, ed. *Toni Morrison.* New York: St. Martin's Press, 1998. Focuses on interpretation and criticism of Morrison's works and examines African American women in literature. Provides a bibliography and an index.

Riley, Jeannette, Kathleen Torrens, and Susan Krumholz. "Contemporary Feminist Writers: Envisioning a Just World." *Contemporary Justice Review* 8, no. 1 (March, 2005): 91-107. Looks at the work of Joy Harjo, Barbara Kingsolver, Toni Morrison, and Adrienne Rich, proposing that each of these authors creates a concept of justice that is more in touch with notions of ethics and equality than are traditional ideas.

Samuels, Wilfred D., and Clenora Hudson-Weems. *Toni Morrison.* Boston: Twayne, 1990. This study analyzes five of Morrison's novels, including *Beloved.* The authors explore common themes such as black folklore and mysticism in Morrison's writings. Contains excerpts from interviews.

Watson, Reginald. "The Power of the 'Milk' and Motherhood: Images of Deconstruction and Reconstruction in Toni Morrison's *Beloved* and Alice Walker's *The Third Life of Grange Copeland.*" *CLA Journal* 48, no. 2 (December, 2004): 156-183. Discusses the importance of maternity and maternal images in the two works. Also comments on the general nature of sexual relationships between African American men and African American women in the books.

— *Kate Begnal; Nika Hoffman*

Walter Dean Myers

Novelist, biographer, and poet

Born: Martinsburg, West Virginia; August 12, 1937

CHILDREN'S/YOUNG ADULT LITERATURE: *Where Does the Day Go?*,
1969; *The Dancers*, 1972; *The Dragon Takes a Wife*, 1972; *Fly,
Jimmy, Fly!*, 1974; *Fast Sam, Cool Clyde, and Stuff*, 1975; *The
World of Work: A Guide to Choosing a Career*, 1975; *Social Welfare*,
1976; *Brainstorm*, 1977; *Mojo and the Russians*, 1977; *Victory for
Jamie*, 1977; *It Ain't All for Nothin'*, 1978; *The Young Landlords*,
1979; *The Black Pearl and the Ghost: Or, One Mystery After An-
other*, 1980; *The Golden Serpent*, 1980; *Hoops*, 1981; *The Legend of
Tarik*, 1981; *Won't Know Till I Get There*, 1982; *The Nicholas Fac-
tor*, 1983; *Tales of a Dead King*, 1983; *Motown and Didi: A Love
Story*, 1984; *Mr. Monkey and the Gotcha Bird*, 1984; *The Outside
Shot*, 1984; *Sweet Illusions*, 1987; *Crystal*, 1987; *Fallen Angels*,
1988; *Me, Mop, and the Moondance Kid*, 1988; *Scorpions*, 1988;
The Mouse Rap, 1990; *Now Is Your Time! The African-American
Struggle for Freedom*, 1991; *Mop, Moondance, and the Nagasaki
Knights*, 1992; *The Righteous Revenge of Artemis Bonner*, 1992;
Somewhere in the Darkness, 1992; *Brown Angels: An Album of Pic-
tures and Verse*, 1993 (poetry); *Malcolm X: By Any Means Necessary*, 1993; *A Place Called Heartbreak: A Story of Vietnam*, 1993;
Young Martin's Promise, 1993; *Darnell Rock Reporting*, 1994; *The
Glory Field*, 1994; *Glorious Angels: A Celebration of Children*, 1995
(poetry); *One More River to Cross: An African-American Photograph Album*, 1995; *Shadow of the Red Moon*, 1995; *The Story of
the Three Kingdoms*, 1995; *How Mr. Monkey Saw the Whole World*,
1996; *Slam!*, 1996; *Smiffy Blue, Ace Crime Detective: The Case of
the Missing Ruby, and Other Stories*, 1996; *Toussaint L'Ouverture:
The Fight for Haiti's Freedom*, 1996; *Harlem*, 1997; *Amistad: A
Long Road of Freedom*, 1998; *Angel to Angel: A Mother's Gift of
Love*, 1998; *At Her Majesty's Request: An African Princess in Victorian England*, 1999; *The Journal of Scott Pendleton Collins: A*

WWII Soldier, 1999; *The Journal of Joshua Loper: A Black Cowboy,* 1999; *Monster,* 1999; *The Blues of Flat Brown,* 2000; *145th Street,* 2000 (short stories); *Bad Boy: A Memoir,* 2001; *The Journal of Biddy Owens: The Negro Leagues,* 2001; *Three Swords for Granada,* 2002; *The Beast,* 2003; *Blues Journey,* 2003 (Christopher Myers, illustrator); *The Dream Bearer,* 2003; *Antarctica,* 2004; *Here in Harlem: Poems in Many Voices,* 2004; *I've Seen the Promised Land,* 2004 (Leonard Jenkins, illustrator); *Shooter,* 2004; *USS Constellation: Pride of the American Navy,* 2004; *Autobiography of My Dead Brother,* 2005 (Christopher Myers, illustrator).

Achievements

Walter Dean Myers writes realistic stories about young African Americans coping with complex social and ethical issues and finding values to live by. His writings range from picture books to short stories to young adult novels to nonfiction books.

Myers's career was launched when he won the Council on Interracial Books for Children Award in 1968 for *Where Does the Day Go?* He has since won several American Library Association (ALA) Notable Book Awards and Best Books for Young Adults Citations, Newbery Honors, Parents' Choice Awards, and Coretta Scott King Awards. He was the first recipient of the Michael L. Printz Award for excellence in young adult literature in 2000 for his powerful book *Monster.*

Biography

Walter Dean Myers was born in West Virginia into a large family. When he was three years old, his mother died. Burdened by poverty, his father sent Myers to live with foster parents in New York City. The foster parents, Herbert and Florence Dean, raised the boy in Harlem, which Myers remembers as teeming with life and excitement. Myers changed his original middle name, Milton, to Dean in honor of his foster parents.

Myers's foster mother read to him every day until he could read for himself. Myers was a good student in the sense that he was literate, but he became known as a discipline problem in school. He had a speech impediment that prevented people from understanding what he was saying. His classmates teased him, and Myers responded with anger. He spent many days in the principal's office or on suspension.

He received some guidance from his fifth-grade teacher, who thought that writing words down would help him with his speech problem. He filled notebooks with poems and stories but did not consider writing as a career. When not in school, Myers hung out with the street gangs and played basketball until it was too dark to see. Later in his life, the game of basketball would be a prominent feature in several of his books.

At age sixteen, Myers dropped out of school and joined the Army the next year. After his tour of duty, he returned to Harlem and worked in a series of low-paying jobs. At the same time, he began to write for magazines. Myers entered a writing contest sponsored by the Council on Interracial Books for Children and won first place in the picture book category. Myers wrote a few more books for preschoolers before directing his efforts toward teenagers. *Fast Sam, Cool Clyde, and Stuff* was his first young adult novel.

For twenty years, Myers worked as an editor during the day and wrote fiction at night. When he was laid off by the company for which he worked, he became a full-time writer. As a result, Myers has been prolific, publishing more than sixty books for young people. He became the father of three children and made a home with his wife in New Jersey.

Analysis: Young Adult Literature

One of Myers's primary goals as a writer is to create novels that intrigue and instruct children and teenagers. He realistically portrays contemporary and historical figures with whom his young readers can identify. His plots are action-packed and fast-moving, and yet his settings and descriptions are rendered in great detail. His contemporary characters tend to be drawn from the ghetto world he once knew intimately.

A thread that runs through many of his books for teenagers is the search for ideals. Myers writes about young people overcoming a harsh environment, senseless violence, and dysfunctional families by developing inner values. His characters face complex ethical choices but usually find an honorable path. It is Myers's intent as an author to instill values in young people who have been devalued or who have undervalued themselves.

Myers believes that in order to reach his readers, they must be able to identify with the actions, thoughts, and emotions of his protagonists. The language, settings, and plots must be relevant to young people, especially marginalized African Americans. He often uses the first-person viewpoint, which provides immediate access to the protagonist's mind. In seeking to establish common ground with his adolescent readers, he uses slang frequently. There is a danger that today's readers might find some of the language dated. However, the plotlines and themes that inform Myers's work have already endured—and been enjoyed—for decades.

Although his books tend to be written from the perspective of an inner-city, African American male, his coming-of-age theme is universal. The crisis may vary from book to book, but each protagonist endures a rite of passage from childhood into adulthood. In essence, Myers writes about young people making choices. This is not unique in young adult fiction. However, Myers's characters tend to be faced with choices that have life-or-death consequences. The subject matter and language in Myers's books are often raw. Gambling, war, drug use, suicide, teen pregnancy, homicide, adoption, and parental neglect are subjects that have brought three of his books to the edge of censorship by school systems. While these topics may seem dramatically harsh to some readers, they are merely reflections of daily life to others. One of Myers's gifts is showing young people, regardless of age, race, and social status, that they can live up to their ideals in any situation.

Hoops

In *Hoops*, Myers makes the game of basketball symbolize the game of life. Basketball was one of Myers's loves; it was an escape from the frustrations of school, a time to bond with other kids his age, and just plain fun. He depicts the basketball scenes in his books with astounding clarity and from an insider's perspective. *Hoops* seems at first to be an action-packed sports novel, but it is revealed as a moral tale about choices and integrity.

The main character in *Hoops* is seventeen-year-old Lonnie Jackson, who clings to a dream that he will become a professional basketball player. He is a senior in high school and is feeling tense about what his next steps in life will be. Basketball could be a way out of Harlem, a way to accrue status in the world, and a way to gain some self-esteem. Lonnie is one of the best players in Harlem. He believes a real chance exists that his dream could come true.

Lonnie rarely stays at home with his mother. He has an arrangement with the manager of a hotel called The Grant where he does some cleaning in exchange for a place to sleep. One of the first incidents in the book is a robbery at a liquor store across the street from the hotel. While the criminals are herding staff and customers into the back, Lonnie grabs a case of Scotch to sell. This incident paints a picture of Lonnie's environment and of his own cunning adaptation to it.

Myers often uses the first-person viewpoint to engage his young adult readers. Lonnie's thoughts and feelings are skillfully articulated, exposing conflicts and concerns about love, sex, money, family, and honor. Specifically, Lonnie's conflicts in *Hoops* revolve around basketball, his mother, his girlfriend, and Cal. Cal, a former pro player who was ousted from the league for gambling, coaches Lonnie's team. He is now a semi-homeless alcoholic, but still possesses enough caring to warn Lonnie about the ugly side of the game. Lonnie starts to look up to Cal, whom he at first considered a useless wino. As Lonnie grows closer to Cal, however, he sees a broken man with a broken past who still manages to instill trust in the team members.

The story builds to its climax with the team playing in a tournament, with big gambling money riding on the outcome. Cal is ordered by mob leaders to keep Lonnie out of the game, which would result in the team's loss. Cal tells Lonnie that basketball is like life: "Everybody plays the game with what they got." At first, Cal does sit Lonnie down, but as the tournament game progresses, he suddenly calls for Lonnie and the team wins the game. However, this spells doom for Cal, who is viciously stabbed in the team locker room.

Hoops takes place in a terrifying world where gangs roam the streets in malicious packs and Lonnie's girlfriend is injected with heroin because she learns about a mobster's involvement in the tournament fix. The reader follows Lonnie's growth from a tough, self-centered kid who cares about nothing except basketball to a more mature young man who sees that even a person as fallen as Cal can overcome his weakness and become a moral force in the midst of corruption.

Fallen Angels

Myers dedicated *Fallen Angels* to his brother who was killed in the Vietnam War. Myers himself joined the Army at age seventeen because it seemed to him that he had few other options. The protagonist of *Fallen Angels*, Richie Perry, is also seventeen when he enlists in the Army. The young man believes at first that he will not see any combat because he has injured his knee stateside. However, he soon discovers that the wheels of paperwork processing grind slowly in the Army, and he finds himself in the muggy jungles of Vietnam.

The story is one of courage, conflict, and deep numbing confusion about a soldier's role in the Vietnam War. Myers tells the story from Richie's point of view and spares the reader no detail of the young man's terror, the firefights and bombings, the killings, and the deaths of his companions, who are the fallen angels to which the book's title refers. Realistic language and settings play an important role in helping contemporary readers relate to the environment of brutal fighting in a Southeast Asian jungle.

There is racial tension in the novel, but it is overshadowed by the intense fear and confusion generated by the war. The language can be vulgar, yet it fits the raw, rugged life that the characters experience out in the jungle. The environment is overwhelming: Death and injury surround Richie and his comrades, dwarfing the concerns of ordinary life (otherwise known as the World).

Initially, Richie yearns to get back to the World, back to his stateside, civilian life. Gradually, he begins to shed his childlike dream of being a hero to his younger brother and focuses on the crucially important issue: staying alive. He realizes that he does not know how to pray and starts to form a spiritual outlook. He begins to love the men that fight alongside him, to think not only of himself but also of his comrades in arms. Myers makes it clear that the war has changed Richie forever and that the World has become the foreign land.

Monster

Monster is presented in an unusual format: a screenplay interspersed with facsimiles of a handwritten journal. The book is illustrated with photographs, court sketches, even fingerprints. It won for Myers the first Michael L. Printz Award for excellence in young adult literature.

The fictional author of this screenplay/journal is sixteen-year-old Steve Harmon. He has been accused of acting as a lookout during a homicide. If he is convicted, he could spend the rest of his life in prison. The book describes his weeks of incarceration, his trial, and its outcome. Steve writes in the screenplay format because he wants to become a filmmaker, and because it is a way to distance or disassociate himself from the unfolding nightmare of his life. He can see himself and others as simply actors in a motion picture.

As the book opens, Steve has already learned that the best time to cry in jail is at night. When other prisoners are screaming and yelling, a little sniffle cannot be heard. He realizes that he must not show weakness in jail, just as he could not show weakness on the street. When he looks in the small scratched mirror over the steel sink in his cell, he does not recognize himself. He starts to wonder if he is becoming some kind of evil changeling. Within the first page of the book, Myers characteristically creates a clear picture of Steve and his predicament. Myers grabs the reader's attention immediately by using the first-person viewpoint to express the character's emotions and by describing a harsh, disturbing setting in sharp physical detail.

The prosecutor calls Steve a monster during opening arguments. Steve begins to wonder obsessively if he is a good person or a monster after all. What constitutes a good person? In

Steve's milieu, drug use, petty crimes, and running the streets are just a part of life. His alleged presence during the robbery/homicide raises questions about his choices. Just as his survival in prison depends on displaying a hardened exterior, so his survival on the streets depended on doing little jobs for gang leaders.

Steve insists in his journal that "he didn't do nothing." However, his defense lawyer, Ms. O'Brien, has some concerns. She is afraid that the jury will not "see a difference between [him] and all the bad guys taking the stand," that Steve might be tarred with the same brush as his fellow defendants. Steve intuits that Ms. O'Brien thinks he is guilty and is merely doing her job in the courtroom. Myers does not state the facts of the crime in the book, so the reader is left wondering if Steve was or was not a lookout at the crime scene. This question is literally illustrated by two captioned photographs in the book. They both appear to be stills from a store's videotape, showing Steve in the store. The captions read: "What was I doing?" and "What was I thinking?" It is not clear if the photographs are anxious figments of Steve's imagination or telltale hints that he was actually in that store.

Finally, Steve is found not guilty. He spontaneously reaches out to hug Ms. O'Brien, who turns away stiffly, indicating that there is something bad about Steve despite his acquittal. *Monster* is thoroughly ambiguous about Steve's role in the crime. It is ambiguous about Steve's basic nature, his goodness or badness. The book leaves the reader to ponder about whether guilt equals goodness and whether acquittal equals innocence.

Other Literary Forms

Myers won his first literary prize for a picture book. He has since also written nonfiction for children and young adults, including biographies of Muhammad Ali and of Sarah Forbes Bonetta, an African princess of the Victorian era. At least two of his highly acclaimed history books are hard to categorize: *Brown Angels* and *One More River to Cross* are designed as photograph albums. The former also includes Myers's poetry. Both books richly display historical images of African Americans from all walks of life.

Bibliography

Bishop, Rudine Sims. *Presenting Walter Dean Myers.* Boston: Twayne, 1990. A study of Myers for young adults which was chosen as a selected book by the New York Public Library.

Brown, Jennifer M. "Walter Dean Myers Unites Two Passions." *Publishers Weekly* 246, no. 12 (March 22, 1999): 45-46. This examination of Myers's love for antique photographs and African American history shows how the author created history books for children. The article points out that Myers reaches out to children with "triumphant images" rather than portrayals of African Americans as victims.

Burshtein, Karen. *Walter Dean Myers.* New York: Rosen, 2004. A biography of the author that frequently references his own words, giving young adult readers insights into his personality and purpose.

Jordan, Denise M. *Walter Dean Myers: Writer for Real Teens.* Berkeley Heights, N.J.: Enslow, 1999. An in-depth biography for young adults which highlights Myers's childhood and teenage years.

McElmeel, Sharron L. "A Profile: Walter Dean Myers." *Book Report* 20, no. 2 (September/October, 2001): 42-45. An insightful view into Myers's motivation as a writer, as well as an overview of his life and works.

— Janet M. Ball

Gloria Naylor

Novelist

Born: New York, New York; January 25, 1950

LONG FICTION: *The Women of Brewster Place: A Novel in Seven Stories,*
1982; *Linden Hills,* 1985; *Mama Day,* 1988; *Bailey's Café,* 1992;
The Men of Brewster Place, 1998; *1996,* 2004.

NONFICTION: *Conversations with Gloria Naylor,* 2004 (Maxine
Lavon Montgomery, editor).

EDITED TEXTS: *Children of the Night: The Best Short Stories by Black
Writers, 1967 to the Present,* 1995.

Achievements

Enjoying both critical and popular acclaim, Gloria Naylor's
work has reached a wide audience. *The Women of Brewster Place*
won the 1983 American Book Award for best first novel and was
later made into a television miniseries. Naylor's other awards include a National Endowment for the Arts Fellowship in 1985
and a Guggenheim Fellowship in 1988.

Surveying the range of black life in America, from poor
ghetto to affluent suburb to Southern offshore island, Naylor's
work examines questions of black identity and, in particular, celebrates black women. In the face of enormous problems and
frequent victimization, black women are shown coping through
their sense of community and their special powers. Male readers
might find less to cheer about in Naylor's early works, as she
writes from a feminist perspective. Later works, however, recognize the plight of black males, acknowledging their struggles
and celebrating their achievements. Though Naylor's focus is
the black experience, her depictions of courage, community,
and cultural identity have universal appeal.

Biography

The oldest child of parents who had migrated from Mississippi, Gloria Naylor was born and reared in New York City; her parents left the South the year before her birth. An avid reader as a child, Naylor seemed to have inherited her passion for reading from her mother, a woman who would go to great lengths to purchase books to which she was denied access in Mississippi libraries since blacks were not allowed inside. The year Naylor graduated from high school, Martin Luther King, Jr., was assassinated, and the shock of this event caused Naylor to delay her college education. She chose instead to become a missionary for the Jehovah's Witnesses in New York, North Carolina, and

(AP/Wide World Photos)

Florida. She eventually found missionary life too strict, but her zeal apparently carried over into her later feminism. Although her writings are not religious, a fundamentalist pattern of thinking pervades them. She tends to separate her characters into the sheep and the goats (the latter mostly men), the saved and the damned, with one whole book, *Linden Hills*, being modeled after Dante Alighieri's *Inferno* (c. 1320).

In high school Naylor read widely in the nineteenth century British novelists, but later in a creative writing course at Brooklyn College she came across the book that influenced her most—*The Bluest Eye* (1970), by the black American novelist Toni Morrison. The example of Morrison inspired Naylor to write fiction and to focus on the lives of black women, who Naylor felt were underrepresented (if not ignored) in American literature. Naylor began work on *The Women of Brewster Place*, which was published the year after her graduation from Brooklyn College with a B.A. in English. By that time, Naylor was studying on a fellowship at Yale University, from which she received an M.A. in African American studies in 1983.

Naylor's background and literary achievements won for her numerous invitations for lectureships or other appointments in academia. She held visiting posts at George Washington University, the University of Pennsylvania, Princeton University, New York University, Boston University, Brandeis University, and Cornell University. Diverse in her pursuits, Naylor wrote a stage adaptation of *Bailey's Café*. She founded One Way Productions, an independent film company, and became involved in a literacy program in the Bronx. She lives in Brooklyn, New York.

Analysis: Long Fiction

White people do not appear often and are not featured in the work of Gloria Naylor. Yet their presence can be felt like a white background noise, or like the boulevard traffic on the other side of the wall from Brewster Place. White culture is simply another fact of life, like a nearby nuclear reactor or toxic waste dump, and the effects of racism and discrimination are omnipresent in Naylor's work. Against these stifling effects her characters live their lives and try to define their sense of black identity, from the ghetto dwellers of Brewster Place to the social climbers of Linden Hills to the denizens of Willow Springs, a pristine Southern island relatively untouched by slavery and segregation.

Naylor writes about these settings and characters in a romantic mode that sometimes verges on the melodramatic or gothic. The influence of her earlier reading—such authors as Charlotte Brontë and Emily Brontë, Charles Dickens, William Faulkner, and Morrison—is apparent. The settings have heavy but obvious symbolic meanings, some derived from literary references: Brewster Place is a dead-end street, Linden Hills is a modern version of Dante's Hell, and Willow Springs recalls the magical isle of William Shakespeare's *The Tempest* (1611). The weather and numerous details also carry symbolic freight, almost as much as they do for such an emblematic writer as Nathaniel Hawthorne. In addition to literary influences, the symbolism seems to draw on Hollywood, particularly Hollywood's gothic genre, horror films; for example, in *Linden Hills* the character Norman Anderson suffers from attacks of "the pinks"— imaginary blobs of pink slime—while the rich undertaker Luther Nedeed locks his wife and child away in the basement.

These two examples also show, in an exaggerated fashion, how Naylor's characters fit into the Romantic mode. Her characters tend to go to extremes, to be emotional and obsessive, or to have a single trait or commit a single act that determines their whole life course. While rather one-dimensional and melodramatic, they nevertheless linger in the memory. Such is the case with Luther Nedeed, who represents Satan in *Linden Hills*, and with the old conjure woman Miranda "Mama" Day, who represents Satan's usual opposition in the scheme of things.

In Naylor, this scheme of things illustrates how she has transferred her former missionary fervor, along with the framework of religious thought, to her feminism. Luther Nedeed's behavior is only the most sensational example of men's cruelty to women in Naylor's work; he has a large following. On the other hand, the mystical ability of Mama Day, the Prospero of women's liberation, to command the forces of nature and the spirit world is only the most sensational example of women's special powers in Naylor's thinking. Even the women of Brewster Place demonstrate these powers through their mutual love and support, enabling them to triumph over devastating personal tragedies and demeaning circumstances.

Naylor's men are another story: If not outright demons or headed that way, they seem to lack some vital force. Even the best men are fatally flawed—they are subject to "the pinks," are addicted to wine, or have weak hearts. Failing at key moments, they are useful only as sacrifices to the feminine mystique. A prime example is the engineer George Andrews of *Mama Day*, who, for all his masculine rationality and New York smarts, does not know how to handle (significantly) a brooding hen. A close reading of Naylor's works reveals the men's victimization, along with the women's; however, Naylor is concerned with the women in her earlier novels. Naylor's later works indicate that she has expanded her vision to include men.

The Women of Brewster Place
Naylor began fulfilling her commitment to make black women more prominent in American fiction with *The Women of Brewster Place*, subtitled *A Novel in Seven Stories*. The seven stories, featuring seven women, can be read separately, but they are connected by their setting of Brewster Place and by characters who appear, or are mentioned, in more than one story. The women arrive on the dead-end street by different routes that exhibit the variety of lives lived by black women, but on Brewster Place they unite into a community.

The middle-aged bastion of Brewster Street is Mattie Michael, who over the course of her life was betrayed by each of the three men she loved—her seducer, her father, and her son. She mothers Lucielia Louise Turner (whose grandmother once sheltered Mattie) when Ciel's abusive boyfriend destroys her life. In addition, Mattie welcomes her close friend Etta Mae Johnson, who also once gave Mattie refuge. Etta Mae is a fading beauty who has used men all of her life but is now herself used by a sleazy preacher for a one-night stand. The other women featured are the young unwed Cora Lee, a baby factory; Kiswana Browne, an aspiring social reformer who hails from the affluent suburb of Linden Hills; and Lorraine and Theresa, two lesbians seeking privacy for their love.

Few men are in evidence on Brewster Place, and those who do appear inspire little confidence. C. C. Baker and his youth gang lurk about the alleyway and, in the novel's brutal climax, rape Lorraine. The crazed Lorraine in turn kills the wino Ben, the old janitor who earlier had befriended her. Yet Naylor acknowledges the plight of the men. In her description of the gang members, she says,

> Born with the appendages of power, circumcised by a guillotine, and baptized with the steam of a million nonreflective mirrors, these young men wouldn't be called upon to thrust a bayonet into an Asian farmer, target a torpedo, scatter their iron seed from a B-52 into the wound of the earth, point a finger to move a nation, or stick a pole into the moon—and they knew it. They only had that three-hundred-foot alley to serve them as stateroom, armored tank, and executioner's chamber.

As these scenes suggest, Brewster Place is located in a ghetto plagued by social ills. The women must face these on a daily basis in addition to their personal tragedies and dislocations. Instead of being overcome by their sufferings, however, the women find within themselves a common fate and a basis for community. They gain strength and hope from their mutual caring and support. Besides their informal support system, they form a block association to address larger problems. The ability of women to unite in such a community inspires admiration for their courage and their special powers.

Linden Hills

The community feelings of Brewster Place, from which the women gain a positive sense of identity, somehow make the ghetto's problems seem less awesome, paradoxically, than those of Linden Hills, an affluent suburb. If Brewster Place is a ghetto, Linden Hills is a hell. Naylor underlines this metaphor by deliberately modeling her novel *Linden Hills* after Dante's *Inferno*. Linden Hills is not a group of hills, but only a V-shaped area on a hillside intersected by eight streets. As one travels down the hill, the residents become richer but lower on the moral scale. Lester and Willie, two young unemployed poets who perform odd jobs for Christmas money (they are the modern counterparts of Vergil and Dante), take the reader on a guided tour.

Lester's sister Roxanne deems black Africans in Zimbabwe unready for independence; one young executive, Maxwell Smyth, encourages another, Xavier Donnell, no longer to consider Roxanne as a prospective corporate bride; and Dr. Daniel Braithwaite has written the authorized twelve-volume history of Linden Hills without making a single moral judgment. Other sellouts are more personal: The young lawyer Winston Alcott leaves his homosexual lover to marry respectably, and Chester Parker is eager to bury his dead wife in order to remarry.

Significantly, Linden Hills is ruled by men. The archfiend is Luther Nedeed, the local undertaker and real estate tycoon who occupies the lowest point in Linden Hills. Speaking against a low-income housing project planned for an adjacent poor black neighborhood, Nedeed urges outraged Linden Hills property owners to make common cause with the racist Wayne County Citizens Alliance. Most damning of all, however, is that Nedeed disowns his own wife and child and imprisons them in an old basement morgue; the child starves, but the wife climbs up to confront the archfiend on Christmas Eve.

Mama Day

It is clear that, while examining problems of middle-class black identity in *Linden Hills*, Naylor has not overlooked the plight of black women. In *Mama Day*, Naylor returns to a more celebratory mood on both subjects. The setting of *Mama Day* is a unique black American culture presided over by a woman with even more unique powers.

The coastal island of Willow Springs, located off South Carolina and Georgia but belonging to no state, has been largely bypassed by the tides of American history, particularly racism. The island was originally owned by a white man, Bascombe Wade, who also owned slaves. Bascombe married Sapphira, one of his slaves, however, who bore their seven sons. In 1823 Bascombe freed his other slaves and deeded the island to them, his sons, and their respective descendants in perpetuity (the land cannot be sold, only inherited). Bascombe was more or less assimilated, and a black culture grew up on the island that was closely tied to the land, to the culture's beginnings, and to African roots. In other words, Willow Springs is definitely a mythical island—a tiny but free black state flourishing unnoticed under the nose of the Confederacy. Naylor underlines the island's mythic qualities by drawing parallels between it and the magical isle of *The Tempest*.

If Prospero presides over Shakespeare's island, then Prospero's daughter, Miranda "Mama" Day (actually a great-granddaughter of the Wades), presides over Willow Springs. Known and respected locally as an old conjure woman, Mama Day is a repository and embodiment of the culture's wisdom. In particular, she is versed in herbs and other natural phenomena, but she also speaks with the island's spirits. Mama Day uses her powers to heal and aid new life, but other island people who have similar powers are not so benevolent. One such person is Ruby, who stirs her knowledge with hoodoo to kill any woman who might take her man.

Unhappily, Mama Day's grandniece Cocoa, down from New York on a visit with her husband George, arouses Ruby's jealousy. By pretending to be friendly, Ruby is able to give Cocoa a deadly nightshade rinse, scalp massage, and hairdo. Just as a big hurricane hits the island, Cocoa begins to feel the effects of the poison. George, an engineer, native New Yorker, and football fan, works frantically to save Cocoa, but he is overmatched. With his urbanized, masculine rationality, he cannot conceive of what he is up against or how to oppose it. Suffering from exhaustion and a weak heart, he is eventually killed in an encounter with a brooding hen.

Meanwhile, Mama Day has been working her powers. She confronts Ruby in a conjuring match, good magic versus bad magic, just as in Mali's oral epic tradition of the thirteenth century ruler Sundjata and in other traditions of modern Africa. Ruby is destroyed by lightning strikes, and Cocoa is saved. It is too late for George the doubter, however, who learns about the mystical powers of women the hard way.

Bailey's Café

In each of Naylor's first three novels, clear links to the work that follow it are evident. The character Kiswana Browne in *The Women of Brewster Place* serves as the connection to *Linden Hills*, having moved from that bourgeois community to Brewster Place in order to stay in touch with the struggles of her people. Willa Prescott Nedeed, the imprisoned wife in *Linden Hills*, points the way to *Mama Day*, since she is grandniece to Mama Day and first cousin to Cocoa. It is George, Cocoa's husband, who provides the link to *Bailey's Café*, Naylor's fourth novel.

In perhaps her most ambitious work yet, Naylor moves her readers from the magical island of Willow Springs to an equally intriguing site, for *Bailey's Café* is both nowhere and everywhere. It is sitting at the edge of the world yet is found in every town. As the café's proprietor, Bailey (though that is not his real name), tells readers, "Even though this planet is round, there are just too many spots where you can find yourself hanging onto the edge . . . and unless there's some place, some space, to take a breather for a while, the edge of the world—frightening as it is—could be the end of the world." His café offers that breather, though some who enter the front door decide not to take it, instead going right through the café out the back door and dropping off into the void.

Like the inhabitants of Brewster Place, the customers in Bailey's Café are marginalized people. Their lives have taken them beyond the poverty and hard times of their urban sisters and brothers to the very edge of despair. However, for the women who people this extraordinary novel, Bailey's is simply a place to get directions to Eve's boardinghouse. Sweet Esther, abused to the point that she will receive visitors only in the dark; Peaches, whose effect on men drives her to mutilate her face with a can opener; Jesse, whose loss of marriage, child, and good name lead her to female lovers and heroin; and the pregnant virgin Mariam, ostracized from her village and bearing the effects of female circumcision—all find at Eve's a haven for their battered souls.

Throughout the individual stories of these women, Naylor uses unifying imagery: flower imagery, since each woman is associated with a particular bloom; musical imagery, jazz mostly, though the chords of the broken lives suggest the blues; religious imagery, figuring heavily in Eve and her garden, but most noticeably in the virgin birth at the end of the novel. This birth is where the connection to *Mama Day* is made clear. Explaining the circumstances of his birth to Cocoa, George told of being left as an infant outside Bailey's Café by his mother, who was later found drowned. The last few pages of *Bailey's Café* reveal George as the drowned Mariam's child, recursively pointing back to *Mama Day*.

Similar to Naylor's other novels in its concentration on the diverse lives of black people, *Bailey's Café* nonetheless marks a shift for Naylor. This shift is evident in her inclusion of Mariam, from Ethiopia, who broadens the depiction of the black experience by encompassing an African one. Mariam is also Jewish, a fact which links her to the Jewish shopkeeper, Gabriel, in the novel. The coming together of the characters in celebration of the baby's birth—a celebration which intermixes different cultural and religious beliefs—brings a multicultural component to the novel absent in Naylor's other works.

Another notable change is Naylor's foregrounding of male characters. Bailey himself, the novel's narrator, is an example. His running commentary on the customers who find themselves in his establishment, his knowledge of the Negro Baseball Leagues, and his narration of his courtship of his wife Nadine make him a central and engaging figure throughout the book. Another example is Miss Maples, the cross-dressing male housekeeper at Eve's boardinghouse. His rather lengthy individual story is included with those of the women; it points to Naylor's intention to portray a different kind of male identity as well as her desire to cultivate a different relationship with her male characters. This shift links *Bailey's Café* to *The Men of Brewster Place*, Naylor's fifth novel.

The Men of Brewster Place
Naylor's return to Brewster Place gives readers the opportunity to revisit the male characters introduced in the first book (generally portrayed negatively) and see them in a different light. No

longer assuming background roles, they are up front, giving an account of their actions in the first book. In *The Women of Brewster Place*, Mattie's son Basil skipped town while awaiting sentencing, causing his mother to lose the property she had put up for his bail. Here Basil does return, check in hand, to repay his mother for her loss; however, she is dead, and his unfulfilled desire to make amends leads him into a detrimental relationship and a prison sentence. Eugene, absent from his daughter's funeral in the first book, is in fact on site. His grief compels him to undergo a harsh punishment, one that has much to do with the fact that he could never tell Ciel that he is gay. C. C. Baker, responsible for the vicious gang rape of Lorraine, executes another heinous crime in this book but gives the reader insight into his tragic character. When he squeezes the trigger to kill his brother, he does so with eyes closed, thanking God "for giving him the courage to do it. The courage to be a man."

In *The Men of Brewster Place*, Naylor seems to be acknowledging that there is after all more than one side to a story and that she is ready to let the whole story be known. Passages from the first book provide continuity between the two works, as does the resurrected voice of Ben, the janitor killed by Lorraine. Reminiscent of the character Bailey in *Bailey's Café*, Ben is both character and narrator.

However, Naylor brings some new voices to Brewster Place when she introduces Brother Jerome and Greasy. These characters link together the lives of the men living in Brewster Place. Brother Jerome is a retarded child with an ability to play the piano that speaks of genius. The blues that pour from his fingers speak to the lives of each man, rendering their conditions tangible. Greasy makes his brief but memorable appearance in the story called "The Barbershop," leaving the men to carry the burden of his self-inflicted demise. Naylor's portrayals of these two characters are perhaps the most moving of the book. These characterizations, along with the complexity of all the male characters, point to a Naylor who is taking a broader view. She had prefaced *The Women of Brewster Place* with a poem by Langston Hughes that asked the question, "What happens to a dream deferred?" In *The Men of Brewster Place*, she seems ready to acknowledge that deferred dreams are not only the province of women.

Other Literary Forms

In 1986, Gloria Naylor wrote a column, *Hers,* for *The New York Times.* She is also the writer of a number of screenplays, short stories, and articles for various periodicals. She is known primarily, however, for her novels.

Bibliography

Blyn, Robin. "The Ethnographer's Story: *Mama Day* and the Specter of Relativism." *Twentieth Century Literature* 48, no. 3 (Fall, 2002): 239-264. Valuable for its explanation of the novel's themes and for its discussion of the importance of relativism to ethnography and to the novel.

Braxton, Joanne M., and Andrée Nicola McLaughlin, eds. *Wild Women in the Whirlwind: Afro-American Culture and the Contemporary Literary Renaissance.* New Brunswick, N.J.: Rutgers University Press, 1990. This wide-ranging collection of critical articles brings the cultural history of black women's writing up to the 1980's. Barbara Smith's article "The Truth That Never Hurts: Black Lesbians in Fiction in the 1980's" discusses the section of *The Women of Brewster Place* entitled "The Two," but other articles also bear indirectly on important themes in Naylor's work.

Carby, Hazel V. *Reconstructing Womanhood: The Emergence of the Afro-American Woman Novelist.* New York: Oxford University Press, 1987. While this book includes nothing on Naylor, it is good background reading. Tracing black women's writing from early slave narratives through the first two major black women novelists in the early twentieth century, it provides a cultural history that reveals the forces and assumptions that black women faced.

Hawkins, Alfonso W. "The Nurture of African American Youth in the Fiction of Ann Petry, Alice Childress, and Gloria Naylor." *CLA Journal* 46, no. 4 (June, 2003) 457-478. Provides interesting insights into the influence that nurture—and many other societal forces—have over African American youths, both in fiction and in life.

Hayes, Elizabeth T. "The Named and the Nameless: Morrison's 124 and Naylor's 'The Other Place' as Semiotic 'Chorae.'" *African American Review* 38, no. 4 (Winter, 2004): 669-682. An interesting article that explores the role of houses as physical manifestations of their inhabitants' personalities.

Ivey, Adriane L. "Beyond Sacrifice: Gloria Naylor Rewrites the Passion." *MELUS* 30, no. 1 (Spring, 2005): 85-109. Studies the ways in which Naylor uses biblical imagery to examine and critique Western culture's most fundamental assumptions. Views the story of Christ's death and resurrection as a tool used to justify oppression.

Kelley, Margot Anne, ed. *Gloria Naylor's Early Novels*. Gainesville: University Press of Florida, 1999. A good study of Naylor's early works. Includes bibliographical references and an index.

Montgomery, Maxine Lavon. "Authority, Multivocality, and the New World Order in Gloria Naylor's *Bailey's Café*." *African American Review* 29, no. 1 (Spring, 1995): 27. Montgomery discusses *Bailey's Café* as a woman-centered work that draws on black art forms and biblical allusions. Though she fails to recognize the true identity of Mariam's child (George of *Mama Day*), Montgomery otherwise provides a valid reading of *Bailey's Café*, commenting on the "more mature voice" with which Naylor addresses the concerns of her earlier novels.

Naylor, Gloria, and Toni Morrison. "A Conversation." *The Southern Review* 21 (Summer, 1985): 567-593. In this recorded conversation, Naylor visits her role model, Toni Morrison, whose novel *The Bluest Eye* (1970) had the deepest influence on her. Their conversation ranges over men, marriage, the inspiration for their various books, how they went about writing them, and the characters in them. Naylor says that she tried in *The Women of Brewster Place* not to depict men negatively and thought that she had succeeded.

Puhr, Kathleen M. "Healers in Gloria Naylor's Fiction." *Twentieth Century Literature* 40, no. 4 (Winter, 1994): 518. Puhr discusses the healing powers of Naylor's female characters, principally Mattie Michael (*The Women of Brewster Place*), Willa

Nedeed (*Linden Hills*), and Miranda (*Mama Day*), as well as Naylor's healing places, particularly the café and Eve's garden in *Bailey's Café*. She also discusses Naylor's works in terms of African American ancestry, generational conflicts, and broken dreams.

Rowell, Charles H. "An Interview with Gloria Naylor." *Callaloo* 20, no. 1 (Winter, 1997): 179-192. Rowell discusses a range of topics with Naylor, including her educational background, her feelings about writing, the genesis of *The Women of Brewster Place* and *Bailey's Café*, and her feelings about the novel she is intending to write, which turns out to be *The Men of Brewster Place*.

Stave, Shirley A., ed. *Gloria Naylor: Strategy and Technique, Magic and Myth*. Newark: Delaware University Press, 2001. A collection of essays focusing on *Mama Day* and *Bailey's Café*. Stave argues for an elevation of Naylor in the American literary canon.

Whitt, Margaret Earley. *Understanding Gloria Naylor*. Columbia: University of South Carolina Press, 1998. A thoughtful book of criticism of Naylor's novels.

— *Jacquelyn Benton; Harold Branam*

Gordon Parks, Sr.

Memoirist and poet

Born: Fort Scott, Kansas; November 30, 1912
Died: New York, New York; March 7, 2006

LONG FICTION: *The Learning Tree*, 1964; *Shannon*, 1981; *Sun Stalker*, 2003.

SCREENPLAYS: *The Learning Tree*, 1969 (adaptation of his novel).

POETRY: *Gordon Parks: A Poet and His Camera*, 1968 (poetry and photographs); *In Love*, 1971; *Gordon Parks: Whispers of Intimate Things*, 1971 (poetry and photographs); *Moments Without Proper Names*, 1975 (poetry and photographs); *Arias in Silence*, 1994 (poetry and photographs); *Glimpses Toward Infinity*, 1996 (poetry and photographs); *A Star for Noon: A Homage to Women in Images, Poetry, and Music*, 2000 (poetry, music, and photographs); *Eyes with Winged Thoughts*, 2005 (poetry and photographs).

NONFICTION: *Flash Photography*, 1947; *Camera Portraits: The Techniques and Principles of Documentary Portraiture*, 1948; *A Choice of Weapons*, 1966; *Born Black*, 1971; *Flavio*, 1978; *To Smile in Autumn: A Memoir*, 1979; *Voices in the Mirror: An Autobiography*, 1990; *Half Past Autumn: A Retrospective*, 1997.

Achievements

Gordon Parks was a versatile man who, at a very early age, had the determination and talent to succeed and excel in several fields. His creative and artistic achievements in a career spanning more than six decades earned for him numerous accolades and awards. Some of the most prestigious include a Julius Rosenwald Fellowship in 1941 for his photography, a Notable Book Award from the American Library Association for his autobiographical work *A Choice of Weapons*, the Spingarn Award in 1972, the National Medal of the Arts in 1988, the 2002 induction into the International Photography Hall of Fame and Museum, more than forty honorary degrees, and, in 2002, the Jackie Robinson Foundation Lifetime Achievement Award.

Biography

The youngest of fifteen children, Gordon Parks was born on a farm to Sarah Ross Parks and Andrew Jackson Parks. His mother died when he was sixteen, and he was sent to St. Paul, Minnesota, to live with a married sister and her husband. Parks clashed with his brother-in-law and, within a few weeks of his arrival, he was forced out of the home. With no money or place to live, Parks was on his own in St. Paul, far from familiar territory in Kansas. He tried to continue with his high school classes, but it was difficult: He could only find refuge during the day in the school building or hanging out in a neighborhood pool hall. He finally found work in various jobs, such as hotel busboy, piano playing in a brothel, playing semiprofessional basketball, and even touring with a jazz band.

In 1933, at the age of twenty-one, he joined the Civilian Conservation Corps (CCC) and married Sally Alvis. This marriage, the first of three, produced three children. He continued to work at various jobs, and it was while working as a railroad porter and bar car waiter that he discovered he had a talent for photography. He bought a cheap camera and taught himself the basics of photography, practicing by shooting pictures in the poor black neighborhoods of Minneapolis. A series of pictures of ordinary African Americans and their lives in black ghettos that he shot in Chicago received considerable attention and won for him a Julius Rosenwald Fellowship in 1941. He moved to Washington, D.C., where he worked at the Farm Security Administration. Later he became a correspondent for the Office of War Information but never received an overseas assignment.

Between 1944 and 1948, he was part of a team at Standard Oil of New Jersey that made documentaries. In 1948 he became the first African American photographer on staff for *Life* magazine. Between 1949 and 1951, he lived in Paris, France, enjoying the comparatively racially neutral climate there. But the Civil Rights movement was getting underway in the United States, and he re-

(AP/Wide World Photos)

turned to the States because he wanted to be a part of the struggle. During the 1950's he became involved with film and television production. These experiences made it easier for him to become the first black film director of a major motion picture: He directed the commercially successful *Shaft* in 1971 and *Shaft's Big Score* in 1972.

He had already published a couple of books by 1966, when his autobiographical work *A Choice of Weapons* came out. Between 1966 and 1975, other works, including photographic exhibits, poem collections, essay collections, films, and documentaries were produced. In 1975, at age 63, he married his third wife, Genevieve Young, and published a book of photographs,

Moments Without Proper Names. His second autobiographical volume, *To Smile in Autumn: A Memoir,* was published in 1979.

In 1995, after years of productive, creative activity, Parks donated his films, photographs, writings, and memorabilia to the United States Library of Congress, where he felt they would be respectfully stored and preserved.

In October, 2004, his hometown, Fort Scott, Kansas, honored him with the first Gordon Parks Celebration of Culture and Diversity, a four-day event celebrating Parks's amazing contribution to American culture. Indeed, Parks was widely considered a renaissance man, almost equally respected as a writer, photographer, musician, composer, and filmmaker. He most certainly excelled in these areas, but, by his own admission, his main loves were music and poetry. His autobiographical works, including the fictional *The Learning Tree,* present a man whose life is filled with people, places, and events, which he captured in his written memoirs, his poetry, his music, and perhaps most memorably in his photographs. His nonfiction—his memoirs and essays—put into words those things that moved him and motivated him to reach the goals he set for himself as a youth.

Analysis: Nonfiction

Aside from his novel *The Learning Tree,* most of Parks's written works are nonfiction. The longer works are autobiographical in nature; his shorter pieces, which are sometimes supplemented with photographs, are either technical (like his *Flash Photography*), poetic (like his *Moments Without Proper Names*), or photojournalistic (like his *Camera Portraits: The Techniques and Principles of Documentary Portraiture*).

A Choice of Weapons

A Choice of Weapons is the first of three nonfiction autobiographical works. The other two continue his life through his prominent career as a photographer and filmmaker. This one starts when he is sixteen years old and his mother has died, essentially the point at which his autobiographical novel *The Learning Tree* ends. In *A Choice of Weapons,* he details the clash with his brother-in-law that causes the man to throw him out of the house and describes the nearly destitute life he is forced to live for weeks as a homeless, penniless teenager. Parks goes to school or to a pool hall during the day and rides streetcars at night because he has no place else to spend the nights. He finds a job playing jazz piano at a brothel, which in one way is fortunate: After he hones his skill as a piano player, a white bandleader hears him play and offers him a job touring with his band. Before this opportunity comes along, though, he works at other jobs, as a busboy and a flophouse cleaner. Sometimes he has no work and no money. One such time he actually fights a hungry dog for a pigeon. He wins, plucks the bird, cooks it on an open fire, and eats it. Another time, he has no money and has been stranded in New York City by the very bandleader who recruited him for his piano playing. This time he is forced to make ends meet by working for a drug dealer, delivering dope.

Occasions arise when he is tempted to take the path that is easier and handier, to do something that is immediately profitable but is also either illegal or immoral. Once, when he was still riding the streetcars as a way to spend his homeless nights, he was accosted by a streetcar conductor and he pulled a knife on the man. These tribulations serve to show Parks the limited options available to a young black man in the early 1930's. He could have gone a violent, criminal route; he chose instead to join the Civilian Conservation Corps, get married, become a father, and seek personal as well as financial fulfillment through a career in photography.

His introduction to photography comes about quite implausibly. Working as a railroad porter on a run between St. Paul and Seattle, he becomes fascinated with the photo stories in the *Life* magazines left behind by departing passengers. The work of the Depression-era photographers leads him to decide he can document in pictures the same kinds of things, and, with that in mind, he buys his first camera at a pawn shop in Seattle, Washington. He leaves his film for developing at Eastman Kodak in Minneapolis, and when he picks them up is complimented for their quality and offered his own show if his work continues to improve.

It does, of course, and he soon gets his own exhibit in Chicago and a subsequent chance to work with Roy Stryker at the Farm Security Administration in Washington, D.C. His most famous photograph, "American Gothic," a stark portrait of a black charwoman holding a mop and broom in front of the American flag, is one result of this experience. He goes on to work at *Life* magazine, becoming the first African American to join the staff of a major American magazine. Some of his most striking photojournalistic work is done during this period in his life.

All is not smooth sailing for him, however. He faces prejudice and even violence in the pursuit of his career. Once he is nearly assaulted by three Texans who object to his being kissed on the cheek in public by a white colleague. Then, when Malcolm X is assassinated, the Federal Bureau of Investigation fears Parks and his family might be targeted because of his friendship with Malcolm, and he is persuaded to take his family abroad for safety.

The memoir's title, *A Choice of Weapons*, suggests he is aware of his options and makes a conscious decision to follow his mother's teachings to make his life worthwhile. He chooses not to follow the readily expedient route so often taken by those who are disadvantaged. When he chooses a camera instead of a gun as his weapon against poverty and racism, he has already seen and experienced the side of life that drove other African American men to desperate measures. When he uses his camera to document and display those who have not escaped despair and hopelessness, he begins an odyssey of creative achievement unparalleled by any other African American man of his time.

Voices in the Mirror
Voices in the Mirror takes up Parks's story from where he left off in *To Smile in Autumn*, the second memoir, which opens in 1944, when his career as a photographer really takes off. It covers his career from 1978, when he worked as a photographer of the rich and famous and, more significantly for him as an artist, as a photographer of the poor, the downtrodden, and the desper-

ate. The memoir covers several decades of his life as he develops his craft. He works in the world of fashion, taking pictures for *Vogue* magazine, but he also works as a photojournalist at *Life* magazine taking pictures of life in black America and in other parts of the world. One of his more memorable stories captured in photographs is of an impoverished Brazilian boy, Flavio. The photo-essay had such an impact that thousands of dollars were donated to help the boy, who was close to dying, enabling Parks to bring the youth to the United States for treatment and eventual cure.

His encounters with famous people are recorded in some of his best-received portraits. He shoots activists such as Malcolm X and Elijah Muhammed, music and film legends including Duke Ellington, Louis Armstrong, Ingrid Bergman, and Roberto Rossellini, prominent athletes such as Muhammed Ali, artists such as Marcel Duchamp and Alexander Calder, and celebrities such as Gloria Vanderbilt. He conveys the glamour of Paris as well as the often-overlooked misery of Rio de Janeiro and the well-known but ignored, downtrodden, and newly militant section of New York's Harlem. His tales of encounters with the many different segments of national and international society communicates his intent to call attention to their often-undetected or unappreciated significance.

This volume not only records Parks's life during a significant time in his evolution as an artist, but it also provides insight into an important period of American history. The recounting of the harshness of African American existence during the Civil Rights movement is both informative and fascinating, and it reveals the paradoxes inherent in the oddly distorted African American dream.

Other Literary Forms

Parks published three novels: *The Learning Tree, Shannon,* and *Sun Stalker. The Learning Tree* is a young adult novel about an African American family in a small Kansas town in the 1920's. The protagonist is a teenage boy dealing with adolescence and racism. *Shannon,* his first attempt at an adult novel, is set in New

York in the early twentieth century and tells the story of a New York family and its tragic rise to prominence during the World War I era. He has several volumes of poetry, often accompanied by photographs, including *Gordon Parks: A Poet and His Camera*, *Gordon Parks: Whispers of Intimate Things, In Love, Moments Without Proper Names, Arias in Silence, Glimpses Toward Infinity, A Star for Noon*, and *Eyes with Winged Thoughts*. A collection of essays titled *Born Black* was published in 1971. A commentary accompanying a traveling exhibit of his photographs was published in 1997, titled *Half Past Autumn: A Retrospective*. He also published two technical books, *Flash Photography* and *Camera Portraits*.

Bibliography

Bohlen, Celestine. "Portrayer of the Black Experience Reflects on His Own." *The New York Times*, November 26, 2000, section 2, p. 36. Provides a brief profile of Parks's work in several genres, paying special attention to his work with photographic essays and his experiences working for *Life* magazine.

Boyd, Herb. "Gordon Parks: Still Smiling at Autumn." *Amsterdam News*, January 29, 2004, p. 8. Examines Parks's life and work shortly after his ninety-first birthday. Especially useful for those looking for information on his film *Solomon Northrup's Odyssey*.

Donloe, Darlene. *Gordon Parks*. Los Angeles: Melrose Square, 1993. Discusses his career as a photographer and the impact of his photographs, especially his serious documentaries of the poverty-stricken.

Halpern, David, ed. *Anteus 61*. New York: Ecco Press, 1988. Insightful selections from Parks's diary.

Harnan, Terry. *Gordon Parks: Black Photographer and Filmmaker.* Champaign, Ill.: Garrard, 1972. An illustrated, juvenile version of his biography that details the many obstacles Parks overcame on his way to fame as a photographer and filmmaker.

Henry, Matthew. "He Is a 'Bad Mother*$%@!#': *Shaft* and Contemporary Black Masculinity." *African American Review* 38, no. 1 (Spring, 2004): 119-126. Compares Parks's 1971 film with John Singleton's 2000 remake while exploring the changing notion of "blaxploitation" and gender relations.

Keller, Jullie. "The Living Tree: Gordon Parks." *Art Business News*, September, 2004, 1. Contains biographical information as well as comments by Parks about the most important episodes and persons in his life.

Miskowitz, Milton. "Gordon Parks: A Man for All Seasons." *Journal of Blacks in Higher Education*, July, 2003, 1. An interesting assessment of Parks's life and work.

Trachtman, Paul. "Too Hot to Handle." *Smithsonian* 34, no. 9 (December, 2003): 27-28. Explores Parks's work and reputation in the field of photography, looks at his experiences working at the Farm Security Administration in Washington, D.C., and summarizes the plot of his book *Sun Stalker.*

—*Jane L. Ball*

Suzan-Lori Parks

Playwright

Born: Fort Knox, Kentucky; May 10, 1963

LONG FICTION: *Getting Mother's Body*, 2003.
DRAMA: *The Sinner's Place*, pr. 1984, pb. 1995; *Betting on the Dust Commander*, pr. 1987, pb. 1995; *Imperceptible Mutabilities in the Third Kingdom*, pr. 1989, pb. 1995; *The Death of the Last Black Man in the Whole Entire World*, pr. 1990, pb. 1995; *Devotees in the Garden of Love*, pr. 1991, pb. 1995; *The America Play*, pr. 1993, pb. 1995; *The America Play, and Other Works*, pb. 1995; *Venus*, pr. 1996, pb. 1997; *In the Blood*, pr. 1999, pb. 2000; *Fucking A*, pr. 2000, pb. 2001; *The Red Letter Plays*, pb. 2001 (includes *In the Blood* and *Fucking A*); *Topdog/Underdog*, pr., pb. 2001.
SCREENPLAYS: *Anemone Me*, 1990; *Girl 6*, 1996.
RADIO PLAYS: *Pickling*, 1990; *The Third Kingdom*, 1990; *Locomotive*, 1991.

Achievements

Suzan-Lori Parks produced her first play, *The Sinner's Place*, in 1984, as a student at Mount Holyoke College. Her second, *Betting on the Dust Commander*, debuted in a Brooklyn garage in 1987, with Parks purchasing five folding chairs to accommodate the audience. From these modest beginnings, Parks has become one of the most celebrated American playwrights of her generation. *Imperceptible Mutabilities in the Third Kingdom*, produced in 1989, earned for Parks her first Obie Award for best new American play, and *The New York Times* named her the year's most promising playwright. Parks received her second Obie, for *Venus*, in 1996. Her next play, *In the Blood*, was a Pulitzer Prize finalist in 2000.

Parks has received numerous fellowships and grants, including the Guggenheim Fellowship in 2000 and the MacArthur Foundation Fellowship in 2001. In 2002, Parks became only the fourth African American and the first African American woman to receive the Pulitzer Prize in drama for her play *Topdog/Underdog*. She has taught at the University of Michigan, Yale University, and New York University. She also served as writer-in-residence at the New School for Social Research (now New School University) in New York from 1991 to 1992. In 2000, Parks became director of the Audrey Skirball Kernis Theatre Projects Writing for Performance program at the California Institute of the Arts.

Biography

Suzan-Lori Parks was born in Fort Knox, Kentucky, in 1963, the daughter of a career army officer. She spent her early childhood in several cities across the United States and lived in Germany, where she attended high school. She began writing short stories as a third grader and continued to focus on prose writing until her undergraduate years at Mount Holyoke College in Massachusetts. There, she met the distinguished author and essayist James Baldwin, who recognized her gift for dialogue and suggested that she explore drama.

Parks wrote her first play, *The Sinner's Place*, in 1984 as a student at Mount Holyoke. Though she earned an honors citation for her work, the college's theater department refused to stage the play. Parks graduated with honors in 1985 and moved to London for a year to study acting. *Betting on the Dust Commander*, her first play to be produced in New York City, debuted in 1987. Two years later, Parks received an Obie Award for *Imperceptible Mutabilities in the Third Kingdom*, and *The New York Times* named Parks the most promising playwright of 1989.

Following the successful production of *The Death of the Last Black Man in the Whole Entire World* at the Brooklyn Arts Council's BACA Downtown Theatre in 1990, Parks produced her next two plays, *Devotees in the Garden of Love* and *The America Play* on smaller stages in Lexington, Kentucky, and Dallas, Texas, respectively. *The America Play* later opened Off-Broadway at the Joseph Papp Public Theatre in New York City in 1994. Parks earned a second Obie Award in 1996, for her play *Venus*, which

845

also debuted at the Joseph Papp Public Theatre. Also in 1996, Parks wrote the screenplay for director Spike Lee's film *Girl 6.*

The productions of *In the Blood,* which was nominated for the Pulitzer Prize in drama in 2000, and *Fucking A,* both of which draw on elements in Nathaniel Hawthorne's classic novel, *The Scarlet Letter* (1850), continued to earn for Parks wide critical acclaim. She received the prestigious Guggenheim Fellowship in 2000 and the MacArthur Fellowship in 2001. Parks's growing reputation as a brilliant young playwright reached new heights in 2001 with the production of *Topdog/Underdog.* The play opened on July 22, 2001, at the Joseph Papp Public Theatre in New York City to rave reviews and earned for Parks the Pulitzer Prize in drama in 2002. *Topdog/Underdog* opened on Broadway in April of 2002, the first Broadway opening for an African American woman since Ntozake Shange, whose *for colored girls who have considered suicide/ when the rainbow is enuf* opened in 1976.

"I think it's a great moment for all African-American women

(AP/Wide World Photos)

writers," Parks has explained about becoming the first African American woman to receive the Pulitzer Prize in drama. "And anytime America recognizes a member of a certain group for excellence—one that has not traditionally been recognized—it's a great moment for American culture." Parks married Paul Oscher, a blues musician, in 2001, and joined the faculty of the California Institute of the Arts in Valencia, California, as the director of the Audrey Skirball Kernis Theatre Projects Writing for Performance program.

Analysis: Drama

"I am obsessed with resurrecting," Suzan-Lori Parks explained in a 1996 interview, "with bringing up the dead . . . and hearing their stories as they come into my head." Parks has often described the characters she creates as independent beings, as voices that relate their stories to her. Rather than writing them into existence, Parks allows the characters to speak themselves into being. Drawing on history, myth, and fantasy, she populates her plays with conventional and unconventional characters whose stories excavate the past in order to expose the truths and misconceptions about African American and American history. "Every play I write is about love and distance. And time," she explained in 1994. "And from that we can get things like history." She elaborates further in her essay "Possession," collected in *The America Play, and Other Works.* "Through each line of text, I'm rewriting the Time Line—creating history where it is and always was but has not yet been divined."

Language plays a vital role in this creation of history. Using what she calls "rep and rev" (repetition and revision), Parks often employs language as a musical refrain, with characters repeating phrases throughout her plays, the repetition of which adds different shades of meaning. In *Topdog/Underdog,* Booth rehearses his three-card monte street routine, addressing his imaginary audience: "Watch me close watch me close now: who-see-thuh-red-card-who-see-the-red-card?" As the words recur at various points in the play, they take on the quality of a chant, or a chorus that signifies the building tension between the brothers.

The question of identity in Parks's drama, as self-awareness and the identification of an individual within a group, is of central importance. As characters attempt to identify themselves, they must destroy the false identities and histories that have been attributed to them. In *Imperceptible Mutabilities in the Third Kingdom,* the characters Mona, Chona, and Verona, whose names have been changed to Molly, Charlene, and Veronica, meditate on the apparent mutability of their characters. "Once there was uh me named Mona who wondered what she'd be like if no one was watchin," Mona/Molly says. The Foundling Father of Parks's *The America Play,* whose setting is the Great Pit of History, is obsessed by Abraham Lincoln and decides to reenact his assassination in a traveling show. Like the character of Lincoln in *Topdog/Underdog,* who earns his living by reenacting Abraham Lincoln's assassination in a local arcade, the Foundling Father is a captive of history.

Imperceptible Mutabilities in the Third Kingdom
Rather than separating her first major play into traditional acts, Parks creates four separate stories that provide a nonlinear and sometimes surreal look at aspects of the African American experience in her *Imperceptible Mutabilities in the Third Kingdom.*

"Snails," the first section of the play, looks at a contemporary group of women who possess two names, one they have chosen and another that has been imposed on them. The second section, "Third Kingdom," re-creates the tragic Middle Passage, through which enslaved Africans journeyed on their way to America, and the details of which are narrated by characters such as Kin-Seer, Us-Seer, and Over-Seer. "Open House," the third section, depicts the life of Aretha Saxon, a black servant/slave in the household of the white Saxon family. Aretha's departure from the family is occasioned by the removal with pliers of all of her teeth. The play's final section, "Greeks," is a modern interpretation of Homer's *Odyssey* (c. 750 B.C.E.; English translation, 1614), with Mr. Seargant Smith in the role of Odysseus. Hoping to earn "his Distinction" in the army, Seargant Smith spends most of his life away from his family, who await his return and the honor he hopes to bring back with him.

The four stories in *Imperceptible Mutabilities in the Third Kingdom* depict characters whose identity and culture are marginalized by others. From the three women in "Snails," whose identities are studied and inevitably altered by the invasive Lutsky, to Miss Faith's extraction of Aretha Saxon's teeth in an act that functions metaphorically as a means of extracting Aretha from the Saxon family history, Parks dramatizes the struggle of African Americans against cultural, historical, and linguistic sabotage. A critical and popular success, *Imperceptible Mutabilities in the Third Kingdom* earned for Parks her first Obie Award for best new American play. *The New York Times* also named her 1989's most promising young playwright.

Venus

Venus received mixed reviews for its portrayal of an African woman whose unconventional physiognomy becomes the basis for her exhibition in a traveling sideshow in Europe. Parks based her play on a historical character, Saartjie Baartman, a South African woman whose body was displayed publicly in London and Paris in the early nineteenth century. Dubbed the Hottentot Venus, Baartman became a popular spectacle for white audiences who were fascinated and revolted by her appearance. After her death, Baartman's sexual organs and buttocks were preserved and housed in the Musée de l'Homme in Paris until the late twentieth century.

As the play opens, Venus is a popular attraction in Mother Showman's traveling show of Nine Human Wonders in London. Because slavery has been outlawed in England, Mother Showman's captivity of Venus sparks a debate about whether such exhibitions constitute slavery. Venus eventually escapes to Paris, where she falls under the influence of the Baron Docteur, who falls in love with Venus but also assures his colleagues that he intends to make her the object of scientific study. A twisted custody battle ensues as Mother Showman and Baron Docteur fight over who has the right to exhibit Venus.

In the character of Venus, Parks explores the objectification of human beings, and particularly African Americans, whose humanity was denied in the nineteenth century (and beyond) on the basis of pseudoscientific theories that reinforced prejudices against physical and cultural difference. Venus, a woman who desires to be treated with love and respect, becomes an oddity in a circus sideshow, reduced to little more in the public consciousness than her "great heathen buttocks."

In the Blood

A modern interpretation of Nathaniel Hawthorne's novel *The Scarlet Letter, In the Blood* depicts a homeless woman's struggle to care for herself and her family. Hester, La Negrita, and her five children, all from different fathers, live under a bridge, making what little money they have from collecting cans. Hester spends much of her time practicing her writing (she knows only the letter *A*). As her health declines, Hester appeals for assistance to a street doctor, her welfare caseworker, a former lover and father of her first child, and eventually a local reverend, who is the father of her youngest child.

The actors who portray Hester's five children also double as adult characters. In a series of stage confessions that resemble the chorus of a Greek tragedy, these characters (Amiga Gringa, Chilli, The Doctor, The Welfare Lady, and Reverend D) explain the ways in which they have taken advantage of Hester, who has been sexually exploited by almost everyone whom she knows.

In the Blood is a hopeless tale of a woman undone by poverty and a social system that cannot meet her needs. Individuals in a position to help Hester can think only of how to use her. The word "slut," scrawled on the wall of Hester's makeshift home under the bridge in the play's opening scene, serves a purpose similar to Hawthorne's scarlet letter on Hester Prynne's chest. Both Hesters are defined almost exclusively by what their societies perceive as aberrant sexuality. When every means of salvation is exhausted, Hester is left, in the final scene of the play, with the word "slut," this time on the lips of her oldest child. Hester's murder of her son Jabber at the end of the play functions as an attempt to efface the word, and the identification, both of which have followed her throughout the play. A critical and popular success, *In the Blood* was named a finalist for the 2000 Pulitzer Prize in drama.

Topdog/Underdog

Departing from the unorthodox staging and characterization of her previous plays, Parks presents what appears on the surface to be a traditional tale of sibling rivalry in *Topdog/Underdog*, which opened at the Joseph Papp Public Theatre on July 22, 2001, and opened on Broadway at the Ambassador Theatre in New York less than a year later. However, Parks links the struggle of her two characters, named Lincoln and Booth, to more complex and historical struggles of race, family, and identity.

The two brothers, Lincoln and Booth, share a seedy urban apartment. Lincoln, a former street hustler whose skill at the card game three-card monte is legendary, now works at an arcade where he impersonates Abraham Lincoln for patrons who pay money to reenact his assassination. Booth, who aspires to his brother's greatness at three-card monte, relies on Lincoln's paychecks and whatever he can steal to make ends meet.

As Lincoln and Booth, so named as a joke by their father, try to plan for their future, they confront the realities of the past: their abandonment by their parents and the buried animosities toward each other. In the play's final scene, Booth flies into a rage when Lincoln bests him at three-card monte, thereby winning the family legacy (five hundred dollars rolled in a stocking) left to each son when their parents fled. Lincoln's violent end is foreshadowed by his job at the arcade and by his and Booth's names. How each brother accepts and realizes the roles imposed by family history, circumstance, and the inherent opposition of their names, however, makes the play a deeply compelling one. In 2002, shortly after its debut on Broadway, *Topdog/Underdog* earned for Parks the Pulitzer Prize in drama.

Other Literary Forms

Though her literary reputation rests primarily on her dramatic writing, Suzan-Lori Parks has also written several screenplays: *Anemone Me*, an independent film released in New York in 1990, *Girl 6*, directed by Spike Lee and released in 1996, and two scripts for Jodie Foster and Danny Glover. Parks has also written several essays that have been published in theater journals.

Bibliography

Brantley, Ben. "A Woman Named Hester, Wearing a Familiar Letter." *The New York Times*, March 17, 2003, p. E1. A review of Parks's controversial play and discussion of its name and cast members.

Brown, Rosellen. "Stumbling from Stage to Page." Review of *Getting Mother's Body*, by Suzan-Lori Parks. *New Leader* 86, no. 3 (May/June, 2003): 37-39. A good review of Parks's first novel.

"For Love or Money." Review of *Getting Mother's Body*, by Suzan-Lori Parks. *Ebony* 58, no. 11 (September, 2003): 28-30. A brief but accessible review of Parks's first novel.

Frieze, James. "*Imperceptible Mutabilities in the Third Kingdom*: Suzan-Lori Parks and the Shared Struggle to Perceive." *Modern Drama* 41, no. 4 (Winter, 1998): 523. Frieze provides a detailed analysis of Parks's Obie Award-winning play, emphasizing the significance of identity in shaping the actions and thoughts of the play's characters.

Garrett, Shawn-Marie. "The Possession of Suzan-Lori Parks." *American Theatre* 17, no. 8 (October, 2000): 22. This essay provides some background on Parks's beginnings as a playwright and her unconventional approach to the writing process. Garrett provides a good overview of Parks's development as a playwright and the historical, political, and racial forces that inform her work.

Kakutani, Michiko. "First Novel by a Hand Already Famous." Review of *Getting Mother's Body*, by Suzan-Lori Parks. *The New York Times*, June 3, 2003, p. E1. A strong review of Parks's first novel.

Parks, Suzan-Lori. *The America Play, and Other Works*. New York: Theatre Communications Group, 1995. This volume combines a sampling of Parks's early plays, including *Betting on the Dust Commander* and *Devotees in the Garden of Love*, with three essays that provide insight into the aims and methods of Parks's writing.

Pochoda, Elizabeth. "I See Thuh Black Card . . . ?" *Nation* 274, no. 20 (May 27, 2002): 36. A review of Parks's *Topdog/Underdog*, following its Broadway debut at the Ambassador Theatre in New York, which touches on the major themes of the Pulitzer Prize-winning play.

Wilmer, S. E. "Restaging the Nation: The Work of Suzan-Lori Parks." *Modern Drama* 43, no. 3 (Fall, 2000): 442. Examines the postmodern elements of Parks's drama and provides analysis of most of her major plays.

Writer. "Suzan-Lori Parks." 117, no. 1 (January, 2004): 66-67. Contains a brief biography, a summary of her first novel, a general look at her works, and her advice for those beginning a writing career.

— *Philip Bader*

Ann Petry

Novelist and short-story writer

Born: Old Saybrook, Connecticut; October 12, 1908
Died: Old Saybrook, Connecticut; April 28, 1997

LONG FICTION: *The Street*, 1946; *Country Place*, 1947; *The Narrows*, 1953.
SHORT FICTION: *Miss Muriel, and Other Stories*, 1971.
CHILDREN'S/YOUNG ADULT LITERATURE: *The Drugstore Cat*, 1949; *Harriet Tubman: Conductor on the Underground Railroad*, 1955; *Tituba of Salem Village*, 1964; *Legends of the Saints*, 1970.

Achievements

Ann Petry's receipt of a Houghton Mifflin Literary Fellowship in 1945 (and an award of twenty-five hundred dollars) enabled her to complete *The Street*, which went on to become the first novel by an African American woman to sell more than one million copies. In 1977 she was awarded a National Endowment for the Arts grant and in 1983 received a D. Litt. from Boston's Suffolk University. In 1992 the reissuing of *The Street* renewed Petry's reputation as an important American writer and introduced a new generation to her work. Her death in April, 1997, was eulogized publicly by Connecticut senator Christopher Dodd, and the following year MacArthur Fellow Max Roach premiered "Theater Pieces" (December, 1998), an adaptation of Petry's tale of a jazz love triangle, "Solo on the Drums," featuring Ruby Dee, Ossie Davis, and Roach.

Biography

Ann Lane Petry was born to Peter Clarke Lane and Bertha James Lane on October 12, 1908, joining a family that had lived for several generations as the only African American citizens of the resort community of Old Saybrook, Connecticut. The descendant of a runaway Virginian slave, Petry admitted to never having felt herself to be a true New Englander; her cultural legacy was not that of the typical Yankee, and as a small child she came to know the isolating effects of racism after being stoned by white children on her first day of school. Nevertheless, her family distinguished itself within the community and boasted numerous professionals: Her grandfather was a licensed chemist; her father, aunt, and uncle became pharmacists; and her mother worked as a chiropodist. In 1902 Peter Lane opened a pharmacy in Old Saybrook, for which Ann herself trained. Inspired by the example of her many independent female rela-

(AP/Wide World Photos)

tives—women who had, she explained, "abandoned the role of housewife in the early twentieth century"—in 1931 Ann secured a degree in pharmacology from the University of Connecticut, the only black graduate in her class. She worked in family-owned pharmacies until 1938, when she met and married Louisiana-born George D. Petry and moved with him to his home in Harlem.

Petry had begun writing fiction seriously in high school after an antagonistic teacher grudgingly praised her work as having real potential, and she wrote steadily thereafter (although to no immediate success). With the move to New York City, her writing career began in earnest. She quickly secured jobs with various Harlem newspapers as a reporter, editor, and copywriter, working for the *Amsterdam News* and *The People's Voice* (the latter a weekly begun by African American clergyman and politician Adam Clayton Powell, Jr.). She also briefly acted in the American Negro Theatre and worked on a study conducted by the New York Foundation investigating the effects of segregation on black children.

Participation in a creative writing seminar at Columbia University greatly influenced Petry during this time. Her first published short story, "On Saturday the Siren Sounds at Noon," appeared in a 1943 issue of *The Crisis* (a magazine published by the National Association for the Advancement of Colored People) and not only earned her twenty dollars but also led to her discovery by an editor at Houghton Mifflin. He encouraged her to submit preliminary work on what would become *The Street*, for which Petry received the 1945 Houghton Mifflin Literary Fellowship and a stipend of twenty-five hundred dollars. Thus she was able to complete her novel, translating nearly a decade spent observing the difficulties of aspiring African Americans in the urban North into the powerful story of single mother Lutie Johnson and her star-crossed eight-year-old Bub. While her trenchant insights into the play of race and class as conjoined factors stifling Lutie's dreams recall Richard Wright's landmark *Native Son* (1940), Petry's recognition of the role of gender in the discriminatory equation made *The Street* a groundbreaking work on its own and another expression of the woman-centered ethic she had learned from her family. Published in 1946, *The Street* received both critical and popular acclaim and sold 1.5 million copies—at the time the largest audience ever reached by an African American woman. The fame accompanying that success overwhelmed Petry, however, and in 1948 she and George returned to the obscurity of Old Saybrook, where they bought the two-hundred-year-old house of an old sea captain and reared their daughter Elizabeth Ann.

Petry's subsequent fiction did not receive the same kind of praise accorded her first novel, despite her continued willingness to tackle difficult racial themes in *The Narrows* and, in *Country Place*, explore the terrain of small-town white America from its own assumed vantage point, a project seldom undertaken by black writers even today. In 1971 she issued a collection of her short fiction, *Miss Muriel, and Other Stories*. She also contributed stories and essays to numerous magazines and journals. Perhaps in response to the indifference accorded her adult fiction, she began writing for children during the time she was raising Elizabeth and produced such classics as *The Drugstore Cat, Harriet Tubman,* and *Tituba of Salem Village.* The latter two novels, about actual historical personages, reflect her determination to place art in the service of an honest picture of American racial history; they have become young adult classics and are perhaps more widely read than the adult fiction on which her initial reputation was built.

Petry spent the second half of her life away from the hurly-burly of publishing centers and for the most part outside the rarefied walls of the university; David Streitfeld of *The Washington Post* said that she "had little tolerance for fools or academics, two categories she regarded as essentially synonymous." She did hold a visiting professorship at the University of Hawaii in 1974-1975 and in 1977 received a grant from the National Endowment for the Arts. Boston's Suffolk University awarded her a D.Litt. degree in 1983. She had the satisfaction of seeing her daughter continue the legacy of strong female achievement by becoming an attorney.

Petry died at the age of eighty-eight in a convalescent home in the same community where she was born, still married to the man who had briefly taken her out of New England and made possible the launching of her lifelong career.

Analysis: Short Fiction

While Ann Petry's fiction typically involves African Americans struggling against the crippling impact of racism, her overarching theme involves a more broadly defined notion of prejudice that targets class and gender as well as race. Thus her aims are consistently broader than racial critique, since she regularly exposes the consequences of America's hierarchical social systems and its capitalistic materialism. That vision explains what might otherwise seem to be inconsistencies of direction in Petry's career: her decision, for example, following the potent racial protest of *The Street* to focus her next novel, *Country Place*, on a white community's postwar crises of adjustment or her movement into the realm of children's literature. Like her contemporaries, black and white alike, who came of age in the 1930's, she adopted a social realist aesthetic committed to documenting the obstacles to human fulfillment imposed on those at the margins of American prosperity. As she explained,

> I find it difficult to subscribe to the idea that art exists for art's sake. It seems to me that all truly great art is propaganda . . . [and fiction], like all other forms of art, will always reflect the political, economic, and social structure of the period in which it was created.

Her work also reveals an increasingly overt Christian existentialist vision celebrating the individual's potential for spiritual liberation, through which an entire culture might come to relinquish its crippling prejudices.

Rather than celebrating the American ideal of self-making with which her native New England is so closely associated, Petry exposes the illusions it has fostered and depicts their graphic costs to those relegated to the periphery of American possibility. Racism invites Petry's most scathing attacks, not only for the material hardship it forces upon people of color but also for the psychological and cultural distortions it produces. At her most biting, Petry lampoons the absurdist systems of human classification into which racist societies ultimately fall. Generally, her perspective is a tragic one, however, grounded in the recognition that confronting racism necessitates confronting history itself.

One of Petry's most insistent indictments of America's hypocrisy targets the class distinctions that parallel and overlap racism as forces negating individual hope for a better life, a more just world. Repeatedly she shows how Americans in quest of the material security, comfort, and status that propel middle-class striving acquiesce to soul-numbing labor and retreat into a moral inflexibility that blindly sanctions aggressive self-interest. In Petry's fiction the culture's high-flown rhetoric is belied by rigid social hierarchies that produce venal, grasping have-nots at the bottom, whose ambitions mimic the ruthless acquisitiveness of those at the top.

Petry's most important characters are those who reject the fallacy of the self-made individual existing independently of the world or the continuing legacy of the past. Though that perspective assumes certain mechanistic dimensions in her work, she does not concede full authority to deterministic necessity; the dice may be loaded against her protagonists, but the game is not inexorably mandated to play itself out to any single predetermined end. Her characters sometimes prove capable of personal growth that moves them toward a common humanity with the potential to fuel real and far-reaching change in the social order itself. Petry's narratives of personal transformation often grow from characters' chance movements across rigid cultural boundaries; the resulting crises test the spiritual flexibility of many others besides her protagonists.

Overlooked by academic critics, Petry's children's books offer tantalizing clues to her larger agenda. Their emphasis upon personal fearlessness in rethinking entrenched assumptions and disengaging from unjust systems invites comparison with numerous figures from her adult fiction. Moreover, in applying their new insights, these characters undertake subtly revolutionary actions that defy the cultural boundaries that had previously defined their lives. It takes a saint, perhaps, to challenge a predatory universe with an alternative vision of love, but having told children in *Legends of the Saints* that true sanctity is a function of bravery, Petry seems to evaluate her other fictional characters on their receptivity to grace as an antidote to hate.

Miss Muriel, and Other Stories
While Petry's reputation rests primarily on her novels, she saw herself quite differently at the start of her career:

> I set out to be a writer of short stories and somehow ended up as a novelist—possibly because there simply wasn't room enough within the framework of the short story to do the sort of thing I wanted to do.

Yet the pieces in *Miss Muriel, and Other Stories*, written over the course of several decades, provide a compact and provocative introduction to her imaginative concerns, chief among them her sensitivity to racism's psychological as well as material consequences.

"Like a Winding Sheet"
In the prizewinning story "Like a Winding Sheet," she depicts the physical and mental toll exacted by the nature of work in an industrial society where laborers are treated as interchangeable machines. The story dramatizes how the corrosive humiliations of prejudice, when added to work stresses, can trigger blind and catastrophic violence. A husband's inability to challenge the string of racist assaults on his dignity delivered both during and after his exhausting night shift at a World War II defense plant not only make him incapable of imagining benign white behavior (even in the face of apologies) but also cause him to respond to his wife's affectionate teasing with the beating he is forbidden to direct at his real oppressors. While racism provides the context for his rage, however (her unwitting use of the word "nigger" echoing the hostile epithet regularly used against him by the outside world), his reaction exposes the starkness of the struggle between male and female in Petry's world and the so-

bering betrayals it can provoke. The title image begins as the bedsheet in which he has tossed and turned all day in a futile effort to sleep, but his wife jokingly casts it as a burial linen—a reference ironically appropriate to his sense of himself as the walking dead. By story's end that reference has assumed sinister dimensions as he feels trapped by the violence he is committing but cannot control, "and he thought it was like being enmeshed in a winding sheet."

"In Darkness and Confusion"

"In Darkness and Confusion" fictionalizes the Harlem riot of 1943, an event sparked by the wounding of a black soldier whose uniform provided scant protection on his own home front. The story's protagonist, William Jones, a drugstore porter who, despite endless humiliations, has worked hard all of his life to secure a better world for his son Sam, suddenly loses that son to the wartime draft and the dangers of a Jim Crow world at the southern training camp to which he is sent. When Sam, who once aspired to college and his share of the American Dream, protests an order to move to the back of the bus and then shoots the aggressive military police officer who gave it, he is court-martialed and sentenced to twenty years of hard labor.

As Jones broods over this news in a Harlem bar, he watches as another uniformed black G.I., this one standing in the supposedly more egalitarian north, tries to help a black woman being beaten by a white policeman, punches the lawman, runs, and is summarily gunned down. Jones erupts into a violence ignited by grief and rage and becomes the leader of a mob. When his churchgoing wife learns of their son's fate, she too turns to retributive action with an explosive passion that kills her: Her religion proves unable to provide her with the strength to resume her burden and go on with her life. Nor is the mob's looting of local merchants legitimized, for it is produced by the intoxicating siren song of white capitalist materialism, with which the culture regularly deflects attention from matters of real social justice. The riot leaves Jones more completely bereft than he had been before, for it literally costs him his heart and soul, even as it finally allows him to understand the anomie of his disaffected teenage niece, who has baldly scorned his lifetime of exhausting effort for the whites, who in the end allow them "only the nigger end of things."

"The New Mirror"

Petry as skillfully evokes the impact of racism on the black bourgeoisie as she does on the proletariat, and in several tales she demonstrates how a lifetime of belittlement and intimidation can erode one's ability to act ethically in the world. In "Miss Muriel" and "The New Mirror," Petry creates a black family much like her own—the Layens are professionals who own the pharmacy in a small New England town. The adolescent girl who narrates these tales speaks of "the training in issues of race" she has received over the years, not only through the casual bigotries she has witnessed but also through the painful self-consciousness of respectable people like her parents, whose behavior is a continual exercise in refuting cultural stereotypes while carefully preserving proudly held racial loyalties. In "The New Mirror" the ironies are more overt, cleaner. Mr. Layen's decision to take a day off to outfit himself with a new pair of false teeth leads his unknowing wife to an excruciating encounter with police, from whom she withholds her fear that the absent Layen may have become another black man who deserts his family as a delayed response to a lifetime of indignities within the white patriarchal social order. Layen's surprising secrecy leads his daughter to realize that even securing a new set of teeth subjects a black male to humiliation, in this case taking the form of the grinning Sambos and toothless Uncle Toms he fears his dental problems will call to mind. The child learns to use the codes by which the black middle class shields itself from white contempt—just as she shoulders her own share of the burden of always acting with an eye on the reputation of "the Race": She thus learns why "all of us people with this dark skin must help hold the black island inviolate."

"Miss Muriel"

The title story of the volume, "Miss Muriel," operates more subtly in its exploration of the racist preoccupations inculcated within and often unwillingly relinquished by its victims. The title itself refers to a white racist joke the young narrator innocently relates to one of Aunt Sophronia's black suitors—a joke in which an African American trying to buy a Muriel cigar is up-braided for not showing the proper respect for white woman-hood by asking instead for a "Miss" Muriel. The child is bluntly chastised for voicing such "nigger" put-downs in one of the many moments of confusion she suffers over the inconsistent and seemingly arbitrary management of prejudices operating among the adults around her: her aunt's unpopular courtship by Bemish, a white member of their upstate New York commu-nity; the equal dismay with which Mr. Layen regards Sophronia's other suitor, the "tramp piano player" Chink, who evokes the "low" culture of the black masses, from which the bourgeois Layen has distanced himself as part of his accommodation to a scornful white world; the contempt quietly directed against the homosexual partner of her cherished Uncle Johno; the colorist hierarchies of all the African Americans she knows (even when the lightest-skinned among them eschew the opportunity to "pass"). At the end of the story, when the black men in her circle have effectively driven Bemish out of town for his persistent wooing of Sophronia, the narrator brokenheartedly confronts their hypocrisy, yelling, "You both stink. You stink like dead bats. You and your goddamn Miss Muriel." Internalizing such divi-siveness as they have just enforced directly clashes with the other set of values she has been taught, and the two are starkly juxta-posed early in the story when the child muses:

> If my objections to Mr. Bemish are because he's white . . . then I have been 'trained' on the subject of race just as I have been trained to be a Christian. . . .

It is one of the paradoxes of bigotry that its victims may become its emissaries, at the price of their most cherished beliefs.

"The Witness"

Petry revisits this theme in a number of ways throughout the col-lection. Against the most aggressive forms of white hatred directed at her characters, there is no defense except a temporary abandonment of one's human dignity. "The Witness" presents the case of a retired black college professor who takes a high school teaching position in a northern white community. Called upon to assist the local pastor in counseling delinquent adolescents, he finds himself their prey as they kidnap him and force him to watch their sexual abuse of a young white woman. Having at one point coerced him to place his hand on the girl, they effectively blackmail him into complicit silence about their crime, for he is paralyzed by the specter of being publicly accused of the ultimate racial taboo. His exemplary life and professional stature cannot protect him from such sordid insinuations, and he bitterly describes himself in his moral impotence as "another poor scared black bastard who was a witness."

"The Necessary Knocking on the Door"

In "The Necessary Knocking on the Door" a similar loss of agency is made bitingly ironic by the context in which Alice Knight's dilemma unfolds: A participant at a conference about the role of Christianity in the modern world, she finds herself unable to master her dislike for a white woman dying in the hotel room across the hall from hers—a woman who had earlier in the day refused to be seated next to a "nigger" and had thus awakened in Alice the bitterness that a lifetime of such indignities has nurtured. Her hardened heart is jolted the next day by news of the woman's death during the night—and her own guilty knowledge that she alone had heard the woman's distress but had let the hated epithet reduce her to that "animal," "outcast," "obscene" state it implies—not because it had been leveled at her but because she had let it rob her of her Christian commitment to do good to those who harm her. Even her own dreams indict Alice: "The octopus moonlight" pitilessly asserts, "Yours is the greater crime. A crime. A very great crime. It was a crime. And we were the witnesses." Like other African American writers before and since, Petry warns that prejudice delivers its most sinister harm when it saps its victims' capacity for decency and compassion and enlists them in the service of a gospel of irreparable division. In these stories Petry vividly captures the spiritual anguish of discovering that one's own grievances can weaken rather than deepen one's moral courage.

"The Bones of Louella Brown"
Her handling of white perspectives on racism is more unyielding. The absurdities into which segregationist practices lead multiracial societies (including the pseudosciences hunting frantically for physical evidence of racial "difference") are lampooned in "The Bones of Louella Brown." The most prestigious family in Massachusetts, the Bedfords, find their plans to build a chapel for its deceased members compromised when an undertaker's assistant confuses the bones of an African American maid with the sole noblewoman in their clan and, because of the "shocking" similarities of hair, teeth, height, and bone mass between the two skeletons, cannot differentiate the two. That alone is newsworthy enough to attract a Boston reporter sniffing for scandal, but the story gets juicier when it becomes clear there is every likelihood that the segregation that has been a hallmark of the cemetery in question will be permanently breached once it can no longer guarantee that "black" bones will not commingle in the same park with "white" bones. After Mrs. Brown makes a series of ghostly visitations to principals in the story, they decide to acknowledge the truth with an epitaph explaining that either woman (or both) may lie in the crypt, along with the admission of their common humanity: "They both wore the breastplate of faith and love, and for a helmet, the hope of salvation." Here too Petry moves her reader beyond social contexts and into metaphysical ones by reminding readers that this story of dry bones (an unmistakable homage to a favorite trope of black oral tradition) is also a meditation on mortality itself, which exposes such preoccupation with earthly pecking orders for the consummate folly it is.

"The Migraine Workers"
"The Migraine Workers" offers another example of white protagonists brought up short in the knowledge of their moral blindness in following the unquestioned attitudes of a lifetime. Pedro Gonzalez, proud owner of a successful truckstop, sud-

denly finds himself staring into a trailer full of migrant laborers exuding a human misery more palpable than anything he has ever encountered. Outraged by the black driver, who blithely explains how he usually hides such scenes from public scrutiny, Pedro feeds the people with the surplus food left on his premises by other haulers. When he later discovers that an elderly man from the crew has hidden himself in the area and is living off what he can scavenge from the truckstop, his first impulse is to have the man removed by the police. It is only when his longtime assistant challenges his callousness and points to the resources they could easily spare for the man's upkeep that Pedro realizes how his own fleshy body indicts him of complicity in a system of polarized haves and have-nots: migraine-producing epiphanies indeed in the land of equal opportunity.

"Mother Africa"

Other stories in the collection evoke the mysterious private centers of grief hidden in the human heart: "Olaf and His Girl Friend" and "Solo on the Drums" show Petry's interest in African American music as an exquisite, untranslatable evocation of that pain. "Mother Africa" introduces Emanuel Turner, another of Petry's junk men, whose business indicts the acquisitive mandate of American consumer culture. Years earlier, the loss of his wife and baby in childbirth had robbed him of any further desire for self-improvement; as a junk dealer he is free from anxious adherence to other people's standards of worth or accomplishment, and because he is his own man, he is a welcome figure to those around him. All that changes when a friend blesses him with the huge sculpture of a female nude being discarded by a wealthy white woman. The statue seduces Turner back into a realm of self-conscious striving as he tries to live up to its grandeur; in the process he loses his liberty and the easy rapport he has had with his neighbors. Convinced that she is a mythic evocation of Africa itself, he resents the prudish efforts of others to clothe her as missionaries had once done to his ancestors. Thus he is stunned to learn that this dark madonna is not a black woman at all but a white woman—the oxidized metal had misled him.

By parodying the assumed black male obsession with white women in this way, Petry implies that the real hunger at work is for authentic enunciation of the African American experience, a hunger left unsatisfied when Turner hurriedly rushes to sell the piece for scrap. In succumbing to the desire to make a world fit for his queenly companion, Turner submits himself for the first time in twenty-five years to the pressures of conformity and material acquisition. Is it love which so compromises him?—or are the statue's racial associations Petry's warnings against the lure of cultural standards derived from the spiritually bankrupt spheres of white consumer capitalism? Taken together, the stories in this collection offer tantalizing variations upon Petry's most insistent themes.

Other Literary Forms

Ann Petry has received critical recognition for her adult novels: *The Street, Country Place,* and *The Narrows.* In 1949 she began a distinguished career as a writer of children's literature with the publication of *The Drugstore Cat,* to be followed by the now-classic biographical novels *Harriet Tubman: Conductor of the Underground Railroad* and *Tituba of Salem Village.* She has also published a devotional work, *Legends of the Saints,* in addition to various articles for small periodicals.

Bibliography

Bell, Bernard. "Ann Petry's Demythologizing of American Culture and Afro-American Character." In *Conjuring: Black Women, Fiction, and Literary Tradition,* edited by Marjorie Pryse and Hortense J. Spillers. Bloomington: Indiana University Press, 1985. An argument for moving Petry out of the shadow of male contemporaries like Richard Wright to permit her fiction the proper reevaluation it deserves.

Bernard, Emily. "'Raceless' Writing and Difference: Ann Petry's *Country Place* and the African American Literary Canon." *Studies in American Fiction* 33, no. 1 (Spring, 2005): 87-120. Examines the significance of *Country Place*'s exclusion from the canon. The author argues that the novel does in fact deal with race, but that it does so in a subtle and complex but ultimately very important way.

Bryant, Jacqueline. "Postures of Resistance in Ann Petry's *The Street.*" *CLA Journal* 45, no. 4 (June, 2002): 444-460. A discussion of the importance of racism and resistance against it in Petry's book. Also includes an explanation of some of Petry's later thoughts on racial issues.

Clark, Keith. "A Distaff Dream Deferred? Ann Petry and the Art of Subversion." *African American Review* 26 (Fall, 1992): 495-505. A study of Petry's interest in the ways black women respond to the American Dream while subverting it to their own ends.

Dubek, Laura. "White Family Values in Ann Petry's *Country Place.*" *MELUS* 29, no. 2 (Summer, 2004): 55-77. Discusses the intersection of ideas about whiteness and blackness in Petry's novel, arguing that *Country Place* completely rejects the racist attitudes common in postwar America.

Ervin, Hazel Arnett, and Hilary Holladay, eds. *Ann Petry's Short Fiction: Critical Essays.* Westport, Conn.: Praeger, 2004. A collection of essays addressing Petry's less well studied short stories, including issues of gender, race, and folklore.

Gross, Theodore. "Ann Petry: The Novelist as Social Critic." In *Black Fiction: New Studies in the Afro-American Novel Since 1945,* edited by A. Robert Lee. New York: Barnes and Noble, 1980. A discussion of Petry's strong commitment to an aesthetic of social realism that puts art in the service of political, economic, and societal transformation and justice.

Hawkins, Alfonso W. "The Nurture of African American Youth in the Fiction of Ann Petry, Alice Childress, and Gloria Naylor." *CLA Journal* 46, no. 4 (June, 2003) 457-478. Provides interesting insights into the influence that nurture—and many other societal forces—have over African American youths, both in fiction and in life.

Hernton, Calvin. "The Significance of Ann Petry." In *The Sexual Mountain and Black Women Writers.* New York: Doubleday, 1987. An analysis of the relationship between Petry's fiction and that of contemporary black women writers, particularly in its wedding of social protest and violence.

Hicks, Heather J. "Rethinking Realism in Ann Petry's *The Street*." *MELUS* 27, no. 4 (Winter, 2002): 89-106. Provides an interesting analysis of the novel's characters and selected passages and compares the work with that of Henry James.

_____. "'This Strange Communion': Surveillance and Spectatorship in Ann Petry's *The Street*." *African American Review* 37, no. 1 (Spring, 2003): 21-38. Argues that the literary community was right to acknowledge Petry's feminist ideals, a return to group Petry with African American male writers like Richard Wright and Chester Himes is also appropriate.

Petry, Ann. "A *MELUS* Interview: Ann Petry—The New England Connection." Interview by Mark Wilson. *MELUS* 15 (Summer, 1988): 71-84. A discussion with Petry about her early life and the first decades of her writing career.

Washington, Gladys. "A World Made Cunningly: A Closer Look at Ann Petry's Short Fiction." *College Language Association Journal* 30 (September, 1986): 14-29. A critical argument for tracing Petry's important themes and their evolving nuances through her understudied short stories.

— *Barbara Kitt Seidman*

Dudley Randall

Poet and publisher

Born: Washington, D.C.; January 14, 1914
Died: Southfield, Michigan; August 5, 2000

POETRY: *Poem Counterpoem*, 1966 (with Margaret Danner); *Cities Burning*, 1968; *Love You*, 1970; *More to Remember: Poems of Four Decades*, 1971; *After the Killing*, 1973; *A Litany of Friends: New and Selected Poems*, 1981, revised 1983.

NONFICTION: *Broadside Memories: Poets I Have Known*, 1975.

EDITED TEXTS: *For Malcolm: Poems on the Life and the Death of Malcolm X*, 1967 (with Margaret G. Burroughs); *Black Poetry: A Supplement to Anthologies Which Exclude Black Poets*, 1969; *The Black Poets*, 1971; *Homage to Hoyt Fuller*, 1984.

Achievements

Beyond his own poetry, it was as an editor and publisher that Dudley Randall's literary talents were most significant. Randall's principal literary accomplishment was the founding of Broadside Press in September, 1965. With an initial investment of twelve dollars, he began by issuing a run of one broadside (a poem printed on a single sheet). These inexpensive broadsides could be folded and carried to be read on lunch breaks, on buses, or virtually anytime, anywhere. They could also be posted just about anywhere as well; thus, Randall's idea succeeded in bringing poetry to the ordinary citizens of the community: The venture was more educational than commercial. (This idea has since been imitated by small presses all over the country.) Within a few years, Broadside was publishing anthologies, volumes by new poets, criticism, and recordings. By example, other black writers also began to establish independent presses that specialized in reaching the black community with inexpensive editions of poetry, most notably Haki R. Madhubuti's Third World Press.

One can fairly credit Randall, then, as one of the most influential black publishers of his time: His refusal to place commercial interests ahead of literary education helped to inform a whole generation of the richness and diversity of black poetic traditions. In doing so, he introduced new African American writers, and he fostered an awareness of the reciprocity between black writers in the United States and Africa.

Randall's own poetry, however, was not without acclaim in its own right. While the critical reception in reviews was laudatory, however, thorough critical appraisal was oddly sparse, at best. Despite the lack of proper critical assessment, Randall remains a significant member of the "postrenaissance" generation that followed the Harlem Renaissance. Along with Robert Hayden and Gwendolyn Brooks, he assimilated into his poetry the variety of techniques and experimentation offered by modernism without extensive imitation of any of the modernists. Despite his lack of wide publication until the early 1960's, Randall pursued poetry consistently with an openness to sources the world over as well as with a persistent study of the literary heritage of blacks. Fusing the eloquence and power of the classical lyric with the terseness and common sense of the oral tradition, yet remaining in the context of modernism, Randall's voice concentrates on the integrity of craft, music, and delight in his poetry. His rhythm is graceful without becoming strained, his tone compassionate without becoming sentimental. Randall's images are precise without becoming obscure and his diction is relevant without becoming contrived. His themes are universal without becoming clichéd.

Even without widespread critical evaluation, Randall's work did not go unnoticed. In 1962, he received the Tompkins Award from Wayne State University for both poetry and fiction, and in 1966, he received the same award for poetry. In recognition of his contributions to black literature, he received the Kuumba Liberation Award in 1973. He was awarded National Endowment for the Humanities Fellowships in 1981 and 1986, and was named the first poet laureate of the city of Detroit in 1981. In 1996, Randall received a Lifetime Achievement Award from the National Endowment for the Arts.

Biography

Born in 1914 to Arthur and Ada Randall, Dudley Felker Randall spent his childhood in Washington, D.C., his birthplace, and in East St. Louis. His father was responsible for the young Randall's awareness of political commitment; he frequently campaigned for blacks seeking political office, and he took Randall with him to hear such speakers as James Weldon Johnson and W. E. B. Du Bois (although Randall reports that at the time he "preferred playing baseball"). Randall's public education continued when his family moved to Detroit. By this time, he was conscious not only of the political process, but also of black literature. Having first begun to write poetry at the early age of thirteen, Randall purchased a copy of Jean Toomer's *Cane* (1923) when he was sixteen; he was so impressed by Toomer's precise images and powerful symbolism that Toomer became—and remains—his favorite black poet. By 1930, the time of his graduation from the public school system, also at sixteen, Randall was well read in the major writers of the Harlem Renaissance.

After graduation in the midst of the Great Depression, Randall eventually found work as a foundry worker for the Ford Motor Company from 1932 to 1937. Sometime in 1933, he met the poet Robert Hayden, also living in Detroit, with whom he shared his poetry and discussed the major poets of the time. Their exchange of poems and ideas was to help him sharpen his skills and was to remain a mutually enriching friendship for many years. By 1938, Randall had taken a job with the U.S. Post Office as a letter carrier, work he was to continue until 1951, except for his service in the United States Army during World War II as a member of the signal corps in the South Pacific (1942-1946). After returning from military duty, Randall attended Wayne State University and was graduated in 1949. While still working for the post office, Randall also managed to complete work for a master's degree in library science from the University of Michigan in 1951.

Degree in hand, Randall began his career as a librarian by accepting an appointment with Lincoln University in Jefferson City, Missouri, where he remained until 1954. He was promoted to associate librarian when he moved to Baltimore to work for

Morgan State College for the next two years. In 1956, he returned to Detroit, where he was to work for the Wayne County Federated Library System until 1969, first as a branch librarian and then as head of the reference and interloan department (1963-1969). Randall's introduction to several relatively unknown black poets from Detroit at a planning meeting for a special issue of *Negro History Bulletin* in 1962 led to his determination to see more work by new black poets become available; thus, he became the founding editor of the Broadside Press in 1965. His collaboration with Margaret Danner, who had founded Boone House, a Detroit cultural center, produced his first published book of poems, *Poem Counterpoem* from Broadside Press (its first publication as well).

With the publication of Randall's second book, *Cities Burning*, his reputation as a poet and publisher grew, and he doubled as poet-in-residence and reference librarian for the University of Detroit from 1969 to 1975. During this time, he also taught courses in black literature at the university, gave a number of readings, and was involved in conferences and seminars throughout the country. In 1966, Randall, with a delegation of black artists, visited Paris, Prague, and the Soviet Union, where he read his translations and his own poems to Russian audiences. In 1970, he visited West Africa, touring Ghana, Togo, and Dahomey, and meeting with African writers. After his retirement in 1975, Randall continued his involvement in writing conferences and readings, but he devoted the majority of his time to the Broadside Press and his own writing. Melba Boyd's well-received documentary film on Randall's life and work, *Black Unicorn*, was released in 1996. Randall died of congestive heart failure on August 5, 2000.

Analysis: Poetry

Like fellow black writers of the "postrenaissance" school that followed the Harlem Renaissance, Dudley Randall embraces not only the concerns of modernism in discovering new modes of expression and technique, but also the increasing awareness of a black literary heritage that begins in slave songs and spirituals.

While much of his earlier work experiments with classical forms, primarily the rhymed lyric and the sonnet, Randall also works in free verse and with the terseness of folk expression. He cherishes the freedom of the individual poet to explore ideas and forms central in his poetry. Although he is primarily lyrical in his tone, his work demonstrates sensitivity to the ordinary experiences of the working man, the political struggles of black Americans, and the sanctity of personal relationships. Cognizant of new developments and "trendy" fashions in poetry, Randall never allows himself the comforting isolation of an art-for-art's-sake poetics; instead, he insists on the integrity of the fundamental values of joy, music, and craft in his poetry while lyrically rendering common experiences in the form of new insights which are comprehensible for the majority of readers. He embodies, in short, that sometimes too-often-neglected maxim of Sir Philip Sidney's in *Defence of Poesie* (1595) that poetry ought "to teach and delight." That Randall achieves both while using an essentially modern black idiom ensures him of a significant place among his generation of poets.

Poem Counterpoem
The polarities of tension in Randall's poetry seem to be the necessity of personal love and social change. These themes underlie most of his poems, which sometimes focus on the one value while faintly suggesting the other but more often than not are characteristic of a tension between the two. In one early poem from his first book, *Poem Counterpoem*, Randall reflects on his youthful experience as a foundry worker while he visits an ailing coworker many years later in a hospital. In "George," the speaker recalls "the monstrous, lumpish cylinder blocks" that too often "clotted the line and plunged to the floor/ With force enough to tear your foot in two." George's response to the industrial hazards of the assembly line was to step calmly aside; working side by side with the older man in his younger days, the speaker looked to George as an example of quiet endurance, even though George, "goggled, with mask on [his] mouth and shoulders bright with sweat," was not particularly articulate in his guidance of the young Randall. George's "highest accolade,"

in fact, following the clean-up of "blocks clogged up" which came "thundering down like an avalanche," was the gnomic folk expression: "'You're not afraid of sweat. You're strong as a mule.'" As the speaker visits George in a "ward where old men wait to die," he realizes that George "cannot read the books" brought to him while he sits "among the senile wrecks,/ The psychopaths, the incontinent." In the transition from the first stanza (set in the past) to the second (set in the present), the long lines of the first (which suggest the rhythm of the assembly line) give way to a shorter line that underscores George's confinement. When George falls from his chair in the course of the visit, his visitor lifts him back into it "like a cylinder block" and assures him: "'You'll be here/ A long time yet, because you're strong as a mule.'"

While the poem relates little more than the memory of assembly line comradeship and the subsequent visit many years later, it suggests a great deal more than that. The sheer physical drudgery of the foundry site is apparent in both imagery and rhythm; George's quiet but resolute determination to survive the toll of accidents is also implicit, but he survives only to find himself relegated to little more than a warehouse for the aged. Juxtaposed, however, with the dismal irony of George's fate is Randall's emphasis on the personal bond of mutual respect between the two men. Just as George encouraged him, the younger man now offers the aging George the same encouragement that he once offered the young worker. George's persistence in overcoming his fear of death, however, is not enough to restore his dignity. The social conditions must change as well, and that will necessitate formal education; this, too, as Randall's own biography might suggest, has been an inadvertent gift from the older man. In stressing the personal bond between them and yet not losing sight of their common experience in the workplace, Randall celebrates the endurance of friendship while condemning the dehumanizing factors of the assembly line and the hospital. That all of this is expressed in one brief mirrored, metaphorical aphorism suggests that the simple eloquence of the poem itself is, like George, rich beneath its surface.

Cities Burning

Randall's second book, *Cities Burning,* focuses on the disintegrating cities during the urban riots and civil struggles of the 1960's. His observations on social change are not, however, solely the result of the 1960's, for several of these poems were written much earlier. "Roses and Revolution," for example, was written in 1948 and attests to Randall's exploration of the dual themes of personal love and social change long before that tumultuous decade. Hauntingly prophetic, Randall's apocalyptic poem speaks of "the lighted cities" that "were like tapers in the night." He sees "the Negro lying in the swamp with his face blown off" and "in northern cities with his manhood maligned." Men work but take "no joy in their work." As a result of the inner turmoil caused by prejudice and oppression, love becomes severely distorted; they greet "the hard-eyed whore with joyless excitement" and sleep "with wives and virgins in impotence." While the poem's speaker searches for meaningful value "in darkness/ and felt the pain of millions," he sees "dawn upon them like the sun," a vision of peace and beauty in which weapons are buried "at the bottom of the ocean/ like the bones of dinosaurs buried under the shale of eras." Here people "create for others the house, the poem, the game of athletic beauty." Having described the misery in the first stanza and the vision of deliverance in the second stanza, Randall proceeds to analyze its meaning in the third: "Its radiance would grow and be nourished suddenly/ burst into terrible and splendid bloom/ the blood-red flower of revolution."

As it is for many of the poems in this volume, the title of the collection is somewhat misleading with respect to "Roses and Revolution," for the city in *Cities Burning* is humankind and the fires are transforming agents. While acknowledging the violence and destruction as literal events, Randall also sees revolution occurring within the heart of man as well. The real revolution is "not for power or the accumulation of paper," greed for money, but for a blossoming of love that can occur when the black American no longer feels "the writhing/ of his viscera like that of the hare hunted down or the bear at bay." The symbolic rose no longer holds its power for transformation unless it is "blood-red" in its "terrible and splendid bloom," for Randall does not sentimentalize love at the expense of the political process.

In "Ballad of Birmingham," for example, Randall dramatically presents a dialogue between a black mother, who fears for her daughter's safety and forbids her to "march the streets of Birmingham/ to make our country free," and the girl herself, who is willing to risk the "clubs and hoses, guns and jails" in order to assert her rights. Obeying her mother, the daughter goes "to church instead" to "sing in the children's choir" rather than join the other children in the freedom march. The historical event on which the ballad is based was the bombing of a black church in Birmingham on September 15, 1963, when four teenage girls were murdered in a dynamite explosion while they were attending a Bible class. When the mother hears the explosion, she rushes to the scene of the violence; although she claws "through bits of glass and brick," she finds only a shoe: "O, here's the shoe my baby wore,/ but, baby, where are you?" Her protective reluctance to become involved in the Civil Rights struggle, although understandable, has failed to preserve her loving security for her daughter or even her daughter herself. Despite the elegiac ballad form, Randall's dramatic irony here is politically and personally potent: Love cannot hide from death in the pursuit of freedom; it must risk it.

Randall, however, is unwilling to endorse violence for its own sake—in revolution or in literature. In "The Rite" and in "Black Poet, White Critic," he addresses, respectively, both the young militant black poet who would annihilate the pioneers of the black literary tradition and the white critic who would deny that such a tradition even existed. The young poet in "The Rite" murders an older poet, whom he views as reactionary, but in sacrificing him to the new revolutionary program, the young poet ritually "drank his blood and ate his heart," thus drawing his revolutionary sustenance from his forebears without conscious knowledge of doing so. That the older writer provides continuing life for the younger one—and is conscious of that fact—not only endorses the persistence of the political struggle, but also establishes a political context for black literature that reaches back to protest elements in the slave songs. The struggle is nothing new to Randall's generation, or to those generations before him; yet the older poet is quite willing to offer his life in order to broaden the continuity of that protest. On the other hand, Randall challenges—in "Black Poet, White Critic"—the establishment critic who "advises/ not to write on controversial subjects/ like freedom or murder" to reexamine his own critical premises. The critic suggests "universal themes/ and timeless symbols/ like the white unicorn," to which Randall responds: "A *white* unicorn?" Refusing to deny his own heritage and experience as a black man, he realizes that the argument is bogus in any context: The timeless drama of Sophocles or William Shakespeare can hardly be said to ignore freedom and murder. Randall, then, implies that the critic who so blatantly misreads his own literary tradition fears not so much a lack of quality on the part of black poets as the fulfillment of that advice on "universal themes" and "timeless symbols" that would indict the critic's own racism and shoddy intellect as a result of that racism. Black poets might, indeed, write *too well.*

Love You, After the Killing, and A Litany of Friends
Randall's third volume of poems, *Love You,* consists entirely of lyric love poems, but unlike those in *Cities Burning,* these poems more frequently use open forms and free verse. While the previous volume is more likely to explore ideas, the poems in this one concentrate on feelings (although the poems in both volumes, of course, embrace both ideas and feelings). The emphasis in *Love You* shifts from the complexity of the political struggle to the complexity of interpersonal conflicts and seems to suggest that social change requires the resolution of such conflicts before its advances can be permanent. These poems, like those in *More to Remember: Poems of Four Decades,* are drawn from several decades, and they offer the intimate but not confessional experience of the classical lyricist. Along with his selected poems, those in *Love You* offer a full range of poetic device and subject matter, although the themes generally oscillate between the polarities of personal love and social change. In his 1973 volume, *After the Killing,* Randall moves to a lyrical form that is closer to

free-verse folk expression than the lyric poems of his earlier work. The themes, however, remain generally the same, although he introduces an emphasis on Pan-African concerns, particularly in the section "African Suite," which is based in part on his travels to West Africa.

A stanza from "A Poet is not a Jukebox," from *A Litany of Friends*, perhaps sums up Randall's position on the role of the poet as an artist above all, who will write of matters such as race and politics only as these subjects inspire him, not out of any requirement laid on him by his skin color:

> Telling a Black poet what he ought to write
> Is like some Commissar of Culture in Russia telling a poet
> He'd better write about the new steel furnaces in the
>   Novobigorsk region
> Or the heroic feats of Soviet labor in digging the trans-
>   Caucasus canal,
> Or the unprecedented achievements of workers in the
>   sugar beet industry who exceeded their quota by 400
>   percent (it was later discovered to be a typist's error).

Randall may be remembered as an outstanding publisher and editor who was also a poet, but he wrote a sufficient number of moving poems to keep him in anthologies for many years to come. Some of his ballads, such as "Ballad of Birmingham," have been set to music and popularized in that fashion. His terse expression and probing voice in poems such as "Black Poet, White Critic" will remind readers that poetry can indeed teach much about what it means to be human without compromising the inherent delight in reading—and living.

Other Literary Forms

Despite his primary interest in poetry, Dudley Randall wrote short stories, articles, and reviews. In the mid-1960's, he founded the Broadside Press, which thereafter consumed much of his energy, as he began to direct most of his writing toward poetry and critical articles. For the Broadside Press he edited, with Margaret G. Burroughs, *For Malcolm: Poems on the Life and the Death of Malcolm X*, the press's second publication. His introductory essay succinctly foreshadowed the influence that Malcolm X was to have on many of the newly emerging black poets of the 1960's; it also helped to introduce many of the contributors to readers of black literature.

In 1969, aware that many current anthologies excluded or gave only limited representation to black poets, Randall edited and published *Black Poetry: A Supplement to Anthologies Which Exclude Black Poets*, which brought such omissions to the attention of larger publishing houses in the country. By 1971, a number of anthologies of African American poetry were in circulation, but many of them were seriously flawed by too-narrow criteria for selection. Randall's *The Black Poets* enjoyed wide distribution in an inexpensive paperback format and corrected many of the deficiencies of previous black poetry anthologies. Presenting a full range of African American poetry from folklore and spirituals to the Black Nationalist poets of the late 1960's, the anthology offered a substantial selection from each of its contributors and stressed the continuity of a rich oral tradition while delineating various periods in the history of black American poetry. It quickly became one of the most widely read and influential anthologies of its kind.

In his critical writings, Randall came to be known as a moderating voice, maintaining respect for poets of earlier periods while accepting the new directions of black poetry since the 1960's. One important article, "The Black Aesthetic in the Thirties, Forties, and Fifties" (*The Black Aesthetic*, 1971), clearly establishes the vital role of such poets as Sterling Brown, Margaret Walker, Melvin B. Tolson, Robert Hayden, and Gwendolyn Brooks, among others who wrote in the wake of the Harlem Renaissance. In providing an essential chapter in black literary history, Randall, here and in other essays, countered eloquently the tendency for young black poets in the 1960's to dismiss gifted, significant writers because they seemed too accommodationist. On the other hand, Randall's productive generosity in publishing and reviewing introduced a great variety of young black poets to literary America and provided an unparalleled availability of black poetry, in general, not only to the black community but also to the mainstream reading public.

Two additional literary forms must be mentioned in assessing Randall's career: interviews and translations. His insights into literary history, political developments, and his own methods of composition can be found in published interviews. While such interviews are frequently useful in understanding his own work, they are also immensely instructional in the field of African American poetry. Randall's translations from Russian, Latin, and French are also worthy of note. He published translations from major figures influential on his own poetic sensibilities, from Alexander Pushkin to K. M. Simonov. Translating from the Latin, he has mastered the classical lyricism of Catullus. From Paul Verlaine, Randall assimilated the influence of the French Symbolists.

While he became well practiced in classical and European forms and techniques, Randall studied equally thoroughly the folk forms of the African American heritage. In these forms, he absorbed the patterns of dialect and commonsensible observation that informed much of the black poetry in the 1960's. Much of this poetry—including some of Randall's own—he made available on tape recordings, through Broadside Press. These tape recordings highlight the performance qualities of the black oral tradition. Randall himself was known as a gifted and effective reader of his own works.

Bibliography

Boyd, Melba Joyce. "'Roses and Revolutions' Dudley Randall: Poet, Publisher, Critic, and Champion of African American Literature Leaves a Legacy of Immeasurable Value." *Black Scholar* (Black World Foundation) 31, no. 1 (Spring, 2001): 55-58. A tribute to Dudley's life and works. Contains information on his family, education, and career achievements.

_____. *Wrestling with the Muse: Dudley Randall and the Broadside Press.* New York: Columbia University Press, 2003. Boyd, a former friend and colleague of Randall, presents an affectionate authorized biography.

Madhubuti, Haki R. "Portrait of a Founding Father." *Black Issues*

Book Review 2, no. 6 (November/December, 2000): 14-16. A tribute to Dudley that also discusses his education, career, and achievements in the literary community.

Melhem, D. H. "Dudley Randall: A Humanist View." *Black American Literature Forum* 17 (1983): 157-167. This excellent article surveys Randall's poetry and includes a biographical overview of his life and career and brief analyses of significant poems. Melhem stresses that Randall was a humanist, a label the poet himself accepted. Includes notes that are somewhat useful in finding other sources on Randall, especially general surveys and interviews.

Randall, Dudley. "Black Publisher, Black Writer: An Answer." *Black World* 24 (March, 1975): 32-37. This article records Randall's own reflections about the world of black publishing houses and the pros and cons concerning a black writer's use of a black or white publisher. Although interesting, the article does not address Randall's profession as a poet. He does, however, make several general remarks concerning other black poets, and he does comment on the role of oral tradition in poetry.

_____. "In Conversation with Dudley Randall." Interview by Charles H. Rowell. *Obsidian* 2, no. 1 (1976): 32-44. In this important interview focusing primarily on Randall's poetic career rather than his role as a publisher, the poet discusses his background and the influences on his life and work. Includes some useful discussion of Randall's indebtedness to the Harlem Renaissance, his views of poetry, and his process of composition. Randall also comments on his poems collected in *Cities Burning* and *After the Killing*, among others. Notes leading to other sources are included.

_____. "Interviews: Dudley Randall." *Black Books Bulletin* 1 (Winter, 1972): 23-26. An informative but short article dealing mostly with Randall's involvement with Broadside Press. Includes some discussion of Randall's poetry and the earlier African American poets who have influenced him. Randall makes general comments about African American poetry which may shed some light on his own poems.

_____. "The Message Is in the Melody: An Interview with

Dudley Randall." Interview by Leana Ampadu. *Callaloo* 22, no. 2 (Spring, 1999): 438-445. A conversation in which Dudley compares his poetry with that of Robert Hayden, discusses his opinions on popular music and on prominent female writers like Toni Morrison and Zora Neale Hurston, and talks about the process he underwent in writing the poem "George."

Redding, Saunders. "The Black Arts Movement in Negro Poetry." *The American Scholar* 42 (1973): 330-336. This article attempts to criticize the "increasing rigidity" of the Black Arts movement, with particular regard to the "new concept of the black and blackness." In contrast to those within this movement, Randall, though a publisher of many poets in the movement, exhibits an earlier, more humanistic tradition in touch with the American past.

Thompson, Julius Eric. *Dudley Randall, Broadside Press, and the Black Arts Movement in Detroit, 1960-1995.* Jefferson, N.C.: McFarland, 1999. A history of the Broadside Press founded by Randall and his subsequent involvement in the Civil Rights movement. Through Randall and the Broadside Press, hundreds of black writers were given an outlet for their work and for their calls for equality and black identity.

Waters, Mark V. "Dudley Randall and the Liberation Aesthetic: Confronting the Politics of 'Blackness.'" *CLA Journal* 44, no. 1 (September, 2000): 111-139. A summary of Randall's efforts as both publisher and poet. The platform for black poetry of diverse style, language, and theme maintained by Randall helped counter the rising influence of radical and militant black poetry that threatened to engulf the larger array of black poetic expression under its own political agenda.

— *Leslie Ellen Jones; Michael Loudon*

Ishmael Reed

(Emmett Coleman)

Novelist and poet

Born: Chattanooga, Tennessee; February 22, 1938

LONG FICTION: *The Free-Lance Pallbearers*, 1967; *Yellow Back Radio Broke-Down*, 1969; *Mumbo Jumbo*, 1972; *The Last Days of Louisiana Red*, 1974; *Flight to Canada*, 1976; *The Terrible Twos*, 1982; *Reckless Eyeballing*, 1986; *The Terrible Threes*, 1989; *Japanese by Spring*, 1993.

POETRY: *Catechism of D Neoamerican Hoodoo Church*, 1970; *Conjure: Selected Poems, 1963-1970*, 1972; *Chattanooga*, 1973; *A Secretary to the Spirits*, 1977; *Cab Calloway Stands In for the Moon*, 1986; *New and Collected Poems*, 1988.

NONFICTION: *Shrovetide in Old New Orleans*, 1978; *God Made Alaska for the Indians*, 1982; *Writin' Is Fightin': Thirty-seven Years of Boxing on Paper*, 1988; *Airing Dirty Laundry*, 1993; *Conversations with Ishmael Reed*, 1995; *Another Day at the Front: Dispatches from the Race War*, 2002 (essays); *Blues City: A Walk in Oakland*, 2003.

EDITED TEXTS: *Nineteen Necromancers from Now*, 1970; *Yardbird Lives!*, 1978 (with Al Young); *Calafia*, 1979 (with Young and Shawn Hsu Wong); *The Before Columbus Foundation Fiction Anthology: Selections from the American Book Awards, 1980-1990*, 1992 (with Kathryn Trueblood and Shawn Wong); *Multi-America: Essays on Cultural Wars and Cultural Peace*, 1997; *From Totems to Hip-Hop*, 2003.

MISCELLANEOUS: *The Reed Reader*, 2000.

Achievements

Ishmael Reed has earned a place in the first rank of contemporary African American authors, but such recognition did not come immediately. Most established reviewers ignored Reed's first novel, *The Free-Lance Pallbearers*, and many of the reviews that were written dismissed the novel as offensive, childish, or self-absorbed. Although *Yellow Back Radio Broke-Down* was even less traditional than its predecessor, it received much more critical attention and became the center of considerable critical debate. Some reviewers attacked the novel as overly clever, bitter, or obscure, but many praised its imaginative satire and technical innovation. Moreover, the controversy over *Yellow Back Radio Broke-Down* stirred new interest in *The Free-Lance Pallbearers.* Reed's increasing acceptance as a major African American author was demonstrated when his third novel, *Mumbo Jumbo*, was reviewed on the front page of *The New York Times Review of Books.* Both *Mumbo Jumbo* and *Conjure*, a poetry collection published in the same year, were nominated for the National Book Award.

Subsequent novels maintained Reed's position in American letters. In 1975, Reed's *The Last Days of Louisiana Red* received the Rosenthal Foundation Award, and some reviewers viewed *Flight to Canada* as Reed's best novel. Yet his work proved consistently controversial. His novels have, for example, been called sexist, a critical accusation that is fueled by comparison of Reed's novels with the powerful fiction written by African American women such as Alice Walker and Toni Morrison. The charge of sexism is further encouraged by Reed's satirical attack on feminists in *Reckless Eyeballing.* Reed has also been called a reactionary by some critics because of his uncomplimentary portrayals of black revolutionaries. His fiction has been translated into three languages, and his poetry is included in *Poetry of the Negro, New Black Poetry, The Norton Anthology of Poetry,* and other anthologies. In 1998, Ishmael Reed was awarded the MacArthur "Genius" Fellowship. This is fitting recognition for a writer who consciously attempted to redefine American and African American literature.

Biography
The jacket notes to *Chattanooga* glibly recount Ishmael Scott Reed's life: "born in Chattanooga, Tennessee, grew up in Buffalo, New York, learned to write in New York City and wised up in Berkeley, California." Each residence played a crucial role in Reed's development.

(AP/Wide World Photos)

Reed was born the son of Henry Lenoir and Thelma Coleman, but before he was two years old, his mother remarried, this time to autoworker Bennie Reed. When he was four years old, his mother moved the family to Buffalo, New York, where she found factory work. Reed was graduated from Buffalo's East High School in 1956 and began to attend Millard Fillmore College, the night division of the University of Buffalo, supporting himself by working in the Buffalo public library. A satirical short story, "Something Pure," which portrayed Christ's return as an advertising man, brought Reed the praise of an English professor and encouraged him to enroll in day classes. Reed attended the University of Buffalo until 1960, when he withdrew because of money problems and the social pressures that his financial situation created. He married Priscilla Rose Thompson and moved into the notorious Talbert Mall Projects. The two years he spent there provided him with a painful but valuable experience of urban poverty and dependency. His daughter, Timothy Bret Reed, was also born there. During his last years in Buffalo, Reed wrote for the *Empire Star Weekly*, moderated a controversial radio program for station WVFO, and acted in several local stage productions.

From 1962 to 1967, Reed lived in New York City. As well as being involved with the Civil Rights movement and the Black Power movement, Reed served as editor of *Advance*, a weekly published in Newark, New Jersey. His work on the *Advance* was admired by Walter Bowart, and together they founded the *East Village Other*, one of the first and most successful "underground" newspapers. An early indication of Reed's commitment to encouraging the work of minority artists was his organization in 1965 of the American Festival of Negro Art.

In 1967, Reed moved to Berkeley, California, and began teaching at the University of California at Berkeley. In 1970, Reed and his first wife divorced (after years of separation), and he married Carla Blank. In 1971, with Al Young, Reed founded the Yardbird Publishing Company, which from 1971 to 1976 produced the *Yardbird Reader*, an innovative journal of ethnic writing and graphics. The Reed, Cannon, and Johnson Communications Company, which later became Ishmael Reed Books, was founded in 1973 and has published the work of William Demby, Bill Gunn, Mei Mei Bressenburge, and other ethnic writers. In 1976, Reed and Victor Cruz began the Before Columbus Foundation. In 1977, Ishmael Reed's daughter Tennessee was born, and he was denied tenure in the English department at the University of California at Berkeley. He continued to serve as a lecturer at Berkeley, however, and also taught at Yale, Harvard, Columbia, Dartmouth, and a number of other colleges and universities. In 1995, he was awarded an honorary doctorate in letters from the State University of New York at Buffalo.

Reed made important contributions as a poet, novelist, essayist, playwright, and as an editor and publisher. He has stated that he considers himself a global writer, and his success at writing poetry in the African language of Yoruba and his study of Japanese language and culture for his novel *Japanese by Spring* support this assertion. He also extended his literary range to include plays, such as *The Preacher and the Rapper,* and jazz albums, such as *Conjure I* and *Conjure II,* and he even completed a libretto and served as the executive producer for a cable television soap opera called *Personal Problems.*

In the early 1990's, Reed was, perhaps, best known for his controversial essays on such issues as the Rodney King and O. J. Simpson trials and the U.S. justice Clarence Thomas hearings, some of which were collected in *Airing Dirty Laundry.* However, his most important contribution to American letters may well be his work as an editor and publisher for other ethnic writers. In all of his publishing ventures, Reed tries to expose readers to the work of Asian Americans, African Americans, Chicanos, and Native Americans in an effort to help build a truly representative and pluralistic national literature.

Analysis: Long Fiction

Ishmael Reed is consciously a part of the African American literary tradition that extends back to the first-person slave narratives, and the central purpose of his novels is to define a means of expressing the complexity of the African American experience in a manner distinct from the dominant literary tradition. Until the middle of the twentieth century, African American fiction, although enriched by the lyricism of Jean Toomer and Zora Neale Hurston, concentrated on realistic portrayals of black life and employed familiar narrative structures. This tendency toward social realism peaked with Richard Wright's *Native Son* (1940) and *Black Boy* (1945), but it was continued into the late twentieth century by authors such as James Baldwin. Reed belongs to a divergent tradition, inspired by Ralph Ellison's *Invisible Man* (1952), a countertradition that includes the work of Leon Forrest, Ernest J. Gaines, James Alan McPherson, Toni Morrison, and Alice Walker.

Believing that the means of expression is as important as the matter, Reed argues that the special qualities of the African American experience cannot be adequately communicated through traditional literary forms. Like Amiri Baraka, Reed believes that African American authors must "be estranged from the dominant culture," but Reed also wants to avoid being stifled by a similarly restrictive countertradition. In *Shrovetide in Old New Orleans*, Reed says that his art and criticism try to combat "the consciousness barrier erected by an alliance of Eastern-backed black pseudo-nationalists and white mundanists." Thus, Reed works against the stylistic limitations of the African American literary tradition as much as he works with them. Henry Louis Gates, Jr., compared Reed's fictional modifications of African American literary traditions to the African American folk custom of "signifying," maintaining that Reed's novels present an ongoing process of "rhetorical self-definition."

Although Reed's novels are primarily efforts to define an appropriate African American aesthetic, his fiction vividly portrays the particular social condition of black Americans. In his foreword to Elizabeth and Thomas Settle's *Ishmael Reed: A Primary and Secondary Bibliography* (1982), Reed expresses his bitterness over persistent racism and argues that the personal experience of racism that informs his art makes his work inaccessible and threatening to many readers: "I am a member of a class which has been cast to the bottom of the American caste system, and from those depths I write a vision which is still strange, often frightening, 'peculiar' and 'odd' to some, 'ill-considered' and unwelcome to many." Indeed, Ishmael seems to be an ironically appropriate name for this author of violent and darkly humorous attacks on American institutions and attitudes, for the sharpness and breadth of his satire sometimes make him appear to be a man whose hand is turned against all others. His novels portray corrupt power brokers and their black and white sycophants operating in a dehumanized and materialistic society characterized by its prefabricated and ethnocentric culture. Yet Reed's novels are not hopeless explications of injustice, for against the forces of repression and conformity he sets gifted individuals who escape the limitations of their sterile culture by courageously penetrating the illusions that bind them. Moreover, in contrast to many white authors who are engaged in parallel metafictive experiments, Reed voices a confident belief that "print and words are not dead at all."

Reed's narrative technique combines the improvisational qualities of jazz with a documentary impulse to accumulate references and allusions. In his composite narratives, historical and fictional characters coexist in a fluid, anachronistic time. In an effort to translate the vitality and spontaneity of the oral, folk tradition into a literature that can form the basis for an alternative culture, Reed mixes colloquialisms and erudition in novels which are syncretized from a series of subtexts. The literary equivalent of scat singing, his stories-within-stories parody literary formulas and challenge the traditional limits of fiction.

Reed claims that his novels constitute "an art form with its own laws," but he does not mean to imply that his work is private, for these "laws" are founded on a careful but imaginative reinterpretation of the historical and mythological past. The lengthy bibliography appended to *Mumbo Jumbo* satirizes the documentary impulse of social realist authors, but it also underscores Reed's belief that his mature work demands scholarly research in order to be decoded. This artistic process of reinterpretation often requires the services of an interlocutor, a character who explicitly explains the events of the narrative in terms of the mythological past. Reed's novels describe a vision of an Osirian/Dionysian consciousness, a sensuous humanism that he presents as an appropriate cultural alternative for nonwhite Americans. His imaginative reconstructions of the American West, the Harlem Renaissance, the American Civil War, and contemporary U.S. politics, interwoven with ancient myths, non-European folk customs, and the formulas of popular culture, are liberating heresies meant to free readers from the intellectual domination of the Judeo-Christian tradition.

The Free-Lance Pallbearers
Reed's first novel, *The Free-Lance Pallbearers*, takes place in a futuristic America called HARRY SAM: "A big not-to-be-believed out-of-sight, sometimes referred to as O-BOP-SHE-BANG or

KLANG-A-LANG-A-DING-DONG." This crumbling and corrupt world is tyrannized by Sam himself, a vulgar fat man who lives in Sam's Motel on Sam's Island in the middle of the lethally polluted Black Bay that borders HARRY SAM. Sam, doomed by some terrifying gastrointestinal disorder, spends all of his time on the toilet, his filth pouring into the bay from several large statues of Rutherford B. Hayes.

The bulk of the novel, although framed and periodically informed by a jiving narrative voice, is narrated by Bukka Doopeyduk in a restrained, proper English that identifies his passive faith in the establishment. Doopeyduk is a dedicated adherent to the Nazarene Code, an orderly in a psychiatric hospital, a student at Harry Sam College, and a hapless victim. His comically futile efforts to play by the rules are defeated by the cynics, who manipulate the unjust system to their own advantage. In the end, Doopeyduk is disillusioned: He leads a successful attack on Sam's Island, uncovers the conspiracy that protects Sam's cannibalism, briefly dreams of becoming the black Sam, and is finally crucified.

The Free-Lance Pallbearers is a parody of the African American tradition of first-person, confessional narratives, a book the narrator describes as "growing up in soulsville first of three installments—or what it means to be a backstage darky." Reed's novel challenges the viability of this African American version of the *Bildungsroman*, in which a young protagonist undergoes a painful initiation into the darkness of the white world, a formula exemplified by Wright's *Black Boy* and James Baldwin's *Go Tell It on the Mountain* (1953). In fact, the novel suggests that African American authors' use of this European form is as disabling as Doopeyduk's adherence to the dictates of the Nazarene Code.

The novel is an unrestrained attack on U.S. politics. HARRY SAM, alternately referred to as "Nowhere" or "Now Here," is a dualistic vision of a United States that celebrates vacuous contemporaneity. The novel, an inversion of the Horatio Alger myth in the manner of Nathanael West, mercilessly displays American racism, but its focus is the corruptive potential of power. Sam is a grotesque version of Lyndon B. Johnson, famous for his bathroom interviews, and Sam's cannibalistic taste for children is an attack on Johnson's Vietnam policy. With *The Free-Lance Pallbearers*, Reed destroys the presumptions of his society, but it is not until his later novels that he attempts to construct an alternative.

Yellow Back Radio Broke-Down

Yellow Back Radio Broke-Down is set in a fantastic version of the Wild West of popular literature. Reed's protagonist, the Loop Garoo Kid, is a proponent of artistic freedom and an accomplished Voodoo *houngan* who is in marked contrast to the continually victimized Doopeyduk. Armed with supernatural "connaissance" and aided by a white python and the hip, helicopter-flying Chief Showcase, the Kid battles the forces of realistic mimesis and political corruption. His villainous opponent is Drag Gibson, a degenerate cattle baron given to murdering his wives, who is called upon by the citizens of Yellow Back Radio to crush their rebellious children's effort "to create [their] own fictions."

Although *Yellow Back Radio Broke-Down* satirizes Americans' eagerness to suspend civil rights in response to student protests against the Vietnam War, its focus is literature, specifically the dialogue between realism and modernism. The Loop Garoo Kid matches Reed's description of the African American artist in *Nineteen Necromancers from Now*: "a conjurer who works JuJu upon his oppressors; a witch doctor who frees his fellow victims from the psychic attack launched by demons." Through the Loop Garoo Kid, Reed takes a stand for imagination, intelligence, and fantasy against rhetoric, violence, and sentimentality. This theme is made explicit in a debate with Bo Shmo, a "neo-social realist" who maintains that "all art must be for the end of liberating the masses," for the Kid says that a novel "can be anything it wants to be, a vaudeville show, the six o'clock news, the mumblings of wild men saddled by demons."

Reed exhibits his antirealist theory of fiction in *Yellow Back Radio Broke-Down* through his free use of time, characters, and language. The novel ranges from the eighteenth century to the 1960's, combining historical events and cowboy myths with modern technology and cultural detritus. Reed's primary characters are comically exaggerated racial types: Drag Gibson represents the whites' depraved materialism, Chief Showcase represents the American Indians' spirituality, and the Loop Garoo Kid represents the African Americans' artistic soul. Reed explains the novel's title by suggesting that his book is the "dismantling of a genre done in an oral way like radio." "Yellow back" refers to the popular dime novels; "radio" refers to the novel's oral, discontinuous form; and "broke-down" is a dismantling. Thus, Reed's first two novels assault America in an attempt to "dismantle" its cultural structure.

Mumbo Jumbo

In *Mumbo Jumbo*, Reed expands on the neo-hoodooism of the Loop Garoo Kid in order to create and define an African American aesthetic based on Voodoo, Egyptian mythology, and improvisational musical forms, an aesthetic to challenge the Judeo-Christian tradition, rationalism, and technology. Set in Harlem during the 1920's, *Mumbo Jumbo* is a tragicomical analysis of the Harlem Renaissance's failure to sustain its artistic promise. Reed's protagonist is PaPa LaBas, an aging hoodoo detective and cultural diagnostician, and LaBas's name, meaning "over there" in French, reveals that his purpose is to reconnect African Americans with their cultural heritage by reunifying the Text of Jes Grew, literally the Egyptian Book of Thoth. Reed takes the phrase Jes Grew from Harriet Beecher Stowe's Topsy and James Weldon Johnson's description of African American music's unascribed development, but in the novel, Jes Grew is a contagion, connected with the improvisational spirit of ragtime and jazz, that begins to spread across America in the 1920's. Jes Grew is an irrational force that threatens to overwhelm the dominant, repressive traditions of established culture. LaBas's efforts to unify and direct this unpredictable force are opposed by the Wallflower Order of the Knights Templar, an organization dedicated to neutralizing the power of Jes Grew in order to protect its privileged status. LaBas fails to reunify the text, a parallel to the dissipation of the Harlem Renaissance's artistic potential, but the failure is seen as temporary; the novel's indeterminate conclusion looks forward to a time when these artistic energies can be reignited.

The novel's title is double-edged. "Mumbo jumbo" is a racist, colonialist phrase used to describe the misunderstood customs and language of dark-skinned people, an approximation of some critics' description of Reed's unorthodox fictional method. Yet "mumbo jumbo" also refers to the power of imagination, the cultural alternative that can free African Americans. A text of and about texts, *Mumbo Jumbo* combines the formulas of detective fiction with the documentary paraphernalia of scholarship: footnotes, illustrations, and a bibliography. Thus, in the disclosure scene required of any good detective story, LaBas, acting the part of interlocutor, provides a lengthy and erudite explication of the development of Jes Grew that begins with a reinterpretation of the myth of Osiris. The parodic scholarship of *Mumbo Jumbo* undercuts the assumed primacy of the European tradition and implicitly argues that African American artists should attempt to discover their distinct cultural heritage.

The Last Days of Louisiana Red

In *The Last Days of Louisiana Red*, LaBas returns as Reed's protagonist, but the novel abandons the parodic scholarship and high stylization of *Mumbo Jumbo*. Although LaBas again functions as a connection with a non-European tradition of history and myth, *The Last Days of Louisiana Red* is more traditionally structured than its predecessor. In the novel, LaBas solves the murder of Ed Yellings, the founder of the Solid Gumbo Works. Yellings's business is dedicated to combating the effects of Louisiana Red, literally a popular hot sauce but figuratively an evil state of mind that divides African Americans. Yelling's gumbo, like Reed's fiction, is a mixture of disparate elements, and it has a powerful curative effect. In fact, LaBas discovers that Yellings is murdered when he gets close to developing a gumbo that will cure heroin addiction.

In *The Last Days of Louisiana Red*, Reed is examining the self-destructive forces that divide the African American community so that its members fight one another "while above their heads . . . billionaires flew in custom-made jet planes." Reed shows how individuals' avarice leads them to conspire with the establishment, and he suggests that some of the most vocal and militant leaders are motivated by their egotistical need for power rather than by true concern for oppressed people. Set in Berkeley, California, *The Last Days of Louisiana Red* attacks the credibility of the black revolutionary movements that sprang up in the late 1960's and early 1970's.

Flight to Canada

Flight to Canada, Reed's fifth novel, is set in an imaginatively redrawn Civil War South, and it describes the relationship between Arthur Swille, a tremendously wealthy Virginia planter who practices necrophilia, and an assortment of sociologically stereotyped slaves. The novel is presented as the slave narrative of Uncle Robin, the most loyal of Swille's possessions. Uncle Robin repeatedly tells Swille that the plantation is his idea of heaven, and he assures his master that he does not believe that Canada exists. Raven Quickskill, "the first one of Swille's slaves to read, the first to write, and the first to run away," is the author of Uncle Robin's story.

Like much of Reed's work, *Flight to Canada* is about the liberating power of art, but in *Flight to Canada*, Reed concentrates on the question of authorial control. All the characters struggle to maintain control of their stories. After escaping from the plantation, Quickskill writes a poem, "Flight to Canada," and his comical verse denunciation of Swille completes his liberation. In complaining of Quickskill's betrayal to Abraham Lincoln, Swille laments that his former bookkeeper uses literacy "like that old Voodoo." In a final assertion of authorial control and the power of the pen, Uncle Robin refuses to sell his story to Harriet Beecher Stowe, gives the rights to Quickskill, rewrites Swille's will, and inherits the plantation.

The Terrible Twos

In *The Terrible Twos*, Reed uses a contemporary setting to attack Ronald Reagan's administration and the exploitative nature of the American economic system. In the novel, President Dean

Clift, a former model, is a mindless figurehead manipulated by an oil cartel that has supplanted the real Santa Claus. Nance Saturday, another of Reed's African American detectives, sets out to discover Saint Nicholas's place of exile. The novel's title suggests that, in its second century, the United States is acting as selfishly and irrationally as the proverbial two-year-old. The central theme is the manner in which a few avaricious people seek vast wealth at the expense of the majority of Americans.

Reckless Eyeballing

Reckless Eyeballing takes place in the 1980's, and Reed employs a string of comically distorted characters to present the idea that the American literary environment is dominated by New York women and Jews. Although *Reckless Eyeballing* has been called sexist and anti-Semitic by some, Reed's target is a cultural establishment that creates and strengthens racial stereotypes, in particular the view of African American men as savage rapists. To make his point, however, he lampoons feminists, using the character Tremonisha Smarts, a female African American author who has written a novel of violence against women. Reed's satire is probably intended to remind readers of Alice Walker's *The Color Purple* (1982).

Because the novel's central subject is art and the limitations that society places on an artist, it is appropriate that Reed once again employs the technique of a story-within-a-story. Ian Ball, an unsuccessful African American playwright, is the novel's protagonist. In the novel, Ball tries to succeed by shamelessly placating the feminists in power. He writes "Reckless Eyeballing," a play in which a lynched man is posthumously tried for "raping" a woman with lecherous stares, but Ball, who often seems to speak for Reed, maintains his private, chauvinistic views throughout.

The Terrible Threes

The Terrible Threes, a sequel to *The Terrible Twos*, continues Reed's satirical attack on the contemporary capitalist system, which, he argues, puts the greatest economic burden on the least privileged. (Reed was also planning a third book in the series, *The*

Terrible Fours.) In the first book, there appears a character named Black Peter—an assistant to St. Nicholas in European legend. This Black Peter is an imposter, however, a Rastafarian who studied and appropriated the legend for himself. In *The Terrible Threes,* the true Black Peter emerges to battle the false Peter but is distracted from his mission by the need to do good deeds. Black Peter becomes wildly popular because of these deeds, but a jealous St. Nick and concerned toy companies find a way to put Santa Claus back on top. Capitalism wins again.

Japanese by Spring

Japanese by Spring is postmodern satire. Like much of Reed's imaginative work, the book mixes fictional characters with "fictionalized" ones. Ishmael Reed himself is a character in the book, with his own name. The protagonist of *Japanese by Spring* is Benjamin "Chappie" Puttbutt, a teacher of English and literature at Oakland's Jack London College. Chappie dabbled in activist politics in the mid-1960's, but his only concern in the 1990's is receiving tenure and the perks that accompany it. He will put up with virtually anything, including racist insults from students, to avoid hurting his chances at tenure. As in many of Reed's books, Chappie is passive in the face of power at the beginning of his story. He is a middle-class black conservative, but only because the climate at Jack London demands it. Chappie is a chameleon who always matches his behavior to the ideology of his environment. However, when he is denied tenure and is about to be replaced by a feminist poet who is more flash than substance, Chappie's hidden anger begins to surface. Chappie has also been studying Japanese with a tutor named Dr. Yamato. This proves fortuitous when the Japanese buy Jack London and Dr. Yamato becomes the college president. Chappie suddenly finds himself in a position of power and gloats over those who denied him tenure. He soon finds, however, that his new bosses are the same as the old ones. Dr. Yamato is a tyrant and is eventually arrested by a group that includes Chappie's father, a two-star Air Force general. Dr. Yamato is released, though, and a surprised Chappie learns that there is an "invisible government" that truly controls the United States. Chappie has pierced some of his illusions, but there are others that he never penetrates, such as his blindness to his own opportunism.

The novel's conclusion moves away from Chappie's point of view to that of a fictionalized Ishmael Reed. This Reed skewers political correctness but also shows that the people who complain the most about it are often its greatest purveyors. Reed also lampoons American xenophobia, particularly toward Japan, but he does so in a balanced manner that does not gloss over Japanese faults. Ultimately, though, Reed uses *Japanese by Spring* as he used other novels before, to explore art and politics and the contradictions of America and race.

Other Literary Forms

Ishmael Reed may be best known as a satirical novelist, but he also gained a reputation as a respected poet, essayist, and editor. His poetry collections, which include *Catechism of D Neoamerican Hoodoo Church*, *Conjure: Selected Poems 1963-1970*, *Chattanooga*, *A Secretary to the Spirits*, and *New and Collected Poems*, established him as a major African American poet, and his poetry has been included in several important anthologies. In well-received collections of essays, including *Shrovetide in Old New Orleans*, *God Made Alaska for the Indians*, and *Writin' Is Fightin','* Reed forcefully presented his aesthetic and political theories. He also proved to be an important editor and publisher. *Nineteen Necromancers from Now* was a breakthrough anthology for several unknown black writers. *Yardbird Lives!*, which Reed edited with novelist Al Young, includes essays, fiction, and graphics from the pages of the *Yardbird Reader,* an innovative periodical that published the work of minority writers and artists. Reed's most ambitious editing project resulted in *Calafia*, an effort to gather together the forgotten minority poetry of California's past.

Bibliography

Anderson, Crystal S. "Racial Discourse and Black-Japanese Dynamics in Ishmael Reed's *Japanese by Spring*." *MELUS* 29, nos. 3/4 (Fall/Winter, 2004): 379-397. Examines Reed's transference of the traditional black/white dynamic onto the more-uncommon juxtaposition of African and Japanese Americans.

Chaney, Michael A. "Slave Cyboros and the Black Infovirus: Ishmael Reed's Cybernetic Aesthetics." *Modern Fiction Studies* 49, no. 2 (Summer, 2003): 261-284. An analysis of *Flight to Canada* that proposes that the novel be read from the apex forward, keeping in mind that Reed's discussion of technology is only a piece of a larger puzzle that also includes the language and literature of slave narratives.

Fabré, Michel. "Postmodern Rhetoric in Ishmael Reed's *Yellow Back Radio Broke-Down.*" In *The Afro-American Novel Since 1960*, edited by Peter Bruck and Wolfgang Karrer. Amsterdam: Gruener, 1982. A valuable addition to the study of Reed regarding his postmodernism.

Fox, Robert Elliot. *Conscientious Sorcerers: The Black Post-Modern Fiction of LeRoi Jones/Amiri Baraka, Ishmael Reed, and Samuel R. Delany.* New York: Greenwood Press, 1987. Situates Reed within both the tradition of black fiction and the self-conscious style of contemporary postmodernist fiction.

Gates, Henry Louis, Jr. *The Signifying Monkey: A Theory of Afro-American Literary Criticism.* New York: Oxford University Press, 1988. The section on Reed examines his fiction, especially the novel *Mumbo Jumbo*, as an extension of the tendency of black English to play deliberately with language.

Hogue, W. Lawrence. "Postmodernism, Traditional Culture Forms, and the African American Narrative: Major's *Reflex*, Morrison's *Jazz*, and Reed's *Mumbo Jumbo.*" *Novel: A Forum on Fiction* 35, nos. 2/3 (Spring/Summer, 2002): 169-193. Takes a closer look at the roles of postmodernism and jazz in works by Toni Morrison, Clarence Major, and Reed.

Lee, A. Robert, ed. *Black Fiction: New Studies in the Afro-American Novel Since 1945.* New York: Barnes and Noble Books, 1980. Frank McConnell's essay on Reed uses a quotation about him from Thomas Pynchon's novel, *Gravity's Rainbow*, in order to speak broadly about parody in Reed's novels.

McGee, Patrick. *Ishmael Reed and the Ends of Race.* New York: St. Martin's Press, 1997. Looks at Reed's refusal to meet expectations associated traditionally with African American writers, and examines his use of satire and his antagonism toward political correctness.

Martin, Reginald. *Ishmael Reed and the New Black Aesthetic Critics.* New York: St. Martin's Press, 1988. A comprehensive and important look at Reed's work and theories in relation to the evolution of the black aesthetics movement.

Nixon, Will. "Black Male Writers: Endangered Species?" *American Visions* 5, no. 1 (February, 1990): 24-29. An interesting study of the reasons why African American male writers were largely ignored during the 1980's. Also looks at the rise of African American female writers.

Reed, Ishmael. *Conversations with Ishmael Reed.* Edited by Bruce Dick and Amritjit Singh. Jackson: University Press of Mississippi, 1995. A collection of twenty-six interviews with Ishmael Reed, which cover the years 1968-1995. Includes one self-interview and a chronology of Reed's life.

_____. "*Konch* Magazine." http://www.ishmaelreedpub.com/ default_other.htm. Accessed September 1, 2005. Reed has started an internet-based magazine, called *Konch*, that offers nonfiction articles, poetry, and short narratives.

The Review of Contemporary Fiction 4 (Summer, 1984). A special issue devoted to Reed. Especially important is an essay by James Lindroth, "From Krazy Kat to Hoodoo: Aesthetic Discourse in the Fiction of Ishmael Reed," and an interview with Reed by Reginald Martin.

Velikova, Roumiana. "*Flight to Canada* via Buffalo: Ishmael Reed's Parody of Local History." *ANQ* 17, no. 4 (Fall, 2004): 37-45. An article that focuses on Reed's influences, which range from Harriet Beecher Stowe and Charles Waddell Chesnutt to the slave narratives of Frederick Douglass and William Wells Brown.

— Carl Brucker; Charles A. Gramlich